AF798600

OPERATONAL EXCELLENCE HANDBOOK: AN ENTERPRISE APPROACH

CERM Academy Series on Enterprise Risk Management

Greg Hutchins PE CERM
CERMAcademy.com
QualityPlusEngineering.com
GregH@QualityPlusEngineering.com
503.233.1012
800.COMPETE

HOW TO ORDER:

Cost is $89.00 per copy plus $6.00 Shipping/Handling in U.S. Offshore orders are based on the form of delivery. Quantity discounts are available from the publisher.

Quality Plus Engineering	503.233.1012
4052 NE Couch St.	800.COMPETE
Portland, OR 97232	800.266.7383
USA	GregH@CERMAcademy.com

For bulk purchases, on company letterhead please include information concerning the intended use of the books and the number of books to purchase.

© 2019 Quality + Engineering/CERM Academy

This publication is designed to provide accurate and authoritative information regarding the subject matter covered. It is sold with the understanding that the publisher is not engaged in rendering legal, accounting, professional risk management, or engineering services. If legal, risk, engineering, or ISO 9001 advice or other expert assistance is required; the service of a competent professional person should be sought.

The author and publisher specifically disclaim any responsibility for any liability, loss, and risk or otherwise, which is incurred as a consequence, directly or indirectly, of the use and application of any element of this book. From the Declaration of Principles jointly adapted by a Committee of the American Bar Association and a Committee of Publisher and Associations.

All rights reserved. No part of this book can be reproduced or transmitted in any form or by the means, electronic, or mechanical including photocopying, recording, or by an information storage or retrieval system without written permission from Quality + Engineering, except for the inclusion of quotations in a review. No patent or trademark liability is assumed with respect to the use of information contained in this book. Every precaution has been taken in the preparation of this book. The publisher and author assume no responsibility for damages resulting from the use of information herein.

All brand names, trademarks, and intellectual property belong to their respective holders. Patents, trademarks, and copyrights have been applied for and are pending for many of the processes described in this book. Future of Quality: Risk®, Certified Enterprise Risk Manager: Risk Based Problem Solving | Risk Based Decision Making®, Proactive, Preventive, Predictive, Preemptive™.

TABLE OF CONTENTS

CHAPTER 1

GLOBAL COMPETITIVENESS

There is no such thing as a free lunch.
Anonymous

The need for competitiveness is now a given. All companies, plants, and individuals have to be competitive if people are going to buy their products or services. Operational management or continuous improvement incorporates a set of flexible principles, policies, and methods that arose largely because of the need for companies to improve their competitiveness.

GLOBAL COMPETITION

GA number of years ago, the President's Commission on Industrial Competitiveness issued a seminal report entitled "Global Competition, The New Reality." The report came to the sobering conclusions that U.S. ability to compete in world markets is eroding; U.S. productivity growth and innovation lags our foreign competitors; U.S. leadership in world trade is declining.[1]

These changes occurred over the last 20 years. During this time, European, South American, and Pacific Rim industries grew rapidly. They invested heavily in plants and modern equipment so they could manufacture attractively priced products.

These countries were very successful as can be seen by the high U.S. trade deficits. The President's Commission on Industrial Competitiveness suggested that part of the solution to lowering the trade deficit is to manufacture high quality, competitively priced products, which is very much what our competition has done.[2]

The authors of the report defined national and organizational competitiveness a number of years ago said:

> "A firm is competitive if it can produce products or services of superior quality or lower cost than its domestic and international competitors. Competitiveness is then synonymous with a firm's long-run profit performance and its ability to compensate its employees and provide superior returns to its owners. The definition of competitiveness for a nation must similarly be tied to its ability to generate the resources required to meet its national goals."

While business competitiveness and national competitiveness seem to be rising, the incomes of many American citizen is diminishing in real terms. The signs can be seen through the downsizing, merging, and outsourcing manias over the last ten years.

Even with the weak dollar, Americans are still Supply Management foreign-made goods even though American-made goods are sometimes less costly than similar goods made offshore. American products which had been considered to be superior, are now perceived as being equal to products made offshore. In any event, U.S. consumers are still Supply Management more foreign-made goods and services.

Industrial Supply Management decisions, which historically were made based on product price, availability, and service are also changing. If a Supply Management manager was interested in buying a piece of industrial equipment, he or she first looked at the lowest price when evaluating competitive bids. Sometimes product availability was important if the piece of equipment was needed quickly. Service was important if the product was subjected to abuse, prone to failure, or designed to run continuously. Nevertheless, price was the primary consideration when buying a product.

This situation has now changed. The primary factor influencing the purchase decision is quality, which is an output of Op Ex. While still important, cost, service, and availability are lower priorities. The importance of operational excellence as a business and public policy issue can now be seen. Competitively priced quality products sell. Sales drive profits. Profits do two things. They maintain the current level of employment and create additional jobs. The maintenance and creation of jobs is now an important public policy concern of city, state, and federal governments.

GLOBAL COMPETITIVENESS

The expression "global competitiveness" has almost become clichéd. This statement is particularly evident in Asia as fast track companies are securing market share and leadership positions in very fast-growing economies. Japanese companies are now competing ferociously with those from Singapore, Thailand, Hong Kong, China, Korea, and Taiwan. In many parts of Asia, labor is no long cheap or plentiful due to increasing consumer demands as well as the cheap dollar.

The world has become an international marketplace. In this marketplace, products from Europe, the Pacific Rim, and South and North America compete for the customer's buying dollar. The money spent on a product by a customer means the company that made the product will have the capital to maintain and expand its operations. It also means the company will be able to keep its people employed making more products to sell in the international marketplace.

A number of factors, some would say opportunities and risk, are increasing the importance of operational excellence and of operational management. In this book, we will abbreviate operational excellence as OpEx. These factors include a global economy, soaring costs, rising customer demands, low-price competition, environmentalism, consumerism, technological changes, and reduced product lifecycles.

The good news about U.S. competitiveness is good. According to surveys, U.S. strengths are in management, Op Ex, technology, and graduate education. Weaknesses are in what's called society infrastructure, specifically low savings, low investment rates, insufficient worker training, and inadequate elementary education.

Occurring simultaneously, customers are demanding quality products and services that are delivered quickly and courteously. As well, products and services are tailored to satisfy national and local requirements.

THE PACIFIC TIGERS

Japanese companies in much of the 1980s were heralded as the epitome of competitiveness, ruthless competitors that captured market share in significant areas, such as steel, consumer electronics, computers, and so on. But this too has changed. American Op Ex in many cases is as high or surpasses Japanese. American design and innovation is definitely higher in many products and industry sectors. As well, the high yen has driven many Japanese products to be unaffordable. The Japanese are now reassessing the traditions of lifetime employment, seniority, consensus decision making, and hierarchal organizations.

Chinese, Thai and Korean companies are becoming fitter, leaner, and faster just as American companies in the pursuit of competitiveness. Management technologies are imported and implemented within months of their introduction in Europe or in the United States. For example, Thai companies were implementing ISO 9001:2015, self-managed teams, and operational management techniques soon after their introduction in the United States. Thai companies are focusing on the same management and organizational initiatives that companies throughout the world are pursuing. Thai companies are becoming less bureaucratic and more customer focused. Responsibility for decision making is becoming decentralized. Plants are becoming entrepreneurial. Quality is improving. Efficiencies and effectiveness are improving. These changes are occurring for companies all over the world.

TODAY'S ORGANIZATIONAL STRUCTURES

Structure is not organization.
Robert H. Waterman, writer and consultant

Companies are focusing on core processes while other work is outsourced. Key skills are retained through partnerships which result in the growth of virtual corporations. The virtual corporation is an amorphous entity that delivers products or services to customers with the external appearance of a single company. Virtual corporations will become more prevalent as small companies develop state-of-the-art, world-class skills, technologies, capabilities, information or other resources. These unique assets are pooled and integrated with other companies to form an integrated network of turn-key capabilities.

SEARCHING FOR THE BEST ORGANIZATIONAL STRUCTURE

In the last 20 years, a number of organizational structures has been introduced. These include: traditional-hierarchical, matrix, virtual etc. Is there one best structure? No. The only important element for an effective structure is flexibility. The appropriate organizational structure is one that satisfies stakeholders at the lowest possible cost. An effective and efficient organization is a group of people who must work together to satisfy customers and meet objectives while using the fewest resources possible. Within this structure, congruent, and supportive systems are created that reinforce the organizational culture.

The hierarchical form of business organization still predominates. It follows the military model and is extensively used because it works but this is also changing. Now, the hierarchal model is much flatter and amorphous. Innovative organizations models are springing up based on interlocking groups, virtual partnerships, strategic alliances, and matrix organizations.

GENERALS, COLONELS AND SO ON

The traditional organizational form consists of a general, colonels, majors, captains, lieutenants, and troops. The business analogue consists of a president, vice-presidents, directors, managers, supervisors, and employees. Work is organized by functional area that is headed by a department manager. Department managers usually direct areas such as Quality, Engineering, Manufacturing, Accounting, or Sales. In larger organizations, these positions may be vice-president level. In the hierarchal structure, all work flows through functional departments.

Functional and area work structures work well in production, operational, and technical areas. This structure encourages professionalism and specialization. For example, Customer Service representatives are well trained to serve customers. Or in a production environment, workers are familiar with all the machines, methods, problems, and specifications in that area. If both areas, employees develop a can-do professionalism about their work. Specifications are jointly developed and everyone is familiar with them. Processes are stabilized, documented, and capable. If there are process deficiencies, workers have the skills to solve them.

The challenges and problems of a vertical structure stem directly from the advantages of vertical compartmentalization of work. In vertical structures, or sometimes called silos, work and authorizations flow up and down the structures sequentially while more work is considered a horizontal, smooth process.

The vertical structure has corresponding disadvantages. One of the advantages is strong vertical control, communication, and responsibility. But, if work flows horizontally, then control, communication, and responsibility flows can stymie smooth process flow. In horizontal work flow if a problem arises, workers must have the authority to solve problems quickly if the flow is to be continuous. In a vertical structure, communication and requests for resource authorization flow up the organizational ladder. If the problem originates in another part of the organization, if technical assistance is required from others, or if politics enters into the picture, then work productivity and Op Ex may be compromised. Information basically goes up the organization, then across and then down again as it filters through many organizational layers.

BENEFITS AND CHALLENGES OF HIERARCHICAL ORGANIZATIONS

This traditional structure has worked and still works very effectively for many organizations because:

- Control of budgets and work is well established.
- Project monitoring is easier.
- Authority and responsibility rests in one area.
- Employees are well trained.
- Policies, procedures, and work instructions are well developed.
- Specialists can support problem solving.
- Problems tend to be function specific and solvable.
- Specifications and work requirements are known.
- Equipment and instrumentation are function specific.

However, vertical structure benefits can become hindrances, such as:

- Departmental budget controls may hinder work flow.
- Departmental procedures and policies may conflict with other departments.
- There is little external or internal customer focus.
- Competition among departments increases instead of coordination and cooperation.
- Decisions take much longer.
- Horizonal work processes require multidisciplinary solutions.
- Teams of workers must be familiar with work outside their work area.
- Process specialists and engineers must know the entire process.
- Authority and responsibility rests with the people actually doing the work.

FLATTER ORGANIZATIONS

Companies are becoming flatter, sometimes this is called delayering or rightsizing. The goal is to make decision making and operations more efficient. All employees are trained, given authority and responsibility to do their jobs. Companies are also focusing on core processes, emphasizing what is essential to maintain externally and internally satisfied customers.

Rigid, hierarchal, and authoritarian styles of management and organizations are becoming history. Employees are encouraged and rewarded to make decisions as a part of a team. There is much less hierarchy. The organization is much more fluid, some say virtual, as teams are established to get a job done and are then disbanded. Command and control first-line supervisors become facilitators. Middle managers become coaches. Senior managers become stewards and champions of the Op Ex initiatives.

What happens to middle management? Middle managers assume different roles and more accountability? If senior management considers middle management frozen and unresponsive then obsolescent managers may be outsourced or whatever the current euphemism is for being fired. Flexible middle managers prosper with more responsibility and authority.

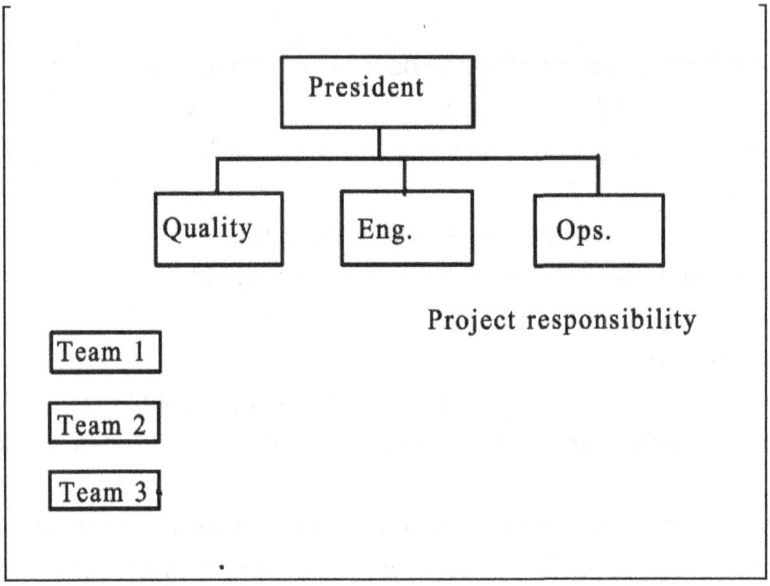

What happens to first level supervision, the group of managers who were responsible for directing day-to-day operations? With the rise of employee involvement through self-managed, high-performance teams, the first-line supervisor has a new role. The supervisor supports problem solving teams in his or her area. The supervisor may become coach, facilitator, trainer, problem solver, assistant, motivator, or assume other roles. The supervisor needs to create a climate of motivation and commitment on a daily basis. First-level supervision can make or break the operational improvement initiative.

MATRIX

A matrix organization is just what the name implies. A matrix reporting structured is overlaid the traditional organizational structure. Groups or teams report up and across the organizational structure as the figure above illustrates. Authority and responsibility for a project is shared among several groups. This structure works well with teams but has problems when it becomes institutionalized. Several disadvantages to matrix structures include reporting and responsibility ambiguities, implementation conflicts, and additional costs.

Participatory management and high-performance teams lend themselves to a matrix organization. The team may well have multiple reporting routes.

An improvement team may report to the Op Ex function and to the line organization where the improvement project is being conducted. As well, individual multidisciplinary team members may report to different organizational areas.

Authority and resources come from a functional or operating area while staff assistance comes from the Op Ex organization. The improvement team is accountable for its success and may have the full backing of the operational group. The operational group may be a business unit, division, plant or department. The operational group has resources to directly influence the success of the project. The Op Ex group has consulting and support resources to aid implementation. The Op Ex group may also provide training, problem solving capability, auditing, consulting or other staff activities.

Matrix organizations became popular in the 60s and 70s as a way to satisfy internal customers or multiple stakeholders. Matrix organizations have been especially popular in aerospace and high-tech organizations In the traditional aerospace matrix organization, special projects and programs usually had multiple reporting structure.

Operational improvement teams tend to succeed in a matrix organization because:

- Team members understand requirements of team participation.
- Team members are loyal.
- Team leader understands organizational culture.
- Commitments are made and followed.
- Conflict resolution is fair and quick.
- Good communication channels exist horizontally and vertically.
- Everyone participates in the planning process.

VIRTUAL ORGANIZATIONS

Information is often seen as the enabler and driver of networked organizations. Examples of virtual organizations include: supplier partnering, global consulting organizations, franchising, joint ventures, strategic alliances,

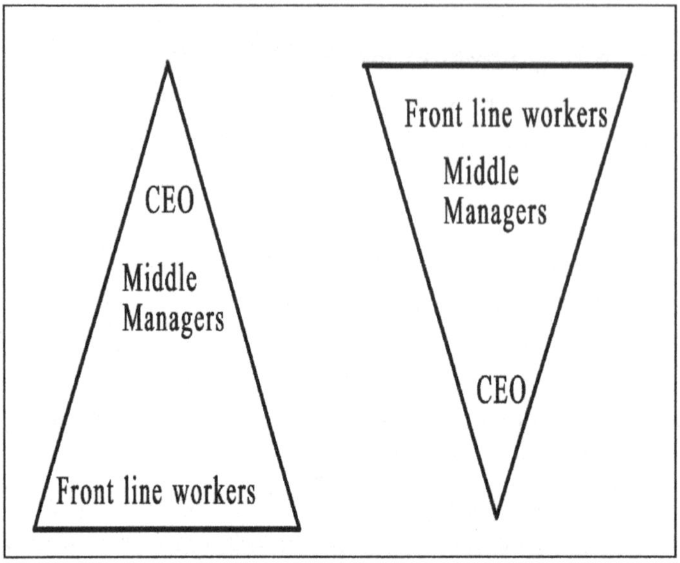

and telecommuting. What pulls everyone together in the virtual organization is synergy - the awareness that the sum of individual skills and knowledge are greater than the individual parts. To make the virtual organizational work, people must bring something of value to the table. It may be money, contacts, special knowledge, or other resources. When the project is over, the virtual group may attempt another project or the group may disband. The advantages of the virtual organization include lower overhead, lower risks, flexibility, and improved performance.

In the virtual group, everyone is an expert at what he or she does. Value-added capabilities are brought in. Synergies arise. The output is greater than the sum of the parts. Each person basically becomes a consultant with marketable and transferable skills that are almost being contracted to the virtual entity.

THE INVERTED ORGANIZATION

The inverted organization was a concept developed several years ago. The traditional organization is a hierarchical pyramid. The Chief Executive Officer (CEO) is at the top and line personnel are at the bottom. The problem is this organizational style doesn't seem to deliver products and services quickly because there are too many barriers for decision making as well as too many hindrances for customers to be satisfied. So what is the solution? Why not invert the pyramid? Line personnel are at the top and theoretically, management is at the bottom. Of course, this is more symbolic than real. However, the point is clear. Customers come first. Front line personnel are next because they are responsible for the product and service quality. What is the best way to deliver this but through empowering customer service representatives.

OP EX DEFINITIONS

WHAT IS OP EX?

Operational excellence is a bundle of technologies and systems that are called different names, such as:

- Companywide operational control
- Continuous Op Ex
- Lean
- Six Sigma
- Total customer satisfaction or service
- Total employee involvement
- Integrated process management

Sometimes, Op Ex initiatives are described in terms of customers. In some organizations, total customer service is preempting total Op Ex and continuous process improvement as the key to profitability. Customer satisfaction is often pursued because it is the means to profitability. Customer satisfaction has become increasingly important as the number of products and service providers has increased in the global economy.

Total Quality Service (TQS) is a bundle of interrelated methodologies for identifying customers, assessing customer service, and improving delivery options. TQS also involves customer assessment, measurement, and feedback; market and customer research; education and training; and delivery process improvement.

Op Ex is basically a way to manage. Op Ex is a way to continuously improve every element of the organization. Improvement includes using resources more efficiently, effectively, and economically. Resources include time, people, monies, machines, and materials. Op Ex also includes concepts such as total cost, Op Ex, service, delivery, and technology.

Op Ex as used in day-to-day conversation means all the elements that remove waste and improve quality. Some Op Ex definitions are synonymous with perceived excellence or absolute perfection which in conversational use, refers to a product or service that has set or met a mark of high achievement.

Op Ex, as the equivalent of excellence, is often a gut level reaction, a feeling that cannot be quantified. In this context, Op Ex is not precise and usually cannot be measured. Rather, Op Ex is a property or characteristic of a product or service recognized through use or experience. It is generally acknowledged that Rolls-Royce, Infiniti, and Mercedes cars have perceived Op Ex. They are styled well, reliably made, and represent excellence.

Today, the search for excellence is synonymous with the search for Op Ex. Creating and pursuing excellence was the theme of two best sellers, **In Search of Excellence, Good to Great,** and **A Passion for Excellence**. These books popularized the idea that Op Ex is a necessary condition for survival in a global economy.

OP EX RESULTS FROM A SATISFIED CUSTOMER

Customers are assumed to have different wants, needs, and expectations. Products that best satisfy these requirements have the highest perceived quality, which is often an outcome of Op Ex.

A company may establish a level of product quality that it feels is appropriate to satisfy certain customers and still maintain an acceptable profit. The company then makes a calculated decision to make and market a product to a target group that is the result of Op Ex.

However, it is difficult to design and develop a product with all the features that everybody wants. So, a product is designed that:

- Has universal features that please the largest number of people.

- Is a basic product with additional features that are added at an extra cost in order to personalize the product?

Features
A product may have universal functional or aesthetic features that many people desire. This product satisfies the needs of the largest number of people possible. For example, in the early days of the automobile, the Ford Model T served the basic transportation needs of the entire country. The Model T was competitively priced, highly reliable, and maintainable.

Additional Features
A product may satisfy a basic need, such as transportation. But, the customer wants the trip to be more comfortable in a nicer looking vehicle. As the automobile became more prevalent and people more affluent, people wanted special and sometimes unique features in or on the automobile, such as bigger engines or different colors. The Ford Escort is basic transportation that can be transformed into a highly personalized vehicle by adding special features.

Unique Attributes
A product may have unique attributes that a target demographic group may desire and can afford. For example, a Jaguar is not looked upon as a basic means of transportation but as an image enhancer, because it has the styling and performance that one would associate with the rich and famous.

OP EX IS CONFORMANCE TO A SPECIFICATION

Op Ex is sometimes defined in terms of compliance or conformance-based definitions, which are precise and measurable. The common feature of these definitions is that Op Ex is defined as conformance to a specification, standard, rule, policy, or regulation.

The conformance-based definition establishes a benchmark or guideline against which Op Ex can be measured, controlled, and ensured. Once a design or service specification has been established, any deviation outside the boundaries, scope, intent, or tolerance limits of a specification implies poor Op Ex. This definition of Op Ex is used in both manufacturing and service industries.

SPECIFICATION DEVELOPMENT

Each product or service has standards and specifications to which it must conform. Product development teams specify standards which include such features as product characteristics, performance characteristics, physical dimensions, and process requirements. Specifications are then placed on engineering drawings. As products are produced, measurements are taken to determine if dimensions are within an allowable specification range. If a product measures outside the allowable tolerance range, production returns the machine or process into the acceptable specification range.

This goal of this approach is to control the process of making a product. If the process is in control and the product is made to conform to a specification, costs can be controlled. The product can be optimized. Excess features that do not serve any function or those that the customer does not want can be eliminated. Also, if the manufacturing process is controllable then waste can be minimized. Waste includes rework, scrap, or warranty expenses.

OP EX IS VALUE

Op Ex is also defined in terms of systems and processes that add value. Value-based definitions compare the cost of achieving a certain level of Op Ex with the benefits accrued. This type of cost-benefit analysis is important, because it is possible to make a high-priced product that nobody will buy. How many people would or could buy a high Op Ex $900 shirt? If nobody buys it, it does not make sense to mass produce it.

Op Ex being synonymous with affordable excellence is becoming an accepted definition. However, this definition is imprecise because the value or worth of a product or service is often subjective and therefore difficult to measure.

OP EX AS REAL AND PERCEIVED VALUE

Op Ex can also be viewed in terms of the real and perceived utility a customer or user has in a product or service. To add value or utility to a product or service means that a feature has been added or performance has been improved so the product's image is enhanced and therefore, the product is more marketable. Op Ex can be thought of generating a combination five value-based factors:

1. **Form.** Form value is the aesthetic, external features of a product. Depending on the nature of the product, such as fashion or consumer products, form may be the most important product attribute. Form Op Ex is established when a manufacturer makes or creates a product out of raw or stock material. The product must be something that the buyer wants, otherwise there is no Op Ex because no need or want has been established or satisfied.
2. **Time.** Time value means having the product available when the customer wants it. This is important to suppliers of manufacturing companies. Firms do not want a large inventory on their books because it is expensive. Today, the goal is to keep all costs low, including the cost of carrying inventory. Firms now ask their suppliers to provide products just-in-time to be used or assembled into a finished product.
3. **Place.** Place value means having the product available where the customer wants it. In the preceding example of JIT and lean production, manufacturers want parts delivered directly to the location on the manufacturing line where it will be used. For example, an industrial customer may ask a supplier to deliver parts to loading dock No.10 at 9:00 am on December 6th in Portland, Oregon so they can be assembled onto the finished part.
4. **Possession.** Possession value means completing the transaction and gaining possession so the customer has the legal right to use the product. Information, warranties, spare parts, and instructions have been provided to the customer so he or she can use the product safely.

5. **Perceived.** Perceived value is the overall perception of a product or service. Often, this involves intangible product and service attributes. Positive perceptions in a restaurant may result from its ambiance, service, food, service, location, reputation, colors, name, and the many little things that create perceptions.[3]

SIGNIFICANCE OF MULTIPLE DEFINITIONS OF OP EX

Each function in an organization may interpret the word Op Ex differently, which affects its implementation. For example, Marketing takes a user or customer approach to the subject. Engineering and Manufacturing pursue a specification approach to the subject. Supply Management takes a value approach to the subject.

All of these approaches are acceptable. Each department, function, and even profession is looking at the same subject, Op Ex, from a different perspective. It is important for each operating department to recognize that operationally (tactically) the definition of Op Ex may differ but the strategic focus is the same, which is to satisfy the needs of the customer with a quality product or service.

OP EX AND COMPETITIVENESS

The only thing that we can predict with certainty is change.
Jayne Spain, writer

Op Ex, reengineering, lean, and JIT are paradigms. They are philosophies, beliefs and practices that properly implemented can result in dramatic organizational changes and enhance profitability. A major element of all paradigms is doing only what needs to be done to create customer value. Waste and redundancy throughout the organization are eliminated.

PARADIGM SHIFTING

Many companies are shifting their paradigms to remain competitive. What does this mean? They have had to shed or discard many cherished beliefs, concepts, assumptions, standards, technologies, operational systems, and compensation systems. The critical question is what will replace these? It is not good enough to simply discard the old and replace it with something new unless it is somehow better.

Which is the best method or paradigm for becoming competitive? This is the key question that senior management is asking. The list of options is long and includes benchmarking, reengineering, Op Ex, and organizational transformation, ISO 9001:2015, and the list continues. Many of these are discussed in the next chapter. The Op Ex manager must be adaptable and go with the flow.

Recent surveys reinforce the competitive importance of Op Ex. According to a recent Harvard Business Review article the 7 deadly sins leading to competitive loss are:

1. Inconsistent product quality
2. Slow response to the marketplace
3. Lack of innovative, competitive products
4. Uncompetitive cost structure
5. Inadequate employee involvement
6. Unresponsive customer service
7. Inefficient resource allocation[4]

As the above survey indicates, certain fundamental concepts and beliefs have survived the fad stage. Operational management is one of those. Operational management, whether it is called Customer Value, Continuous Process Improvement, or Total Quality Excellence Management, has become an umbrella for diverse methods, principles, and ideas. Operational management is all inclusive.

What does this mean for the Op Ex manager? He or she must be more flexible by learning, implementing and measuring the effectiveness of each new technology and paradigm. Each tool or technique offers new insights and ways of affecting efficiency, effectiveness, and profitability. Flexibility is encouraged. Failure is OK as long as lessons are learned and mistakes are not repeated. Continued failure through repeating the same mistakes is systemic, chronic, and stupid.

OP EX MYTHS AND REALITIES

Peters and Waterman a number of years ago pointed out in their book **In Search for Excellence** that while many factors interact to create a corporate culture: three are dominant: leadership, myths, and reinforcement.

- **Leadership.** The leader, usually the Chairman or Chief Executive Officer decides what shared values he or she wants to instill in the organization. The leader establishes Op Ex values through policy statements, reward mechanisms, and selection of subordinates. The leader also establishes a personal style that employees in the organization may want to emulate.
- **Myths.** Myths and stories are created around the leader or selected individuals of an organization. In some organizations, the leader such as an Iacocca of Chrysler, sets the direction and tenor of the organization. Year ago, Iacocca appeared in Chrysler ads selling the company's quality automobiles. In other organizations, heroes are employees who have excelled in some fashion. At 3M, the inventors of Post-It note pads are corporate heroes. Heroes are carefully selected so their accomplishments reinforce the corporate Op Ex message.
- **Reinforcement.** Finally, positive reinforcement, judiciously used, communicates consistent messages of basic values, behavior, and ideas. Employees whose actions support the organization's basic Op Ex values and beliefs are publicly heralded in the company's magazine, receive a badge or emblem of accomplishment, or receive an outstanding bonus.

In an analysis of organizational change, Harvard professor Michael Beer discovered that by adopting and internalizing a theme, credo, or belief, people can mobilize and support change. Beer reports that Op Ex was one of the themes that served most companies well. He explains: "This is probably because it is the one theme all stakeholders - workers, management, unions, and shareholders - can support."[5]

OP EX FUNCTION CHALLENGES

A box in the organization chart is not sufficient to get an operation going; it must have the backing of an important leader.
Joseph Froomkin, Management consultant

Op Ex at its core is about people, people who do the work and the people who buy products and services. We've discussed the importance of the customer and in this chapter, we discuss the leadership and management of the Op Ex function and of teams.

The velocity of the changes occurring in Op Ex function is due to changing customer requirements, technology, competitive environment, organizational culture, globalization, and other factors. While every organization may not demonstrate all these changes, sufficient number of Op Ex organizations are facing challenges in these areas:

- Chief Operations Officer
- Changing reporting relationships
- Operational focus
- Interfacing and coordinating responsibilities
- Authority and responsibility
- Span of control
- Organizational example
- Operational management opportunities

RESTRUCTURING PRESSURES

Organizational transformations are not easy. A company going through a transformation, not a transition or change implies it can be wrenching and abrupt. The transformation process is both external and internal to the organization.

Executives and managers must live in a constantly changing and some would say, chaotic world. Why? The marketplace is global. Developing nations are becoming formidable competitors. Customer requirements are changing in the U.S. and throughout the world. As more companies see offshore markets growing faster than the U.S., companies must adapt their sales strategies and product mix to these markets.

The critical element of a successful transformation is senior management who must create an organizational climate that is respectful to the individual and the team. This climate is sometimes called the organizational Op Ex culture or ethos. The culture must support a climate where new ideas can take hold and risk taking is safe.

NEXT CHAPTER

In the next chapter, Leadership Op Ex Commitment is discussed. The number #1 indicator of Op Ex success is the commitment of senior management, in particular the Chief Executive Officer (CEO). Commitment can range from lip service to active, almost daily involvement. For the Op Ex manager, senior management commitment is the benchmark for determining how successful and rapid the organizational transformation will be.

CHAPTER 2
OP EX LEADERSHIP COMMITMENT

Successful Op Ex initiatives and projects require the full participation and cooperation of an organization's management. If an Op Ex initiative is imposed without the full participation and acceptance of an organization's management, it will fail.

ROLE OF LEADERSHIP

Whenever you see a successful business, someone once made a courageous decision.
Peter F. Drucker

Senior management may be a different person depending on the scope of the project. For example, if the project deals with organizational transformation or starting an Op Ex initiative, then the board and CEO commitment are critical. If the project is a supplier improvement project, then senior Supply Management, Production, and operational management support is essential. If the project deals with customer service training, then Customer Service, Marketing and Sales management support is required.

An organization gets its messages and rewards from senior management. If employees don't believe senior management is committed they won't be committed. Executives must be willing to attend the same courses as everyone, learn Op Ex concepts, implement technologies, attend critical operations meetings, and communicate the importance of customer satisfaction. Executives should be willing to practice Op Ex in their own jobs so they become part of the organizational way of life.

Attitudes and actions that reflect the organization's Op Ex policy are then reinforced by strong and consistent messages from middle and first line management. Senior management can emphasize continuous, long-term improvement by establishing and developing an Op Ex ethic and culture. If middle management supports Op Ex in policy as well as in action, employees learn that Op Ex is important.

However, strong and consistent management signals on the importance of Op Ex can be undermined by conflicting operational realities. If management only pays "lip service" to Op Ex, employees receive the reverse message that Op Ex is an expedient measure, here today and gone tomorrow. Management may talk about Op Ex and exhort everyone to action through slogans like "the essence of Op Ex is doing the job right the first time." But when a conflict arises between product delivery and management say, "shove the product out the door" the Op Ex initiative is dismissed because it has been subordinated to operational expediency.

SENIOR MANAGEMENT INFLUENCES

No commitment - no total Op Ex. It's pretty straightforward. Senior management leadership and involvement influence the following:

- **Culture.** Senior management cultivates, encourages, and reinforces an organizational culture that values customer satisfaction, employee empowerment, and continuous improvement.
- **Climate of trust.** Only leaders can create an environment of trust.
- **Importance.** Senior management emphasizes the importance of Op Ex practices, principles, and behavior. Senior management provides reinforcers of approved behavior. Senior management establishes clear corporate Op Ex mission, vision, customer and Op Ex goals. As well, management integrates Op Ex into large business issues.
- **Communication.** Senior management has the ability to communicate performance expectations and understanding of strategic and operational plans. Management also communicates and reinforces the Op Ex message.

- **Empowerment.** Management has the ability to increase the authority and responsibility of people to pursue Op Ex and empower people to think and to act.
- **Recognition.** Only management has the ability to recognize and reward individual and team accomplishment.
- **Role modeling.** Leaders role model the behavior they expect from others. They define core Op Ex values and ensure behavior is consistent with the values.
- **Ethical practices.** Management sets the expectations and policies for the organization's business ethics and standards.
- **Authorize.** Senior management authorizes the development and installation of Op Ex systems, processes, and procedures.
- **Resources.** Resources must be authorized and allocated to projects, systems, and processes.

THE FUTURE OF THE CHIEF EXECUTIVE OFFICER

With all these different management methods and philosophies, is there a need for a Chief Executive Officer (CEO)? Chief executives will always be around. Someone, or a central group, has to lead, even nominally in a technologically, diverse organization. The important point is this person or group much be adaptable and quick on its feet.

So, what characterizes an obsolescent chief executive? The following are somewhat tongue in cheek examples of what an outdated CEO or organization might look like:

1. Still uses hierarchical organization charts.
2. Still heads multinational company instead of a global one.
3. Still thinks of computers as MIS (Management Information Systems).
4. Still considers shareholders to be individuals who should be dealt with or appeased.
5. Still has a management group predominantly composed of white males.
6. Still has a board packed with beholden directors.[6]

CHIEF OPERATIONS OFFICER

The corporate head of Op Ex, the Chief Operations Officer, may have different titles depending on the size of the organization, competition, products, Op Ex processes, and a host of other factors. A larger Op Ex organization in a competitive market will have highly evolved Op Ex systems. In such organizations, Op Ex will be at an executive, corporate vice president or director position.

The senior Op Ex executive, called the Chief Operations Officer, usually reports to a senior executive which may be the Chief Operatlons or Chief Executive Officer. This reporting relationship sends an important message to the organization regarding the importance of Op Ex, including the following:

- Only the Chief Executive or Chief Operating Officer can make the commitment and signal the need for major changes, such as in culture, Op Ex, teams, etc.
- The Op Ex group is responsible for facilitating Op Ex initiatives throughout the organization as well as in the supplier base. The Op Ex manager thus reports to the person who can influence the entire organization.
- The Chief Operations Officer has access to the entire organization's resources.
- A Chief Operations Officer by title confers respect and commitment to the Op Ex initiative. This conveys to customers, suppliers and other stakeholders that the organization is fully committed to Op Ex.

LEADERSHIP ROLES AND RESPONSIBILITIES

Leadership is action, not position.
Donald McGannon

Leadership is a principle element of operational management. Leadership and operational management seem synonymous. Leadership is an art. Depending on the requirements of the market, organizational culture, and abilities of the people, leadership may involve "command and control" elements to coaching and mentoring. More often, leaders are closely involved with employees, suggesting and demonstrating as opposed to directing what needs to be done.

What makes a leader? Is a leader made, nurtured, or self-selected? Leadership is still a difficult issue to understand and to explain. More and more, leaders are seen as people who can guide themselves or a group to do what needs to be done as well as reach ever higher goals. In general, these are normal people who possess high energy, are committed to a cause, can share responsibility, have high values, and are highly credible.

A leader is a person who can adapt and learn in different circumstances. One element of leadership is the ability to communicate at a visceral level. The leader does not simply communicate information but also has the ability to communicate vision. Often this type of communication means sharing information and becoming actively involved in discussions. The leader questions, listens actively, and surfaces issues that are important to individuals, to teams, and to the organization.

An interesting question is whether leadership can be learned and if it can be shared. Pursuing and sharing leadership with others in the organization is a fundamental element of team problem solving, self-directed teams, and process ownership. People and teams must take responsibility and leadership for the Op Ex of their efforts. Everyone in the organization is empowered to make a maximum contribution to improving the effectiveness of their process.

The following elements of Op Ex leadership are discussed below:

- Visionary
- Leader
- Role Model
- Initiative or Project Sponsor
- Change Agent
- Ombudsperson
- Champion
- Manager/Administrator

- Coach
- Organizer
- Mentor
- Enabler
- Cheerleader
- Delegator
- Entrepreneur
- Compliance officer
- Translator
- System Architect
- Internal Consultant
- Management Representative

Visionary

The Chief Operations Office or manager must have the necessary vision to establish the function as an example for the organization and to position it for future change. Some Op Ex managers understand what is ahead of the change curve and can provide direction for the change. Within this change, the role of the emerging Op Ex manager must be to reinvent the Op Ex organization. The new Op Ex manager must know Op Ex technologies but also understand how to organize, motivate, coach, train, mentor, and energize employees.

Leader

Op Ex managers often must lead through example rather than through hierarchal authority. As operational manager's responsibilities and authorities have been downloaded to people actually doing the work, the Op Ex function has evolved into a staff, support group for operating units. The Op Ex manager can't insist, push, or require a certain Op Ex initiative or improvement project. Supporting and implementing Op Ex requires new skills in this unstructured atmosphere. The Op Ex manager must lead by example and support operating personnel across functional areas and work processes. The Op Ex manager must develop the relationship, trust, and credibility with other operating managers.

Role Model

Integrity is a belief and moral principle that is often cited as a guide for personal and organizational performance. Integrity is also the essential foundation of trust for all team empowerment efforts. Integrity, or the lack of it, is the reason why some operational management initiatives have failed while others have flourished. Integrity is the ability to honor commitments and promises to employees, team members, suppliers, customers, communities, and other critical stakeholders. Integrity is an ethic that reinforces an organization's vision, mission and values.[7]

Initiative or Project Sponsor

A senior Op Ex executive may sponsor the Op Ex initiative. In a large organization, the project sponsor provides guidance to operational management and line managers on the Op Ex initiative. If the Op Ex initiative is new to the organization then a senior executive sponsor vouches for its importance.

The advantages of using an executive sponsor include:

- Provides access to top management
- Provides resources
- Handles major problems
- Provides instant credibility to the project
- Keeps senior level management informed
- Advises the team
- Sits in on senior level meetings
- Vocally and actively supports the initiative

Change Agent

Change agent is a relatively new term to describe the role of a person or a group to move the organization in a new direction. The Op Ex manager may be the change agent. Sometimes, the initial change agent is the CEO who assigns the transformational responsibilities to a senior management team charged with transforming the organization.

Usually a competitor or a customer initiates or signals the need for the change. Old ways of business are no longer sufficient. An organization may have to change from an engineering to a customer-focused organization. Or, it may have to evolve from product oriented to a systems and process orientation.

The Op Ex manager should be familiar with emerging social and technical change paradigms. This person must be familiar with the tools for process modeling, simulation, reengineering, self-managed teams, learning organizations, and other change models.

Ombudsperson

In some organizations, the Op Ex manager serves as the ombudsperson on critical Op Ex issues. In much the same way, the human resources manager is the ombudsperson on organizational and cultural matters. The Op Ex manager, as an ombudsperson, is a designated neutral person to resolve Op Ex, customer satisfaction, and customer-supplier issues among teams, departments, and other business units. The Op Ex manager serves as an impartial listener and a means for resolving conflicts.

Champion

The champion of the Op Ex initiative may be the Chief Operations Officer, other senior executives, or even the Chief Executive Officer. In formal and informal settings and activities, the champion reminds the organization of the importance of Op Ex. Championing Op Ex activities has evolved into the most visible way an executive can provide active and continued internal and external support.

Coach

In the athletic metaphor, the coach is nominally in charge. The coach decides who's on the team, who plays, and so on. But the coach is not responsible for the big play or the series of downs that allow points to be scored. The coach broadly establishes the game plan, provides training, encourages self-sacrifice, mentors players, and serves other facilitating roles. The manager of the future may well be the coach of a work team composed of experts performing the work.

Op Ex managers and coaches have similar goals to be competitive and to win games. This requires getting the best from his or her players. Success depends on how players follow through on their assignments.

The relationship between management and sports is close. Organizations are developing into teams. Team structure is flat. The manager is the coach. The manager works through his or her employees. Coaching requires the ability to encourage teamwork, motivate employees, and provide rewards.

Organizer
A major responsibility of the Op Ex manager is to interface, organize, and monitor companywide Op Ex projects. The Op Ex manager may have a dotted line, indirect responsibility for the project. However, the manager may be responsible for organizing, facilitating, monitoring and reporting progress.

The Op Ex manager interfaces with operational units such as Engineering, Manufacturing, Supply Management, and other functions. The Op Ex manager or representative reports progress, communicates progress, schedules activities, facilitates meetings, provides administrative support, and provides training.

Mentor
An Op Ex manager must be a mentor and be capable of being mentored. Mentoring for employee, especially high potential employees, may be as little as guiding new employees in the organization's culture and value systems. Or, mentoring may entail a long-term relationship of providing guidance to a team or individual.

Enabler
The enabler assists functional personnel and process owners establish and meet their goals. This may mean reviewing plans, reviewing processes, training personnel, monitoring improvement, and otherwise supporting Op Ex initiatives. The enabler does not control, punish, or financially reward team personnel. The enabler basically aids and counsel to process owner's goal. The Op Ex enabler walks a fine line. The enabler can provide

assistance and guidance but can't take ownership away from teams or employees. Ownership for Op Ex and productivity performance still rests with the people doing the work.

Cheerleader

Cheerleading managers are optimistically realistic. Cheerleading may involve a number of activities such as uplifting talks, encouraging improvement teams, recognizing accomplishments, thanking personnel, being a mentor, or defusing tension. They are infectious self-starters who generate enthusiasm in others. Cheerleader management is not rose colored or polyannish.

Cheerleader management is tightly focused on raising awareness on challenges and opportunities. Management cheerleaders don't look at the glass as half empty or half full. They look at the glass as an opportunity to fill it and try to convince others of the wisdom of filling it.

Cheerleaders also focus energies on meeting the organization's mission and objectives. They empower teams to target their energy and the company's resources on opportunities for success and high promise outcomes.

Cheerleading is one of the more difficult challenges for the Op Ex manager. Disillusionment over an Op Ex initiative can take its toll. Cynicism or defeatism can result and become self-fulfilling. The Op Ex manager may cheerlead when a project flags because of rising expectations, poor results, internal resistance, conflicting projects, ego-gratification, selfishness, poor communications, or slow progress.

Delegator

Delegation is another important skill for the Op Ex manager. Delegation means empowering people often subordinates to perform a specific task, complete a project, or manage a process with little or no interference. Delegating may entail shared responsibility or a total hand-off of responsibility for the successful completion of a project.

Delegation works if there is trust between parties, the delegator and the receiver and if the receiver knows what is expected and required. For example, the delegator should communicate specifically what is to be done by what time. The how's of the project, how it will be done, is usually the responsibility of the receiver. Also, the delegator should be aware of the capabilities of the team or individuals responsible for a task. The delegator may provide resources or authorize the team to acquire the resources to get the job done on time and on budget.

Entrepreneur

The Op Ex department may become a small business, a profit-loss department. The Op Ex department must understand its internal customer requirements and how to satisfy them. The department bills user departments for training, consulting, and other services. These services must add value and be priced competitively. An Op Ex department may compete directly with external providers of the same services. This keeps internal staff departments competitive and ensures they keep providing value. If operating groups don't want to use the Op Ex department's services, the message is loud and clear - no business, no monies, no Op Ex personnel.

Compliance Officer

Every manager is aware of workplace regulations such as sexual harassment, equal opportunity, and disability. Regulations affect all elements of the work place and place obligations on employers for safety, health, and access.

Perceived and real fairness may be the most difficult challenge for an Op Ex manager who must face the equity and fairness issues throughout the organization. While a manager must be aware and comply with regulations, the manager must also be sensitive to workplace issues of pay equity, fairness, family leave, scheduling, and maternity leave. However, there are other workplace issues dealing with the quality of work life that are eminently important to workers, many of whom have to work long hours and balance work and family issues.

Translator

Each discipline has its own language including Mechanical Engineering, Op Ex, Finance, and Sales. The language of Op Ex is a process driven language which affects every area of the organization as well as the supplier base. Another role of the Op Ex manager is to assist in understanding and implementing Op Ex systems. As Op Ex issues arise concerning customer requirements, process requirements, product attributes, or supplier capabilities, everyone should be speaking the same language.

System Architect

The Op Ex manager may be a system architect. The Op Ex manager may work with Human Resources to facilitate organizational change or transformation. The Op Ex manager may also work with consultants to reengineer technical systems and processes. The conventional wisdom is that to survive global competition, companies will have to radically redesign processes, systems and even basic organizational structures. Reengineered processes result in streamlined work flows which require fewer managers and workers.

Organizational and process redesign is a never-ending process to accommodate new products or new customer requirements. Organizations are also transformed to accommodate new people, new ideas, and new competitive requirements. This change offers the Op Ex manager the opportunity to expand his and her abilities as well as influence internal processes.

Internal Consultant

The Op Ex function is often a staff function. The function may have few full-time employees and a small budget. The department must leverage itself through operating departments to get the job done. The Op Ex department may not have the staff to support a major Op Ex initiative, such as ISO 9001:2015 registration.

As Op Ex is being operationalized, what is the role of the Op Ex manager in this type of organization or even is an Op Ex department required? The Op Ex manager may become an internal consultant. The manager works with operational groups, process owners, and plant managers to initiate Op

Ex initiatives, develop unit Op Ex strategies, and install the proper mechanisms to ensure Op Ex thrives. This role requires a special individual who has developed "real" world consulting expertise. A consultant must first be a self-starter and be able to discover opportunities for improvement and innovation. As well, the internal consultant needs strong interpersonal skills plus a strong desire to learn new skills on the job.

Is the typical Op Ex manager ready for the challenges discussed in this section? Does the typical Op Ex manager have the skills to serve as an internal consultant on organizational redesign or reengineering? The Op Ex manager must be willing to intervene in difficult situations, remain calm, and do what's necessary to change the organization from the inside. Internal consultants must offer hard suggestions to those who may not want to hear it as well as receive feedback from people.

Management Representative
ISO 9001:2015 requires a company appoint an executive to ensure Op Ex systems are established, implemented, and maintained. This person reviews and reports on Op Ex system performance to senior management. If a management review indicates the Op Ex system is not suitable or effective in satisfying ISO 9001:2015 requirements then this person has the authority and resources to ensure they are working properly and improving over time. The management review may evaluate Op Ex problems and actions taken, outstanding actions, areas for improvement, customer complaints, field failures, customer-supplier problems, process capability, and training requirements.

MANAGER ROLES AND RESPONSIBILITIES

People ask the difference between a leader and a boss. The leader works in the open and the boss in covert. The leader leads and the boss drives.
Theodore Roosevelt, President

Operational management is a broad field incorporating new concepts and practices that focus on enhancing customer satisfaction. More often, operational management represents good management practices.

OP EX MANAGERIAL RESPONSIBILITIES

Every manager has to evaluate employees. The evaluation is usually based on objective criteria that were often negotiated at the beginning of the year. The evaluation may be a vertical evaluation, manager to direct reports, a 360-degree evaluation, or something in between. Evaluations involve a number of compensation factors including performance, salary, promotion, bonuses, overtime pay. As well, the following year's objectives, responsibilities, authorities may be discussed and negotiated.

Performance feedback is often the toughest job and biggest concern for any manger or supervisor. It is personal. It is on-on-one. It can be painful, but is necessary. Evaluations and corrections were often based on Hays points, management by objectives and were fairly straight forward. Now the risks are greater because fairness must be ensured and documented. It often means there must be a face-to-face assessment that if negative can lead to disagreement or confrontation. The following are informal and formal tips for evaluating performance:

- Evaluate performance not the person
- State factual information
- State beliefs and feeling of performance
- Solicit understanding, agreement, and commitment
- Offer suggestions and assistance for improvement
- Reinforce support

In the traditional evaluation, the supervisor or manager evaluates the yearly performance of the person's direct reports. The manager may also participate in the performance evaluation of those two levels down.

A team or a person's stakeholders may also evaluate an individual performance. A person's stakeholders are people who a person works with including bosses, employees, customers, and suppliers. These evaluations tend to present more information however they take longer. This assessment receives feedback from more sources and provides more tips for improvement.

THE NEW OP EX MANAGER

Control circumstances and do not allow them to control you.
Thomas A. Kempis

The Op Ex manager, like all managers, has certain management functions, specifically:

- **Planning.** The Op Ex manager plans and designs Op Ex initiatives.
- **Organizing.** The Op Ex manager organizes staff to effectively and efficiently meet its functional objectives.
- **Controlling.** The Op Ex manager oversees the effectiveness and improvement of Op Ex function processes and products.
- **Directing.** The Op Ex manager directs and oversees Op Ex staff activities.
- **Staffing.** The Op Ex manager hires, trains, and evaluates Op Ex staff performance.

MANAGER/ADMINISTRATOR

The Op Ex manager or administrator still needs to provide effective and efficient leadership to accomplish departmental and business tasks. An Op Ex manager still has certain traditional managerial functions, specifically to:

- **Plan.** The Op Ex manager plans and designs Op Ex initiatives.
- **Organize.** The Op Ex manager organizes Op Ex control and assurance activities.
- **Control.** The Op Ex manager oversees the effectiveness and efficiency of Op Ex staff processes and products.
- **Directs.** The Op Ex manager directs and oversees Op Ex staff activities.
- **Staff.** The Op Ex manager hires, develops, and evaluates Op Ex staff performance.

OP EX MANAGER

Op Ex manager also works closely with operational managers. The Op Ex manager must understand the roles, requirements, and expectations of operational management. This is especially critical as more functional Op Ex responsibilities are being downloaded on operational management and teams.

MANAGERIAL FUNCTIONS

An Op Ex manager in many organizations still has traditional managerial functions of planning, organizing, directing, and controlling:

- Planning
    - Assist in the development of strategic and Op Ex plans.
    - Assist in the development of Op Ex vision and mission documents.
    - Identify key customer/stakeholder requirements.
    - Prioritize customer requirements.
    - Develop plans to satisfy customer requirements.
    - Direct the development of Op Ex policies, procedures, and work instructions.
    - Develop the function budget.
    - Schedule projects and assignments.
    - Develop function objectives and metrics.
    - Monitor objectives and metrics periodically.
    - Correct systems and processes as required.
    - Acquire resources.
    - Develop team structures.
    - Develop metrics.

CHANGING NATURE OF OPERATIONAL ASSURANCE AND CONTROL	
Old Approach	**New Approach**
Op Ex is inspected into a product	Op Ex is controlled and assured
Op Ex department is responsible for Op Ex	Op Ex is everyone's responsibility
Technical skills, such as statistics, are for specialized personnel	Everyone has the opportunity to learn and develop technical skills
Op Ex department polices Op Ex problems	Op Ex department facilitates the solution of Op Ex problems
Op Ex control is a functional area	Op Ex is a state of mind

- Organizing
    - Develop organizational chart.
    - Review employee requirements.
    - Review latest regulatory workplace requirements.
    - Identify improvement projects.
    - Participate in selection of key personnel.
    - Review position descriptions, responsibilities, and capabilities.

- Directing
    - Direct growth and development of personnel.
    - Establish objectives and performance metrics for key personnel.
    - Sustain positive environment for business.
    - Establish and maintain clear policies and procedures.

- Controlling
    - Monitor improvement projects.
    - Monitor Op Ex system documentation.
    - Track progress of teams.
    - Conduct gap analysis - actual to forecasted.
    - Assist and coach the teams.
    - Intervene and shepherd as required.

NEW TYPE OF OPERATIONS MANAGER

A new Op Ex manager and professional is emerging. This person is skilled in many management methods and skills that were not even defined ten years ago, such as reengineering, change methods, benchmarking and the list goes on.

This new Op Ex person has the required technical knowledge but is also comfortable with the strategic business direction and the tactical Op Ex implementation. This new Op Ex manager must be equally conversant with marketing, sales, Supply Management, administration, manufacturing and product development since each has an important Op Ex component.

This new Op Ex manager must also have strong interpersonal skills because senior management may look at the Op Ex function as change agents. While Human Resource professionals or external consultants are retained to serve as change masters, they will work closely with the Op Ex organization. Op Ex professionals may be the bridge between the technical and the people sides of the transformation.

Op Ex professionals may have technical backgrounds and operational experience. They know operations intimately through exposure to Op Ex systems, processes, and products. They know the key players having worked with them to solve problems. As well, they have the confidence of site management and the teams having debriefed, consulted, and facilitated improvement groups.

This person must be flexible and have management skills to make the organization more responsive to customer requirements. The Op Ex organization must be able to influence the organization and be adaptable to fit into many different roles. As well, the organization must:

- Be aware that good is simply not "good enough" anymore.
- Upgrade skills continuously.
- Develop portable, transferable, and marketable skills.
- Be nimble - be quick in anticipating opportunities.
- Seek opportunities and be risk-taking.

- Develop core skills outside of Op Ex disciplines.

GOOD MANAGEMENT OP EX PRACTICES

When many people think about a leader, the company CEO or President come to mind. They are still perceived as organizational generals who point the company in new directions and new markets. The entire organization and its stakeholders then mobilize to go in that direction. This image of leadership is changing for a number of reasons. One person or even a small group of high-level managers don't have the breadth of vision to understand the global marketplace and how an organization can satisfy many customer needs. The marketplace is now segmented by national, cultural, governmental, and other types of requirements. As well, individual customer groups in large markets have their own requirements. It's not possible for an executive group to identify and understand how to satisfy all these groups.

There are now a number of different management practices and styles, including:

- Scientific management - Taylorism
- Situational leadership
- Self-managed teams
- Stewardship management
- Activity based management
- Management by fact
- Management by objectives
- Management by walking around
- Process management
- Project management
- Boundary management

Scientific Management and Taylorism

Frederick Winslow Taylor is considered the father of scientific management. Taylor believed that supervision and efficient experts can determine the precise actions to make work ultimately efficient and scientific. Work could be segmented, precisely defined, and optimized. Workers were considered mechanistic cogs that could be moved and exchanged to determine the optimal methods for working. Mechanistic work managed in hierarchical "command and control structures" became the model for many organizations.

Now while much work is still mechanistic, more and more work requires ingenuity and flexibility to deliver specialized products to different customers. In other words, repetitive tasks can be done through automated machinery, but thinking employees must still manage and organize work in effective and efficient ways.

Situational Leadership

Another leadership style may be called situational. Situational leaders do what is necessary to get the job done with the available human resources in the best possible way. Paul Hersey and Kenneth Blanchard, who developed this model, suggest that situational leaders are directive and supportive. Situational leaders direct teams and individuals in terms of who, what, where, why, when, and how to perform tasks. The other element of a situational leader is to support a team by encouraging, helping, mentoring, and training team members. Teams and individuals are empowered with a vision and mission of success.[8]

Self-Managed Teams

Information, wisdom, and resources can't reside in a group of a few people. The fundamental principle to self-managed teams is to use people, the human resources, in the organization to make decisions. If a company has been hiring the best and brightest for years, why not use their capacity and capability to solve problems, find new customers, and in general make the organization more effective. Employees, either individuals or preferably teams, can take the initiative and maybe even share in the benefits. This type of thinking in many organizations seemed revolutionary when it was first proposed that employees could become leaders, masters of their destiny, and the organization would recognize and even reward them for their initiative.

This can now be seen in many newer organizational models. Front line supervisors often are called team leaders. Supervisors are responsible for coordinating and integrating work of the group. Supervisors are no longer responsible for all process monitoring, control, and improvement. A self-managed team may have hiring and firing authority.

Stewardship Management

Some management styles are more creative and innovative. Peter Block and others advocate a stewardship management style. Organizations that practice stewardship succeed because they place service over self-interest, partnership over patriarchy, responsibility over entitlement, accountability over power, cooperation over competition. Instead of the traditional management tools and concerns of consistency, command and control, organizations focus on partnering with stakeholders.[9]

Activity Based Management

Activity based management was developed from activity-based costing. Fundamental to activity-based management is that an organization can be broken down into a set of activities or processes. An activity is basically what an organization does. An activity like a process has inputs and outputs. The objective of an activity is to convert input into value-added outputs. Value can be added through people, machines, or materials. Activity based management identifies the activities performed in an organization and optimizes their performance and cost. Performance can be measured by Op Ex, service, delivery, or time requirements.

Management By Fact

Management by fact and data allow workers to do the job right the first time. But, people must be able to access and understand data to manage and operate by facts. Employees must have some technical training in computers, data base management, and so on.

Much has been written about the intuitive or gut-level elements of management. The good thing is that when it works, people are called leaders and visionary. When something fails, people are called irresponsible. There is now much more emphasis to provide facts, data, and information to decision makers to ensure decisions are made with all the information at hand. A decision maker can be a person on the line or a senior manager.

There is now much more emphasis on data collection, analysis, and interpretation than ever before. Everyone in the Op Ex function and some companies maintain that everyone in the organization, should be familiar with problem solving tools such as flowcharting, histograms, process capability charts, and Pareto charts.

Management By Objectives
Management by objectives is still the prevalent method for evaluating and directing employees and teams. The essence of MBO is that objectives are tangible, verifiable, measurable, and attainable. The objectives are linked to performance and financial rewards.

The challenge is that objectives are often intangible, can't be verified, are difficult to measure, are attainable only by a super person, and are subjective. The results are lagging performance and cynical employees.[10]

Op Ex by Walking Around
Tom Peters in his management books popularized the phrase, management by walking around, MBWA. From the Op Ex manager's perspective, this can be turned to Op Ex by walking around which is an important function of a newly minted Op Ex manager. The Op Ex manager assumes different roles as Op Ex responsibility is operationalized. The Op Ex manager becomes a coach, supporter, and facilitator of the Op Ex initiative. The Op Ex manager may visit a supplier, department, business unit, and plant to support the Op Ex initiative.

The Op Ex manager may have a floating or virtual office. The Op Ex manager may have an office at corporate headquarters, at a business unit, plant, or even at home. Electronic communications become an important part of the manager's life, using laptop computers, e-mail, cellular telephones, and personal pagers.

Process Management

Most companies are organized in terms of vertical, functional silos also called departments or functions. Accounting, Engineering, Manufacturing, and Sales are examples of silos. These silos have functional specialists who provide one service or function to the organization. These silos are usually organized in terms of a traditional hierarchical groupings. In place of these vertical silos, horizontal processes are being formed with the purpose of integrating work and communications along logical paths to optimize external and internal customer satisfaction.

Project Improvement

Project improvement may be a one-time effort to solve a specific problem or it may be operationalized as a normal part of daily improvement efforts. Op Ex projects may include customer complaint analysis, operational problem solving, supplier improvement, or ISO 9001:2015 registration.

Boundary Management

A popular concept in management is called boundary management. Most employees know their jobs, are accountable for their processes, and then satisfy internal/external customer needs. Many of today's jobs are actual horizontal processes. In this convoluted organizational arrangement, what is the role of the manager? Some say that managers and supervisors now manage organizational boundaries between functional areas while teams manage their processes. In other words, boundary managers ensure information, material, monies, and other resources are provided to make value-adding processes seamless.

MANAGING THE OPERATION FUNCTION

Op Ex managers continuously work with managers throughout the organization. Op Ex managers must understand the roles, requirements, and expectations of operational management. This is especially critical as more functional Op Ex responsibilities are being downloaded on line and operational managers and team.

The Op Ex manager's role more and more are coordinating and integrating Op Ex initiatives, activities, and projects across functional areas and along value adding processes. Work is often organized through critical, core processes instead of vertical functional areas. Op Ex is also integrated across core processes.

The Op Ex manager has to work through and with operational management. The Op Ex manager needs strong interpersonal skills, have knowledge of the organization's core processes and have a general knowledge of how Op Ex adds value to each core process. From a business perspective, the Op Ex manager must:

- Consider the future direction of the function.
- Align the function with the organization's objectives, and vision.
- Be able to demonstrate how the function adds value to the organization and what it will be doing in the future to add value.
- Think strategically and demonstrate how the function will address marketplace concerns and future competition.
- Benchmark best Op Ex practices in industry.
- Ensure the Op Ex function represents and reinforces best industry practice.
- Practice daily what it preaches.

NEXT CHAPTER

Managing change is a difficult process. The process has to respect individual rights, comply with regulations, comply with work agreements, be ethical, and in the end be effective. Challenges also increase if international boundaries, financial exigencies, political constraints. cultural changes, and other factors are involved.

CHAPTER 3
CONSTANT CHANGE

There are a number of early indicators of business trouble. Profits are low. Customer satisfaction is low. Costs are high. Field failures are high. The preferred solution is to increase sales but that may be impossible if a company's reputation for product Op Ex and customer service are poor. The solution is to look internally to determine the root cause of the troubles. While reengineering seems to be the most current attention getting fad, companies are also downsizing, trimming excess capacity, discarding low profit businesses, improving training, and transforming organizations.

CHANGE IS COMING

Leadership appears to be the art of getting others to want to do something you are convinced should be done.
Vance Packard

How does a company become competitive? This is a critical question to all companies and all organizations. Companies are investing in improvement activities when the need is not fully understood or articulated. The following are early warning signs that change, evolutionary, progressive, or transformational, may be necessary:

- Changing competitive environment.
- Low internal and external customer satisfaction.
- Low performance measures in Op Ex, cost, or product development.
- Slow or very fast company growth.
- Mergers, acquisitions, reengineering or other organizational transformation.
- New management.

CHARACTERISTICS OF THE PERFECT CHANGE AGENT

- Flexibility and adaptable
- Excellent communicating abilities
- Leading by example
- Persistence
- Group leadership
- Persuasive
- Organizational and relationship building awareness
- Excellent planning and organization skills
- Adopting a can do and will do attitude
- Promoting a spirit of cooperation

- Competitive loss
- Inflexible organization
- Strong departmental silos
- Low profit margins
- Poor intra and inter organization communications
- More talk and planning than action
- Unclear goals
- No emphasis on training or learning
- Resistance to change
- No top-level management commitment

CRISIS AS STIMULANT FOR CHANGE AND ACTION

An ounce of emotion is equal to a ton of facts.
John Junor

The driver to establishing an Op Ex initiative may be external or internal. Whatever the driver, it is critical the Op Ex strategy evaluates external and internal factors such as business climate, competition, customer expectations, current business practices, organizational culture, and current systems. The rapid rate of change in customer expectations and in com petitive pressures has also created the need for new organizational structures for conducting business. Traditional hierarchical, bureaucratic structures have had to adapt by becoming flat, transformed organizations.

Often crisis is the stimulant for change and action. However, crisis management over the long term can be dangerous because it can lead to dispirited employees and flagging sales. Now, competitive companies seem to be in a permanent crisis state moving from one special project or fad to another. Without hard evidence most managers and teams won't change. What happens if survey data suggests that a major change, transformation, or reengineering may be required instead of simply tweaking the systems. People will resist this radical change intensely. The issue for many Op Ex managers is how to stimulate and reinforce Op Ex over the long haul.

There is no successful approach or standard for starting an organizational transformation or Op Ex initiative. Some companies pursue an incremental or companywide approach. The incremental approach is pilot, plant, or area driven. Lessons learned are translated to new improvement targets and this approach continues throughout the organization. Another approach is to pursue companywide Op Ex where a central core group provides loose direction and support for the initiative. The latter approach is common in large companies that have dozens of locations and hundreds of Op Ex activities. Each Op Ex activity is tailored to the plant or site where the corporate steering committee provides direction, support and continuity to the local activities.

MANAGING CHANGE

Change and transformation may involve a certain amount of discomfort. The challenge is to almost institutionalize discomfort so it becomes part of the organizational fabric, ethic, or culture. In other words, marketplace pressures are communicated internally so people become flexible and almost anticipate the need for change. This is difficult because extreme, external pressures can stymie initiative. People become frozen through fear. Other organizational changes also occur. Change involves disruption. Work and processes may be redesigned. Teams may be formed. The organization is flattened. Suppliers are integrated into the design process.

Resistance is normal and expected when an organization must change. Resistance may occur initially, disappear, or continue throughout the change process. What is the change agent or team supposed to do with pockets of resistance? Communications of the need and urgency of the change is critical. Most people are rational and will understand the need for change if it is plainly explained and if the urgency is particularly evident. Change may also be induced through money, training, promotion, or other mechanisms.

TRANSFORMATION PROCESS

An organizational transformation usually occurs at two levels, establishing drivers and eliminating inhibitors. Drivers for the transformation include senior management commitment, customers, and competitors. Eliminating inhibitors include those elements that obstruct the development of organizational Op Ex initiatives. Inhibitors may include departments, internal functional boundaries, fear, politics, and other forms of resistance.

If senior management feels comfortable with command and control, the driver approach can be used by the organization. Management will establish and drive the mandate for change whether it is reengineering or ISO 9001:2015 registration throughout the operation or into the supplier base. Driving a partnering or employee involvement process may cause additional organizational stress and strains. It is often more effective to use drivers as well as to eliminate inhibitors through decreasing internal resistance and eliminating obstructions. Freeing the organization from existing ways of doing things is difficult but is recognized as an effective means for inducing change. In general, it is wiser to proceed slowly, show daily commitment to the process, understand that actions speak louder than words, couple job security with empowerment, and reinforce actions that support the initiative.

Who is going to be the change agent or facilitator? This person may be from the Op Ex, Human Resources, operational departments, or an outside consultant. Sometimes, organizational development (OD) practitioners are called upon to assist and facilitate the transformation. OD consultants can:

- Provide a roadmap to changing the organizational culture.

- Facilitate meetings.
- Provide training and role model team leaders on facilitating meetings.
- Analyze operational problems and offer solutions.
- Intervene at critical project junctures.
- Resolve conflicts.
- Provide objective and independent evaluations of the process.
- Provide suggestions for improvement.

CHANGE VS. TRANSFORMATION

It is better to be the reorganizer than the organizee.
Normal R. Augustine, CEO Martin Marietta

Some companies are more conducive to change than others. Mature companies in commodity or regulated industries are less likely to change because of entrenched practices, top-heavy hierarchies, and inflexible cultures. Continuous improvement tends to flourish in companies and industries where the marketplace requires speed and flexibility. Op Ex systems and processes must be flexible to adapt to dynamic marketplace and customers. Op Ex systems must be congruent, supportive, and reinforce the culture of the organization.

Many companies are changing but are not transforming themselves but are only tweaking existing systems. Continuous improvement is often associated with 10% or 20% improvements while transformational change may mean 10-fold improvements. Incremental change focuses on establishing Op Ex systems, getting back to basics, reducing costs. Transformational change challenges the basic assumptions of the organization.

Organizational change and transformation processes are fundamentally different. According to Richard Pascale, author of **Managing of the Edge,** change is incremental improvement while transformation is a "discontinuous shift in capability." He defines transformation as a discontinuous shift in bottom line results, in industry standards, benchmarks, and employee perceptions. The transformation process results in major changes in Op Ex or service levels that is brought about by engaged employees. Engaged

TEN RULES FOR CEO'S LEADING ORGANIZATIONAL TRANSFORMATION

1. A strategic framework
2. Top-down involvement
3. Organizational assessment
4. Clarification of core values
5. Work force involvement and participation
6. Inspirational leadership
7. Communications
8. Financial focus
9. Training
10. Personal recognition program[12]

employees view a transformed company almost as a different organization from that of 5 years ago. While change is sufficient for many companies that are performing well, a company in competitive market segment may have to transform itself.[11]

ORGANIZATIONAL TRANSFORMATION PROCESS

In the simplest terms, a leader is one who knows where she or he wants to go and gets up and goes.
John Erskine

A fundamental challenge to all executives, including the Op Ex executive, is managing change. For some managers, this involves being proactive, embracing change, searching for new opportunities and capitalizing on them. For others, this means surviving the latest management fad or simply maintaining operations in a changing workplace.

WHO LEADS AND FACILITATES THE TRANSFORMATION?

Cultural change is an organizational transformation. The Op Ex or Human Resource manager may lead it. However, the transformation can't be delegated. The CEO or another senior manager must make it a personal challenge. The CEO must make it a top priority otherwise it won't happen.

The essential element behind any transformation is a person or team that catalyzes the transformation. Often, this is the Chief Executive Officer or a core group of senior executives. If senior management and the board of directors makes the transformation a priority, devotes times, assigns resources, and manages it then it has a much higher chance of success.

Successful organizational transformations usually require:

- Sense of mission and vision.
- Sense of external urgency.
- Active CEO and senior management involvement.
- Long term view and mandate.
- Involvement and acceptance by all organizational stakeholders.
- Extensive individual and team training and development.
- Customer driven orientation.

CHANGING MANAGEMENT RULES

A critical question is to whom and where should the Op Ex function report? Conventional wisdom says the Op Ex organization should be on the same level as other groups it monitors or audits. The Op Ex organization is at the level where it can do its job. It's reporting relationship has changed as it has evolved from inspection, Op Ex control, operational assurance to operational management. More often, Op Ex is being placed at the same level as major functional groups, such as Engineering, Supply Management, Materials, and Production. The important point is the Op Ex function should be sufficiently high to affect the Op Ex of products and services.

Reporting relationships are critical and communicate important information. Again, there is no one approved reporting structure. However, the following is a common structure. The Op Ex director or vice president reports to the Chief Operating Officer (COO) or to the business operating head. The operating unit Op Ex manager has a solid line reporting relationship to the VP of Op Ex or to the unit manager. This reporting structure communicates important information. If the operating unit or plant Op Ex manager reports to the unit manager then this communicates the operating unit is responsible for Op Ex. If the operating unit Op Ex manager reports directly to the corporate Op Ex vice president, then this communicates there is central control of Op Ex.

ENDANGERED MIDDLE OPERATIONAL MANAGER

Some say the middle Op Ex manager is an endangered species especially in light of rightsizing, team management, instant access to information, and the tendency to push authority and responsibility to the lowest organizational level. Let's look at the role of the middle level Op Ex manager in terms of two tendencies, organizational restructuring and instant information access.

Organizations are getting flatter. Self-managed teams are taking on many of the responsibilities of first level supervision. First level line supervision is taking on the authorities and responsibilities of their supervisors. Something has to give which is middle management. Mid-level Op Ex managers especially may feel left out as organizations are restructured and power shifts to those actually doing the work. Too many companies are asking why do we need middle level management when he or she has little to do? This may be exacerbated when senior management is frustrated by the lack of organizational change, slow Op Ex and stagnant customer satisfaction.

As organizations link their information via networked computers, what is the role of the supervisor or first line manager? Traditionally this middle person evaluated designs, managed operations, and communicated operational information to senior management. Now, team members can evaluate designs. Teams may also self-manage projects. And, senior management can access project, process and product files to assess progress, evaluate budgets and check performance.

These trends create risks and opportunities for middle level Op Ex managers. True, there are and will be fewer middle managers in future organizations. Those left will have broader and deeper spans of control in the flatter organization and have instant access to information for Op Ex decision-making.

The op ex manager must position himself or herself as an agent of change or be perceived as a roadblock to innovation. The mid-level op ex manager may be forced to take early retirement if he or she is perceived as part of the problem. The op ex manager may have to redefine himself or herself as being part of the team to lead the change. One role of the op ex manager is to participate on corporate strategic teams, work with consultants in redesigning the organization, reengineering internal processes, and facilitating problem solving teams to eliminate chronic problems.

NEXT CHAPTER

In the next chapter, Op Ex Empowerment is discussed. Empowerment is more than a buzzword. Employees who are expert at what they do have an active stake in the decisions that affect their processes and work area. Some teams are responsible for and empowered to plan their activities, recruit new members, delegate responsibility, develop procedures, enforce rules, and monitor Op Ex.

CHAPTER 4
OP EX EMPOWERMENT

People support what they help to create.
Anonymous

We've all heard of workplace transformations but in reality, how many companies are going through it? A recent survey sheds some light. Recently 35% of the businesses with 50 or more employees made substantial use of flexible organizational philosophies such as teams, job rotation, and self-managed teams. A number of factors accelerated the adoption of these practices, including an internationally competitive product market, technologies that require high levels of skills, and a total Op Ex emphasis that requires everyone's participation.[13]

WHAT DOES EMPOWERMENT MEAN?

What is empowerment? It seems to mean different things in different companies. Probably, the most common element of empowerment is that decision making is shared horizontally and vertically in the organization. In a team environment, empowerment is the ability to change a process or system. Self-managed teams are probably the most notable example of empowerment.

Empowerment is not a selfless mechanism for sharing or even relinquishing power. In companies where excellence is a daily objective, empowerment has become a way of doing business. Supervisors are no longer responsible for work in an area. Responsibility is now shared with supervision and employees.

Team members in one company are called associates and are real process stakeholders. They participate in decisions that traditionally was the purview of middle management such as deciding whether to buy a major piece of equipment. Everyone has a direct stake in the machine's operation. If process owners are truly responsible then they should have input in the purchase decision. In this plant, hiring is also a joint process involving a hiring board consisting of the personnel director and 3 hourly people. After the orientation and review period, team members and the area supervisor jointly evaluate the new employee's performance, including Op Ex training and team responsiveness.[14]

Empowerment attempts to change the fundamental relationship between management and workers. Instead of having management hold all authority and responsibility, employees share in authority and responsibility. Front line employees have the power and knowledge to do their jobs properly.

Empowerment is more than a slogan, it is an attitude and a way to conduct business. Specifically empowerment incorporates four factors:

1. Authority and responsibility are delegated to the level where the action is taken.
2. Team members have sufficient knowledge and skill.
3. Adequate and timely information is shared among all team members.
4. Confidence and self-esteem are high among members.

INFLUENCING THE ORGANIZATION

Downsizing, rightsizing, or whatever is the current euphemism used to occur only during recessions. Now, it is a fact of business life. There is no lifelong employment and little stability. This creates new and worrisome challenges for the Op Ex professional. Op Ex priorities become unclear during such times. Everyone is looking for cost cutting opportunities which may conflict with Op Ex messages and opportunities. What's the role of the Op Ex professional in these turbulent times especially if he or she is the change agent?

The role of the change agent is difficult in the best of times and is very difficult in these downsizing times. In change resistant organizations, the change agent may feel she or he has a bulls-eye on her back. Why? Change may be revolutionary instead of evolutionary. Senior management may not totally support the initiative. There may be pockets of resistance. The organization is not adaptable or people don't have the skills to affect the change. Cynicism becomes widespread over the newest fad. People already are too busy on day-to-day operations and don't have time for the new project. The wrong person may have been chosen to lead the change initiative. Whatever the cause, the result is the same. Organizational transformation and Op Ex initiatives tend to bog down or get sidetracked. Key people including Op Ex professionals become discouraged over the floundering initiative.

The Op Ex professional and manager may have to refocus on the basics as dictated by the organization's strategic and tactical plans. The Op Ex professional should demonstrate management commitment to improving work processes, enhancing the organizational work ethic, empowering teams, satisfying customers, cutting costs, facilitating inter/intra departmental relations, and improving overall operational efficiencies. For example, senior management will never criticize efforts that support customers in cost-effective ways.

An Op Ex manager can support, reinforce and influence the organizational transformation in a number of ways. One way is through developing trust and commitment through operating management. Operational management support is critical because they have the authority, responsibility and resources to get Op Ex initiatives started and finished.

IT'S ALL ABOUT PEOPLE

Command and control are still an important management method in many organizations. The major difference is that in an empowered work environment, command and control is being exercised over systems and processes instead of over employees.

The process is fundamental to all operational management. Traditional management focused more on the person than on the process. If there was a product nonconformance, blame was immediately placed on the person - he or she screwed up. It was assumed he or she had the capability to improve the process. As emphasis shifted from the product to the process, the individual and process became more linked. The individual, the process owner, is now responsible for understanding, controlling, and improving his or her process which may be answering the phone, designing products, delivering products.

MAINTAINING MOTIVATION AND DIRECTION

After an Op Ex initiative has been running for a while, inertia may set in. Energy flags. The hard work now sets in as results are harder to demonstrate quickly. The steering committee may want to stop and sharpen its vision and mission. The entire organization, not only the Op Ex teams, may want to evaluate where the organization is in regards to Op Ex and where it wants to go. A critical part of the evaluation is to determine the returns on the time, energy and resources invested in Op Ex. After the organization and Op Ex teams have discussed the benefits and costs of previous Op Ex projects, its future direction can be determined.

Maintaining motivation is especially difficult in the service environment where wages, morale, and skills are low. Incentives are used to reward and motivate employees for suggesting improvements or improving operations. Incentives may on the spot rewards such as a prize or a financial bonus. Some companies reward employees by entering them into weekly prize drawings. The prizes are an effective morale booster adding to the excitement of "thank god it's Friday" atmosphere. Prizes can be awarded for team participation, team building, operational suggestions, customer service, following procedures, or going to school. Winners can be nominated by a supervisor, customer, or a team.

PARTICIPATION - INVOLVEMENT - EMPOWERMENT

Empowerment just doesn't happen. The process follows a natural progression from participation to involvement to empowered work teams. Participation is the first step where employees work together in ad hoc teams. In the next step, employees become more involved and show more commitment and caring about work processes and the quality of work life. The employee becomes a process stakeholder. In the empowered workforce, employees and teams do something about what they care about, whether it is improving safety or developing more effective methods for doing a job.

Another term often heard is employee involvement, EI, which is a broad category of people and team technologies to empower people to make decision and to solve problems not only in their work area but throughout the organization. EI is a process where teams try to find creative solutions to chronic or systemic problems. As well, EI strives to standardize business operations with the goal of having consistent output.

Involvement or empowerment are not sufficient in themselves. Employees and teams must be able to work together to get the job done. Training ensures employees have the right skills and know how to do the right thing at the right time. With training and empowerment, employees and teams can then develop workable, creative solutions. However, this process doesn't come naturally. The process may require a dramatic change, some say a transformation in how a business is run.

Specifically, empowerment only works as well as senior management supports it. Other critical success factors include:

- Middle management and first line supervision actively support it.
- Training is provided to all employees.
- Accountability, responsibility, and authority are fully understood and accepted by all.
- Limits of power are understood and not transcended.

What's the best way to start? The empowerment process takes time. Total Op Ex and team involvement can be stressed on a short-term project and can evolve over time. One approach is to focus on an important problem. Members are trained and given the opportunity to work on what concerns the team. The team and its members show that they can change systems. Eventually, the team focuses on new projects.

Some companies are making each person responsible for problem recognition, solving, and improvement of their Op Ex systems. Individuals are empowered and responsible for their system or process step. Teams are still created as needed. For example, a team may be created for a special project or to solve a chronic problem The team stays together as long as it is needed and then it is disbanded.

MANAGEMENT BY OBJECTIVES

Management by objectives works if you know the objectives. Ninety percent of the time you don't.
Peter F. Drucker, writer

Management by objectives (MBO) is relatively straightforward and well known since everyone has been evaluated by the method. If the performance objective is subjective, it can lead to misinterpretations and disagreements.

OBJECTIVES

Management by Objectives (MBO) is probably the most commonly used management tool. It works this way. Senior management determines the objectives of the organization based on strategic plans and mission. These objectives get translated into operational objectives for lower management and the process cascades throughout the organization. Managers, teams, and individuals are rated based on meeting these objectives. Individuals are promoted based on demonstrating superior results. Sometimes, entire teams are compensated based on achieving these objectives.

The major criticism of MBO is that evaluations of individuals can lead to individual competition resulting in highly efficient individuals but ineffective organizations and teams. One response has been to reward and recognize team performance. In progressive organizations, teams often are process owners, responsible for their systems and processes.

OP EX AND MBO

Organizational objectives are usually developed top-down based upon the strategic direction of the company. Objectives can be thought as the steps in the journey to achieve business objectives. Several years ago, the Op Ex director determined the objectives for the function. A conventional wisdom now is that Op Ex is everyone's responsibility.

What is the role of the corporate Op Ex director if operational units are responsible for Op Ex? The Op Ex director assists senior and operational management into developing and monitoring plant, department, and work area business objectives. Performance monitoring is essential in Op Ex. Traditional performance monitoring was usually based on management by objectives where a person was evaluated periodically on meeting pre-agreed upon objectives.

An Op Ex objective should be:

- **Relevant.** Objectives should be aligned and reinforce the organization's strategy and tactics.
- **Doable.** Objectives should be attainable with present resources.
- **Challenging.** Objectives should stretch the individual or team.
- **Measurable.** Objectives should be measured using hard data.

Measure the System Not People

Op Ex pundits believe the process and system should be measured and not particularly people because it takes fear out of the job. The objective is to improve the system not to negatively reinforce individuals in the system. As well individual performance is largely determined by the system in which the individual has little control. People are one of the critical variables in a system or process. The challenge is to measure system performance as well as evaluate team or process owner performance and improvement.

OP EX ACCOUNTABILITIES

There is nothing wrong with making mistakes. The only crime is to make the same mistake over and over again.

Paul F. Orreffice

Corporate Op Ex objectives can only be achieved when Op Ex accountabilities have been defined clearly and assigned. Accountabilities state who is responsible for what Op Ex objective and when it will be achieved. Top management defines and assigns Op Ex accountabilities to divisions, departments, and work units. Each organizational level should have Op Ex accountabilities and objectives. If management does not assign accountabilities, Op Ex plans will not be adhered to and Op Ex objectives will not be achieved.

ACCOUNTABILITY ANALYSIS

Accountability is similar to responsibility. Accountability is the acceptance of responsibility to achieve specific results within a mutually agreed time and to report results back to the customer. The customer may be a manager, team, or other stakeholder. There also has to be a clear understanding of what needs to be done, who will pursue the task, when it will be done, and how the task will be measured. The how's it will be done is usually left to the accountable party. As well, the party needs resources to complete the job whether they are people, tools, materials, knowledge, or monies.[15]

If an organization says that everyone is responsible for Op Ex and accountabilities have not been assigned, then no one is really responsible and virtually nothing is achieved. All too often, it is assumed that the "other person" is accountable for Op Ex and the result is that no one is really accountable. This is exacerbated with employees who are buried 10 levels down in an organization often do not have the external customers' interests in mind because they are so removed from customer concerns.

Enhancing Op Ex and increasing productivity are sometimes pursued concurrently in many organizations. However, emphasizing productivity sometimes leads to lowered Op Ex. Labor, as we mentioned, is an important input of the productivity equation. If productivity is increased by requiring workers to increase their rate of work beyond a comfortable level, the result can be diminished Op Ex. If productivity increases are accomplished without the approval of workers and the support of their union, product quality may decrease.

LEGAL AND REGULATORY ISSUES

The biggest tragedy in America is not the waste of natural resources, though this is tragic. The biggest tragedy is the waste of human resources.
Oliver Wendell Holmes, jurist

Safety is an important element in Op Ex because it affects the quality of work life. It is estimated that employee behavior accounts for 85 to 90% of workplace accidents which is the reason why safety and Op Ex experts are embracing behavioral modification techniques to lower workplace accidents.

SAFETY AND HEALTH

Workplace safety enhances the quality of work life. Ensuring workplace safety is one of the first steps to develop a spirit of error-free work. The risks of a dangerous workplace known for a high incidence of injuries and illnesses are much higher these days due to recent safety legislation, workmen's compensation, and the litigious nature of our society. Multiple workplace stakeholders, including management, union, regulatory authorities, and insurance carriers are working together to make the workplace safer.

At G.M. Saturn, the company safety director and the union health and safety representative have joint responsibility for coordinating the safety and health process at Saturn's 5 million square foot facility. Trained and empowered production teams are responsible for their safety and health. Using an operational management approach, teams set their own safety goals and strive for continuous improvement throughout operations.[16]

Many organizations now employ joint labor/management safety committees which identify critical behaviors in work performance that affect job safety. Line employees, supervision, and staff review coworkers' performance to identify risky behaviors. When unsafe behaviors are identified, they are root cause corrected. An important element is to recognize and reward safe behavior.[17]

Continuous improvement techniques, such as minimizing variation and constancy of purpose, are widely used to minimize the frequency and severity of harmful workplace accidents. The following describes a generalized Op Ex model for monitoring and improving workplace safety:

1. Stress constancy of purpose.
2. Implement a process, not a program.
3. Do it right the first time.
4. Don't blame employees.
5. Assess performance.
6. Improve the process, not the downstream results.
7. Use statistical techniques to identify unusual patterns of variation.[18]

WORKPLACE HARASSMENT

Sexual, physical, and other types of harassment are also major work life issues. Harassment depreciates the quality of an organization – quality of production, safety, security, and work life. As well, harassment is illegal and can result in very high damage awards.

What can be done to stop workplace harassment? First a harassment policy is absolutely essential. The policy states that all harassment is absolutely forbidden at work. Zero-tolerance is becoming the norm in many companies. If an incident is found to be true, the result is dismissal. The hope is zero tolerance may preclude damaging litigation.

The harassment policy should be written and include a clear detailed policy outlining the organization's position on all forms of harassment, a complaint procedure that encourages employees to come forward with harassment complaints, investigative strategies to protect the privacy of the alleged offender and victim, and periodic organizational training stressing the importance of the policy.[19]

WORKPLACE DRUGS

Drugs and substance abuse are another explosive workplace issue that affects the work life. Substance abuse at the least is damaging to productivity and at most can result in loss of life. For example, substance abuse in airlines, trucking, nuclear power plants, pharmaceutical companies can result in catastrophic loss of life.

Drug testing has now become a condition of employment in many companies. Companies have implemented random drug testing for new and existing employees. If an employee fails, the result is immediate dismissal. If the employee voluntary submits to a test then the employee is offered counseling and other forms of assistance.

To communicate the importance of the process, companies are explaining the purpose of the process, explaining how the process works, offering employee assistance, and explaining the consequences of a positive test result.

BUDGETING

Cast thy bread upon the water; for thou shalt find it after many days.
Ecclesiastes

Senior management looks to the Chief Operations Officer and to the Op Ex function to implement elements of its the strategic vision and mission. Each manager is expected to know how their contribution fits into the organization's goals. The Op Ex function and all Op Ex projects must be budgeted, approved and result in measurable savings.

The role of senior management is to determine where the company is going and what its goals, objectives, and priorities are. Senior management relies on operational management to determine how overall goals will be achieved. Senior management develops budget targets for the organization that satisfy shareholders, bond holders, and other financial stakeholders. Budgeting is a management tool to get things done. It operationalizes the strategic plan, objectives, and priorities of the organization.

Long term goals provide direction for the organization to meet its yearly objectives. In the budgeting cycle, middle management proposes and senior management disposes funds to meet its yearly objectives. Once objectives have been developed, then operational and functional management develop plans to achieve the desired objectives. Staff accountants then apply their financial and cost criteria to determine if the proposals pass certain financial criteria, which may be return on investment, internal rates of returns, or cash flow criteria. If they do then funds are allocated to functions and projects. Senior management is primarily concerned with how much a new project will return, how soon returns will occur, and what the risks in the project are.

Budgeting involves four discrete efforts, 1) planning next year's activities, 2) identifying resources, 3) estimating costs for accomplishing the activities, and 4) communicating the requirements to management.

In general, budgeting is a rational planning and decision-making tools to:

- Provide and authorize resources.
- Indicate how time and resources will be allocated and used.
- Prioritize work.
- Communicate the importance of activities.
- Control activities.
- Reinforce and remunerate performance.
- Ensure all organizational areas are going in the same direction.
- Provide resources to get things done.

Budgeting is often the bane of many managers. It takes too long. It starts too early. Management wants more done with fewer resources, including people. The list of complaints goes on.

Budgeting is difficult because:

- Corporate goals, strategies, and plan are sometimes vague or unknown.
- Competition for finite resources is fierce.
- Future is uncertain and unknown.
- Internal politics and game playing are inherent in budgeting process.
- External requirements change rapidly.

RESOURCE REQUIREMENTS TO MANAGE THE OP EX FUNCTION

Once the toothpaste is out of the tube, it's hard to get it back in.
H. R. Haldeman

Capitalizing and expensing are two concepts critical to all managers. Op Ex function operating expenses are charged to the profit and loss statement during the periodic in which they are incurred. Typical operating expenses for the Op Ex department include administration, salaries, consumables, supplies, training, rent, and small purchases.

Major expenditures that are expected to be used for several years are capitalized and entered as assets on the company's balance sheet. These capital expenditures are depreciated and amortized over the expected useful life. Depreciation is the gradual decline of the value of the asset over its useful life. There are a number of acceptable methods for depreciating an asset such as straight-line or accelerated methods. Straight line depreciation for a product with a ten years useful life would have one-tenth of its cost charged or expensed to the Profit/Loss (P&L) account in each of the ten years.

The Op Ex manager needs resources to get a job done on time and on budget so customers and stakeholders are satisfied. The Op Ex manager must justify, authorize, and monitor resource flows including people, equipment/technology, facilities, materials, and technology.

Depending on the level of the Op Ex organization, the organizational culture, policies, and expectations, the Chief Operations Officer or functional Op Ex manager may have extensive or little direct control of these resources. As Op Ex is being operationalized, the Op Ex organization is changing. The Op Ex group has more visibility, stature, and authority but less direct responsibility for the control of Op Ex. Op Ex responsibility rests with the person doing the job.

Business unit, line, functional, and team leaders often have control of the resources that affect Op Ex. The role of the Op Ex manager is to advise, request, convince, negotiate or do whatever is necessary to funnel resources into Op Ex initiatives. The successful Op Ex manager must be able to work with operational management to authorize and assign resources to Op Ex projects. The Op Ex manager thus needs a good working relationship with others.

NEXT CHAPTER

An Op Ex system works best in companies where it has become part of the value or corporate culture of the company. Once Op Ex is perceived as a necessary element to the pursuit of profits, then Op Ex and the pursuit of excellence become part of a company's philosophy for success. The pursuit of Op Ex then provides a sense of common direction for all employees to guide their daily behavior.

CHAPTER 5
OP EX TEAMING

Well run organizations, regardless of their size, promote a distinct culture. The Op Ex culture defines how quality and lean are pursued. It is the explicit and implicit rules that people follow to transact business. The culture adopted by many American companies is excellence through some form of operational management. As we mentioned, sometimes it is called Op Ex, Management Systems, Total Customer Value, Total Customer Satisfaction, or Continuous Improvement. Regardless of the name, for people who work in these companies Op Ex is the shared value and common vision of the organization.

OP EX CULTURE

A company in which anyone is afraid to speak up, to differ, to be daring and original, is closing the coffin door on itself.
Leo Burnett

The culture of an organization consists of the beliefs, values, and actions shared among most of its members. A total Op Ex culture implies that most of the organization shares consistent and core Op Ex values and beliefs. Op Ex culture is a matter of attitude, the commitment and belief by employees of the importance of listening to the customer, designing reliable products, manufacturing products according to specifications, and delivering cheerful service. Much of this sounds like advertising copy but companies that pursue these goals of excellence see the result in higher earnings.

Once introduced, the Op Ex system is internalized by reinforcing and rewarding individual and group efforts that embody the Op Ex culture. A corporate Op Ex culture creates a sense of identity for those who work in the organization and makes employees feel special. Everyone pulling together in the same direction to achieve a common goal engenders corporate unity and strength.

WHY IS CULTURE IMPORTANT?

Before embarking on a total Op Ex initiative, the Op Ex executive must determine whether the organizational culture is appropriate or conducive to total Op Ex. Who should do this? Sometimes, the Human Resources, Training, or Op Ex organization may conduct an environmental assessment. How is the culture assessment conducted? The cultural assessment is a gap analysis or survey of "what is" and "what is required." The "what is" is the current culture. The "what is required" is the core values and culture change senior management and other stakeholders want of the organization.

Words must be used carefully and clearly. Words convey data, information, and ideas when conducting the assessment. The Op Ex executive must pay particular attention and be sensitive to the cultural related issues, including gender, race, age, language, lifestyle, sexual preference, and abilities, each of which is protected by statute.

If senior management mandates or imposes Op Ex on an organization and the people within, employees may perceive this as another mandate from above and just another fad. And, management fads, such as MBO, Op Ex, and automation, have come and gone. Seldom are fads around long enough to be internalized into an organization. There is little time for the initiative to be evaluated before something else takes its place. This too can happen with the Op Ex system unless there is a companywide culture that supports the Op Ex effort.

Senior management is critical to redesigning the workplace because they:

- Lead the transformation.
- Make a case for the change.
- Use organizational behavior and design as part of their business strategy.

- Ensure a successful change effort is collaborative, systemic, and competently managed.
- Promote a continuous learning environment.
- Are keepers of the organizational vision.

CULTURAL AWARENESS

Before Op Ex can be applied to an organization, its culture, values, and workforce must be understood. More of the American workforce is multicultural. Before an organization introduced a new system of behavior or skills, Op Ex or Human Resource management should determine if the technology will take hold. It is essential to understand the culture of the various groups of employees and understand obstacles to learning and adopting a new culture.

Depending on the size and the composition of the organization, a full-blown organizational assessment doesn't need to be conducted. A process as simple as asking impacted employees and supervisors what their concerns are of adopting and adapting to a new culture may be sufficient.

When an organizational change is implemented, a pilot or a controlled implementation may be considered. Many organizational transformations start large and become complicated very quickly. It may be wise to consider a small pilot that addresses the following questions:

- What is the objective of the transformation?
- What transformational methods should be applied?
- Who is responsible for the transformation?
- How will it be known that the transformation results in improvement?
- Who is impacted by the transformation?

CULTURE IS DYNAMIC

Culture is a dynamic not a static concept. Culture must reflect the environment and competitive marketplace. Culture must also be flexible to change with the times. For example, AT&T for a hundred years had a culture that stressed the highest production standards and highest service. For many years, AT&T, as a regulated monopoly provided a high level of service. Customers were willing to pay for the service through their rate structure.

Now, this has changed. Customers want competitive rates for their telephone service at the same level of Op Ex service. Unfortunately, there is a trade-off because customers want the same level of service at the same price. AT&T changed its culture of service at any cost to a culture that pays attention to optimizing design, Op Ex, delivery, and value.

The culture of lifetime, womb-to-tomb, employment changed at AT&T. This culture attracted, rewarded, promoted, and nurtured risk-averse behavior. Lifetime employment, internal promotion, Op Ex service, and technical excellence were messages that AT&T management communicated to its employees.

The competitive marketplace is forcing change. Current AT&T management encourages intelligent risk-taking. Employment reflects market demand. Unprofitable operations are shut down. AT&T outsiders are hired to manage profit-oriented operations. Op Ex service is balanced against service, price, and availability.

ESTABLISHING AN OP EX CULTURE

Attitudes and feelings influence day-to-day behavior which is often more important than policies, procedures and work instructions. But, capturing hearts and minds is more difficult than developing the documentation infrastructure. Companies can establish and reinforce a positive culture by:

- Establishing a consistent vision, mission and plans.
- Empowering all employees.
- Pushing decision making to the lowest possible level.
- Providing employees tools through up to date training.
- Improving intra and intercompany communications.

ETHICS AND CORE VALUES

Ethics basically is the ability to determine right from wrong. In an Op Ex sense, ethics is the ability to do the right things right. Or, as Philip Crosby eloquently said: "Do it right the first time." Ethical lapses happen and may involve improper waivers, negligent corrective action, fraudulent certifications, and sexual harassment.

Ethics should be a part of an organization's Op Ex culture and ethic. Ethics should strike to an organization's core values which reflect on its overall reputation. For example, Motorola, ATT, Fidelity Investments are companies with strong ethical core values that reinforce their reputation as world class organizations.

Core values are as important as core competencies. Each reinforces the other. Core values establish the principles and attitudes for an organization. Core values include organizational beliefs, attitudes, principles ethics, and culture. Core values may mean the difference between success and failure of the Op Ex initiative.

The area of Op Ex is fraught with opportunities to do the wrong things. Op Ex professionals must pay attention to due professional care, ethical duties, professional conduct and responsibilities, and regulatory compliance. The Op Ex function and management specifically should be exemplars of ethical behavior. The Op Ex manager should assess the ethical risks throughout the Op Ex organization, communicate clear standards of behavior, develop reporting and corrective systems for unapproved behaviors.

Establishing and maintaining a core set of values is difficult. It's not something that can be mandated from above and then installed upon the organization through policies and procedures. Ethics goes beyond standards of conduct. Values and ethics are a personal commitment to do what's right, right what's wrong, and to improve continuously.

TYPES OF TEAMS

The power of the waterfall is nothing but a lot of drips working together.
Anonymous

D. Quinn Mills in **The Rebirth of the Corporation** describes the new organization as composed of clusters, teams of employees, working for similar larger goals. The clusters of employees may share the following:

- Handle their own administrative functions.
- Develop their own expertise.
- Express a strong customer orientation.
- Are action oriented.
- Share information broadly.
- Accept accountability for business results.[20]

Teams can be loose clusters of individuals or they can be highly structured bound by contracts and mutual obligations. They can be self-managed or can be tightly managed. They can be permanent or temporary. The form and shape of a team is largely dictated by its purpose and effectiveness. A conventional wisdom is the shape and form have to be flexible depending on skills, purposes, objectives, culture, company politics, technology, and a number of other factors. Technology is one of the more powerful drivers in the formation of the team. Technology has made the flow of data, information, and ideas much easier. Computer networks and groupware allow different team members to share information.

EXAMPLES OF TEAMS

The following are examples of teams:

- Self-managed teams
- Work area or process teams
- Task groups
- Customer-supplier teams
- Op Ex teams
- Virtual teams

Self-Managed Teams

Self-managed teams are a common form of bottom-up management where workers constructively participate in finding answers to problems that directly affect them and more importantly doing something about them. No one knows better how to improve product or service Op Ex than the people directly involved. Self-managed teams provide employees more control over their jobs, encourage creativity, and give employees a bigger stake in the organization.

Effective self-managed teams focus on core processes, products, and critical organizational points that provide the highest organizational leverage and rewards. In order to do this, the team needs the following:

- **Sense of mission.** The team has to be motivated, maybe at a visceral level, to get a job done.
- **Value driven.** The team has to understand, reinforce, and operate within the organization's values and culture.
- **Knowledge and skills.** The team has to have the skills to get the job done.
- **Resources.** The team must have resources to get the job done, including, people, authority, monies and other resources.
- **Deployment.** The team must be able to implement its objectives throughout the organization.

Work Area Or Process Teams

Sometimes improvement teams are formed from process owners. This team understands the process, can identify its key variables, and is continuously responsible for it. The improvement team usually rotates people from the work area so over a two-year period everyone has a chance to participate. New people continually provide fresh ideas and perspectives.

Customer-Supplier Team

Customer-supplier teams may be formed if a supplier is not meeting customer expectations. A team may be formed to determine why the supplier's shipments are being rejected. The customer wants the supplier's shipment to go directly to production. The project team would consist of the procurement engineer, buyer and design engineer.

The customer team may review specifications with the supplier during an on-site audit. Specifications may be rewritten to conform to customer needs and to supplier capabilities. The team investigates the supplier's production and Op Ex processes to ensure the supplier's processes meet customer requirements. The team may provide the supplier with corrective action information or conduct an initial production audit of the supplier's facility.

Op Ex Teams

The Japanese developed quality circles as part of their drive to apply Statistical Process Control (SPC) techniques. Once established, quality circles broadened the scope of their responsibility beyond improving product quality. Workers presented proposals on improving productivity, improving material distribution, increasing shop safety, and enhancing product design. Management listened and accepted these ideas. As a result of Japanese successes, the quality circle concept was exported to the United States in the 1980s, where it was integrated into Op Ex.

Virtual Teams

As more people work off-site, on the road, in a plant, at headquarters, at home, and throughout the world, virtual teams are becoming more common. A virtual team is a distributed work group who work closely together to accomplish a project. Individuals may be separated by many miles but work together to solve a problem, design a product, or implement a software system.

Instant communication and transfer of information allow people to work as part of a team. Electronic communication through email, fax machines, telephones computers, groupware, and video-conferencing allow teams to be linked almost as if they were in the same building. For example, if one person needs some information, he or she can retrieve it through email.

Virtual teams while seemingly positive still have some drawbacks, specifically:

- Face-to-face contact is still important.
- Computer communications misses subtleties.
- Virtual team commitment and trust are not as strong as real-time teams.

HOW OP EX TEAMS WORK?

There is no way to make people like change. You can only make them feel less threatened by it.
Frederick Hayes, business person

An Op Ex team often has an objective which is to solve a problem. A team follows a logical cycle, specifically:

- Steering committee is formed
- Facilitator is selected
- Problem is identified
- Problem is analyzed
- Solution is presented
- Solution is implemented

STEERING COMMITTEE IS FORMED

A management steering committee is formed to develop the overall goals and objectives of all Op Ex teams. The steering committee can be at the division or plant level. The steering committee, composed of management and labor, selects the overall coordinator, allocates resources, develops policy, and establishes the direction of the Op Ex initiative.

While, the steering committee establishes the broad objectives of the empowerment process, the team may choose the project to work on. For example, if the steering committee mandates cost-reduction objectives then a team may decide to reduce costs in customer service.

FACILITATOR IS SELECTED

A facilitator or leader may coordinate meetings and direct the team. The facilitator is either a staff member from corporate training or an outside consultant. The facilitator ensures meetings do not become gripe sessions, going nowhere. The facilitator structures meeting agendas so teams focus on doable, measurable, and cost-effective projects.

PROBLEM IS IDENTIFIED

The team first identifies problems common and familiar to the team members. Problems and issues are uncovered by brainstorming or through some other technique. Team members identify problems that are aligned with management concerns and the company's mission. Team members are considered experts on what is important in their area of work, since they perform certain tasks daily. Team members will be more committed if they can identify or have input in the projects they work on.

PROBLEM IS ANALYZED

Team members then analyze the problem and propose solutions by brainstorming or by obtaining expert information from staff specialists.

SOLUTION IS PRESENTED

The problem and proposed solution are then presented to the steering committee. The steering committee reviews the proposal and decides whether or not to implement recommendations. Regardless of the decision, team feedback is essential so enthusiasm is maintained and reinforced.

SOLUTION IS IMPLEMENTED

If the steering committee blesses the recommendations, the team implements the solution. If recommendations cannot be implemented because of excessive costs or for some other reason, then management communicates its decision to team members in a supportive, positive manner. Otherwise, team members may get the message that management is using the Op Ex theme to manipulate them.

HOW TO FORM AN OP EX TEAM

Never one thing and seldom one person can make for a success. It takes a number of them merging into one perfect whole.
Marie Dressler

Team building is a critical responsibility of the Op Ex manager. The Op Ex manager may be called upon to build a team internally or externally. Internally, the Op Ex manager has to establish teams and integrate groups to accomplish Op Ex function tasks. Externally, the Op Ex manager commits function resources and facilitators for Op Ex projects. The Op Ex manager may even facilitate senior level management teams.

Team building is often an evolutionary process. Self-managed teams may have to evolve in vertically structured organizations because of a fear of the unknown or insecurity about new reporting relationships.

Building a team does not end when it is first formed. Team building is pursued throughout the team's existence. Issues or problems will arise on a daily basis that need resolution. Decisions must be made. Resources must be allocated. Things must get done. Information is transmitted and received. All of these processes require interaction and interfacing among team members. As long as this occurs, the team leader must shepherd, tweak, and correct the process, if necessary.

The following are critical issues in the formation of a team that must be understood and addressed:

- Alignment of team objectives with the organization's
- Stakeholders and customer identification
- Team recruitment
- Reporting structure
- Reporting results
- Team success metrics
- Employee/team evaluation
- Team support

- Having fun
- Maintaining motivation and direction

TEAM RECRUITMENT

Op Ex teams may be composed of part time or full-time employees. If an improvement project requires immediate attention, such as a product recall, then the team may require full time participation to contain the damage, fix the problem, implement the root cause solution, or satisfy customers. Daily, maybe hourly meetings, are held until the problem is solved. In this case, the Op Ex team may have to put their daily work on hold or put in long hours until the problem is resolved. Or, a team may work on minor, chronic problems that require continual participation.

Many problems can be resolved during selection or recruitment of team members. If the team leader, Op Ex manager, or whomever is doing the recruitment communicates requirements and benefits of project participation, there is a higher chance people will volunteer for the team. If people are assigned to the Op Ex team, there may be resentment especially if the person has good reasons for not participating. The person may work reluctantly with others. In a worst case, the person may sabotage the project or directly impede its development.

Should team members be assigned or have the option to volunteer? This is a key question. Some unions have objected to Op Ex team assignment and have taken it to the National Labor Relations Board. There are a number of elements that affect the composition of the team. A major element is whether the team is composed of supervisory and professional personnel or union personnel. Work rules, contracts, and regulatory rulings may affect how to approach recruitment.

While there are no strict guidelines for recruiting and staffing a team, the following are suggestions for effective recruitment and staffing:

- Recruit from appropriate operating and staff departments.
- Recruit, don't assign, personnel to the team.

- Explain the purpose, objective, outcomes, and deliverables of the project.
- Explain the benefits to the individual.
- Explain why the person is being asked to participate.
- Explain the level of commitment and participation.
- Explain the process, techniques, and skills required for a successful project.
- Explain the risks in the project.
- Surface and resolve potential conflicts.
- Allow a person to decline participation.
- List the people on the team.
- Encourage candor and honesty in recruiting discussions.

TEAM BUILDNG

There are literally hundreds of books on team building, each with its own prescription for total success. What's the truth for team success? There is no one set of prescriptions, except that the team should be tailored to the organization, processes, systems, and stakeholders.

Many experts include the following recommendations:

- Ensure senior management support.
- Create a sense of urgency.
- Encourage team diversity.
- Celebrate successes.
- Encourage honesty and trust building.
- Establish team vision and mission.
- Obtain sufficient funds and resources.
- Establish lines of communication.
- Make decisions by consensus.
- Provide direction, policies, and standards.
- Respect the individual.
- Focus on doable and results oriented projects.
- Establish clear rules of behavior.
- Seize the moment.

- Challenge the team.
- Communicate clearly.
- Understand the culture of the organization.
- Identify people's needs and how to satisfy them.
- Choose champions from management and from line employees.
- Ensure there is an immediate payoff in the improvement.
- Choose realistic improvement projects.
- Make team participation voluntary.
- Provide positive feedback, recognition and rewards.

TEAM EMPOWERMENT

The authorities, responsibilities, ethics, policies, procedures and protocols associated with empowerment should be explained and discussed with team members. These topics should be explained, discussed, and reinforced in an early meeting:

- Understand organizational directions and customer requirements.
- Be able to meet timetable and commitments.
- Operate efficiently and effectively.
- Be composed of motivated people.
- Focus on relevant, operational problems.
- Follow proper protocols.
- Make decisions based on real data and information.
- Understand internal systems and process.
- Give credit where it belongs.
- Thank operational management for their help.
- Document and deliver on promises.
- Be willing to try new ideas and methods.
- Stress open communication.
- Treat team members with respect.
- Use facilitators to guide the team if necessary.
- Attempt not to disrupt operations.
- Understand and articulate "what's in it for me".
- Establish project plan, objectives, and metrics.
- Focus and prioritize projects.

TEAM CHALLENGES

Certain people and certain things require to be approached on an angle.
Andre Gide, Writer

There are many challenges to forming and maintaining a supportive team environment. Highly creative employees sometimes can't work as part of a team. Also people may have been hired, trained, rewarded for one set of behaviors and now must change behaviors. For example, people may have to be coached and rewarded to change from competition to collaboration.

Challenges to the team also include:

- Vague objectives
- Breakdown of trust
- Expectation creep
- Looking out for #1
- Team assignment conflicts

VAGUE OBJECTIVES

If the team doesn't have a clear objective, it will wander aimlessly. Team meetings become a chance to visit. Or, arguments and power struggles will occur because everyone wants to go in a separate direction.

Sooner or later, supervision and management will wonder what's going on and what's being done. Management will feel that resources are being squandered. Supervision may say that "I told you it wouldn't work." The team must specify expected outcomes or results. Resources are then provided and the team is accountable for achieving results.

BREAKDOWN OF TRUST

Many organizations in the U.S. had a simple approach to organizational commitment - trust coming down the organization was rewarded with trust going up. This compact has recently been broken. Employees seem to believe that trust has been broken with downsizing, reengineering and their other initiatives that have resulted in many employees departing and those who remain having to work longer hours for less remuneration. Employees, including many managers, feel they have little reason to trust senior management.

Some of the problem can be laid to poor communications about expectations. Lately many employees believe the organization does not recognize, care, trust, listen or reward people appropriately. Senior management believes employees don't understand global competitive pressures or customer requirements.

EXPECTATION CREEP

Expectation creep is common in implementing projects. After consulting with stakeholders, the team develops realistic objectives. These are written and everyone agrees to them. As the project evolves, stakeholders or team members sometimes want the team to solve a wider problem. The team however was charged with a much narrower scope. The team may not be able to meet the enlarged expectations. This is a recipe for failure. The team should work closely with stakeholders to ensure both party's expectations and requirements are aligned.

LOOKING OUT FOR #1

There is a major struggle going on in business. Companies are downsizing. The implicit contract between employer and employee is disappearing. Many people are taking a "what's in it for me" or "looking out for # 1" attitude. In this environment, operational management is trying to foster collaboration, cooperation, and other types of partnering arrangements in a "me" instead of "we" climate. There is really no easy way to change from "what's in it for me" to a "what's in it for us" attitude. Employees realize they may be rightsized in a month. Or, suppliers know they will be asked to partner with a customer who will be going form five suppliers to a single source in a year.

TEAM CONFLICTS

Often, people conflicts seem to be the most damaging. There may be conflicts because of pressures at work or at home or differences in personal tastes, prejudices, beliefs, actions, and attitudes. The list of reasons goes on. Conflicts should be resolved amicably and fairly. This may be easier said than done. Problems may arise again. Team members may not have ownership in a project. Process owners may not care about their process. Relationships may sour or there may be some other inadvertent outcome.

As people conflicts arise in a team setting, how they are resolved reveals much of the future effectiveness of the team. Team cohesion can be established through reasoning or through emotional responses. In a reasoned response, a person understands what's in it for him or her to resolve a dispute amicably. In an emotional response, a person reacts to a situation, often seeing it from his or her personal point of view.

TEAM ASSIGNMENT CONFLICTS

Most Op Ex teams are part time assignments for their members. Individuals must still go back to their daily jobs. They must satisfy their supervisor's and internal customer's concerns. The time and resources expended working on an Op Ex team and one's job can be a source of conflict.

A person's daily work must still go on. A person still must answer voice mail or a customer's problem. However, conflict can arise about conflicting meetings, paperwork pressures, multiple stakeholders, time and other conflicts. Who or what takes precedence? This is one of the many issues confronting Op Ex teams. As a general rule, one's day job, the full-time job takes precedence over an improvement project. If there is a recall or customer issue that requires immediate attention then these will take precedence.

TIME AND OTHER CONFLICTS WITH OPERATING GROUPS

Often teams must secure resources from operational managers who may be at different organizational levels. For example, the plant manager may become involved if a team wants to change the process, buy equipment, develop new procedures, purchase materials from a new supplier, or reroute materials.

Another conflict involves time. Functional managers have daily operating priorities. For example, a plant manager must produce sufficient, low-cost products to make his or her customers happy. A plant manager may have multiple stakeholders including the controller who wants to keep costs low, a boss who wanted a production report yesterday, employees who want to be treated fairly and so on. As well, senior management may be urging the plant manager to pursue simultaneous initiatives, including cost reduction, reengineering, robotics, MRP, and three Op Ex projects.

The plant manager is going to pick and support those projects that are the most important. How does he or she determine what is most important? A plant manager may determine what is important by how he or she is compensated, by the latest flavor of the month, by what the customer requires, or by what poses the most risk. The bottom line is the Op Ex manager has to get this person's attention. The Op Ex manager understands there are competing projects and only limited resources.

The Op Ex manager has a number of ways to get a project supported by top plant management, including:

- A senior officer supports and champions the project.
- A customer requires it.
- A senior manager, maybe a personal immediate boss, suggests implementation.
- The organization as a strategic mission adopts the project.
- The Op Ex manager may reason with the plant manager.
- The Op Ex manager may ask the plant manager to support and champion the project.

POLITICS

Probably nothing drives an Op Ex manager more crazy than company politics. Politics is basically the organizational process of determining who gets what, when, and where which usually determine who gets ahead. Organizational politics is the ability to get things done. It is the ability to obtain resources, to solicit cooperation, for people to go the extra step, and to harmonize often conflicting organizational concerns. Being comfortable and adept at politics is the bread and butter of any manager, consultant, and employee.

Op Ex professionals sometimes believe decisions should be based purely on technical merit and feasibility without taking into consideration political and organizational factors. Often the culture, ethics, politics, and norms of the organization are more essential to initiative and project success than technical or economic issues.

TEAM AUTHORITY AND RESPONSIBILITY

The classic organizational challenge is balancing authority with responsibility. In the new Op Ex environment, the reverse now occurs. Op Ex is everyone's responsibility. The Chief Operations Officer has authority to directly and indirectly facilitate Op Ex initiatives. However, operational managers are often responsible for initiating, controlling, and allocating resources to the project.

The Op Ex manager does less direct doing but does more supporting. Words that are commonly heard about excellent Op Ex managers include: coaching, supporting, planning, designing, recommending, suggesting, assisting, partnering, and mentoring.
Some Op Ex managers will thrive in these changes and other will resign themselves to flow with the change. Unfortunately, the latter approach can lead to a victim mentality. The prospering Op Ex manager will create an organizational situation as well as a personal vision to prosper from the changes. The role of the emerging Op Ex manager will be to reinvent the Op Ex organization. The new Op Ex manager must know Op Ex technologies but also understand how to organize, motivate, coach, train, mentor, and energize employees.

REPORTING STRUCTURE

A team may report to the Op Ex function, another functional area, higher level project team, or to others. What complicates the reporting relationship of the Op Ex team is that team members may report to different departments with different priorities. For example, a multi-disciplinary technical team may have members from 5 or more groups.

Teams must show results. Teams, sometimes as many as 15 are given 20 minutes in front of senior management to make presentations, to recount their story of Op Ex success. Team leaders describe the Op Ex project, why it was chosen, how the challenge was pursued, and what the outcomes were. Outcomes should result in hard savings, demonstrable customer satisfaction, or new products.

TEAM EFFECTIVENESS

In any organization, employees become dissatisfied because of poor communications, delays, poor material, internal conflicts, or poor supervision. This translates into an "I don't care" attitude, which results in lower Op Ex work, absenteeism, or product waste.

Teams allow workers to identify problems, suggest, and implement solutions. Improved communication and a closer working relationship between management and labor hopefully results. While teams may not transform an adversarial relationship into a cooperative one, teams do provide management and employees a chance to talk to each other, instead of past each other.

Worker perceptions are important to the successful implementation of the empowerment initiative. If workers perceive the team or project as a management tool to impose work rules or productivity/Op Ex quotas, teams will fail. A successful team is an avenue to permit workers to participate in controlling their employment future. A successful project hopes to inspire and guide workers to make better use of their work time to produce a quality product or to better service a customer.

If teams are perceived as a management technique imposed on workers, then the entire Op Ex system may fail even though Op Ex teams are only a small part of the larger Op Ex initiative. Teams should be seen as a useful communication and problem-solving tool that work when applied to specific company and work area needs.

OP EX TEAM PERFORMANCE EVALUATION

People forget how fast you did a job - but they remember how well you did it.

Howard Newton

A fundamental tenet of operational management is that everything including team and individual performance is measured, evaluated, and improved. Another important element of operational management is accountability. A person or team is responsible for getting the job done efficiently, effectively, and economically.

Performance feedback is often the toughest job and biggest concern for any manager or supervisor. Person-to-person, face-to-face, evaluations are hard even to the best managers. When evaluation is positive, everyone wins. When performance has to be corrected, monitored or improved, disagreements may arise. A worker may blame a superior for showing preference or being out of touch.

In the traditional approach to performance appraisal, a supervisor objectively evaluated an individual's contributions and performance. Improperly conducted, performance appraisals can destroy morale, inhibit motivation, or result in competing employees.

TEAM SUCCESS FACTORS

Most Op Ex teams share common features including:

- Team meets frequently and at scheduled times.
- Team membership is voluntary.
- Management is supportive.
- Op Ex culture is actively promoted.
- Team facilitator involves everyone.
- Team members support each other to develop personal growth.
- Team members choose projects to work on, not management.
- Training is provided to workers and to management.
- Projects are measurable and profitable.
- Projects are doable.
- Projects are limited in scope.

TEAM SUCCESS METRICS

The basic metric of success is whether the customer is satisfied with the results. Objectives may be derived or determined by the customer, process owner, or some other stakeholder. Common requirements or expectations of success include attaining process capability and control, increasing customer satisfaction, increasing time-to-market, and lowering costs. Usually the above requirements have a measurement or metric. For example, process capability may be increased from 1.0 to 1.33 to 1.66 to 2.0 over several years. Or, unit product costs may be lowered 5% a year.

Performance review is a reluctant duty of management. It is one of the most painful duties of any Op Ex manager. In the traditional evaluation, supervisor and employee meet across a table once a year to discuss performance while the supervisor rates the employee. In much the same manner, teams must be evaluated in terms of their performance.

The Op Ex organization often will work with operating departments to establish and support their Op Ex implementation teams. A customer organization may provide all the resources for the project, team members, monies, or equipment. The Op Ex department provides the expertise to support the teams. The Op Ex department may facilitate meetings, coordinate meetings, assist in establishing reasonable and doable goals, serve as a communications link, and provide training.

PERFORMANCE INDICATORS

The first 90% of the project takes the first 90% of the time. The last 10% of the project takes the last 90% of the time.
Anonymous

Measurement or metrics should be tied to what matters to the organization, which may be customer satisfaction, time-to-market, profitability, cost reduction, or operational effectiveness. If non-critical or non-essential activities are measured, the rationale of the improvement project and ultimately the Op Ex initiative may be questioned. Over-measurement may be as critical as under-measurement. Some organizations measure everything in sight.

It has become a conventional management wisdom that excellent companies measure critical processes, system, and products. What should be measured? Theoretically, thousands of factors, elements, attributes, features, and characteristics throughout an organization can be measured. But, what critical data should be measured, collated, and analyzed? A few important questions to ask are:

- Is the particular attribute or characteristic related to customer satisfaction or to Op Ex?
- Is the data or information important to other organizational measures, such as productivity, costs, or employee satisfaction?
- Is the data universally understood to be important?
- How will the data be used to improve performance, efficiency, Op Ex, or effectiveness?

Soft and hard attributes or activities can be measured. Soft measures include internal customer satisfaction, team effectiveness, opportunity cost, and quality of work life. Hard measures include capability indices, mean-time-to-failure, Six Sigma, and others. The indicators or metrics of Op Ex may exist in various operating departments or accounting systems.

More companies are pursuing "world-class" measures. "World class" to many companies mean comparing systems and processes with the best in their industry, in the U.S., or in the world. Common manufacturing and operations measures include equipment set-up time, area and machine productivity, cycle time by product, inventory turns by product, and improvement.

360 DEGREE EVALUATION

In the 360-degree evaluation, an employee is evaluated by a number of process stakeholders, the person's direct supervisor, other process supervisors, same-level customers, same-level suppliers, and finally by subordinates. The 360 degree evaluates is usually process instead of function driven and oriented. There are a number of benefits and challenges to the 360-degree evaluation. Let's first enumerate the benefits:

- Strengths and weaknesses are recognized
- Strengths are recognized and rewarded

- Weaknesses are corrected
- Evaluation is more objective and impartial
- Emphasis is on total process
- Favoritism is eliminated

Some of the challenges to a 360-degree evaluation include:

- Is time consuming
- May require consensus building
- May lead to the highest or lowest common denominator evaluations
- May become evaluations by committee

SYSTEM PERFORMANCE EVALUATION

Many Op Ex practitioners suggest management should evaluate the systems and processes for which middle and senior management are primarily responsible. Systems and processes have a strong influence on organizational performance. Operational management is based on the principle that Op Ex is a function of the system which is under management control. Low level employees and supervisors can't change the system in which they operate and are sometimes prisoners of. The primary purpose of the evaluation and measurement then becomes to improve Op Ex systems which are usually beyond a person's or team's control.

Op Ex practitioners believe performance appraisal systems must be consistent with Op Ex principles, specifically:

- Focus on the whole system.
- Gather evaluations from multiple sources.
- Ensure evaluations are team as well as individual focused.
- Tailor performance objectives and measures to a specific process and system.
- Evaluate performance not the person.
- State factual information.
- Solicit understanding, agreement, and commitment.
- Offer suggestions and assistance for improvement.
- Reinforce support and improvement.

GAINSHARING

Fundamental progress has to do with the reinterpretation of basic ideas.
Alfred North Whitehead

What's the best way to motivate people is an ongoing discussion. Some believe that money does not motivate people in the long term. Some experts argue that people don't solely work for money but also for intrinsic motivation. Money will probably continue to be the critical motivator of individual and team performance and will be a major inducement for organizational change.

WHAT'S IN IT FOR ME?

Too many companies sell and promote Op Ex and improvement initiatives from their perspective, in other words what's in it for the company. If Op Ex has to be communicated to line employees it should be done in terms of the employee's self-interest or what's in it for them. Sometimes, Op Ex has to be sold to employees for them to embrace it. Once the benefits of Op Ex are understood then it will be operationalized. Employees won't embrace a new method, idea, or philosophy unless they understand what's in it for them. Otherwise, "this too shall pass" attitude will result. Op Ex may be explained as improving safety, easing work, or enhancing employee bonuses.

A common method of dealing with the "what's in it for me" attitude is to develop compensation and rewards systems that tie Op Ex with team or individual performance. Sometimes these systems are called gainsharing or bonus systems. These systems have significantly increased employee involvement.

COMPENSATION

"OK, what's in it for me?" Employees are asking this basic question. One of most critical inducers is compensation. Employees want to be compensated fairly. The issues and questions that are brought up are not easy to address:

- How should a company reward satisfactory, good or exemplary work?
- How are teams rewarded?
- How is individual performance on a team rewarded?

Not too many years ago, compensation was a nice, tidy system. Every employee from executive to the line worker knew the rules of the compensation game and was rewarded accordingly. Executives and managers knew their Hay points and bonus plan. Line employees knew their salary ranges, yearly incremental increases, and cost of living raises.

Much of this has changed. Companies now reward employees based on performance than on longevity or other factors. Performance measurements are usually tied to important process, plant, business unit, or organizational objectives.

Senior executives often don't have lifetime employment but are employed through contracts which are renewable based on overall business performance or stock price. Managers are rewarded based on business unit performance as well as Op Ex, team performance, external/internal customer satisfaction, and other factors. Sales people are remunerated based on total sales, customer service, and internal customer satisfaction. Engineers may be remunerated based on designing new products, improving time-to-market, working as a team, or improving product reliability. Line employees are rewarded based on skills, attitudes, and acquired knowledge. As well, everyone is rewarded based on internal and external customer satisfaction measures.

Financial rewards are but one method for motivating employees. However, with downsizing and the increase of work, financial rewards or even a paycheck are not enough to motivate and retain excellent workers. Other motivations include freedom, personal growth, flextime, daycare, recognition, and challenging work.

USE AS BASIS FOR CAREER DEVELOPMENT

From the employee's point-of-view, performance-based appraisal discussions should serve as the basis for career development. Since the marketplace is not static, employees can't be static. A conventional business wisdom is that most future employees will have portable, transferable, and marketplace skills that will be sold to the highest bidder. The yearly or quarterly performance appraisal is an excellent time for the employee to adjust his or her skills and aptitudes to the needs of the organization. This ensures his or her continued employability by adding value to the organization.

COMPENSATION, RECOGNITION AND REWARDS

Recognition of a job well done is high on the list of motivating influences for all people; more important in many instances than compensation itself.
John Wilson

The entire recognition and rewards system for recognizing performance is changing. Fewer companies provide automatic cost of living adjustments (COLA) and salary increases. Government, state, and local agencies still follow a matrix based on time in grade and overall increases negotiated by contract.

Companies are moving towards performance-based incentive mechanisms. Each year, a person has a base salary. There is no cost of living adjustment or automatic increase in salary. A person's compensation is based on individual or team performance or adding value to the organization. Depending on performance the person may get a bonus, stock options, comp time, or other perquisites.

In addition, the following are major trends in rewarding employees:

- Rewards are based on measurable performance often based on customer satisfaction and other market measures.
- Lifetime employment is a matter of history.

- Raises based on seniority or cost of living occur less often.
- Incentive compensation is becoming more common.

COMPENSATION

Compensation for work involves salary, benefits, and other inducements. Inducements may include profit sharing, special bonuses, stock options, prizes and other remunerations. Because of the changing competitive marketplace, compensation is changing. Salary is usually pegged to performance or some other key business indicator. Benefits are tailored to individual needs, are menu driven, and are established so costs are shared between employer and employee. Other forms of remuneration are also tied to business performance. As well, education and training has become more critical as employees and organizations must adapt to marketplace pressures.

NEXT CHAPTER

In the next chapter, Op Ex Strategic Op Ex Planning is discussed. An Op Ex project requires extensive planning first among the project stakeholders and then among the team members who are brought together to discuss their expectations and requirements.

CHAPTER 6

STRATEGIC OP EX PLANNING

Are companies profiting from your Op Ex investments? This is becoming the critical question to all Op Ex managers. The days are gone when any Op Ex idea or project automatically was approved and resources allocated. Companies are seeking ways to increase profitability and to provide customers with the highest level of satisfaction.

INVESTMENT AND OP EX

The challenge is figuring the link between Op Ex investments and critical business measurements. It is imperative to determine the overall success of Op Ex projects, programs, and initiatives. The problem is that benefits and costs are difficult to measure and may be unknowable. The Op Ex manager must now determine and measure Op Ex's effect on the bottom line.

The following are tips for determining the relationship between Op Ex and profitability:

- Understand customer Op Ex requirements.
- Tie Op Ex initiatives to satisfying and pleasing customer requirements and expectation.
- Define and understand the relationship between Op Ex investments and gross profits by product line.
- Focus Op Ex projects on providing the greatest returns.
- Establish accounts for tracking the various elements of the cost of Op Ex.

- Measure returns and revenue on Op Ex based primarily on customer satisfaction.
- Measure returns on Op Ex based on stakeholder satisfaction.

TOYOTA EMPLOYMENT

Toyota production depends upon employee commitment to kaizen, a philosophy of continuous improvement. This requires highly motivated and Op Ex conscious employees capable of problem solving and team work. Job applicants are simply not hired off the street. They go through a rigorous screening process to get a sense of the person's personal qualities, values and Op Ex commitment.

Toyota follows a 6-phase hiring process:

- Application completion and a viewing of a video of the work life at the plant.
- Assessment of the applicant's technical knowledge and potential.
- Assessment of the applicant's interpersonal and decision making skills.
- Group interview where candidates discuss their achievements.
- Physical and drug/alcohol tests.
- Assessments of employee performance in the first 6 months on the job.[21]

NATURE OF GOAL/OBJECTIVES

Long and short terms objectives flow out of strategic and tactical plans. A typical strategic Op Ex plan may state that "We will produce a high reliability, competitively priced product that will satisfy our customer's needs." Following this statement, doable and measurable Op Ex objectives are developed and assigned to business units and departments. An Op Ex objective derived from the above plan may state: "In the next year, manufacturing defect rates at XYZ plant will decrease 50% and product reliability will increase 40%."

While Op Ex goals may be vague and general, Op Ex objectives are more precise because they describe what actions are going to be pursued and by whom. Sometimes, they detail how objectives are achieved. More often, unit managers develop specific action plans to meet Op Ex corporate objectives. Objectives form a hierarchy. Op Ex objectives start at the top of the organizational structure and are developed after the companywide Op Ex strategy is formulated. Then, lower tactical level objectives are set and so on down the organizational ladder to the lowest working unit and even to the individual. Objectives are written to be doable and measurable for every manager and supervisor in an organization.

OP EX AND MBO

Organizational objectives are usually developed top-down based upon the strategic direction of the company. Objectives can be thought as the steps in the journey to achieve business objectives. Several years ago, the Op Ex director determined the objectives for the function. A conventional wisdom now is that Op Ex is everyone's responsibility.

What is the role of the corporate Op Ex director if operational units are responsible for Op Ex? The Op Ex director assists senior and operational management into developing and monitoring plant, department, and work area business objectives. Performance monitoring is essential in Op Ex. Traditional performance monitoring was usually based on management by objectives where a person was evaluated periodically on meeting pre-agreed upon objectives.

An Op Ex objective should be:

- **Relevant.** Objectives should be aligned and reinforce the organization's strategy and tactics.
- **Doable.** Objectives should be attainable with present resources.
- **Challenging.** Objectives should stretch the individual or team.
- **Measurable.** Objectives should be measured using hard data.

BUSINESS OBJECTIVES

Since Op Ex is a moving target of ever improving Op Ex, Op Ex objectives and goals change annually so five-year as well as yearly objectives are established. Top management or the corporate steering committee develops the general five-year Op Ex objectives. Typically, five-year objectives are generated for the organization by the individual business units and for individual product lines. The five-year objectives focus on broad goals such as minimizing defect levels, reducing costs by product line, and improving product reliability.

YEARLY OP EX OBJECTIVES

Yearly Op Ex objectives are derived from the five years Op Ex objectives. Yearly objectives may originate from business units or operating departments since it is up to the operating units to ultimately achieve the objectives. Since, productivity improvement is an essential part of every worker's and supervisor's annual review, Op Ex targets are also established for every business unit or department.

VAGUE OBJECTIVES

If the team is assigned to fix a problem and it doesn't have a clear Op Ex objective, it may wander aimlessly. Team meetings become a chance to visit. Or, arguments and power struggles occur because everyone wants to go in a separate direction. Sooner or later, supervision and management will wonder what's going on and what's being done. Management will feel that resources are being squandered. Supervision may say that "I told you it wouldn't work." The solution is to specify expected outcomes or results. Resources are then provided and the team is accountable for achieving results.

PLANNING SKILLS

In organizations with highly developed Op Ex initiatives, Op Ex planning is a high priority and is almost as critical as budgeting. Internal customer groups want to know:

- What Op Ex initiative or project is contemplated?

- How will the Op Ex initiative work?
- What resources are required?
- Will operations be disrupted?
- What are the benefits of the project?
- When will it be implemented?
- How much will it cost and who will pay for it?

While Op Ex knowledge is critical to the Op Ex manager, this person must also learn the language of delivery, cost, service, productivity and technology. The Op Ex manager should be fluent in the language of just-in-time delivery, total customer service, cost containment/reduction, and profitability. Op Ex is integral to all of these and should be factored into any project, process, and product development planning.

TYPES OF OP EX PARTNERSHIPS

Another form of new organization is the strategic alliance or partnership. Partnerships come in various forms:

- **ISO 9001:2015 partnerships.** Companies form an ISO 9001:2015 alliance to share non-proprietary information and experience. They will often share costs, expertise, consultants, and manuals.
- **Virtual partnerships.** Companies form a temporary, virtual partnership to respond quickly to marketing demands or customer requirements.
- **Technical/manufacturing groups.** These groups will share experiences and provide information on technical matters such as bar coding, EDI (electronic data interchange), or other information.
- **Resource centers.** These are public-private partnerships with the goal of strengthening local or statewide economic development efforts. Usually, they are managed by private industry personnel and funded by public monies.
- **University-business partnerships.** These are synergistic programs or partnerships where each party provides unique benefits to the other party. University provides research and other informational resources. Business provides real-life problems, ability for faculty to earn extra income, and so on.

- **Management-union partnerships.** Total Op Ex partnering has been introduced into management-union environment which traditionally has been adversarial. Total Op Ex has slowly made inroads into this environment so there is more cooperation and involvement. Both sides understand that traditional adversarial relationships won't work in a competitive environment requiring everyone's cooperation. Making customers happy will only work in a structure where everyone supports each other's activities. Progressive unions are seeing Op Ex as on opportunity to improve their member's quality of work life as well as provide job security.[22]
- **Customer-supplier partnerships.** The goal of customer-supplier partnering is to establish a mutually beneficial long-term alliance or relationship. In some partnering relationships, external suppliers are treated as an extension of the customer. Key suppliers are provided with demand, price, technical, manufacturing, and other sensitive information so a supplier can match processes and capabilities with that of the customer. In these close partnering relationships, key external suppliers are treated exactly as internal parts suppliers. External suppliers are monitored and expected to improve at the same rate as internal suppliers. External suppliers are also expected to follow the customer's internal procedures, adopt the same processes, and establish the same communication protocols.

GOALS AND OBJECTIVES

Doing little things well is the way towards doing big things better.
Anonymous

Op Ex objectives are statements of how an organization intends to meet its Op Ex goals, including customer satisfaction. An objective can be thought of as a doable, tactical goal to be achieved in the near future. Objectives usually include intended results, units of measurement, plans for action, and timetable.

Goals may be realistic or even outrageous. The pursuit of outrageous goals is a concept that is gaining much credence as companies are not satisfied with incremental improvement. Incremental improvements of 10 or 20% a year are no longer acceptable in many companies where 100% quantum improvement is common.

Regardless, Op Ex goals focus on delivering value and satisfaction to an organization's stakeholders. Op Ex goals serve several important purposes:

- **Can provide a sense of urgency.** Realistic and attainable goals can create a sense of urgency for the entire organization.
- **Provide organizational focus.** Many Op Ex and continuous improvement initiatives emphasize process over results or deliverables. Op Ex initiatives were kicked off with lots of training with a mandate to improve systems and make customers happy. There was little or no focus on how these would benefit the corporation. Now, Op Ex goals are tied to the organization's mission and overall strategy.
- **Provide the basis for measurement.** Op Ex and continuous improvement can only be achieved through establishing baselines and benchmarks and through measuring improvement.

NATURE OF GOAL/OBJECTIVES

Long and short terms objectives flow out of strategic and tactical plans. A typical strategic Op Ex plan may state that "We will produce a high reliability, competitively priced product that will satisfy our customer's needs." Following this statement, doable and measurable Op Ex objectives are developed and assigned to business units and departments. An Op Ex objective derived from the above plan may state: "In the next year, manufacturing defect rates at XYZ plant will decrease 50% and product reliability will increase 40%."

While Op Ex goals may be vague and general, Op Ex objectives are more precise because they describe what actions are going to be pursued and by whom. Sometimes, they detail how objectives are achieved. More often, unit managers develop specific action plans to meet Op Ex objectives. Objectives form a hierarchy. Op Ex objectives start at the top of the organizational structure and are developed after the companywide Op Ex strategy is formulated. Then, lower tactical level objectives are set and so on down the organizational ladder to the lowest working unit and even to the individual. Objectives are written to be doable and measurable for every manager and supervisor in an organization.

FIVE YEAR OP EX OBJECTIVES

Since Op Ex is a moving target of ever improving Op Ex, Op Ex objectives and goals change annually so five-year as well as yearly objectives are established. Top management or the corporate steering committee develops the general five-year Op Ex objectives. Typically, five-year objectives are generated for the organization by the individual business units and for individual product lines. The five-year objectives focus on broad goals such as minimizing defect levels, reducing costs by product line, and improving product reliability.

YEARLY OP EX OBJECTIVES

Yearly Op Ex objectives are derived from the five years Op Ex objectives. Yearly objectives may originate from business units or operating departments since it is up to the operating units to ultimately achieve the objectives. Since, productivity improvement is an essential part of every worker's and supervisor's annual review, Op Ex targets are also established for every business unit or department.

VAGUE OBJECTIVES

If the team is assigned to fix a problem and it doesn't have a clear Op Ex objective, it may wander aimlessly. Team meetings become a chance to visit. Or, arguments and power struggles occur because everyone wants to go in a separate direction. Sooner or later, supervision and management will wonder what's going on and what's being done. Management will feel that resources are being squandered. Supervision may say that "I told you it wouldn't work." The solution is to specify expected outcomes or results. Resources are then provided and the team is accountable for achieving results.

OUT OF BOX THINKING

Many of us take the path of least resistance when analyzing problems or situations. What is comfortable, known, successful, and reinforcing tends to be repeated. This is the same with most of us at work. As well, the organization through its policies, procedures, culture, principles, objectives, and even appraisal systems tend to promote status quo systems. Sometimes, radical change is required to break the organization out of what may be self-defeating patterns.

How can an organization break out of its patterns which may challenge status quo systems or the conventional wisdom of the organization? Insiders who are subject and some would say trapped in the existing systems may not have the perspective or the impetus to transform the system. This is a major reason why many companies have hired external consulting firms to provide out of box thinking and consulting.

Out of box thinking means seeing things differently. Tools for out of box thinking include: scenario building, what if analysis, simulation, contingency planning, or brainstorming. The power of these tools rests with their ability to look at problems differently, with different people using different tools.

Out of box thinking is especially critical for Op Ex managers because the Op Ex function has been instrumental in implementing Op Ex systems and processes which stabilized, proceduralized, and maybe improved existing systems. The operative word is existing systems. A basic shift may be required to breakthrough improvement or reengineering. Examples may illustrate this point:

- Instead of minimizing process variation, what may be the value of eliminating or substantially improving this process.
- Instead of documenting all processes, what are critical Op Ex related processes that require documentation.
- Instead of auditing all Op Ex systems equally, what are the critical Op Ex systems which have the most risk of failure.
- Instead of correcting deficiencies, what can be done to prevent deficiencies from occurring or recurring.

RECOGNITION SYSTEMS

Traditional individual employee recognition involved cash, trips, company gifts, or newsletter recognition. In work environments involving self-directed, empowered work teams, recognition is given to a team composed of process owners. Recognition may include personalized plaques, cash, savings bonds, stock, or gift certificates.

Recognition serves several important purposes. Recognition is a form of motivation that identifies, praises, thanks, and rewards employees or teams for a job well done. As well, recognition reflects what is important to the organization, its culture, values, principles, and goals. For example, if the organization believes customer satisfaction, Op Ex, and personal integrity are important then recognition and rewards are usually tied to these objectives.

The following are key factors that must be established for an employee recognition system to work:

- **Sincerity.** The recognition program is founded on the genuine desire to recognize individual and team accomplishments instead of forcing workers to work faster or harder.
- **Fairness.** Fairness implies that all team and employees are treated equitably and that opportunities are open to all.
- **Appropriateness.** Rewards and recognition are written and are consistently followed. Grounds rules for behavior are understood.
- **Consistently.** Formal policies and procedures are consistently applied throughout organization and into the supplier base.
- **Timeliness.** Recognition and rewards follow quickly upon accomplishment. Rewards reinforce behaviors and rewards accomplishments.
- **Importance.** Recognition is an important incentive to all people. Employees and teams want to be recognized for a job well done.[23]

SHORT TERM (TACTICAL) PLANNING

You never reach the promised land. You march towards it.
James Callaghan, statesman

Many western companies still view Op Ex as a short-term fix which is the reason why so many Op Ex initiatives haven't met objectives and simply fade away. Long term management is essential to a successful Op Ex initiative.

One way to ensure success is to evaluate the Op Ex initiative in terms of meeting stakeholder needs and providing high returns on their Op Ex investment. Each year, the organization should assess Op Ex efforts to determine if the direction is correct and if it has been effective. These yearly audits become part of the annual tactical planning and review cycle of business operations and companywide budgeting.

Tactical planning is often helpful to a small company. A small company has an entrepreneur-owner who has a "show-me" attitude. He or she wants to see immediate benefits from the Op Ex investment. While it's helpful to discuss strategic Op Ex plans, unless there is some strong external force, such as a customer or competitor requiring Op Ex, the small business owner will focus on the tactical plan. The first Op Ex efforts better work and fix problems, otherwise the strategic plans are moot.

TACTICAL PLANNING OBJECTIVES

Op Ex projects are created, authorized and planned with a specific purpose in mind. It may be to reduce the cost of internal failures or to improve the flow of material through a plant. These fairly straightforward projects are well defined and are measurable. In the first instance, the team lowers costs through some form of prevention. In the second case, the team can time the flow of in-process material through the plant and see improvements. Poorly defined projects have fuzzy authorizations, little management backing, and internal resistance which will usually doom the project.

Is there one way to develop doable objectives? No. However, it is better to have well defined, narrow objectives and plans, rather than try to do all things to satisfy all people.

Tactical Op Ex planning has a number of objectives, including:

- Providing an operational roadmap for implementing a company's vision.
- Providing specific explanations, procedures, and even work instructions for employees to follow.
- Providing a template against which day-to-day, weekly, and monthly decisions can be compared.
- Providing a structure for operational or improvement project plans.
- Enhancing communications among stakeholders.
- Justifying and authorizing resources.
- Determining where resources are required.
- Enhancing control of processes.
- Limiting risks.
- Clarifying objectives.
- Identifying project constraints.

ORGANIZATIONAL ASSESSMENTS

Fundamental progress has to do with the reinterpretation of basic ideas.
Alfred North Whitehead

The purpose of the organizational assessment is to diagnose the present state of the organization and offer a prognosis of its ability to change. The change may involve enhancing customer satisfaction, improving processes, registering to ISO 9001:2015, downsizing, outsourcing, developing new products, securing new contracts, designing new organizational structures, or some other major change. After the assessment, objectives and plans are developed to implement change. Readiness to change can be determined by an organizational assessment. This assessment determines internal resistance to change and whether there is sufficient support or understanding for the need to change. Often, the need for change is not understood because it has not been sufficiently explained. Readiness is often a function of the organizational culture. Flat organizations in competitive markets understand the need for and are more adaptable to change.

ORGANIZATIONAL EXAMPLE

The Op Ex function should exemplify the best Op Ex activities in the organization. Credibility for improvement and change will not be accepted unless it is modeled in the Op Ex organization. If the Op Ex function preaches or exhorts something that it doesn't do then cynicism will be bred. In other words, operational management and personnel must walk their talk.

To set an example for the rest of the organization, operational management should remove barriers to personal performance and empower all its employees including administrative personnel. The value of administrative work should be emphasized and genuinely acknowledged. This may be through providing day care and family friendly atmosphere, providing training, and providing access to fitness centers and cafeterias.

ORGANIZATIONAL ASSESSMENT QUESTIONS

A number of structures and methodologies can be introduced into an organization such as reengineering, self-managed teams, learning organization, and continuous process improvement. However, which is the best? A number of factors come into play when evaluating systems including products, processes, technology, personnel, competitive climate, and other factors. It's essential the group or person conducting the organizational or climate assessment asks the right questions. The following paraphrased questions were suggested by Philip Sadler:

- Does the organization require hands-on guidance or control for it to work efficiently?
- What are the requirements of the people doing the work? Requirements may involve needs, attitudes, feelings, beliefs, etc.
- Are there and what are the social groupings in the organization and how do these groups affect the behavior of the people in the group?
- Is there any element of the organization's activities that needs to be closely integrated if overall goals and objectives are to be achieved?
- What organizational measures can be developed that will provide effective control over processes and products while still meeting the needs of the people doing the work?

- Are there environmental or competitive changes that will or can affect operations and if so how can the organization adapt effectively?
- Who should make the above evaluation?[24]

The evaluation should be objective and independent of the organizational area being assessed. So, if the entire organization is being evaluated then outside consultants may have to be brought in to conduct the assessment. If a business unit, plant, or work area is being evaluated then the assessors can be from Human Resources, Training, or Op Ex departments.

Many organizations are redesigning and reengineering their systems, processes, and even their entire operations. Organizational redesign requires different skills than many Op Ex managers have. Organizational redesign basically provides a roadmap for implementing change aligned with the strategic direction of the company. Organizational development includes designing systems, adopting new methodologies, consulting with organizational stakeholders, implementing new practices, advising internal stakeholders, and engaging management in the sociotechnical systems of the organization.

THEORIES OF MOTIVATION

It's what you learn after you know it all that counts.
John Wooden, Basketball Coach

The following theories of motivation have been widely examined:

- Maslow's hierarchy of needs
- Herzberg's hygiene and motivator factors
- McClelland's achievement goals
- Lawler's expectation model
- Latham and Locke goal setting

THEORY X AND Y

The next major contribution to management theory was Douglas McGregor's Theory X and Theory Y principles. Theory X assumes employ ees do not like to work and therefore must be controlled, directed, and punished if work is not properly performed. It also assumes the average employee lacks ambition, is not responsible, and wants to be managed.

On the other hand, McGregor proposed an alternate management style, Theory Y. Theory Y assumes employees develop attitudes about work based on their experiences. Employees can be motivated to work other than through an authoritarian style of management.

Theory Y assumes employees seek responsibility and have abilities to solve problems. Theory X assumes a top-down management style works best while Theory Y assumes a bottom-up style also achieves an organization's objectives.

MASLOW'S HIERARCHY OF NEEDS

Maslow introduced the idea of a hierarchy of needs. In the hierarchy, people first satisfy their physiological needs then their safety, social, ego, and self-actualization needs. Maslow believed that once a lower-level need is satisfied, a person actively seeks to satisfy the next higher-level need and so on up the hierarchy.

People first seek food, water, and shelter as requirements of survival. Once satisfied, people seek safety. Then, people develop friendships and affiliations with others. People improve their sense of self-worth (ego needs) through peer group recognition. Self-actualization, the highest level in the hierarchy, is the need to achieve one's potential in life.

According to Maslow, once lower-level needs have been satisfied then only a higher-level need can motivate behavior. While the model seems overly simplistic, it has received widespread acceptance.

HERZBERG'S HYGIENE FACTORS AND MOTIVATORS

Herzberg developed the two-factor theory of motivation, consisting of hygienes and motivators. Hygiene factors, like a higher salary or better working conditions, satisfy immediate wants but do not motivate employees in the long run. Increasing hygiene factors is a poor way to motivate someone, because lower-level needs, such as hunger, are quickly satisfied. And once satisfied, additional motivators, such as salary increases, have to be offered at an ever-increasing rate. Therefore, hygiene factors are only good for preventing dissatisfaction. This is an inefficient way to motivate workers.

However, motivators such as recognition, advancement, and responsibility can motivate workers because they satisfy an employee's higher-level needs for achievement and self-esteem. Herzberg believed that people have an infinite craving for these needs, so these can never be fully satisfied.[25]

LAWLER'S AND PORTER'S EXPECTATION MODEL

Lawler and Porter propose a different model of goal achievement. The expectancy model proposes that motivation depends on an individual's desire to achieve a certain set of goals. The model starts with the person's end goals and assumes that people modify their behavior to achieve these goals.

MCCLELLAND'S ACHIEVEMENT GOALS

McClelland believes that highly motivated people seek achievement along with affiliation and power. The need for achievement is found in people who set high and attainable goals for themselves. These people choose tasks they can control and receive immediate feedback on how the tasks are performed. According to McClelland, motivation is not something that evolves through life but is a characteristic developed in childhood.

INSPECTION IS STILL NECESSARY

While many companies are abolishing quality control inspectors, inspectors are still necessary and required in industries where public safety is involved. Government regulations in the nuclear, gas, pharmaceutical, and transportation industries require independent audits and product inspections.

Large manufacturers, such as Ford, IBM, General Motors, and Chrysler, expect their suppliers to maintain a separate and independent Op Ex group to perform specialized inspection and audit activities. The independent group monitors in-process control and maintains records for material and product traceability. Inspection is also important for one-of-a-kind or very expensive products. If a loss occurs, the result may be costly litigation. An independent inspection function can also be used for independent management audits. This is especially helpful for measuring outgoing material quality.[26]

COMMUNICATE GENERAL AND SPECIFIC INFORMATION

Marketing communicates general and specific customer information to many parts of the organization. For example, Marketing communicates specific product information such as styling, size, weight, strength, reliability, and features.

Marketing also communicates general customer information on safety, operation, maintenance, transportation, handling/storage/shipping requirements; packaging instructions; warranty information; and environmental requirements. Once expressed, implied, or anticipated customer requirements are understood, the Engineering and Manufacturing can develop detailed technical specifications.

ORGANIZATIONAL STAKEHOLDERS

We've always felt we had an obligation to not only bring home the bacon to our stockholders, and to do that aggressively as well, but also to be a good national citizen.

William Kieschnick, business person

Who are an organization's stakeholder's? A stakeholder may include customers, suppliers, employees, union leadership, regulatory authorities, community groups, and possibly a host of other stakeholders.

Organizational stakeholders form a synergistic and reciprocal relationship with an organization. Each stakeholder provides some value to the organization and in return expects some value. The following list of business and organizational stakeholders illustrates the reciprocal relationship:

- **Employees.** Employees are the means for generating new ideas, developing new products, and satisfying customers. In return, employees expect financially rewarding work or opportunities for personal growth and advancement.
- **Shareholders.** Shareholders provide monies and resources for the company to grow and prosper. Shareholders expect that their assets are invested prudently and the company provides superior investment returns.
- **Customers.** Customers provide monies and cashflow to maintain and grow the business. Customers expect price competitive, safe, environmentally safe, aesthetically pleasing products and services that are delivered just-in-time and in a courteous manner.
- **Suppliers.** Suppliers provide technically advanced, safe, conforming, products and services that are delivered just-in-time to the right location. Suppliers expect invoices to be paid promptly and good works to be rewarded with future contracts.
- **Society/public.** Corporate responsibility means the company demonstrates social responsibility, demonstrates ethical behaviors, complies with regulations, and is an exemplar of good citizenship. Society and the public serve as the marketplace for companies. With no society or customers, there is no business. The public expects a company to be safe and prudent in its activities.
- **Wholesalers/distributors.** Wholesalers provide access to customers and to markets. Distributors want to be treated fairly, maintain a mutually profitable relationship and expect future growth.
- **Regulators.** Regulators ensure that safety, health, and environmental laws are promulgated and consistently enforced. Companies want to be treated fairly and comply with laws that meet cost/benefit criteria.

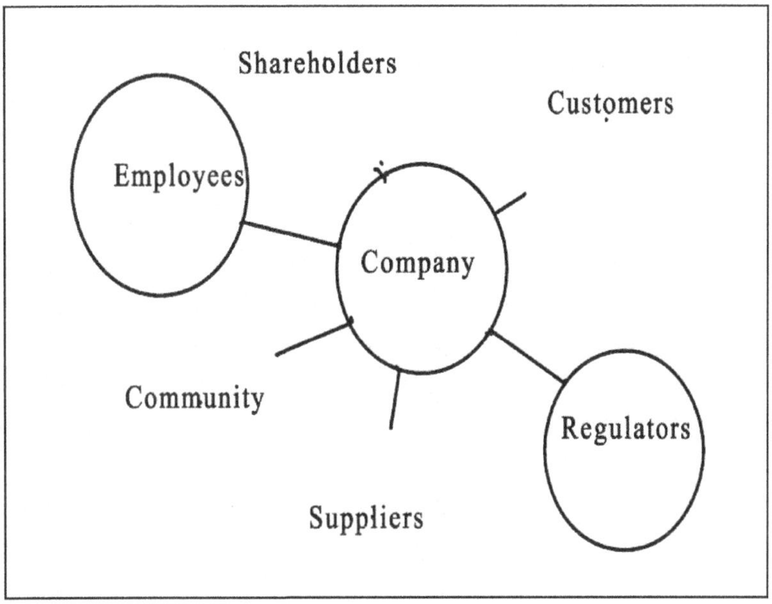

STAKEHOLDER MANAGEMENT

Business and project stakeholder groups overlap in terms of having similar constituency groups, including competitors, intervenor groups and others. The team leader must be able to identify each stakeholder group, work with them, and satisfy their requirements.

Stakeholder requirements may also conflict. For example, the client may want expensive extras to facilitate operations. The accounting or cost group wants to minimize costs. Senior management wants the project done faster because of competitive pressures. Intervenor groups such as regulatory agencies may be impeding the project with new requirements, conditions and stipulations. Project team members are tired of the long hours. In order to resolve the conflicting stakeholder priorities and achieving a balance, the team leader must negotiate with the stakeholders to optimize desires against conflicting politics, resources and timelines. The process isn't easy and usually spells the difference between a successful and a less than successful team leader.

OP EX AND REENGINEERING

Carpe diem. Seize the day.
Horace, Roman poet

Does reengineering conflict with total Op Ex? This question is perplexing many people. Reengineering and total Op Ex are synergistic and complementary. Let's discuss both.

REENGINEERING AND OP EX

Reengineering and operational management should be complementary. Reengineering is basically revolutionary while operational management, specifically kaizen and continuous process improvement are evolutionary. Reengineering is associated with the quantum leap, innovative process redesign. Reengineering looks at systems and processes to ensure they are adding value and it is basically a top-down process. Operational management is associated with the incremental, continuous process improvement relying on the input of teams and individuals.

Which is better? Currently reengineering is the favored approach to organizational redesign. It is new, bold, and adventuresome. The problem is that radical surgery can cause major organizational changes and may even kill the patient. Radical redesigns are risky but have the potential for higher rewards. The high-risk, high-reward approach has become a preferred approach for organizational change and competitiveness. However, the risk is that reengineering may go in the wrong direction or cut into the organization's bone and sinew.

Continuous Process Improvement (CPI) and reengineering sometimes refer to the same set of activities. They are similar in terms of looking at what's done and to find better ways to do them. Better may mean more productive, efficient, effective, or cheaper. Advocates of each say the differences are more fundamental. Continuous process improvement depends upon employee's commitment and cooperation to initiate and maintain changes. Reengineering is revolutionary in terms of asking basic questions: "Why are we doing this and what value does it add?"

Some other differences are also telling. Reengineering is often imposed on the organization. The following sometimes occurs. Senior management wants to change the organization. Exhortation and other techniques did not work. So, external consultants are retained to provide the organization with an "independent and objective" perspective.

In-house expertise and knowledge often drive continuous improvement. Fundamental to CPI is the belief that employee involvement and imagination are key to improving processes that will create new job opportunities. Reengineering, if not used carefully, can create an environment where employees may feel they can't be trusted or don't know how to improve the Op Ex of their process or products.

REENGINEERING CHALLENGES

Reorganization is the permanent condition of a vigorous organization.
Roy Ash

Hammer and Champy in their breakthrough book **Reengineering** proposed that management, specifically middle management, must fundamentally change. They mean radical change, not an evolutionary or tweaking type of change. The basic purpose and value of middle management no longer seem to apply. Middle managers traditionally supervised workers or managed information. Now, these assumptions have changed. Self-managed teams perform many of the tasks traditionally done by middle management. As well, networked computer systems provide everyone in the organization access to information. So, the question being posed is why do we need middle management?

MANAGEMENT - THE KEY TO SUCCESSFUL REENGINEERING

Hammer and Champy believe that managerial jobs will require three skills which don't have much to do with traditional management. Managers must become process owners, coaches-teachers, and leaders.[27]
Hammer and Champy also concluded that:

- Reengineering is here to stay.
- All operational systems and processes must be viewed as integrated systems.
- Fundamental questioning of everything in business is here to stay.
- Current management skills have to be updated.

- Employees will be making more day-to-day decisions.
- Middle managers are an endangered species.
- Learning marketable skills is the only measure for true career success.
- Dislocation may become a fact of work life for many.
- Future job security and satisfaction are linked to skills mastery, not promotion.

REENGINEERING PROPONENTS AND OPPONENT

Reengineering has its strong proponents and opponents. They are both right in some way. The basic approach to reengineering is to look at end-to-end processes to determine if they add value and satisfy stakeholders. Opponents who have either survived or been displaced by this approach call it slash-and-burn management because reengineering is sometimes used to scrap and replace existing process, systems, and personnel. This may be done without regard to people, ostensibly a company's most valuable resource.

Headcount reduction is one of the reasons why reengineering has become synonymous with downsizing which is why it is meeting with resistance. External consultants come in, study processes, and suggest the elimination of non-value adding processes. But, what happens to the people that performed those functions?

Reengineering often starts with an emergency, such as nonconforming products or high cost of Op Ex. A process expert would then ask "if we had to start over again how would we develop Op Ex systems and processes." The opportunities to this approach are huge. The organization can ask fundamental questions, including:

- What business are we in?
- Who are our customers?
- Do our processes add customer value?
- What can be done to improve existing ones or redesign them across functions?

The major challenge to reengineering is that scrapping and starting over is a shock to an organization with strong internal systems that have worked for years. Change is horribly difficult in these companies especially if major surgery is suggested. Too many companies still run on old mindsets, systems, and processes. Just about every element of the organization can be looked at differently and probably improved including: job descriptions, compensation, training, appraisal, rework, processes, and product development. Reengineering communicates a sense of urgency to the organization that business as usual is dead and that improvements should be dramatic.

On the other hand, the incremental or the continuous process improvement (CPI) approach allows one success to build upon the next. Systems and processes can be redesigned with input from many stakeholders. The process is evolutionary instead of revolutionary which can cause turmoil. CPI also emphasizes improving efficiency, effectiveness, Op Ex, cost, productivity, timeliness, and customer satisfaction. As well, CPI can reduce process time, defect levels, and inventory.

In examining any process, the primary emphasis should be on satisfying final customer needs and expectations. Every process and system necessary for satisfying internal and external customers are examined to determine if they need to be modified or even eliminated. What is left after this examination should be the core processes of the organization. If only modification or minor process redesign is required, incremental Op Ex may be pursued. If the process doesn't seem to be adding customer value, a more dramatic implementation is required, specifically rethinking how the entire process should work.

WHY DOESN'T REENGINEERING WORK?

Why doesn't reengineering work? The following reasons are usually offered:

- No senior management active support.
- Middle management fears hinder the process.
- Fear of learning new tasks and methods.
- Little understanding of the technologies surrounding reengineering.
- Fear that reengineering is a euphemism for being fired.
- Lack of reengineering vision.
- No sense of urgency or expediency.
- Belief that reengineering is a flavor of the month.
- Don't know how to meld reengineering, Op Ex, JIT, lean, and other improvement initiatives.
- Underestimating the requirements for implementation.
- People, team, and organizational burnout.
- Long hours and more work because of fewer people.
- Lack of training.
- Disregard of the human side of redesign.
- Faddi

THE IMPROVEMENT PROCESS

H. James Harrington in **The Improvement Process: How America's Leading Companies Improve Quality** showed how AT&T, Avon, Corn¬ing Glass, and GM implemented their improvement programs. Harrington listed the following common elements of most improvement and Op Ex programs:

1. Obtain top management commitment.
2. Establish an improvement steering committee.
3. Obtain total management participation.
4. Secure team participation.
5. Obtain individual involvement.
6. Establish system improvement teams.
7. Develop supplier involvement activities.
8. Establish a systems operational assurance activity.

9. Develop and implement short range improvement plans and a long-range improvement strategy.
10. Establish a recognition system.[28]

NEXT CHAPTER

In the next chapter, Customer Requirements are discussed. The need to continue satisfying and pleasing customers has become a motherhood. The wisdom of this statement is so ingrained there is no reason to defend or support this contention. It is widely understood. The only question is how.

CHAPTER 7
CUSTOMER REQUIREMENTS

Scandinavian Airlines System (SAS) was struggling to survive several years ago. The airline business was in a worldwide slump. SAS was covered in red ink. Something had to be done, quickly and drastically. The company's existence was on the line as well as 20,000 jobs.

CUSTOMER NEEDS AND DESIRES

We have 50,000 moments of truth out there every day.
Jan Carlzon, President of SAS

As so often occurs in times of great need, in walks a visionary called Jan Carlzon. At the time only 39, Jan Carlzon reoriented and transformed the company. He added an external focus to the company which had largely been operationally oriented. The external focus was customer service while still taking care of the important internal needs of the organization, such as the repair and maintenance of the aircraft.

The above quotation Carlzon suggests that in any day customers come into contact with some part of SAS 50.000 times a day. Carlzon calls customer contact the "moment of truth" where a customer's perceptions of a company are first formulated. A positive first impression generates continuing sales. A poor first impression results in a poor reputation and no repeat sales. Carlzon believes the "moment of truth" can be managed so that a positive impression can be left with the customer every time.

The bottom line is "Did a customer-focus help the organization"? In a little more than a year, SAS went from a $8 million dollars loss to a gross profit of $71 million on sales of $2 billion.

KEY POINTS TO CONSIDER IN IDENTIFYING CUSTOMER'S CONCERNS

The following should be considered when identifying customers' concerns:

- Identify existing and prospective groups of customers.
- Identify customer concerns, requirements, and expectations of each group.
- Determine the driver of customer satisfaction.
- Develop customer surveys.
- Align product and service processes with customer concerns.
- Develop action plans and measures for closing the gap between customer requirements and internal systems.
- Monitor and continuously improve systems for monitoring customer satisfaction.

POWER OF THE UNCONDITIONAL GUARANTEE

The unconditional guarantee states that if the customer is not totally satisfied with a product or service that the company will gladly exchange it or reimburse the customer, no questions asked. This is an extraordinarily strong and potent promise by a company. If a company has a high number of returns because of deficient processes or systems then a company could theoretically go broke having to correct the problems and to satisfy the promises. If a company has excellent Op Ex systems then an unconditional guarantee and excellent marketing can be an excellent promotional tool to revitalize customer relations. The worst that may happen is that there are a small number of frivolous and abusive claims. In general, an unconditional guarantee should be offered only after extensive discussions with many stakeholders of the ramifications and significance of the guarantee.

IMPORTANCE OF THE CUSTOMER

You pays your money and takes your choice.
Punch

Alignment of requirements, needs, and expectations between the final customer and the organization that provides the product or service is essential. Customer focus is essential for survival and profitability. The problem is the external customer may have a different view of Op Ex than the organization does.

MANAGING BY CUSTOMER SATISFACTION

The Boston Consulting Group recently surveyed a group of businesses and concluded that 95 to 99% of a company's activities have little or no relevance to the final customer. This is an astounding number when one considers that all organizations are focusing internal operations on adding value and satisfying final customer needs. The final customer doesn't really care what a company does to provide a product or service as long as it satisfies real and perceived needs.[29]

As well, a company these days must do more than satisfy customers. A company must deal with and address the concerns of its stakeholders which may include shareholders, customers, employees, community, suppliers, and regulators.

Too many companies are still managed by priorities and politics that don't matter to the customer or that generate income. The important message of the above survey is that every company must understand its customer priorities and satisfy them in every possible way. This attitude is then transferred internally so everyone's concern is on satisfying first the external and then internal customers. Total Op Ex becomes a comprehensive management system for continuously improving every element of the organization as well as the supplier base to improve total customer satisfaction. Customer satisfaction becomes a company's most important performance indicator. Many companies including Motorola use Total Customer Satisfaction to drive and focus all their Op Ex initiatives and projects.

INDICATORS OF POOR SERVICE

A. C. Rosander, a service expert, identified the following indicators of trouble in service quality:

1. Error rate is too high.
2. Idle time is excessive.
3. Delay is too long.
4. One massive error is found.
5. A violation of a basic procedure is discovered.
6. Length of life is too short.
7. Failure rate is too high.
8. Cost is too high.
9. Too many complaints.
10. Critical or control level is exceeded.
11. Illegal action is discovered.[30]

VOICE OF THE CUSTOMER

Hindsight is good, foresight is better; but second sight is best of all.
Evan Esar

Progressive companies want customer expectations to drive the product development process. In addition, the design team and its marketing representative attempt to understand the values, culture, and principles of different customer groups. This understanding hopefully translates in products and services that satisfy present customer requirements but also provide a starting point for anticipating broad ranging future customer directions. This broadly is called capturing the "voice of the customer."

Market research and a number of other methods discussed in this chapter deal with understanding customer requirements. These methods focus on the status-quo. With the product lifecycle being so short and customer requirements changing so rapidly, there is more attention being focused on how to anticipate customer requirements.

Methods for identifying or capturing the voice of the customer vary depending on the products, services, location, context, culture, expectations, resources and a number of other factors. The basic steps include:

- **Identify customers.** This may involve market segmentation, breaking a market into smaller components until a profitable target market that can be reached is identified.
- **Obtaining the voice of the customer.** The voice can be obtained through focus groups, customer visits, or market research.
- **Collate the data.** Customer responses must be collated and distilled into information that can be analyzed. In an Op Ex sense, the information signal to data noise ratio has to be strengthened.
- **Analyze the data.** Data must be analyzed so it becomes information useful for making decisions. The decisions may involve developing products, predicting customer buy decisions, or identifying customer requirements.
- **Test the analysis.** The previous analysis has to be verified or corroborated. The costs and risks of a wrong decision or wrong direction can be very expensive and time consuming for the product development team. Testing may involve building a prototype, conducting more surveys, or using other methods to corroborate the information originally gleaned.
- **Communicate knowledge to the product development team.** During this process, data evolves to information to knowledge which serves as the justification for developing products and services.

The advantages of this approach include:

- Provides a broader perspective, picture, and context of the customer.
- Breaks the customer profile into sub-groups each of whom has separate needs.
- Allows for meeting more than one customer need.
- Allows for anticipating customer needs.
- Encourages bundling products and services.
- Transfers customer requirements into the organization.

- Offers a holistic approach to delighting customers.
- Provides a structured methodology for delighting customers.

WHAT CAN CUSTOMER SERVICE DO?

As we have mentioned, the service component is as important as the tangible component of a product. Customer Service manages a variety of Op Ex related services, specifically:

- Arranges for maintenance, replacement or repair
- Supplies parts
- Handles claims and warranties
- Supplies critical feedback
- Handles complaints
- Directs customer corrective action

Arranges for Maintenance, Replacement, or Repair

Customer Service arranges for the maintenance, replacement, or repair of defective products. Customer Service may arrange to repair a product in the vicinity of the customer instead of shipping it to the factory. If a large piece of industrial equipment fails, then Customer Service may send a maintenance engineer to repair it in the field. With a consumer product, Customer Service arranges to replace the product if it fails within the warranty period.

Supplies Parts

Customer Service may supply factory parts to repair industrial machinery. For rare, out-of-production, or expensive parts, these are specially made upon demand.

Handles Claims and Warranties

Customer Service handles claim and warranties on defective merchandise. If a product fails within the warranty period, Customer Service replaces or repairs the product.

Supplies Critical Feedback

Customer Service is the primary interface between the customer and the manufacturer after the sale. Customer Service supplies critical feedback to the company about improving the product, such as adding features, re-designing the product, or adapting it for a new use.

Handles Complaints

Sooner or later, a company receives a customer complaint. Customer Service handles complaints by ensuring different departments in the organization listen and satisfy the needs of the customer by following through with corrective action requests, issuing credits, or expediting bottlenecks that may inhibit quick, courteous service.

The manner in which these are handled reflects on a company's reputation for Op Ex service. Complaints can originate from service or product problems. Customers can be dissatisfied with the material, size, delivery, packaging, price, or salesperson.

Directs Customer Corrective Action

Corrective action has to be swift, fair, and courteous. If customers' complaints are not handled satisfactorily, the result is a gradual loss of business. If complaints are handled carefully, then long-term, loyal support can be established. One major retail company uses complaints as a measure of customer satisfaction.

To ensure quality customer service, companies audit customer service operations. The audit assesses the objectives of the customer-service organization, evaluates the effectiveness of the services, compares the quality of the service with the competition, and determines if the services are the type and quality the customer wants.[31]

WHEN LISTENING TO CUSTOMER IS DANGEROUS

It is possible that listening to customers too carefully can be dangerous to a company's business. A company may have hundreds of customers and many other stakeholders. Different customers may want different products, services, each with different features, attributes, and performance levels.

Customers may also demand more product and service choices and levels than ever before. As well, they want it faster, better, cheaper, and so on.

Which customer or stakeholder is the most important, who should be listened to, and who should be satisfied first? It is easy for a sales manager to treat all customers or stakeholders the same way and eventually end up satisfying none. As well, a person's health can deteriorate as workloads, requirements, time, and other resources take their toll trying to satisfy all stakeholders.

CUSTOMERS DON'T ORIGINATE KILLER IDEAS

Customers often don't originate innovative or breakthrough ideas which may seem like heresy. Customer feedback and market research are critical for improving or enhancing existing products. There are several reasons for this. Customers sometimes don't have the perspective or experience to suggest new products because they don't have market knowledge or perspective. A smart manufacturer is one that carefully listens for new ideas that may become the essence of a new product.

RELEVANT STAKEHOLDERS

A common definition of Op Ex quality is the ability to satisfy and please customers. The customer may be internal or external to the organization. In a complex business environment, a better definition of Op Ex is the ability to satisfy many stakeholders, one of whom may be the final product user.

STAKEHOLDERS AND CUSTOMER IDENTIFICATION

A successful Op Ex project meets its objectives and pleases its customers. Customers may be any number of stakeholders. Objectives may be anything from developing procedures to determining why a robotic arm doesn't work. The other element of project success deals with time, cost, delivery, efficiency, effectiveness, and other requirements. A successful project tries to economize and optimize all these variables. Sometimes, each one can be dealt with but more often there are tradeoffs such as a quick project requires spending more resources.

STEPS TO ENSURING TOTAL CUSTOMER SATISFACTION

Rockwell International as well as other companies have developed total customer satisfaction initiatives. Rockwell supplies products to other manufacturers that add value through their technical capabilities. Rockwell's definition of quality or Op Ex is "fitness for use" which is the acceptability of a product or service by the customer. In a commercial transaction, the customer is usually the Supply Management agent who usually requires the following:

1. **Fitness for use.** Is the product ready for the customer?
2. **Outgoing product Op Ex.** How many nonconformances are being shipped to customers?
3. **Delivery conformance.** Does the customer receive the product when promised?
4. **Initial product performance.** Does it work when received by the customer?
5. **Product reliability.** Does the product continue to work over its life?
6. **Responsiveness to the customer.** How good is the organization at resolving customer's problems?
7. **Customer satisfaction.** Are customer's expectations being met?[32]

A customer driven organization emphasizes the total customer experience with a product or service including paying attention to such Op Ex details as branding, packaging, advertising, and installation.

CUSTOMER EXPECTATIONS, PRIORITIES, NEEDS, AND VOICE

Industry Week recently reported that "customer delight, once thought to be an esoteric ideal, is emerging as the single most powerful tool for achieving and sustaining competitive advantage."[33]

HEARING THE CUSTOMER

A well-informed employee is the best salesperson a company can have.
E. J. Thomas

Customer information is often difficult to gather. TARP, Technical Assistance Research Programs, conducted extensive studies of customers. The

results were astonishing. For every 50 to 250 problems experienced by customers, on the average only one customer will complain to the company's headquarters. If a field or customer representative is available, the ratio decreases to one complaint for every 20 to 50 problems. An 800 number will generate about one complaint for every 10 to 50 problems depending on the 800 number's visibility. If the customer has a broken product, only one in three will even bring it back for repair.[34]
Hearing, caring about, and conveying the voice of the customer can be used to drive operations. Some companies survey customers to determining Op Ex areas that provide the greatest impact on customer satisfaction. Successful Op Ex oriented organizations attempt to discern at least five voices of Op Ex including:

1. Voice of the customer.
2. Voice of the best in class.
3. Voice of the process and the people.
4. Voice of suppliers.
5. Voice of the quality system.[35]

CUSTOMER FANS

Tom Peters and others have pushed the customer satisfaction envelope. They say that customers need to be delighted, amazed, stunned, pleased, which is much more than simply being satisfied. The world is changing where simply meeting requirements won't differentiate a company or its products from its competition. A company must go beyond satisfying requirements to anticipating, meeting and surpassing expectations.

To surpass expectations, a company must listen very carefully to the voices of customers and processes. What do these concepts mean? The voice of the customer is what will please the customer at the moment of the sale and throughout his or her history with a product. The customer must have sufficient fond memories of the sales experience or encounter to encourage him or her to be repeat customers.

The voice of the customer is particularly important in this equation. The customer drives the entire process. This is critical to companies that focus on internal needs and requirements. However, the customer doesn't really care about what is occurring inside the company. The customer is concerned about what the product or service can do for him or her.

As the quality of products and services become uniformly high, customer service becomes much more important. Excellent service becomes the variable that separates excellent companies from the simply good ones. The organizational challenge is that customer service personnel sometimes are not appreciated. Customer service, whether it is the receptionist or the person answering questions is often an entry level position.

These five dimensions of service performance are critical to pleasing customers:

- Tangible characteristic including facilities, equipment, and appearance of customer contract personnel.
- Dependable and accurate performance.
- Customer responsiveness.
- Service personnel courtesy and competence which instill trust and confidence in customers.
- Customer empathy which is the ability to understand customer requirements.

CUSTOMER FOCUSED ON VALUE

Be everywhere, do everything, and never fail to astonish the customer.
Margaret Getchell

People are at the center of Op Ex. People buy quality products and services. And people add or detract value when they produce a product or deliver a service. The natural tendency for many of us is to become so preoccupied with improvement programs, processes, and techniques that we forget who implements improvement ideas and for whom they are implemented, people as internal human resources and as final customers.

More companies are using total customer value to drive their Op Ex and continuous improvement initiatives. Some companies even have an officer called the Chief Customer Officer. The benefits of total customer value approach include:

- Recognition the final customer is the primary organizational driver.
- All organizational activities must focus on the final customer.
- All activities, processes, and product must provide value to the customer.
- Value includes cost, delivery, quality, service, technology, and other attributes.

FINAL, INTERNAL AND OTHER TYPES OF CUSTOMERS

Warning - Customers are perishable.
Store Sign

Customer needs, wants and expectations must be met by employees many layers down the organizational structure. In the ideal organization, every employee has direct contact and direct identification with the final customer. Final customers are the end users of a product or service. Final customers can be a retail customer buying a raincoat; a government agency Supply Management a missile system; or a manufacturer Supply Management components for assembly into a larger product. When people think of a customer, it is assumed we mean the end user or final customer.

In this book, we refer to four types of customers:

- Final customer
- Intermediate customer
- Internal customer
- End user

FINAL CUSTOMER

The final customer is the final person who buys a company's product or service. The final customer is sometimes called the consumer, end user, or buyer. The important point is the final customer provides signals to an organization what to produce, when to deliver it, and how to service it.

As the marketplace becomes more competitive, locating, attracting, and retaining the final customer becomes the primary mission of an organization. In this marketplace, the final customer demands high quality, competitively priced products. Quality products and services are essential to the survival in this competitive marketplace. Companies that adapt and satisfy customer requirements survive. Companies that do not adapt, stagnate, and wither away.

The final customer buys goods based on a combination of aesthetics and function. When a final customer buys a product, it must work the first time and every time. Also, it must be attractive and appealing. If a product or service is perceived poorly, a customer will not buy that product or service. No repeat buying means loss of revenue. Also, word spreads to other potential buyers that goods are shoddy, service is poor, and value is not received.

INTERMEDIATE CUSTOMER

The intermediate customer purchases goods and services that satisfy the demands of his or her own customers. An intermediate customer could be an industrial buyer of raw material, partially finished products, fabricated parts, components, or subassemblies that go into a final product. Intermediate customers can be manufacturers, government agencies, wholesalers, or small businesses. Intermediate customers purchase goods or material to be processed or assembled into a finished product. Ford Motor Company purchases glass, ornaments, brake assemblies, and other goods from external suppliers. These goods are assembled into an automobile that is sold to a final customer.

Purchasers of intermediate goods follow a highly structured process for making buy decisions. Formal supplier analyses, audits, inspection, and corrective action are used to select, monitor, and correct suppliers.[36]

INTERNAL CUSTOMER

Customer satisfaction is an eternal truth. So, why not call downstream departments or team's internal customer. This was a flash of genius. By changing the point of view, internal groups became collaborators instead of competitors. In traditional hierarchical groups, the "over the wall" attitude was obliterated just by how internal groups were perceived. As collaborators, internal groups are viewed as partners to please external customers. This is the first step in building internal trust and confidence which are the foundation for building an Op Ex culture.

The internal customer is the person or work unit that uses services or products provided by others in the organization. On a manufacturing line, an internal customer is the next (downstream) operator in a particular operation. Internal customers are the end users of information produced and provided by a staff specialist.

An internal customer can also be a division that receives products from another part of the organization to be machined, cast, or assembled. An internal customer can be a department such as Manufacturing or Engineering that uses cost information from Accounting. Or, an internal customer can be a downstream machinist who takes a partially finished product and performs another task on it.

The internal customer and the supplier of the service have a reciprocal or interdependent relationship. All the processes we discuss in this book, Marketing, Engineering, Supply Management, Op Ex, Manufacturing, and Distribution are internal suppliers and customers of each other. For example, Manufacturing and Engineering must exchange information continually throughout the product life cycle to produce a product that satisfies the external customer.

END USERS

The end user, sometimes called the final customer, is the final person to use a product. In the sourcing chain, a supplier may be four or five tiers removed from the end user. A supplier may supply a screw that fits into a sub-assembly, that fits into the assembly that fits into the product used by the final customer or end user. In this case, the supplier is four tiers removed from the final users. It is difficult for the supplier to understand the requirements or to share a common bond with the customer.

Another example of the difference of customers and users can be found in the military. Military contractors supply products to the customer, the U.S. government that is usually represented by Federal procurement officers. However the ultimate user of a tank or a plane is the officer and person in the field.

INTERNAL STAKEHOLDERS

The biggest challenge and opportunity lies in involving every one of our people in what amounts to an quality obsession. Everyone needs to say by his or her actions that quality is a way of life; to affirm that they apply the same high standards of perfor-mance to their jobs as they do in their personal lives.

Douglas D. Danforth, Chairman, Westinghouse Electric

Five critical internal stakeholders groups influence the direction and implementation of a companywide Op Ex initiative:

- Chief Executive Officer
- Steering committee
- General management
- Op Ex department
- First level supervision
- Partners/Associates

CHIEF EXECUTIVE OFFICER

The Chief Executive Officer (CEO) initiates the Op Ex initiative. He or she then provides personal, continuous, inspirational, visible leadership, and commitment to the initiative. Since the CEO. is the most recognizable leader in an organization, only the CEO. can credibly communicate the purpose and urgency of Op Ex. And only the CEO can lead and inspire others to pursue Op Ex. The CEO leads by communicating a deep personal commitment to values he or she wants the organization to have. Some CEOs are known to have the spirit of an evangelist when they communicate the importance of Op Ex.

STEERING COMMITTEE

Once the CEO starts the Op Ex initiative, a companywide steering committee is formed to ensure the initiative operates as intended and achieves its goals. The steering committee is sometimes called Op Ex Council, Improvement Steering Council, Quality Task Force, or Op Ex Task Group.

A successful steering committee includes significant organizational Op Ex stakeholders because they are responsible for its general direction and can allocate resources for its successful implementation.

The steering committee has representatives from all departments and functions that can affect or are affected by Op Ex. Steering Committee members are selected from management, staff, and operations, senior management, and union personnel. Even union participation is encouraged to ensure long term co-operation.

The corporate level steering committee scans the competitive environment to develop organization's Op Ex strategic vision and strategy. Then, the committee identifies and deploys corporate resources to achieve and implement the organization's Op Ex strategy. Once policies are formulated, the committee continuously directs, monitors, and measures initiative success.

Specifically, the committee:

- Provides visible Op Ex leadership.
- Focuses attention on Op Ex.
- Provides management and labor ownership.
- Provides ongoing direction.
- Defines Op Ex responsibilities.
- Establishes corporate level Op Ex objectives.
- Monitors progress.
- Develops reward and recognition systems.

- Overcomes organizational obstacles to success.

GENERAL MANAGEMENT

For Op Ex to succeed, an organization's general management must support, participate, and reinforce the Op Ex initiative. General management directly establishes standards of Op Ex performance, assigns jobs, establishes operating procedures, and rewards performance.

Once the initiative is established, general management reinforces behavior and activity that lead to continuous improvement. On a regular basis, general management supplies messages about the importance of Op Ex and encourages activities that support the Op Ex initiative.

OP EX FUNCTION

The responsibility for many operational assurance and control activities used to rest in the Op Ex function. These responsibilities are now assigned to people, teams and departments perform-ing the work. While the Op Ex function still has some operational responsibilities, it has acquired more management authority. The Op Ex function is responsible for facilitating the implementation of the Op Ex effort, including training, monitoring Op Ex projects, auditing operations, and surveying suppliers.

The Op Ex function is also responsible for developing "Op Ex literacy" in companies. As the Op Ex function has less direct control of process and product quality, it has increased responsibility for training people and monitoring processes. Op Ex personnel also coordinate interdisciplinary teams that solve operational problems.

FIRST LINE SUPERVISION

On a daily basis, first-level supervision directs teams or workers performing work, whether it is polishing a car or cutting threads on bar stock. First-level supervision is directly responsible for facilitating and overseeing the Op Ex and quantity of daily work. First-level supervision directly imparts to the team and employee the organization's expectations of performance and Op Ex. First-level supervision or teams communicate technical information by interpreting engineering specifications and drawings.

First-level supervision works with line personnel to develop weekly and daily work and Op Ex plans. Work plans include drawings and specifications that detail what a product should look like; what its performance should be; and how it will be measured, inspected, stored, and shipped. Op Ex instructions detail how to monitor work processes; how to inspect material; and, finally, how to control product quality.

PARTNERS/ASSOCIATES

It is clearly important that what people are called affects their job performance and their sense of value. In order to empower front-line teams and to establish continuous improvement culture, employees are called associates, owners, and partners. Are these titles gimmicks or real? Do titles really matter and do they instill caring into the work place? The quick answer is they do seem to work.

TYPES OF CUSTOMERS

Without customers, there is no business and no jobs. It's pretty simple. This is the competitiveness message that companies are conveying to managers and employees. So, companies are focusing on providing products and services that not only meet customer requirements but anticipate and surpass customer expectations.

Usually, the drive to Op Ex starts from a customer or competitor. As a condition of business, a customer may require Op Ex systems to be in place and working consistently before a company can be placed on the approved bidder's list. Or, a benchmarking study may indicate a competitor has developed a new product or a superior service.

These external indicators clarify the need for Op Ex or customer satisfaction which are then communicated internally. The benchmarking study or customer survey can indicate a company is much less competitive than it thinks it is. The survey or study is used to tweak, transform, or revolutionize the way a business is structured and how products are developed. Other factors that encourage management involvement include a major product failure resulting in a death, injury, and litigation, regulatory requirements, or internal concerns about efficiencies and effectiveness.

USING CUSTOMER SERVICE FOR COMPETITIVE ADVANTAGE

How do you make an employee customer sensitive? This is the critical question of all organizations, large and small, public and private. Companies are relying on the Op Ex organization and Op Ex professionals to provide training and to communicate the value of good customer service. But, do these training programs change hearts and minds? Can a training session encourage employees to think and act differently?

Some say formal training can only increase awareness of customer importance. It is up to operational managers to emphasize and reward behaviors that are consistent with the training. Supervisors and team leaders can be coached and taught the value and basics of customer service. In some cases this may not work, processes may have to be redesigned so the right people are doing the right things.

In launching an internal customer service initiative, the following should be considered:

- Identify internal customer requirements.
- Conduct internal customer focus groups and market research.
- Identify individual, team, and department services with satisfying customer requirements.
- Adopt new requirements.
- Provide feedback on internal customer satisfaction.
- Communicate the importance of internal and external customer service.
- Develop process flow charts identifying value adding contributions of each step.
- Encourage and reward employees for working and satisfying internal customers.
- Encourage internal workers to nominate employees for outstanding customer service achievements.
- Train, train, and train employees in a value adding work culture.

As the marketplace becomes more competitive, suppliers to large companies are touting their training initiatives. Technology is accelerating so quickly that companies must support their products with technical services. Services may entail informing customers of new product development, how to solve problems, or how to install a new piece of software. Excellent product and service training is used to differentiate suppliers from their competition. Suppliers are offering training to their customers as part of their product support and are moving further upstream into providing input in design development.

TYPICAL CUSTOMER SURVEY

You, the customer, are important to us. We want to know what you think about the XYZ super tool. Your comments will help us to improve the tool and to serve you better in the future.

1. Usability (comments)
   Serviceability (comments)
   Versatility (comments)
   Power (comments)
   Durability (comments)
2. When using this product:
   a. Is the machine easy to use?
   b. It is safe?
   c. Is it too heavy?
3. Competitive analysis
   a. Who is this product's largest competitor?
   b. What features does the competitor's product have?
4. Has your product been repaired?
   a. By whom?
   b. What was the problem?
   c. Were service people courteous?
   d. What was the turnaround time for repair?
   e. If you repaired it, were supplied instructions understandable?
5. What do you like about XYZ Supertool?
6. What don't you like about the product?
7. What should be modified?
8. How much would you pay for this product?
9. Would you recommend this product to someone else?

CRITICAL QUESTIONS FOR A SURVEY

Critical issues in developing a customer satisfaction survey include:

- Who is the customer or other stakeholders?
- What are the needs and expectations of the customer or the stakeholders?
- Does the survey support overall business objectives?

- Who pays for the survey?
- Who will manage and develop survey?
- Who is surveyed?
- What is the target population?
- How is a representative sample chosen?
- How and where does the survey fit in the customer lifecycle?
- How often should the survey be carried out?
- Has the organization been empowered to act upon the survey information?
- What are appropriate survey methods?
- What questions will be asked?
- What are special cultural, customer, environmental sensitivities?
- What analytical tools will provide the most actionable customer information?
- How does survey maker know he or she is asking and measuring the right things?
- How should the information be communicated to the customer?
- How does the customer information drive improvement?
- What sort of follow-up is required?

SURVEYS

I listen to everybody and take notes. Particularly salesmen. They get close to people.
Leo Burnett

Surveys are a proactive method for determining customer satisfaction. It is estimated that 95% of unhappy customers will not call an offending company and voice their dissatisfaction. The company's competitor will probably get the customer's business. In the mean time, the offending provider is oblivious of why customers are not returning as well as can't correct a problem it doesn't understand.

Customer satisfaction surveys can be used to gather information through the telephone, computer, mailings, and other means. In telephone inter views, a marketing person may ask specific questions related to an experience at a hotel or use of a product. Through the internet or other computer on-line systems, companies are also discussing computer products, software, or services with users. Direct mail to a representative, targeted group is another type of customer survey. The problem is the response rates are low and the respondees may not be representative of the population. Customer surveys are usually structured and systematic. The interviewer may ask specific questions in a survey form designed by a psychologist, marketer, or Op Ex personnel.

CUSTOMER IDENTIFICATION AND SEGMENTATION

Business has only two functions - marketing and innovation.
Peter Drucker, 1971

The marketplace for goods and services is now international. The press calls it the "new global game", or "world economy", or "global economy." This means that foreign competition for customers is intense and serious. Those who identify and satisfy customers will best survive and prosper.

"World-class Op Ex" is recognized as the means for surviving in the global economy. "The Op Ex conscious company that stays tuned to its people, its processes, and its customers will produce not only a quality product, but a world-class product."[37]

To satisfy consumer needs in the global marketplace, Marketing and operational management attempts to:

- Identify prospective users and customers.
- Identify customer requirements, needs, expectations, and wants.

CUSTOMER RETENTION

No customer can be worse than no customer.
Leopold Fechtner

Customer retention is the process of maintaining a loyal customer base. Customer loyalty requires patience and a long-term commitment to continually identifying needs and fulfilling expectations with the right products and services at the right price. If there are problems, these are fixed quickly and affirmatively so the customer is pleased. One faulty experience may sour the customer for life. As well, the customer may regale 20 or more friends of the negative experience.

CHANGING NATURE OF MARKETING	
Old Approach	**New Approach**
Markets are homogeneous and stable	Markets are heterogeneous and unstable
Marketing is responsible for determining customer needs	Multidisciplinary team is responsible for customer needs
Product function is important to customer	Product function, size, shape, appearance, and many other factors are important to the customer
Product lifecycle is long	Product lifecycle is short
Customer expects low product reliability	Customer expects high reliability
Product has simple specifications	Product has complex specifications
Product features are not important	Product features sell products
Service is not specified	Service attributes are specified
Customer service answers questions	Customer service provides soluitons
Choices among consumer products are few	There are many competing consumer products
Installation instructions are unimportant	Installation instructions are complete and complex
Products do not have warranties	Products have extensive warranties
Brands communicate Op Ex image	Brands communicate quality image
Packaging serves as container for goods	Packaging sells, communicates, and provides multitude functions

CUSTOMER RETURNS

"Customer satisfaction is guaranteed or your money back" is the policy of many customer-driven organizations that want to retain customers for life. The guarantee only makes sense if a company has excellent products and service. Otherwise, this customer policy will bomb as the following example illustrates.

Customer returns have sometimes been used to evaluate product quality in inspection mode environments. Products were in-process and final inspected using 100% or statistical sampling plans. However, these methods were ineffective. Nonconforming products still slipped through and were delivered to customers because inspection failed to catch nonconforming products. Customers would get nonconforming products which they would return to the manufacturer for a replacement product, get the damaged product fixed, or obtain a full refund. The manufacturer would then conduct failure tests to determine the root cause. This was after-the-fact problem solving. Disgusted customers wouldn't return to buy more products and would spread the word of the bad experience. This pattern of behavior could destroy businesses.

Customer returns can be used as an early warning system of impending problems and to prevent future recurrences. Customer returns can indicate the cause of the problem is further upstream and has to be fixed quickly. High returns may also indicate higher customer expectations, impulse buying patterns, and upstream Op Ex problems such as in the design process.

Tips for reducing returns include:

- Focus on process controls and stabilizing upstream operations.
- Establish final testing programs.
- Eliminate conflicting testing.
- Install strong design review system.
- Encourage customer input-output feedback mechanisms in engineering.
- Encourage involvement of line personnel to solve problems as they occur.

CUSTOMER SEGMENTATION

Too often, the customer gets treated more like a peasant than a king or queen.

Karl Albrecht/Ron Zemke, writers

Once potential customers and their needs are identified, Marketing develops strategies to sell the product. For example, one automobile cannot appeal and satisfy all possible customers. Customers may be widely scattered with different attitudes, wants, needs, and expectations. Some competitors may be in a better position to sell or deliver products such as those close to their markets.

Four commonly used marketing strategies are:

- Mass marketing
- Mass customization
- Product differentiation
- Target marketing

MASS MARKETING

A company can mass produce and distribute a basic, competitively priced product to attract as many customers as possible. Mass marketing strategy seeks to appeal to the highest common denominator of tastes but does not attempt to satisfy consumers with specific product tastes. The product is sparse on special features but high on reliability. For example, a Ford Escort is basic transportation and appeals to a large user group.

MASS CUSTOMIZATION

Mass customization sounds like an oxymoron, however it isn't. Mass customization means working with customers to develop tailored products that meet generic aesthetic, delivery and functional requirements. This adds value to the customer and allows products or services to be sold at a premium in a variety of models. Mass customization requires that at a manufacturer or service provider have a common platform or standardized product which can be change quickly to meet specific customer needs.

Mass customization requires operational management and just-in- time operations. The customer can order a specific product with the exact requirements and features that he or she wants. The secret of mass customization are flexible, stable, and capable processes coupled with responsive employees.

PRODUCT DIFFERENTIATION

A company can produce products that are designed to look or operate differently than the competition's product. Or a company can design a product to emulate an existing product that is sufficiently different in price or quality. The products can have different product attributes and features. Ford Escort can come with options and features at an additional cost that differentiate it from the basic model. The extra features add real and perceived value to the automobile. This strategy offers variety at an additional cost to the customer.

TARGET MARKETING

A company can produce products to appeal to small segments of customers. A product is specially tailored to customers in these markets by offering different options and features. Customers are offered totally different automobiles at different prices or may be offered one automobile with all of its options preloaded.

CAUSES OF POOR SERVICE

The customer is always right.
Anonymous

Too often, customers perceive that service people do not care or do not take pride in what they do. Repairs on cars, homes, and appliances do not fix products that should not have failed in the first place. The perception of service becomes more tarnished.

REASONS FOR POOR OP EX

Poor operational service continues largely because:

- Products are more sophisticated.
- Entry in many service fields is not regulated.
- Service people are low paid.

- Customers have high expectations.
- Throw away products are produced.

PRODUCTS ARE MORE SOPHISTICATED

Engineers design modular, microprocessed products which are difficult to service. Electronic products often require sophisticated diagnostic and measuring equipment to detect faults. In a car, the sound, ignition, carburetion, and timing systems rely on microprocessors to control their units. An electronics background is necessary to understand and repair these systems.

ENTRY IN MANY SERVICE FIELDS IS NOT REGULATED

Entry into many service fields is not regulated. Often, there are no certification tests for those installing roofs, laying concrete, or building houses. People who have repaired televisions, radios, and small machinery at home may have a sideline appliance repair business. As products become more sophisticated, specialized skills, knowledge, and equipment are required to repair these products.

SERVICE PEOPLE ARE POORLY PAID

Service people are not well paid. As the service market grows, so does the demand for people to deliver services. However, most people do not want to work for the minimum wage normally paid to service workers.

CUSTOMERS HAVE HIGH EXPECTATIONS

Consumers are barraged with advertisements that promise excellent service that is not delivered. Consumers hear about General Motor's "Mr. Goodwrench" or Ford's "Quality-Care" program and expect excellent service. Unfortunately, these examples of excellent service are not universal. Expectations more often than not are built up and then dashed. As a result, consumers become hostile.

THROWAWAY PRODUCTS ARE PRODUCED

Throwaway products are produced so they cannot be repaired. Manufacturers produce products in sealed units which cannot be opened unless the seal is broken which cancels any warranties. So, it is often cheaper to discard a product than to have it repaired.

WORLD-CLASS CUSTOMER SATISFACTION

"World-class companies share the following characteristics:

- Customer requirements and expectations are anticipated through surveys.
- Benchmark comparisons within industry are higher than other companies.
- Company has a customer inquiry center with a toll-free telephone number.
- Corrective and preventive actions result from survey results.
- Formal Op Ex systems are established to improve customer satisfaction.
- Customer relationship management is highly visible.
- Customer service representatives are empowered to solve customer complaints.
- Customer service is periodically audited.
- Customer satisfaction standards and procedures are defined and measurable.
- Customer complaints are logged and trends are analyzed.
- Customer satisfaction is correlated with financial performance.
- Company is recognized for outstanding customer satisfaction performance.[38]

TOTAL CUSTOMER FOCUS

As mentioned above, the goal of every company should be to encourage all employees to focus on external customers. Instead of looking at Marketing or the Sales department as the focus of all customer activities and opportunities, there are now multiple points of customer contact and support. Each contact is viewed as an opportunity to cement the relationship between the customer and the supplier of the product or service.

A customer orientation and focus may mean a number of things for an organization, including:

- Providing exceptional products and services.
- Anticipating and exceeding expectations.
- Providing a friendly and pleasing purchase experience.
- Correcting deficiencies rapidly.
- Redressing grievances fairly and rapidly.
- Committing to delighting customers.
- Responding to marketplace changes quickly and efficiently.
- Developing and maintaining long term-trust.
- Respecting an individual's and group's dignity, culture, and lifestyle.
- Providing real and perceived value to customers.
- Providing innovative and cost-competitive products and services.
- Respecting the customer and the individual.
- Having every employee be a salesperson.

TWELVE RULES OF CUSTOMER RETENTION

Long term customer relationships are critical to long term profitability. The following 12 rules of customer retention are pretty universal. They can be applied in banks, hospitals, or manufacturing companies. For example to retain customers, banks should:

1. Spend more time working with the customer.
2. Read between the lines of conventional customer research.
3. Focus on the 10% of the customers who represent 90% of the business.
4. Allow staff to build retention systems.
5. Start and work from the internal customer out.
6. Focus on solving customer complaints.
7. Invent excuses to be in touch with customer.
8. Work on cross-selling products.
9. Encourage managers to get involved in the process.
10. Hold everyone in the bank accountable for retention results.
11. Use motivators, such as recognition, cash, or training to get employees involved in customer retention.
12. Expect that a customer retention program will need considerable fine tuning.[39]

CUSTOMERS

The following was on the wall of a manufacturer of electronic measurement instruments:

Customers:

Customers...are the most important persons in any business.
Customers...are not dependent on us-but we on them.
Customers...are not an interruption of our work - they are the purpose of it.
Customers...do us a favor when they call us - we are not doing them a favor by serving them.
Customers...are part of our business, not outsiders.
Customers...are human beings like ourselves, with the same feelings and emotions.
Customers...are not people to argue or match wits with.
Customers...bring us their wants, and it is our job to fill those wants.
Customers...are deserving of the most courteous and attentive treatment we can give them.
Customers...are the people who make it possible to pay our salaries, whether we are truck drivers or managers.
Customers...are the lifeblood of this and every other business.
Remember..."It's the service after the sale that counts."

SERVICE GUARANTEES

Guaranteed overnight deliver is an example of a service guarantee which is becoming more common as business defines Op Ex as "anticipating and exceeding customer expectations, one hundred percent of the time." The guarantee basically spells out to the customer what recourse is available if the customer is dissatisfied for any reason. The customer may receive a full refund, replacement, or fixed product.

The challenge to a company is the hollow guarantee, a promise for less than what the customer already expected. For a guarantee to work, it should:

- **Be unrestricted.** The best service guarantee promises to pay without restrictions or exceptions.

- **Be specific and clear.** The guarantee should be clearly spelled out and easy to understand.
- **Be meaningful.** Successful guarantees provide value to the disappointed customer.
- **Be Hassle free.** The customer is already disappointed. The guarantee should be easy to fulfill and provide the customer with enjoyment.
- **Quick to pay out.** The guarantee should provide immediate reward. The longer the payout, the more disappointed the customer will be.[40]

CUSTOMER SERVICE

Marketing: the search for the best possible product at the most possible mark-up with the shortest possible duration for the earliest possible replacement.
Unknown

However good a product is, a customer's perceptions are made at the point of contact between customer and salesperson. Direct contact with the final customer is the first and most important opportunity a company has to convey an Op Ex message and impression. Routine contact with the customer can be at the operational, sales, or maintenance level, specifically with the receptionist, salesperson, service people, applications engineer, or customer service representative.

This contact can convey a positive or negative image depending on whether the receptionist or salesperson was courteous and helpful. The salesperson is the primary contact with the customer. Each salesperson has to be able to answer questions about the product in a friendly and courteous manner.

But, customer service is labor intensive and thus expensive. Companies try to determine the appropriate level of service and then factor this information into the product price. For example, Federal Express discovered that customers want packages delivered overnight. IBM customers want technical assistance on demand, 24 hours a day. Both companies have excellent service reputations and price their products accordingly.

Customer service and product reliability (long-term Op Ex) are inversely related. The greater the reliability of the product, the less the need for customer service. Products are now designed and developed so maintenance and operation are simplified. Products are designed and manufactured so moving parts are reduced. Electronics are widely used. Also, products are designed as modules so if a failure occurs, it can be diagnosed and repaired easily.

WARRANTY/GUARANTEE

If you think you have someone eating out of your hand, it's a good idea to count your fingers.
Martin Buxbaum

Warranties and guarantees are important methods for cementing the relationship between customers and product/service providers. Warranties are a public promise or guarantee to the customer that if a product fails in service, the manufacturer will repair, service, or replace the defective product at no cost to the customer within a prescribed period of time. Warranties enhance a product's image by offering comprehensive protection. Thus, warranties can establish a competitive advantage for a product or service.

Warranties can be a simple guarantee or a statement about a product attribute or product performance such as "satisfaction is guaranteed." "Money back" guaranties are common with consumer products. Or warranties can be complex documents limiting the manufacturer's legal responsibilities. Complex warranties are common with industrial products, such as automobiles or industrial machinery, where the potential for exposure to and risk of product litigation is much greater than consumer products such as lipstick or designer fashions.

Warranties are a remnant of the inspection mode of management. Management believed if a defective product slipped through inspection, the warranty covered the customer and still maintained customer goodwill essential for repeat Supply Management. This was false because defective products result in excessive manufacturing costs and eventually in customer dissatisfaction. Customers do not want to buy defective products.

The Magnuson-Moss Warranty Act, enacted in 1975, requires consumer products conform to Federal Trade Commission (FTC) rules. All warranties must be:

- Disclosed fully in a readable spot on the package in simple and understandable language.
- Labeled as full or limited warranty.
- Provided to customers for reading and comparison before purchase.

SOMETIMES CUSTOMER SURVEYS DON'T WORK WELL

Surveys are an important instrument that may not work because of poor design and complicated analysis. Most customers will respond to a survey if they know it will be used to improve a service or product. The survey must therefore be focused, easy to respond, and preferably hit a visceral nerve in a customer.

Surveys are often driven and justified in terms of pursuing customer satisfaction and customer delight. However, surveys may result in reams of data with little useful information. Customer surveys are often misunderstood, unread, dismissed, or ignored. No action is pursued as a result of the survey. There is little or no time spent evaluating the results and the value of the survey or the resulting actions if there are any. Part of the problem may be due to the fact that surveys are conducted because Sales or Customer Service wanted them, but didn't communicate the importance, action, or need for the surveys to senior management and operational heads.

Factors to consider in developing a survey:

- **Customized questionnaires.** Questionnaires should be tailored to the needs of the customer as well as the abilities of the respondee.
- **Time.** Surveys require time to conduct, to analyze and to respond to. Survey responses are often very low because the survey was

poorly designed and took too long to complete. Customers don't want complete a survey if it exceeds their survey time limit.

- **Distribution.** Surveys can be distributed at the place of business, via mail, electronically, and a number of other ways.
- **Response mechanism.** There has to be some method for the customer to respond. Is there a self-addressed, self-stamped mailer? Who will the information be sent to? Who and how will the information be collated?
- **Costs.** Surveys can become cost-prohibitive if they aren't structured scientifically.
- **Ease of response.** Customers will only respond if the survey isn't a time or convenience imposition.
- **Communicating results.** The customer wants information about the customer that is useful for decision making such as how to improve products and services.

SERVICE IS BIG BUSINESS

Business has only two functions - marketing and innovation.
Peter F. Drucker

The popular media several years ago discovered "quality of service" and still uses it as a business buzz phrase. Major growth sectors in the next decade include service industries such as banking, health care, government, retail, fast foods, utilities, education, and insurance companies. The quality of service is becoming paramount in these industries.

Service is big business. Americans spend more than $50 billion on car repairs, providing work to more than 360,000 people in over 180,000 service stations, garages, and dealerships. One estimate suggests that Americans spend over $19 billion just to repair their televisions, refrigerators, lawnmowers, and air conditioners.

SERVICE BUSINESS

As the U.S. economy evolves into an information-based economy, more of the population works in providing some form of service. Currently, 60 - 70% of the working population is involved in the service economy and the number is expected to go higher as the number of manufacturing personnel steadily declines.

It is interesting to note that the top consumer complaint is over car repairs while the second is over home repair. Americans also spend at least $75 billion dollars fixing, remodeling, and restoring houses. This produces work for at least 150,000 contractors and remodeling companies nationwide.[41]

If service is poor and unreliable, then sales and revenues are affected. Customers are now more sophisticated and better informed with higher expectations. If expectations for product or service are not met, then the customer can purchase other comparable products.

MANUFACTURING AND SERVICE BUSINESSES

Most products are partly intangible service and partly tangible product. Sometimes as the quality of products has improved, service Op Ex has not kept pace. Unfortunately, the highest quality product can be compromised if service delivery is not equally good.

What is service? It is the delivery system of a product. It is a polite voice on the phone. It is reliable phone service. It is prompt delivery of a package. Often, service is what feels right. One knows it when one sees or experiences it.

Manufacturing and service businesses are basically different. Manufacturing is characterized by capital intensity, large inventories, complex operations, and tangible products. On the other hand, service businesses are characterized by labor intensity, paperwork intensity, and simple operations.

The focus of manufacturing and service companies is the same, both focus on satisfying the customer. In manufacturing, interaction with the customer is usually limited to customer representatives, who resolve disputes or provide information over the phone.

Often a customer's first contact with a company is through the receptionist or telephone operator. Too often, telephone operators leave people hanging on the line or receptionists bark instructions to people waiting in a lobby. If the initial contact is not warm, helpful or courteous then the negative attitude will spill over onto the product.

However especially in small service businesses, the interaction with the customer is more direct, intense, and frequent. In some restaurants, customer service directly involves customers from when they enter until they leave. In a restaurant, a maitre'd ushers the couple to a table. A waiter or waitress delivers a meal. A bartender mixes a drink. In some establishments, the cook leaves the kitchen, talks to patrons and inquires if they enjoyed the meal. The owner or manager of the restaurant also talks with customers to determine if everything was satisfactory.

HOW TO IMPROVE SERVICE OP EX

The responsiveness of a firm is directly proportionate to the distance on the organization chart from the consumer to the chairman of the board.
Virginia Knauer, writer

Service Op Ex is attained in a manner similar to manufacturing Op Ex. The following is an abbreviated systems approach to solving service Op Ex problems. Specifically, in order for a service organization to have an Op Ex system, it must:

- Develop performance standards
- Build Op Ex requirements into all activities
- Measure performance

DEVELOP PERFORMANCE STANDARDS

The first task is to define service quality and Op Ex standards. Service Op Ex may be defined as conformance to service Op Ex standards, system procedures, or work instructions. Service standards are the equivalent of product specifications. Often, the causes of poor service are weak, nonexistent, or unfollowed standards of performance. A typical service excellence standard may be "satisfy a customer's request within 30 seconds."

Service requirements define exactly what, how, when, and where the service is to be delivered to the customer.

Standards are developed from customers' requirements of delivery, service, cleanliness, politeness, and value. Commonly used methods of soliciting customer service needs are through market research, focus groups, opinion surveys, returns/claims analysis, and customer complaints analysis.

Each element of the service process is defined precisely in terms of understandable, attainable performance standards. These are then communicated to the people responsible for delivering the service. These may involve helpful expressions, efficient motions, procedures, clean dress, courteous attitude, and promptness.

MEASURE PERFORMANCE

The next goal is to measure performance against these standards. Measurement determines whether the organization is meeting the standards. If not, then measurement indicates areas of improvement.

Performance measurement is not popular with people, but it is essential if a process is to be improved or if problems are to be eliminated. Measurement is also necessary to reward outstanding group and individual performance.

IF NECESSARY, INITIATE CORRECTIVE ACTION

Next, performance gaps are analyzed. If the expected level of performance is not being achieved, this is an opportunity for corrective action. Corrective action should fix the service deficiency, but also eliminate the root cause. For example, poor-quality service may not be the fault of the waitress or server. The poor service may be a symptom of a larger systemic problem of poor training or poor supervision.

In horizontal work flows, responsibility, authority, and resources are pushed to the lowest possible organizational level. Decision making and information access is also at the lowest possible organizational level.

- Develop performance standards.
- Build Op Ex requirements into all activities.
- Measure performance.

THE IMPORTANCE OF CUSTOMER SERVICE SYSTEMS

Personal contact with the customer is the essence of any service business. The front-line customer service representative is the key to excellent customer service because he or she has daily or if not hourly contact with customers. Service must be consistently defined and followed by each employee with every customer contact. There is little or no chance for test or rework if the first customer contact should fail.

The challenges to providing high quality, customer service consistently is imposing. No two people are like. Service is often an individual interpretation based on listening and responding so the customer is satisfied. Often, service employees are paid minimum wage which can affect their self-perception.

Organizational systems should allow employees to improve Op Ex. Training, procedures, information, enlightened supervision, teams, and proper equipment are all essential organizational systems for implementing Op Ex. Training ensures customers are handled consistently and courteously. Procedures detail how customers should be treated and how claims are resolved. Information provides the customer representative with the right information at the right time to answer customer questions or resolve customer claims. Enlightened supervision empowers and allows front-line representatives to do what is necessary to please the customer as well as represent the interests of the company. Self-managed teams energize members and focus on getting the job done the right way, the first time and every time. Tools and equipment are necessary to answer a customer's technical questions efficiently and effectively.[42]

WHAT IS A SERVICE?

Albrecht and Zemke, in Service America, identified the following characteristics of a service:

- The product cannot be demonstrated nor can a sample be sent to the customer in advance of actual practice.
- The sale, production, and delivery of a service takes place almost simultaneously.
- A service takes up no shelf space and cannot be stockpiled.
- The individual who receives the service participates in the production of the service.
- Delivery of a service usually requires human contact; seller and buyer come into contact to create the service.
- The receiver's expectations of the service are integral to his or her satisfaction with the service.
- The person who receives the service owns nothing tangible.
- The experience cannot be sold or passed on to a third party. [43]

ANATOMY OF A CUSTOMER SURVEY

A survey is basically a report card to identify strengths and weaknesses so employees can develop corrective actions to eliminate system weakness and improve delivery. Operational service criteria or attributes include: courtesy, timeliness, accuracy, usefulness, cost, turnaround time, appearance, dependability, accessibility, promptness, and delivery. Methods for gathering customer related information include phone surveys, question and answer cards, anonymous callers, and customer feedback.

A survey can be used for a number of purposes including to:

- Understand customer's reaction to a product or service.
- Define corrective, preventive, or improvement actions.
- Measure customer attitudes and perceptions.
- Measure actual customer buying behaviors.
- Seek business priorities.
- Allocate resources for improvement and customer satisfaction.
- Identify new market and product opportunities.
- Develop business goals and performance standards.
- Enhance marketing and advertising.
- Improve public relations.
- Identify customers and their requirements.

- Provide market segment information.
- Measure customer satisfaction.
- Provide information to improve existing products or develop new products.
- Use as communication tools to determine the "voice of the customer".
- Catalyze for change.
- Internalize the voice of the customer.
- Measure gaps between real and perceived Op Ex levels.
- Prompt changes if required.
- Correct service deficiencies.
- Identify areas of strengths.
- Instill customer awareness and concern.
- Reward strong service.
- Use results for market positioning.

Survey results can be communicated in a numerical score, alphabetical grade, or a narrative. The advantage of a score or grade is it can be used for comparison against competitors and to indicate improvement. However, the grade may not focus on customer concerns. Narratives tend to identify areas of improvements, however most customers don't want to spend the time writing a dissertation. Closure in customer surveys involves a follow-up action which may be preventive, corrective, or improvement.

NEXT CHAPTER

In the next chapter, Op Ex Product Development is discussed. Product design has not always been important to American companies. Profit margins and function were more important. Now, more global and American companies are becoming well known for design excellence, including Apple Computer Company, Nike, Xerox Corp., and Chrysler.

CHAPTER 8
OP EX PRODUCT DEVELOPMENT

Finding what the customer wants is sometimes as simple as asking the customer the right questions. Several methods for finding what the customer wants include focus groups, surveys, customer service personnel asking questions, consultants asking questions, and phone inquiries.

IDENTIFYING CUSTOMER WANTS, NEEDS, AND REQUIREMENTS

Consumerism is getting more important as more business leaders leave their executive suites and go into the marketplace they should have visited before. They are discovering sources of consumer dissatisfaction they never knew existed. They are improving communications and customer relations, checking on services and advertising warranties, finding out what makes customers buy and becoming better chief executives as a result.
Theodore C. Sorensen, writer

What does the customer really want? What is the customer willing to pay for it? These are the critical questions anyone who has developed a product wants to know. Answers to these questions justify developing a product or service. For example, if the customer doesn't want a product with all the bells and whistles, then the product or service will flop. When it costs millions to develop a product, answers to these fundamental questions are essential in making the hard trade-off decisions at each step of the product development process.

How does a company determine what a customer wants? Marketing watches consumer trends and other indicators of public taste. Also, companies track consumer perceptions by surveying existing and potential customers.

Common methods of determining customer needs include:

- Market research
- Contract reviews
- Quality function deployment
- Focus groups
- Surveys
- Customer contacts
- Plant visits
- Analysis of complaints
- Test and evaluations
- Forecasting trends
- Quality image analysis

MARKET RESEARCH

Market research is a commonly used method of determining what customers want. This research investigates the marketplace, examines customer needs, and develops methods for delivering quality products or services in a cost-efficient manner. Market research can provide a company with the following information:

- Trends in Op Ex.
- Cost vs. quality tradeoffs.
- Customer preferences and their impact on product and service quality.
- Industry/market analysis.
- Market threats and opportunities.[44]

CONTRACT REVIEWS

Contract review, commonly used in military procurement, is a method to evaluate new customer's or supplier's Op Ex requirements. A new or modified product may have special or unusual quality-related requirements such as special equipment, fixture, or gage requirements. Once these requirements are specified and understood, a company can develop or purchase the capabilities of meeting the requirements.

QUALITY FUNCTION DEPLOYMENT

Quality function deployment (QFD) is a formal mechanism for translating customer requirements into specific actions. Quality function deployment is a powerful tool in the Op Ex professional toolbox. QFD drives the "voice of the customer" through the organization and especially into product development. QFD is sometimes called the "house of quality" because of the structure and look of the planning tools. The house is really a matrix that correlates critical customer requirements with competitive, design, and delivery factors.

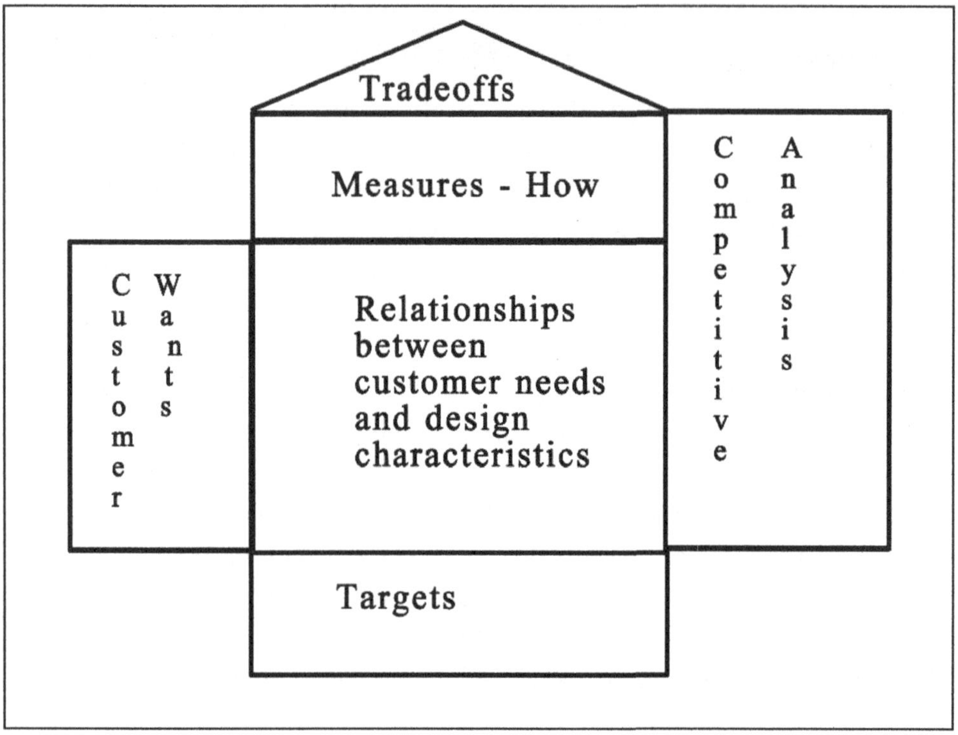

FOCUS GROUPS

A focus group consists of 6 or more people who spend a few hours with a skilled interviewer who directs open discussions around a specific topic, project, service, or other marketing related issue. Focus groups can be used to gage the effectiveness of new or existing services. Users of existing services can suggest improvements or changes to existing services. For example, focus groups can be used to estimate the potential impact of a new product price, taste, or promotion.

A focus group can be thought of as a representative sample of a larger population. The data or information derived from the focus group is used to gain glimpses of the larger population's responses. Tight focus groups are usually representative of the population or a segment to which a product will appeal to. Focus group information should be used as the raw data by which to create a customer survey. Identifying customer needs can be done through focus groups or customer surveys of homogeneous customer segments. In a study identifying customer needs and concerns, 20-30 customer interviews were determined as sufficient for identifying 90% or more of the customer's concerns of a relatively homogenous customer segment.[45]

SURVEYS

A survey, if it is properly prepared and correctly targeted, can provide information on product trends, market trends, and customer attitudes. A survey can also be used as a marketing tool to present a company as a concerned and well-informed expert to potential customers. Customer surveys are explained extensively later in this chapter.

CUSTOMER CONTACTS

Direct customer contact supplies customer information to the manufacturer. Employees who have direct customer contact must be well qualified by temperament, attitude, and training to solicit customer information and provide assistance. Employees who have direct customer contact include: application engineers, design engineers, marketing personnel, customer service representatives, salespersons, receptionists, service personnel, and telephone operators.

PLANT VISITS

Plant visits are a preferred method for a supplier to obtain information from a customer. A plant visit provides the supplier with information directly from the development team on how the supplied material is being processed, machined, or assembled into the finished product.

ANALYSIS OF COMPLAINTS

Customer complaint analysis tells a company what went wrong with the product. A company can then determine how an existing product can be improved, modified, or adapted to a different market.

TEST AND EVALUATION

Product testing evaluates how a product performs in the marketplace. For example, manufacturers may evaluate new autos on a test track to gauge acceleration, braking, cornering, and other factors.

FORECASTING TRENDS

Trend forecasting attempts to anticipate consumer expectations. Useful trends in marketing include societal attitudes, demographic shifts, and buying behavior. Companies obtain trend data from government statistics, Supply Management data, demographic compositions, and news media.[46]

OP EX IMAGE ANALYSIS

Companies also use a technique called "operational excellence image analysis" to assess customers' perceptions of a product or service. The analysis assesses the effect of quality on customers' purchase decisions and appraises Op Ex strategies to deliver a product that satisfies expectations.

Accurate and realistic technical specifications alone do not result in a quality product. A product, especially a consumer product, must satisfy intangible customer expectations. Customers often pay more attention to form, fit, styling, and aesthetics than to its function.

Good design also adds perceived value to a product. Good design makes a product unique, distinguishable and ultimately, more marketable. Good design sells a product and, in some cases, has turned a company's fortunes around. Years ago, Ford's Taurus, the so called "aero jellybean," was a major design statement and contributed to Ford's rise in market share and profits.

Good design blends three important features - form, fit, and function to enhance its marketability. However, form and appearance will not sell products over the long term if functional attributes such as reliability and maintainability are not incorporated into the product. On the other hand, product reliability alone does not sell product.

Taking a customer's conception or feeling and designing an aesthetically pleasing product requires input from:

- Industrial design
- Product engineering

- Manufacturing engineering

INDUSTRIAL DESIGN

Industrial Design focuses on form, appearance, and aesthetics including packaging, styling, decoration, safety, logos, and cosmetic attributes. Industrial designers ask "does the product look good?" instead of "does it work well?"

However, the industrial designer must also be aware of the product's materials, construction, tooling, cost, and function. A product may be aesthetically appealing but may not be manufacturable with today's material or equipment or at a price that will be recovered in current market conditions.

For many years, auto designers seemed to have a herd mentality because too many auto designs looked alike. Auto designers used many identical parts to cut costs. They would disguise the sameness of their body designs by adding chrome strips, flashy adornments, and even vinyl roofs. Unfortunately, consumers did not accept the automotive "jewelry." The "jewelry" was supposed to communicate value at, of course, an additional cost. Unfortunately, the jewelry communicated a sameness that customers did not buy. To distinguish its autos from the competition, auto companies moved away from a boxy look to aerodynamic styling.

Retail consumers are especially concerned with form, styling, aesthetics, and decoration. For example, people buy fashion products based on what the product can do to emphasize their individuality. They may want to feel a spirit of adventure, be different, or be recognized as individuals. Of course, well-designed products sell at a premium. Designer shirts with embroidered logos may cost twice as much as a generic shirt with no logo.

Form is also important to industrial products. If a component is part of a product's exterior, then it must match in form, shape, decoration, and style the other body parts. Otherwise, the new component detracts from its marketability.

However, industrial buyers pay more attention to product function. The industrial buyer asks "does the product do what I want it to do, how well, and how quickly?" Since industrial products often operate continuously, maintainability and reliability are also important.

PRODUCT ENGINEERING

Product Engineering focuses more on function and fit. With a new product, Product Engineering takes the industrial designer's conceptual and tentative ideas and develops drawings, product specifications, and tolerances for Manufacturing Engineering to produce the product. For an existing product, Product Engineering may modify or update drawings to improve manufacturability, lower cost, or update cosmetics. Also, Product Engineering may develop and publish support documentation such as drawings, engineering parts books, and related technical publications.

MANUFACTURING ENGINEERING

And Manufacturing Engineering focuses on manufacturability. Product designs are next converted into detailed drawings suitable for production. Specifically, layout drawings are developed that show the overall configuration of the product. Layout drawings show assembly of parts at each level of design and detail how parts come together. Layouts also show the general configuration, shape, and overall dimensions of the product. Layouts are developed for each level of a product from subassembly, assembly to finished product. Detailed drawings specify dimensions and tolerances for all critical elements including holes and intricate shapes. The bill of materials lists all items such as bolts, nuts, and washers used in assembly.

Detailed drawings specify material as well as how a part is manufactured. If an item is purchased "off the shelf" from a supplier, then a supplier's catalog description is called out on the drawing. If an item is supplied by a vendor, then the part is detailed to the same precision as if it were made in the customer's manufacturing facility.

CHANGING NATURE OF ENGINEERING	
Old Approach	**New Approach**
Products are simple and mechanical	Products are complex, integrating mechanical, and electronic components
Lone engineer or craftsperson designs products	Team of specialists designs products
Engineer designs product then gives it to 'next in line'	Development team follows product through design cycle
Product is designed to operate in controlled environment	Product is designed to operate and survive in many environments
Product lifecycle is long	Product lifecycle is short
Existing products are modified	New products are introduced

Finally, everything is brought together. Layouts, detailed drawings, bills of material, tolerances, cost estimates, lab results, shop manuals, field tests, tooling, document check lists, parts book pages, service manuals, calculations, and government regulations are checked, rechecked, corrected, and updated.

PRODUCT DEVELOPMENT LIFECYCLE

Anybody can cut prices but it takes brains to make a better product.
Philip Armour

The development lifecycle (DLC) is a useful system or framework for understanding how different processes (Marketing, Engineering, Supply Management, Op Ex, Manufacturing, and Distribution) change over time to accommodate customer needs and to bring products to market quickly. The development lifecycle is composed of two parts, the design lifecycle (DLC) and the product lifecycle (PLC).

The design lifecycle (DLC) precedes the product lifecycle. The design lifecycle is divided into four stages:

- Customer wants, needs and expectations identification stage.

- Conceptual stage.
- Product design stage.
- Test marketing assessment stage.

The length of each stage depends on a product's application, complexity, level of innovation, degree of standardization, time-to-market pressures, and similarity of previous designs. These DLC stages can blend into each other, can be carried out concurrently, or can overlap into the beginning stages of the product lifecycle.

CUSTOMERS WANTS, NEEDS, AND EXPECTATION IDENTIFICATION STAGE

First, a market need is identified. A new market may be identified or an established market may have new wants. The product development team attempts to understand preferences, needs, and perceptions of the target market. The development team attempts to identify potential customers; list and prioritize critical needs of each target group; identify tangible and intangible product characteristics critical to the customer target group; and identify environmental, regulatory, and cost constraints to using the product. QFD and similar techniques discussed in the previous chapter are used to understand customer needs.

CONCEPTUAL STAGE

In the conceptual stage, as customer needs are identified and clarified, the development team studies alternative designs. The development team evaluates each design to determine if a proposed product can be designed, produced, and marketed at an economical cost.

Specifically, the development team must:

- **Study applicable technologies.** The development team investigates a product's "state of the art" so current and relevant technology can be used to design the new product.
- **Examine competing products.** Competing products are scrutinized to ensure the new or modified product is sufficiently different

or better than competing products. For example, the distinct advantage of a new laptop PC may be its portability, speed, ease of use, screen, or more options.

- **Determine design constraints.** Once customer needs are understood, the team asks what constraints could cause the product to malfunction, deteriorate, or be nonmarketable. Constraints routinely considered are cost, physical size, maintenance requirements, product life, operating costs, surface finish, delivery date, quantity of production, transportation costs, mechanical/electronic conditions, and environmental conditions.
- **Account for global marketing.** If the product is sold overseas, the team must account for different tastes, technical conditions, climatic conditions, and cultural differences. In many countries, industrial specifications or codes do not exist, are not standardized, or are more stringent. Also, humidity, rain, snow, or heat can adversely influence operating conditions.
- **Consider timing.** The team must consider various lead times in selecting suppliers for component parts, choosing the right timing to introduce the product to market, and considering lead times for manufacturing design fixtures.

PRODUCT DESIGN STAGE

The product design stage is iterative involving the following steps:

- Product brief
- Preliminary stage
- Prototype construction
- Design control, assurance, and review
- Product testing
- Trial production run

Product brief

Once Marketing has determined customer needs then it has to set these needs down in a formal statement or outline of product requirements. This document, sometimes called a product brief, translates customer requirements, needs, and expectations into a preliminary set of specifications that will be used by the organization to design a quality product or deliver a service.

A product brief usually addresses the following:

- Performance characteristics (environmental and reliability)
- Sensory characteristics (style, color, taste, smell)
- Installation configuration or fit
- Applicable standards
- Packaging
- Operational assurance/verification[47]

Preliminary Design

If a product consists of layers of assemblies, subassemblies, components, and parts, the development team divides a product into small, manageable subsystems. Each system can be designed by a separate product development team. Once each functional sub element is designed, these are integrated into the finished product. The design is then reviewed in terms of interaction and function of the different system parts. After assembly interaction is assessed, then the interaction of subassemblies and components is assessed. The review goes from bottom-up as well as top-down. At each level, detailed drawings are generated and refined until finished drawings are developed. Finished drawings include bills of material, drawings of various views, layouts, and work and inspection instructions.

Prototype Construction

Prior to constructing a physical model, products may be tested on a computer to simulate stress, fatigue, and other types of physical conditions. Once constructed, a prototype reveals fit and function problems that may be encountered in production. It is always easier to modify a design before production than try to incorporate changes during production or when the product is in the customer's hands.

Design Control, Assurance, and Review

By this time, the design has gone through many iterations including evaluations of specifications, tolerances, standards, production drawings, manufacturing instructions, assembly procurement, production, and inspection plans. Since each iteration is a potential source of error, each document is checked for consistency, completeness, and correctness. This is called design assurance and control.

Design control and assurance are critical for controlling product design changes. If a product has to be modified, then methods are established to control release, change, and use of specifications, drawings, and other engineering documentation.

Product Testing

The product is tested and evaluated almost continuously during the design lifecycle. Original calculations are verified. Samples are tested to destruction in various reliability tests. Performance, safety, reliability, and maintainability are tested under operating conditions.

Trial Production Run

If a design has been approved and the product is ready for production, the development team secures resources including materials, labor, factory space, components, and fabrication to produce the product. A trial production run allows the development team to debug the product by looking for design flaws and to optimize machinery. Timelines for each project phase are scheduled and planned because machinery selection, delivery dates, supplier selection, and operator training have to be coordinated.

TEST MARKETING ASSESSMENT STAGE

A prototype is usually test marketed prior to full scale production. This stage often overlaps the introduction and growth stages of the product lifecycle (PLC). The company wants to know whether there is a market for the product prior to making the decision for full-scale production. Full-scale production may require a commitment to rearrange production lines; purchase new equipment, fixtures, and tools; train personnel; or approve new plans and drawings.

So, Manufacturing builds a small number of products using existing tooling and equipment. With consumer products, Marketing identifies a geographic location that resembles the target market and test markets the product. Customer impressions are then solicited through customer surveys. Industrial products may be tested and evaluated in a customer's industrial facility.

If survey results are positive, then full-scale production is warranted and authorized. If results are negative or inconclusive, then the product is modified. If a second or third survey substantiates the negative results, the product design may be scrapped.

DESIGN PROCESS

The genius of modern technology lies in making things to last fifty years and making them obsolete in three.
Anonymous

Companies are moving responsibility for Op Ex upstream from the manufacturing process to design. Product value and content is often in upstream packaging and design.

When a new product is planned, a company will form product development teams where designers are placed next to manufacturing engineers. Designing products in a vacuum without input from other parties results in dangerous consequences. Industrial designers may not know how industrial products are produced or how they are used in the customer's facility. Product engineers may be inexperienced in manufacturing and develop specifications that are mathematically correct and appear acceptable on the drawing but introduce unnecessary production difficulties, difficult shapes, or unrealistic or unneeded precision. All of which adds to product cost.

If Engineering has little faith in Manufacturing's seriousness about conforming to specifications, Engineering may deliberately specify tighter specifications believing that Manufacturing may build in extra tolerance. Also, Manufacturing supervisors and machine operators may operate outside product specification limits thinking the product is still safe and reliable.
Realistic product specifications are developed when product engineers, industrial designers, and Op Ex engineers get "hands on" experience on the

manufacturing floor. Manufacturing can provide Engineering information about the ability of machines and processes to meet specifications. Also, Manufacturing Engineering and Production supervisors should spend time with Op Ex, Design and Product Engineering gaining an understanding of their disciplines.

PRODUCT LIFECYCLE

If every new product is stamped "improved," what were we buying before?
Anonymous

The product lifecycle (PLC) is a simple and useful concept to explain how the dynamic nature of the marketplace influences product quality. As we have said, Op Ex is a moving target because customer's expectations change over time. A product is conceived, develops, matures, and then disappears.

The four PLC stages are: introduction, growth, mature, and decline. For most products, the order of the PLC does not change. However, the length of different stages in the cycle may vary between product categories. Consumer products have a much shorter lifecycle than industrial products. Or, a product may emulate an existing product and enter in the middle of the lifecycle.

Some products have sharp growth curves and then die a quick death. Trendy toys exhibit this type of curve with extraordinary sales the first several years that quickly taper off. Or, other products have a relatively slow growth curve which flattens out. These products continue selling well for many years. Maybe, the label will change to reflect the styles of new users, while the ingredients stay the same. Examples of this pattern include: Cheerios cereal, Arm and Hammer baking soda, and Marlboro cigarettes.

At each PLC stage, the development team modifies or adapts a product so it still satisfies the customer. Simple quality features such as branding, advertising, and packaging can be modified to satisfy changing tastes and to extend different parts of the PLC curve.

PRODUCT LIFECYCLE - INTRODUCTION STAGE

As mentioned, this stage often overlaps the design lifecycle. A specific market need has been identified through market research or similar techniques. If a niche is identified in an existing market, then the competition is researched and evaluated. If the market is sufficiently large to accommodate a new product, if the product is sufficiently different from its competition, and if cost/revenue projections look good, then a prototype is developed.

A prototype is then designed and constructed. The prototype is evaluated and tested for potential flaws. Aesthetics, fit, and other quality characteristics are changed as necessary. A prototype can be a radical departure from an existing product or can emulate an existing product. If the new product emulates an existing product, then it should have performance features or cost advantages that differentiate it from previous and competitive products.

The product is then introduced into the marketplace. The product may be distributed to select customers. These early adopters are important for the product's image and for subsequent endorsements. Advertising is used to create product awareness. During product development, product costs increase. Substantial administrative overhead, advertising, sales, and other costs are incurred to introduce the product to market. Initially, products may be priced high in order to recover initial investment in the venture or to garner market share.

During this stage, defect rates are high because products have not been debugged and processes have not been stabilized. Manufacturing processes are continually adjusted to ensure Op Ex is maintained. Suppliers are continually monitored to ensure raw material and parts comply with specifications. Products are distributed mainly through wholesale distributors to keep costs low. Investment in fixed warehouse facilities is kept low. Since the market for the product is developing, timeliness, and reliability of delivery are important Op Ex attributes. Customers want products quickly. Small, value-added products may be shipped directly by air freight. Production runs are short. Inventory stocks are kept low in order not to exceed product demand.

In this stage, production is usually low because products are being manufactured using existing machinery. Existing machinery may have to be modified to produce products. If sales take off, specialized equipment may also be purchased to increase production capacity. Product designs may also be refined.

PRODUCT LIFE CYCLE = GROWTH STAGE

If the product is a success, sales and profits increase because demand is high. If the product fails, the opposite occurs. As the market grows, competitors may offer similar lower priced products. Or competitors may enhance a product design by adding features, by increasing reliability, or by adding cosmetic refinements. As the variety of products increases, sales still increase but profits flatten because of rising competition.

In this stage, cost control is emphasized. Profit margins may be squeezed. Longer, more economical production runs are encouraged. Product warehouses are built and dealer networks are created to deliver high volumes of product. By this time, customers are using the product extensively. Customer feedback through warranty claims and complaints provide the operational assurance group with information of the type and magnitude of product flaws and nonconformances. Production processes are adjusted or the product is redesigned to eliminate nonconformances.

Raw material is purchased in bulk quantities to take advantage of quantity discounts. As product requirements are understood, scheduling is tightened. Mode of transport for raw material is slower, while the delivery of finished product is still speedy and reliable.

Production runs are still high, which requires accurate forecasting of customer demand so the minimum amount of safety stock is on hand. Accurate order processing and tight inventory control become important. Production increases to accommodate increasing customer demand. Production adapts to changes in demand by increasing product variety and restructuring production equipment.

Existing products are often modified or replaced by new models. Products are redesigned to appeal to new market niches. Engineering and Manufacturing work closely together. New or modified products require new drawings, specifications, work instructions, and test procedures. Engineering and production operators communicate during changeovers so operators understand what is expected of them. Without this information, unintentional errors can arise due to operators' inexperience, lack of familiarity, or lack of product or process understanding.

Flexibility in production is required to adapt to customer product changes. Jigs, fixtures, and dies are redesigned so they can be interchanged quickly and easily. Manufacturing operations are finetuned to produce different products on demand. Products are standardized and modularized. Automation is used for repetitive tasks. Process controls are used to monitor measurements and control production.

PRODUCT LIFECYCLE = MATURE STAGE

In the maturity stage, the product has secured a high market share. Sales taper off because of stiffer competition. The firm and its competitors have reached the consumers who are likely to buy the product. The potential for further growth is limited. The market is saturated with products with similar attributes, features, and performance. Offshore, lower priced manufactured products dominate the market. New firms enter the market seeing opportunities to compete by offering a lower price or improved service. Companies emphasize the product's value-added features to differentiate it from others.

Profit margins decrease through this stage because everyone is competing for a smaller piece of the pie. Since the market is static, profits come from eating into someone else's market share or by producing products at lower costs. So, firms concentrate on making better products at a lower price. Less efficient firms that cannot compete, drop out. By this stage, a successful product has a quality image or reputation, consisting of a combination of logo, name, brand, and label.

A company has two strategic marketing options. First, a company tries to find and develop new products to replace those that are no longer wanted by the customer. Second, a company can try to manage the existing product to maximize profits. A company may extend the maturity part of the curve by modifying a product, adding "bells and whistles," or through heavy advertising.

A company reassesses how it wants to deliver and store products, including on deciding transportation modes, optimal location, and number of warehouses. Products are often distributed by dealer networks that sell products and provide customer service. Network supplies are replenished regularly.

In this stage, production is high. To move material quickly, processes are automated and integrated. Production operations become more flexible to produce different products quickly and inexpensively that meet customer requirements and expectations.

PRODUCT LIFECYCLE - DECLINE STAGE

In the decline stage, new products replace older products. Competition is fierce as a shakeout occurs with weaker competitors leaving the market. Profits are squeezed. As in the mature stage, a company may be able to extend product life by adding new features or providing additional services. Or, a company can develop a new product as a substitute for the existing product. Or a company can drop the existing product.

In this stage, sales and revenues drop. Lower production levels result in lower distribution levels. Firms leave the market because of insufficient profit margins. Dealer distribution networks contract.

If the product has strong market recognition and brand loyalty, then the product brand can be updated. Packaging can be changed. If the product does not have sufficient brand recognition, then declining sales volume and rising costs will force the product to be dropped.

PRODUCT LIFECYCLE CONCEPT IS GOOD, BUT!

The PLC is easy to understand, but it is difficult to apply. PLC's curves vary in shape and length across product lines. PLC's have different shapes for consumer and industrial products. A trendy consumer product like a designer dress has a very steep rise in the introduction stage and sharp drop off in the decline stage. The maturity stage is short. On the other hand, an industrial product like a compressor has a flatter introduction and longer maturity and decline stages.

PLC is a good concept, but it does not tell a product manager how long each stage of the cycle will last or when to modify a product to extend its life. So, product managers often do not feel confident of a product's lifecycle. Instead of managing an existing product to lengthen its profitable stages, product managers tend to introduce risky new products which may cause a premature death in an existing product.

Product introduction is always more visible and interesting than product maintenance. However, it sometimes makes sense to milk an existing cash cow than to introduce a new product. The odds are 1 in 4 that a new product will be profitable. The result is new products get all of the attention while the established products languish and die.

PRODUCT LIFECYCLE DEVELOPMENT

Customers late in the product lifecycle can have different requirements than those who purchased the initial product. Competitors or emulators in the mature stage of the PLC may have products that offer better performance at a lower price than the original product.

To keep a product marketable throughout the product lifecycle, the development team can:

- Alter Op Ex characteristics
- Redesign packaging
- Modify or update brand or label
- Add product value
- Modify product line

ALTER OP EX CHARACTERISTICS

By adding, removing, or altering product characteristics, a product's performance, reliability, or appearance can be enhanced to satisfy the changing needs of the marketplace. In this way, the possibility of competitive duplication can be reduced and profit margins maintained with the existing product. Product performance, reliability, maintainability, physical characteristics and other product characteristics can be altered.

For example, product performance may be enhanced by replacing existing materials with technologically superior materials. This may mean replacing heavier steel structural members with lighter and stronger composite material. Using composite in place of steel saves weight. If composite is used properly, it provides higher strength per unit weight than steel and has more resistance to corrosion.

Product characteristics cannot be altered haphazardly. While new technology often stimulates changes in a new or existing product's features or performance, new technology can also threaten an existing product line. Customers may forego Supply Management an existing product because industry rumors speculate a new product may soon be introduced. The existing product may have an early demise, which occurs when product lifecycles are short as in personal computers.

A product can also have its product characteristics changed in response to regulatory mandates, litigation, industry standards, or pressure from consumer groups. The Federal government has suggested or mandated modifications in such products as automobiles, contraceptives, and airlines.

REDESIGN PACKAGING

If a product is reliable, widely used and readily recognized, the development team may decide an aesthetically pleasing and functional package may extend its useful life. Packaging just needs to be redesigned and updated. In consumer products, labels can be updated to show consumers in modern clothing and surroundings.

Changing packaging can also enhance functional and aesthetic qualities. Functionally, a package protects contents during transport, use, or storage. Packaging also protects contents against degradation caused by vibration, pressure, changes in temperature, and humidity. Packaging facilitates product use, such as being able to dispense contents easier or by providing more shelf space.

In recent years, pharmaceutical product tampering has forced manufacturers to design tamper resistant packages. Packages have shrink fit sleeves or twist caps so the consumer can see if it has been used or opened.

MODIFY OR UPDATE BRAND OR LABEL

A new brand or label can extend product life by repositioning the product in the marketplace by enhancing its image. Also, a brand is used to differentiate among good, better, or best. Or a brand can be used to distinguish product features or performance.

ADD PRODUCT VALUE

Manufacturers add features or increase performance to enhance product value. Value can be added to a broad product line or to a single product. Companies manufacture customized or personalized products for special applications.

Manufacturers may offer a basic line of automobiles or may offer limited editions with special performance packages to attract upscale consumers. For example to update a well-known automobile, a manufacturer has added features, increased engine performance, changed its name and image, and charged a premium price.

Customizing a product line also prolongs its useful life. A product can be introduced stripped, and the manufacturer adds features or performance by requiring the consumer to buy additional accessories. Value can also be added by offering consulting, design, or maintenance services.

CHANGING NATURE OF MANUFACTURING	
Old Approach	**New Approach**
Inspect products after production	Monitor processes during production to reduce to find defects
Scrap and rework are expected	Parts per million defect rates are accepted
Production runs are long to reduce unit	Production runs are short
Production jobs are simple	Production jobs are complex
Technology is static	Technology is rapidly changing
Machine set-up time is long	Machine set-up time is short

MODIFY PRODUCT LINE

A manufacturer can penetrate and capture different market niches by modifying a product line. A product line is modified to induce consumers to switch brands because of different tastes, performance expectations or Op Ex desires. A manufacturer can modify a product line by adding, modifying, or withdrawing models, styles, size, price ranges, accessories, flavors, color, or performance. In consumer products, this may entail minor cosmetic changes. In industrial products, changes usually focus on increasing technical or functional capability.

PRODUCT MODIFICATION THROUGH ITS LIFECYCLE

A new idea is delicate. It can be killed by a sneer or a yawn; it can be stabbed to death by a quip and worried to death by a frown on the right man's brow.

Charles Brower, executive

Designing a reliable and aesthetically pleasing product is becoming more difficult because the product lifecycle especially of high-tech products is very short, while the design lifecycle may still be long. Some products that had a 10 years product lifecycle are now compressed into 2 or even 1 year. There is little time to adapt or modify the product. The right product has to be delivered to the customer at the right time. If it is not, the customer will buy another product.

Also, companies have been known to develop, design, and manufacture only one product. This is risky. In this competitive environment, firms bet the company the product will be successful. If the product fails to generate income, then the organization goes "belly up," high risk - high return.

Once a product is developed and in the hands of the customer, the development team is continuously adapting, upgrading, modifying, or enhancing the product to keep it current and to minimize costs. The development team ensures the product does not wear out or become prematurely obsolete.

To minimize risk, companies are ensuring that Op Ex is integrated and considered throughout the product development process by:

- Understanding customer requirements.
- Identifying marketing processes and products.
- Matching and correlating customer requirements to marketing processes and products.
- Eliminating ineffective or non-value-adding processes and products.
- Improving existing processes.
- Adding new processes as required.
- Involving all employees in marketing excellence.

PRODUCT INNOVATION

One reason often mentioned why a company may be losing its manufacturing edge is because it cannot rapidly translate technology and innovation into competitive, marketable products. While technology is available, products are produced that don't satisfy customer needs.

Or, products are designed from the point of view of the designer instead of the customer. For example, products are loaded down with technical features that please the designer but distract the customer. So, as U.S. brand names dominate certain critical markets, such as computers and scientific instruments, many product components are manufactured and assembled offshore.

PRODUCT DIFFERENTIATION

Brands help customers differentiate a product from its competitors. Customers buy products based on the brand name and pay a premium price for its reassurance. A recognizable brand and easily remembered name confers trust onto the product.

Brands are used to communicate excellence in industrial goods and consumer goods. Buyers of Microsoft software feel secure they are receiving the most integrated and widely used software in the computer industry. Microsoft obtains premium prices for its products because of the confidence and trust its name confers.

PRODUCT DEVELOPMENT TEAM

Companies are establishing multidisciplinary teams to develop products. Product development is organized so knowledgeable people in different departments and on different organizational levels contribute to development decisions. Increasingly, a product development team including representatives from Marketing, Engineering, Op Ex, Supply Management, Distribution, and Manufacturing may follow a product from conception through market introduction. Once on the market, the team follows a product through its lifecycle modifying the product over time to meet the changing needs of the marketplace.

Why is this happening? The day of the "lone wolf" engineer designing a technical product is over. Products are now so sophisticated and so complex that they require a multidisciplinary team approach to design. One person no longer has the range of knowledge and experience to design and develop a product from start-to-finish. Only a team has the knowledge and skills to design value into the product.

Several years ago, Hewlett-Packard wanted to develop a new oscilloscope. On the front end, Op Ex and reliability were the goals of the new scope. The reliability goal was to develop a scope three times better than the existing product.

Since the goals for the new product were especially ambitious, a multidisciplinary team from the following functional areas was chosen to design and develop the product:

- R & D project manager
- Production engineering new products manager
- Op Ex engineering manager
- Materials procurement manager
- Product marketing section manager

CONCURRENT ENGINEERING

Competition is now global. Customers are demanding more. Both of these are driving companies to become more competitive which usually means doing things right the first time, faster, and better. A current conventional wisdom is to do things simultaneously instead of serially such as developing products.

Concurrent or simultaneous product development is the process of integrating people, technologies, methods, systems, and processes into cross functional, self-managed teams to develop products. Simultaneous product development tries to develop products in parallel instead of in series. This is a major change from traditional product development. Concurrent product development stresses collaboration and cooperation instead of competition among company departments. Information is shared and communication is open through connected networks of computers. The organization is flat instead of hierarchical. Teams cooperate throughout the development process. The team leader provides the organizational links, resources, and support for the team.

While concurrent engineering is common, the risks are also high. One risk is the possibility of design changes, rework, mistakes, and redundancies. In serial process design, critical process and product parameters were checked, rechecked, and checked again over a long period of time. There were other benefits to serial design. Assumptions could be questioned. Calculations could be rechecked. Suppliers could be selected, evaluated, monitored, and improved. Customer requirements could be fine-tuned and specified in detail. The problem was that product development took a long time. Time-to-market is now a critical competitive weapon.

SHRINKING PRODUCT LIFECYCLES AND INCREASING TIME-TO-MARKET

Many companies are managing product lifecycles continuously, trying to balance Op Ex, cost, efficiency, and innovation factors. Since new products develop quickly from conception to market introduction, companies are able to flexibly monitor and adapt the development process to satisfy changes in the external environment.

Speed and flexibility provide companies with a competitive advantage in the form of increased increased productivity and lowered costs. The rapid introduction of innovative products contribute to increased market share. A recent study concluded the following speeded the development process:

- Top management encouragement and involvement.
- Concurrent or simultaneous product development teams.
- Self-driven and managed project teams.
- Overlapping product phases.
- Devotion to continuous learning and trying new technologies.
- Subtle peer group pressure to perform.
- Rapid transfer of knowledge and techniques.

WHAT IS GOOD DESIGN?

For functional, aesthetic, and manufacturable design, the simplest configurations often work best. For example, complicated configurations, such as thin-wall sections or complex contours magnify tooling and manufacturing problems resulting in rising costs. While there are few universal laws for good design, the following are some good rules of thumb:

- Customer requirements are defined and understood.
- Design control is defined.
- Plans are developed for each design activity.
- Technical interfaces are defined.

WHY NEW PRODUCTS FAIL

A study by the National Industrial Conference Board concluded the following are reasons why new products fail:

1. Inadequate market analysis	32%
2. Product defects	23%
3. Higher costs than anticipated	14%
4. Poor timing	10%
5. Competition reaction	8%
6. Inadequate marketing effort (includes weaknesses in sales force, distribution, and advertising)[48]	13%
	100%

- Design input, output, and process requirements are defined.
- Design is validated.
- Design changes are identified, documented, reviewed, and approved.
- Design is reviewed continuously by the development team.
- Key suppliers are part of design team.
- Design incorporates a minimum number of parts.
- Parts are defect-free.
- Design has a suitable safety margin.
- Design incorporates parallel circuits for redundancy.
- Design is manufacturable and testable.
- Subassemblies are minimized.
- Design reviews are conducted throughout design process.
- Design has been tested.
- Design emphasizes standardization for new or existing models.
- Engineering changes are documented and authorized by appropriate personnel.

NEW PRODUCT SUCCESS

What makes a new product successful? The following are key factors for new product success:

- Product superiority
- Strong market orientation
- Up-front homework
- Early product definition and introduction
- Cross functional team approach
- Focus and project prioritization
- Op Ex of execution[49]

PRODUCT SAFETY

The oil can is mightier than the sword.
Everett Dirkson

Product safety has been important since the beginning of the industrial revolution. Industrial firms during the industrial revolution obtained their power from boilers which were not designed and built to any standard.

While many boilers were reliable and safe, many still exploded. Starting in the 1880's, the American Society of Mechanical Engineers (ASME) developed designs and documentation standards for boilers that are still used today. Every pressurized boiler must have a plate on the outside shell that specifies the pressure rating and other relevant safety data.

Product safety is especially a major concern to companies that are exposed to lawsuits. To ensure product safety, companies are pulling unsafe products off the market, redesigning products, educating customers on proper use, and testing products more thoroughly before they are introduced into the marketplace.

HUMAN FACTORS

Studies reveal that a major cause of industrial accidents are people misusing or abusing machinery. The more complex and sophisticated the machinery, the higher the chance for failure. An Air Force study concluded that as much as 60% of missile system failures were attributed to human error. A relatively new field has evolved called human factors or ergonomic engineering.

Human factors engineering evaluates how people, environment, machines and other factors relate to each other. For example, machines are designed to be "user friendly" by considering the many variables of human judgment that are used to manipulate machinery. A multidisciplinary team may analyze the function and purpose of a machine and ask if the task is reasonable given the operator's abilities. The team may consider:

- User abilities, including physical limitations, strength, co-ordination, and capabilities.
- Environment, including lighting, weather, location, and sound.
- Equipment, including size, color, and shape.

For example, the development team may look at and measure the strength and coordination, sensory capabilities, body dimensions, skills and optimum workload of people. Automobile companies measure the movement and strength of drivers so automobile seats can be designed for driver's comfort and safety.

PRODUCT SAFETY AND LIABILITY PREVENTION

The Consumer Product Safety Commission (C.P.S.C.) is the government agency responsible for monitoring and ensuring the safety of consumer products. The agency recently has been reviewing the safety records of off-road vehicles. These three- and four- wheeled vehicles have had a history of overturning and causing injuries and deaths.

So, when the development team reviews a product's design, they brainstorm solutions to the following reliability and maintainability related questions:

- Is the product safe?
- Is the product easy to use?
- Where and how will product fail?
- Can the product be tested?
- What is the failure rate (reliability) of the product?
- How can the risks be minimized and at what cost?
- Can safety and health standards and specifications be met?

So when a new product is developed, the product development team looks at a number of process and product related factors to improve product safety. The development team evaluates product safety and liability prevention issues in the following areas:

- **Proper Advertising Language.** Advertising copy is carefully written and reviewed so it does not state or imply unachievable product performance because advertisers may puff up product attributes or performance beyond its abilities. A customer purchases a product believing it will perform as advertised. If an accident occurs because of misuse or abuse, the manufacturer may be liable for verbal excesses in the advertising copy.
- **Safety Warnings.** Safety warnings are written carefully so the customer knows where and under what conditions a product can be used. Sales personnel, installers, maintenance personnel, and users are informed of product use, misuse, and abuse.
- **Safety Analyses.** Safety analyses evaluate new products, modified products, or prototypes to ensure they perform as intended under specified conditions. Safety tests may evaluate a product to the point of failure.

- **Environmental Analyses.** Environmental analyses and testing verify a product does not contaminate the environment. Chemicals, pharmaceutical products, power plant controls, and life-enhancing products are extensively tested by government agencies. As well, chemical, power, and industrial processes are scrutinized to assure processes do not fail and dump effluent in the environment.
- **Packaging.** Proper packaging ensures product integrity during shipment, storage, delivery and display. Packaging is especially important to maintain a product's appearance during shipment and storage. Shipping packaging should be durable and functional. Shelf packaging should be attractive, compact, and informative.

RELIABILITY

The decent thing for an inanimate object in America to do is wear out. Most inanimate objects understand and do their duty. Light bulbs are particularly good about it.
Russell Baker

Reliability and maintainability are two important attributes or dimensions of operational excellence. They are important for continued customer satisfaction and for maintaining public safety. After the sale, the customer wants a product to operate satisfactorily. When the customer flips the light switch, the customer wants light not excuses. Or, Management Information Systems wants continuous power to maintain computer memory, otherwise a power bump may erase memory. The customer wants a product to work the first time and every time.

An obvious concern to the development team is how, when, where, and why will a product fail over time. Will the product simply not work or will the product suddenly and completely fail resulting in permanent injury or loss of life? Accidents result in litigation and high insurance premiums.

A product may be defect-free when it is made. But what about 10 or even 20 years in the future? Companies have been held liable for defects or abuse of products made many years ago. To limit product liability and exposure, products are overdesigned or overbuilt to be reliable many years into the future. Product reliability depends on many factors, including product design, component operational excellence, manufacturing operational excellence, packaging, handling, maintenance frequency, test, and operating conditions.

WHAT IS RELIABILITY?

Reliability can be thought of as long-term quality. We have discussed operational excellence in terms of a static notion of control. In other words, dimensions, tolerances, and performance are checked at one point in time.

But what happens to the dimensions and performance of a product over time? While product performance may be satisfactory at one point in time, dimensions obviously change as a product is used. Moreover, modern products are complex, manufactured to tight tolerances, and composed of many parts. These products are prone to failure.

A formal definition of reliability reads:

> "Reliability is the probability that a product will do what it's supposed to do under prescribed operating conditions for a specified period of time."

As seen in the above definition, reliability is a function of three factors: performance, operating conditions, and time or period over which it is supposed to operate.

RELIABILITY SPECIFICATIONS

A user or designer can specify that a 100-Watt light bulb should be 99% reliable during a two-year warranty period or 4000 hours of operation. Specifying product reliability limits defines its design. By setting standards for product performance, the reliability engineer measures actual performance of the product against a standard. The difference between the actual and expected level of performance tells the designer what to change in the product. If the light bulb lasts only 4000 hours, the designer can specify a longer lasting filament or some other change. If the light bulb lasts 10,000 hours, the designer can specify less costly components, modify advertising copy, or raise the product price.

Product reliability can range from 1.0 to 0.0 - 1.0 means the product operates as expected over a specified period of time under the environmental conditions it was placed; 0.0 means that it will fail during the specified period of time or under the prescribed operating conditions.

COMPUTER RELIABILITY

Software reliability is often as important as machine reliability because software instructs complex machinery what and how often to perform a function. Software does not wear out like machinery and can be programmed to perform different tasks. However, when a software defect or bug exists, especially in a large, complex program, it is difficult to detect until extensive damage may have been done. Any bug in source code or an original program will be duplicated in other programs.

A tiny software error can stall or damage very large computers, whole plants, or military systems. Computerized insurance systems serve millions of people. The software directing and transferring data is large and complex. Computerized instructions consist of millions of lines of code that are written by hundreds of programmers each of whom work on small sections of the program. It is possible that a tiny error such as a misplaced period can cause an entire system to fail.

WHEN FAILURE IS BUILT IN?

Following the Challenger shuttle and Chernobyl nuclear power plant disasters, many questioned the reliability of technological products. Editorials in technical journals pointed out that sophisticated, technological products have built-in failure. It is less a question of whether they will fail, rather, it is a question of when they will fail.

Since Three Mile Island and Chernobyl, nuclear power plant safety is an important public policy issue. The dangers of an accident however remote, are vivid reminders that plants must be safe and reliable. All nuclear power plants have safety programs to prevent any release of radiation exceeding 0.5 rem to the whole body. To maintain safety, all critical systems, equipment, and components are designed for reliability. Safety systems have redundant, back-up systems so that if one fails then a parallel one works.

The booster rocket joints of the Challenger had almost failed in previous shuttle flights. The joints remained unmodified until the fatal accident. As well, a poorly designed graphite moderator reactor and water coolant system in the Chernobyl reactor increased the likelihood of a catastrophic accident following a reactor failure.

The moral is that all man-made technological products have a reliability factor so it is not a question if a product will fail, it is just a matter of when.

THE FUTURE

Software is becoming more important than hardware. Hardware is becoming a relatively inexpensive, mass-produced item. The high value-added part of a product can be software that instructs the machine how to perform special functions. Software, the brains inside the product, must be programmed. This is time consuming even for a simple product.

This trend can be seen in industrial and consumer products. Simple telephones and cameras are relatively cheap. When these items are loaded with special features, they can perform varied and complex functions. These models are more expensive. As the price-to-performance ratio of computers decreases, personal computers are also seen as commodity products.

MAINTAINABILITY

GIGO: Garbage in, garbage out.
Anonymous

Products fail. Products are designed to be easily maintained at a minimum cost. When products fail, the customer wants the product repaired quickly. So, products are designed not only to last a long time but to be repaired easily and quickly.

Maintainability is the ability to restore service after a failure. When a product fails in the field or in the customer's hands, the customer is able to have the product repaired or serviced quickly.

Maintainability and reliability are similar but different concepts. Maintainability studies the results of product failures to find ways to minimize them. In contrast, reliability analyzes the cause of product failures to find ways to eliminate them.

MANAGING USING OP EX DOCUMENTATION

Managing ISO 9001:2015 requires a new focus in a team environment. At least superficially, Op Ex functional requirements may not seem like a good fit in team work environments. ISO 9001:2015 Op Ex documentation are customer-supplier contractual requirements. Op Ex policies are "shall" requirements. These should be developed carefully in a participatory work environment. Participatory work environments are characterized by self-managed, high- performance teams. The organization is flat. There are few middle managers. Teams are responsible and have the authority for their operations. Technical staff assists teams and other work groups to do their jobs.

How will teams and more specifically team members feel about ISO 9001:2015 "shall" requirements? Op Ex policies and procedures should be thoroughly explained to the entire organization. If senior management simply mandates Op Ex systems implementation, operations may be disrupted possibly resulting in more scrap and increased rework.

Suddenly in this environment, Op Ex procedures are established and sometimes imposed on accountable work groups. These procedures and work instructions may at first be threatening especially if they seem to be imposed from above or from outside the organization. Op Ex systems should be integrated into existing procedures. Workers and teams should be involved throughout the process.

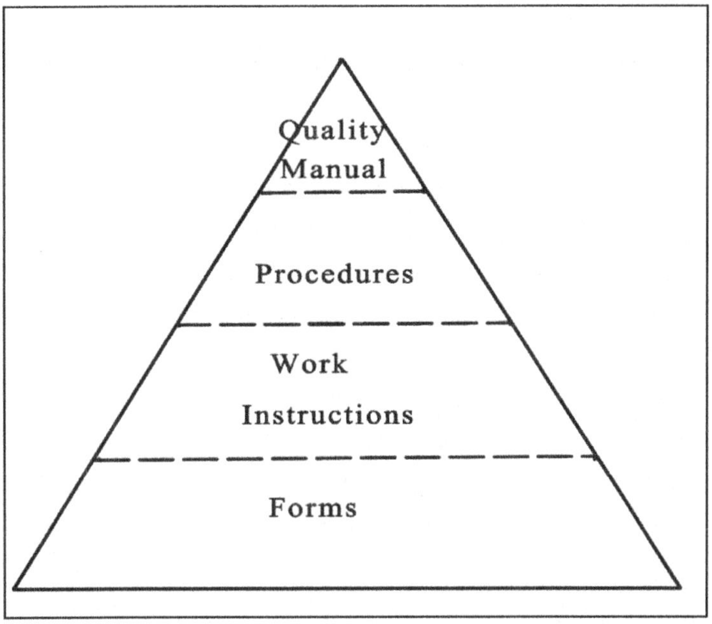

Op Ex paperwork can snowball as more operations are proceduralized. The question arises: "what type of Op Ex system should be implemented, paperwork, computerized, or a combination of both." For small companies a paper-based system should be adequate. Paper can be accessed easily and the number of Op Ex systems is manageable. However, in larger companies a computer may be necessary to manage the Op Ex documentation. Documentation must be kept current, complete, and be usable. However computerization of documentation is difficult. Computerized documentation is expensive because people must be trained, computers purchased, software purchased, and new procedures developed.

Op Ex documentation must be generated, updated, and distributed carefully. The key to documentation systems is finding the optimal balance among competing requirements including the type of records, amount of records, and level of detail in the records.

Properly used, Op Ex documentation are important tools for reducing company and supplier wide variation in critical Op Ex, performance, customer, and operational criteria. As the number of users increases, the potential for variation in implementation, communication, and understanding also increases.

A policy and procedure may look the same. However, a procedure usually addresses the following:

- **Why.** Why is the procedure being developed?
- **Where.** Where will the procedure be applied?
- **What.** What activity or activities will be accomplished?
- **Who.** Which function, team, or individual will accomplish the activity or action?
- **When.** When will the activity be done?
- **How.** How will the activity be accomplished?
- **What.** What equipment are required to accomplish the activity?
- **How.** How will the results of the activity be documented, controlled, or monitored?

MAINTAINABILITY MEASUREMENT

Maintainability is measured in terms of:

- **Mean-time-to-repair (MTTR):** the mean or average time it takes to repair a product.
- **Downtime:** the time that a product is unavailable for use because it is being repaired or people are waiting for parts.
- **Availability:** the time a product is available for active use or is on standby.

What is good maintainability? A system with good maintainability optimizes all system inputs. Good maintainability involves accomplishing all of the required tasks within a minimum amount of time, at the least cost, and with the least number of people.

WHERE IS MAINTAINABILITY USED?

Maintainability techniques are used by:

- **Utilities.** Large power plants use preventive maintenance to schedule repairs of critical equipment. For example, nuclear power plant personnel repair critical pumps and turbines on set schedules to prevent premature failure.

- **Military.** Maintainability is an operational imperative in the aerospace, military, and nuclear industries. Military hardware has to be operational so it can be deployed quickly and effectively, especially in the event of war. Military hardware is designed to be maintained easily and quickly in the field.
- **Automated facilities.** Automated warehouses and factories run continuously. A breakdown in one part of the process can shut an entire factory.

INSTALLATION

We want consumers to say "that's a hell of a product" instead of "that's a hell of an ad."
Leo Burnett

Consumer products are usually ready to be used when received by the customer. If a bicycle has to be assembled, a customer can assemble it easily and quickly. However, industrial products often need to be assembled, installed, constructed, or tested in the field. Industrial products can require special:

- Instructions
- Trained technicians

INSTRUCTIONS

An owner's manual has assembly, installation, test, and maintenance instructions. Complex products may have instructions running hundreds of pages, which may specify how to construct, install, store, move, assemble, test, inspect, and maintain a product.

TRAINED TECHNICIANS

For complex products, industrial firms supply a technician to ensure the product is installed properly, operating smoothly, and field tested. Industrial pumps, turbines, and mainframe computers require installation technicians who have special tools, equipment, and training.

OP EX PACKAGING FEATURES

The package of a product has functional and aesthetic features that enhance its value. Packaging provides the following specific features:

- Protects goods
- Protects customers
- Offers convenience
- Allows convenient display space
- Displays advertising
- Displays content information
- Contains operating, maintenance, and installation instructions

PROTECTS GOODS

Proper packaging protects goods from breaking or spoiling during shipment. Perishable goods require special handling and refrigeration. Electronic assemblies are stored in clean, dry environments and shipped in anti-static containers for fear of damage.

Consumer products are sold based on "fit and finish." Surface blemishes, such as scratches, dents, dings are the first Op Ex characteristics a customer inspects to determine whether to purchase a product.

PROTECTS CUSTOMERS

Proper packaging of industrial or consumer goods protects the customer from possible injuries. Mechanical equipment always has enclosures over moving parts. Shampoo bottles are made of plastic instead of glass because of possible breakage in the shower.

OFFERS CONVENIENCE

Proper packaging offers customer convenience. Customers want products delivered in quantities and in packages that are convenient to use. Working adults want to eat in a hurry and do not have time to cook for several hours to feed a family. Food is packaged so it is microwavable. Also, gourmet microwavable food is packaged in small portions so it appeals to single people or children.

ALLOWS CONVENIENT DISPLAY SPACE

Proper packaging allows a product to be displayed conveniently on a store's shelf. Also, rectangular, narrow boxes are easier to hold and easier to display on store shelves than round containers which require more shelf space than square containers.

DISPLAYS ADVERTISING

Eye catching packaging or labeling advertise products and draw customers to them. Coke logos and Goodyear blimps are immediately recognizable.

DISPLAYS CONTENT INFORMATION

Packages display content information. On consumer products, labels specify net weight, ingredients, grade, calories, and vitamins. On industrial packages, labels display net weight, instructions for operation and maintenance, rating, product grading, certification, and safety information.

CONTAINS OPERATING, MAINTENANCE, AND INSTALLATION INSTRUCTIONS

Packages contain important operating, maintenance, and installation information. Industrial products have safety information and warnings.

PACKAGING

It comes in three sizes. Large, Giant, and Super. I gave you the smaller size - Large.
Anonymous

What is good packaging? The following packages have something in common: cookie boxes, cracker boxes, lunch meat wrappers, flour bags, and cereal boxes. Good packaging keeps its contents safe and secure. Good packaging protects contents while satisfying the customer. Good package design focuses on the utility or function of the package, but also on satisfying the customer through ease of entry, resealing capability, or attractiveness.

BRANDING

The commercial process consists of sensing the existence of latent needs and exploiting them, i.e. converting them into conscious wants by marketing and advertising appropriate products.
Robin Morris, 1964

Brand names are a symbol of quality and operational excellence. Brands are "a name, term, sign, symbol, designer, or a combination of them which is intended to identify the goods or services of one seller or group of sellers and to differentiate between them from those of competitors."[50] Brands are often a name, symbol, or design. Brands communicate product or service goodness or quality. They convey that products were made with integrity.

Brands are also a visual specification of product integrity. Most customers do not read the label or the list of ingredients to find what's in a package. Customers will buy products based on familiarity and trust conveyed by the brand name.

Brands are everywhere; companies identify themselves with a brand name and logo. Brand names are protected by trademarks. Any unauthorized use results in trademark infringement litigation. They can only be used with the permission of the trademark holder. For example, Coca-Cola is a brand name and is usually followed by the Coke trademark.

BRANDS REPRESENT GOODWILL

A reputation of quality promotes continuing sales. A perceived quality sells at a premium, which is the "goodwill" attached to the product. The goodwill can be a brand, logo, or label.

Brands, labels, and name recognition add perceived value which once established is critical to maintain. But once a product's reputation is tarnished, the product is almost impossible to sell. Customer loyalty, maintained through trust in the product, is important for repeat business. If a customer is satisfied with a product and the service, the customer will buy the product again.

Customers are especially loyal to brands in higher priced specialty goods. For example, buyers of Mercedes, Tide, and Coke are loyal because these products have high quality reputations and represent value.

CLASS CUSTOMER SATISFACTION

"World-class companies share the following characteristics:

- Customer requirements and expectations are anticipated through surveys.
- Benchmark comparisons within industry are higher than other companies.
- Company has a customer inquiry center with a toll-free telephone number.
- Corrective and preventive actions result from survey results.
- Formal Op Ex systems are established to improve customer satisfaction.
- Customer relationship management is highly visible.
- Customer service representatives are empowered to solve customer complaints.
- Customer service is periodically audited.
- Customer satisfaction standards and procedures are defined and measurable.
- Customer complaints are logged and trends are analyzed.
- Customer satisfaction is correlated with financial performance.
- Company is recognized for outstanding customer satisfaction performance.[51]

HOW MUCH QUALITY SHOULD BE DELIVERED TO CUSTOMERS?

Since Op Ex is a moving target, the question arises "How much quality should be delivered to customers at any point in time?" The answer is to give customers as much as they want, can afford, and are willing to pay for.

This is difficult for companies to understand because of the temptation to load a product down with as many features as possible. The result, unfortunately, is a product that customers do not want, cannot afford, and will not buy.

A prevalent, market-based definition of operational excellence is "fitness for use." If customers want simple, reliable transportation from point A to point B then in the customers' eyes a reliable Ford has as much perceived utility or value as a Mercedes. Customers should get and pay for what they want or perceive they want.

On the other hand, if customers want a hand-made, high performance, fully loaded automobile, customers expect more and will pay more than for a Ford. A high-performance automobile requires specialized tooling and fabrication. The added investment in time, labor, and material that goes into the exotic car enhances its quality and value at an equivalent increase in price.

So, once companies and their marketing organizations have sensed what customers want, they should deliver the level of product and service quality that customers are willing to pay for and have come to expect. This is the ideal Op Ex level. However, it is difficult to pinpoint precisely what customers require and what they are willing to pay.

Another difficult decision is determining the optimum blend of competing product and service quality attributes. As we discussed in the second chapter, a product is the sum of many attributes such as features, performance, and reliability. Once key product attributes have been identified, they are incorporated or designed into a product. Then the company uses information to develop a market strategy to penetrate a market or raise existing market share.

WARRANTY/GUARANTEE

If you think you have someone eating out of your hand, it's a good idea to count your fingers.

Martin Buxbaum

Warranties and guarantees are important methods for cementing the relationship between customers and product/service providers. Warranties are a public promise or guarantee to the customer that if a product fails in service, the manufacturer will repair, service, or replace the defective product at no cost to the customer within a prescribed period of time. Warranties enhance a product's image by offering comprehensive protection. Thus, warranties can establish a competitive advantage for a product or service.

Warranties can be a simple guarantee or a statement about a product attribute or product performance such as "satisfaction is guaranteed." "Money back" guaranties are common with consumer products. Or warranties can be complex documents limiting the manufacturer's legal responsibilities. Complex warranties are common with industrial products, such as automobiles or industrial machinery, where the potential for exposure to and risk of product litigation is much greater than consumer products such as lipstick or designer fashions.

Warranties are a remnant of the inspection mode of management. Management believed if a defective product slipped through inspection, the warranty covered the customer and still maintained customer goodwill essential for repeat Supply Management. This was false because defective products result in excessive manufacturing costs and eventually in customer dissatisfaction. Customers do not want to buy defective products.

The Magnuson-Moss Warranty Act, enacted in 1975, requires consumer products conform to Federal Trade Commission (FTC) rules. All warranties must be:

- Disclosed fully in a readable spot on the package in simple and understandable language.
- Labeled as full or limited warranty.
- Provided to customers for reading and comparison before purchase.

IDENTIFY PROSPECTIVE CUSTOMERS

Why are customers important? As the marketplace becomes more competitive, locating, attracting, and retaining external customers are the key to a company's strategic thinking. Customers provide cash flow which provides jobs. If a company wants to maintain customer loyalty, a company has to produce and deliver a quality product.

Marketing serves as a company's primary interface with the customer. Marketing communicates customer needs, wants, and expectations to the organization. Marketing constantly reminds an organization to provide customers what they need instead of providing customers what the company can produce.

Marketing is responsible for identifying, understanding, and communicating this information to the company. A company must be constantly alert to the signals and messages of the marketplace so the company can offer product benefits that customers seek, otherwise customers will purchase products elsewhere.

Once a market and customers are identified, an organization develops appropriate products or services to satisfy the particular market. Marketing may recommend a new product or service or may recommend that an existing product or service be modified to satisfy changing market needs.

In some cases, the marketplace changes so rapidly that an organization cannot adapt quickly and eventually fails. For example, if a company makes paper clips in a stagnant market, a firm cannot switch to growing silicon wafers.

IDENTIFY CUSTOMER NEEDS

What do customers want? The common feature of the marketplace is change - change in demographics, customer expectations, product, and customer service. In the global economy, the process of understanding and communicating customers' needs, requirements, and expectations must consider the following:

- Marketplace is global

- Competition is international
- Product lifecycle is short
- Customers speak in generalities
- Customers' tastes change over time

Marketplace is Global

The scope of the marketplace used to be a town, a region or a country. The marketplace is now global. Techniques used to sell fryers in Peoria may not work in Singapore. Product packaging, instructions for use, and marketing approaches may need to be reformulated.

Competition is International

Competition is now international. U.S. manufacturers once only had to worry about competition from domestic producers. Now, automobiles from U.S., Japan, Korea, Italy, Germany, England, France, and Great Britain compete for customers' attention.

Product Lifecycle is Short

The product lifecycle of many consumer products (consumer electronics and fashions) is now measured in terms of a year or two instead of 10 - 20 years. Products are continuously being redesigned or replaced by a new product.

Customers Speak in Generalities

Customers speak in generalities. People express likes and dislikes in terms of vague intangibles such as "I like the fit and finish of the car" or "it just looks great." Customers do not speak in terms of measurable specifications. Customers do not know or do not care about technical specifications or Op Ex standards. Fashion or taste is a feeling at a visceral level instead of a well-constructed thought. Customers have a preconceived idea of what they want. When they see the right Op Ex mix in a product or a service, they buy it.

TASTES CHANGE OVER TIME

Customer needs, wants, and requirements are a moving target. In this marketplace, customers' desires change radically and quickly. What was acceptable in a product 6 months ago is no longer acceptable and saleable. Black and white TV sets were a normal part of most households 15 years ago. Now most homes have sophisticated entertainment centers with 24-inch color TV sets, stereo sound, and laser disks.

NEXT CHAPTER

In the next chapter, Op Ex Management Essentials is discussed. The Op Ex manager must be "able to walk the talk", in others words exemplify the best in his or her department. The Op Ex manager is responsible for maintaining quality of work life and establishing Op Ex systems in the Op Ex department. The Op Ex organization becomes the benchmark department on how to develop and implement Op Ex systems and processes.

CHAPTER 9 OP EX MANAGEMENT ESSENTIALS

Being a successful Op Ex manager in these changing times requires adaptability and the ability to learn quickly. The following seem to be essential for Op Ex managers to survive and prosper in the future:

- Company experience
- Managerial skills
- Technical or Op Ex experience or abilities
- Operational experience
- Personal abilities

OP EX MANAGEMENT

Sometimes, high potential people will be rotated through the Op Ex department. The position has excellent visibility, problem solving and operations exposure. A fast tracker can cut her teeth on significant problems that affect customer satisfaction or the bottom line. The person is also exposed to almost every area of the organization.

However, this person may have been brought in from a prestigious MBA program or is a personal choice of a senior manager. The problem is the person hasn't had exposure to the organization, doesn't understand its culture, doesn't know its power politics, and hasn't built up the system of trustful contacts and doesn't know Op Ex.

Sometimes, much of an organization's work is conducted through back channels. These are based on work relationships, sports, family get-togethers and other social events that cement relationships and build trust. A new person doesn't have these and may not have the same support as an internally promoted person.

TECHNICAL OR HUMAN RESOURCE EXPERIENCE OR ABILITIES

The Op Ex manager should have both technical and human resource abilities. Technical abilities include system, processes and product knowledge. Human resource abilities include team building, facilitating, teaching, and coaching. For example, senior management may promote a generalist, perhaps a trainer, into a technical Op Ex position. The personal has excellent organizational skills but knows little about the technical and operational sides of Op Ex. This can be dangerous for the following reasons:

- This person may lack credibility with operational teams and problems.
- Op Ex manager will have to defer to experts when technical knowledge is required.
- Poor judgements may be made.
- Customers or supplier may require technical information, corroboration, or validation.

OPERATIONAL EXPERIENCE

Lack of operational experience is a problem that arises often. Op Ex professionals have been promoted through the Op Ex function ranks. This person has worked with operational departments but has never worked in an operational area. A certain kinship develops when a person has worked in a high-pressure situation whether it's production or process engineering. There are customer pressures, deadlines to meet, costs to control, special projects to get done and a myriad number of other critical issues that bond people. There is a feeling this person has gone through the fire with us, understands what it's all about and can be trusted to get the job done.

The Op Ex manager is more effective if he or she has had operational exposure. A major criticism through the years is that some Op Ex departments still don't understand internal systems, processes or products. Op Ex encourages continuous improvement but doesn't know how to advise operational groups to achieve it. So, internal departments also have complained that Op Ex departments still have the policing mentality, inspecting and controlling quality instead of assuring the management of Op Ex. Some say that the Op Ex organization and professionals do not have the skills as the stakes have become much higher. Customers want much more, much faster, and cheaper than before.

PERSONAL ABILITIES

In the final analysis, personal abilities make or break the Op Ex manager. These personal skills may be learned on the job. An Op Ex manager should have and demonstrate these personal attributes, skills, and abilities:

- Be honest.
- Be adaptable.
- Be an excellent communicator.
- Have stamina.
- Understand cultural, organizational, and team dynamics.
- Communicate clearly.
- Be able to display and communicate values.
- Manage and defuse conflicts.
- Develop teams.

STARTING A COMPANY-WIDE OP EX INITIATIVE

Ready, fire, aim.
Anonymous

The first steps in an Op Ex initiative must be successful because an initial misstep may end the entire Op Ex initiative. Declining market share, poor customer satisfaction surveys, high cost of Op Ex created awareness that something is wrong and that there is a need for change. Change can be substantive or visual. Substantive change may entail improving research capabilities, reengineering operations, or training employees in customer service. Or change may be more visual, such as a new firm logo, advertising, or articles in the trade press of successes.

The structure of an Op Ex initiative follows a common pattern. The CEO or senior executive champions the initiative. This person actively communicates and rewards commitment and progress. A corporate officer, usually a vice president or a director level, is chosen to lead the effort. This person may lead a corporate Op Ex group or have a small core group supporting the organizational initiative. An Op Ex manager is appointed for each operating unit. Each operating unit may have domestic or offshore plants. Each plant may have an Op Ex manager who has supervisors, process control staff or inspectors reporting to the position.

Most companywide Op Ex initiatives evolve through a similar sequence:

- CEO communicates a sense of urgency about Op Ex.
- Steering committee is formed.
- Orientation seminars are conducted.
- Steering committee develops strategic Op Ex plan.
- General management develops tactical Op Ex plans.
- Op Ex accountabilities are assigned.
- Goals and objectives are formulated.
- Formal training courses on Op Ex are delivered.
- Measurement parameters are chosen.
- Auditing system is developed to measure progress.
- Corrective action loops are designed.

Other Op Ex related initiatives include self-managed teams, product development, process problems solving, constraint elimination, just-in-time, kaizen, MRP, process improvement, reengineering, rightsizing, and work redesign. It should be noted that these can also be projects.

GOOD CORPORATE CITIZENS

More companies are using Op Ex methods to focus on society's good. These companies are called socially responsible, good corporate citizens. What makes a good corporate citizen?

- Focus on the total cost of a product including environmental costs.
- Develop environmentally friendly products.
- Understand and obtain total and lifecycle costs of products.
- Identify societal useful goals and be able to meet them.
- Deliver products and services that result in profits.
- Improve the quality of life in markets where plants are located.
- Encourage individual respect.
- Comply with laws.
- Set national and internal examples for ethical conduct.

WHAT IS TOTAL OPERATIONAL MANAGEMENT?

An airplane is a system of spare parts flying in close formation.
Orville Wright

The Op Ex system starts and ends with the customer. It starts by identifying customer needs, wants, and expectations. It ends by producing a product or delivering a service that satisfies or exceeds these needs, wants, and expectations. In between, a product or service goes through a series of steps, each of which processes labor, information, or other resources.

Each process step from marketing to shipping a finished product adds value or, in other words, quality to the product. Specifically, Marketing determines what customers' needs are and communicates these to the organization. Engineering designs a product to customer's requirements. Supply Management then buys components and parts to be machined or assembled into a finished product. Manufacturing produces the product. Distribution delivers it to the customer. Op Ex monitors processes. This pattern is repeated each time a new product is developed or an existing product is modified.

THE ORGANIZATION AS A SYSTEM

One of the powerful analytical tools in management theory is the systems approach, which explains complex relationships in simple terms. This book presents a systems approach to Op Ex where independent and interdependent business elements work together to deliver quality products and services that satisfy customer's wants, needs, and expectations.

A system is a group of elements or processes that function together to achieve a common goal. Elements can be parts of a machine or actors in a play. In this book, the elements are departments (Marketing, Engineering, Op Ex, and Manufacturing) in an organization. The common goal is a satisfied customer.

USING THE SYSTEMS APPROACH TO SOLVE OPERATIONAL EXCELLENCE PROBLEMS

Op Ex projects can be incremental, continuous, and breakthrough. Regardless of the type, they involve a systematic and structured systems approach to solving problems. The Op Ex systems approach focuses on measurable, simple, and doable solutions. The system approach is common to all Op Ex problem solving and incorporates the following elements:

- **Identify Improvement Project.** An improvement project is first identified. A project may involve customers or suppliers who have requirements, specifications, needs, or expectations which are not being met. Or, a project may be proposed which improves organizational effectiveness, increases operational efficiency, increases market share, adds product value, or minimizes product or process variation. Safety or health issues usually have the highest priority. Customer, market, chronic, major, and cost issues with the greatest potential for gain are then considered. The financial impact of each alternative project is estimated. These are determined by estimating the cost of achieving or not achieving Op Ex. Projects can be identified by performing customer surveys, analyzing warranty claims, and analyzing customer complaints.

- **Define Constraints.** Constraints have to be identified. Constraints are factors that may impede implementation of a solution. Constraints can be lack of financial resources, internal resistance, lack of special skills or equipment.
- **Organize for Implementation.** As emphasized throughout this book, teams are often the best approach to solving a problem. A multidisciplinary team offers knowledge, skills, abilities, perspective, and resources to solving the problem.
- **Identify Possible and Probable Causes.** Those who are impacted by or can solve the problem are asked to identify probable causes. It is important to focus on root causes not symptoms of the problem. The root cause or causes may be people, material, methods or machinery or some combination of these.
- **Select the best solution.** Once root causes are identified, solutions are proposed to eliminate the root cause. Brainstorming is one common technique of soliciting solutions from a group. The "best" solution is selected for implementation. Best may be the solution that is easiest to implement, one that generates the most revenue, leads to lower costs, etc.
- **Implement solution.** Implementation is often assigned to those responsible for the problem. Or, implementation may be assigned to the project team, who performs the work with the blessings of the work area's management. Implementation can cross departmental boundaries or specializations.
- **Audit improvement project.** Improvement is measured to determine the amount of change. Improvement justifies the next improvement project. Improvement is then audited to ensure the root cause or causes are eliminated so the problem does not recur. Once root causes have been eliminated, a new level of Op Ex, hopefully a breakthrough, has been attained.

- **Optimize solution.** Once this level has been attained, the process starts all over again on a new problem. Or, if not enough improvement has been achieved, the Op Ex process repeats the above steps again.

OPERATIONALIZING OPERATIONAL EXCELLENCE

It is a paradox that the greater the decentralization, the greater the need for both leadership and explicit policies from the top management.
Bruce Henderson, consultant

Op Ex has traditionally been viewed as a function with specialized disciplines and techniques. This perception gave rise to the Op Ex professional. But, what is the role of the specialist, the Op Ex professional, when everyone is responsible for Op Ex?

Now, many quality control, assurance and management staff responsibilities are being operationalized. Individual, teams, and process owners are now responsible for their processes and systems. Many quality control and assurance technologies have been integrated into almost all operations. For example, internal auditing, process control, and closed-loop corrective action are considered good business systems. There are many other Op Ex technologies that have been integrated into daily management practices. For example, Marketing and Sales use six sigma, lean, quality function deployment, benchmarking, and customer surveys as a normal part of business.

THE CHANGING OP EX FUNCTION

It is difficult to assess and to justify the value of a staff position unless it directly works with a process that adds value to the bottom line or somehow supports customer satisfaction. Too often, staff are removed from day-to-day operations. Operational managers may ask: "What does this staff group or person do for me?" This is an especially critical question when the operational area is supporting the overhead burden of corporate Op Ex staff. Staff expenses often are disaggregated to operational units.

Op Ex is a staff function that is changing because of this new perspective. All too often operational management see the Op Ex function as requiring personnel, taking care of paperwork, and complying with a myriad of regulations. The Op Ex function is often considered a corporate support function. The department may have a small full-time staff and a part-time staff. Part-time staff consists of borrowed experts from Human Resources, Supply Management, Production, or Engineering. These people may report dotted line to the corporate Op Ex organization but are direct reports to their functional plant, department, or area. For example, Supply Management may provide a buyer to work with the Op Ex Department on customer-supplier partnering, supplier auditing, and supplier training. The Human Resources department may provide Op Ex training to new employees, reengineering assistance, organizational assessments and team facilitation that may have been done by the Op Ex function. Production may provide first line supervisors to provide manufacturing expertise as well as to learn new Op Ex skills such as learning how to conduct FMEA, SPC, or capability studies. Engineering may provide engineers who conduct customer requirement planning.

OBSTACLES TO SUCCESS

You've removed most of the roadblocks to success when you've learnt the difference between motion and direction.
Bill Copeland

Why have Op Ex initiatives failed? Many are searching for the answer to this question. One reason for the failure of Op Ex is because there has been a blurring of lines among competing techniques. Total Op Ex is inclusive. Many different operational, managerial, organizational, and technological practices and concepts have been brought under its umbrella. This has caused resentment in some organizations. Internal obstacles to implementing Op Ex systems include nay-sayers, redundant controls, internal politics, second guessing, and not-invented-here syndrome.

Another set of reasons why Op Ex has been slow to deploy and integrate deal with internal resistance especially when the hard work sets in. There are several sources for this. There is reluctance to change. There is reluctance to maintain a fierce, daily focus on Op Ex. There is reluctance to make the hard choices. There is reluctance to empower employees. There is reluctance to invest in Op Ex. There is reluctance to hear and believe bad news.

Op Ex is a workplace transformation for many organizations. Each step of the Op Ex process or as some say, the Op Ex journey requires significant and increasing levels of attention and participation. Successful Op Ex initiatives require the full participation and cooperation of an organization's management. If an Op Ex initiative is imposed without the full participation and acceptance of much of an organization's management, it will fail.

OPERATIONAL FOCUS

If the Op Ex function is a staff function, it must continually focus on improving operations and satisfying stakeholders. The Op Ex function has technical and organizational expertise that must support line management and process teams.

How can the Op Ex function provide an operational and customer focus? The Op Ex manager should keep senior management informed of all Op Ex developments and be immersed in operational problem solving and in pleasing customers.

EARLY SCIENTIFIC MANAGEMENT

Early in this century, Frederick Taylor, the father of scientific management, studied how workers worked and managers managed. Taylor believed managers could manage in a scientific manner so productivity could be improved by careful and structured analysis of required work. He developed management principles that became the foundation of the scientific management movement:

- Supervisors and managers manage.
- Workers do work assigned to them.
- Managers are taught how to manage.
- Job is broken down into its basic elements.

- Most efficient way is identified.
- Right worker is chosen for each job.
- Workers are rewarded in direct proportion to their contribution to productivity or profits.

Taylor's scientific methods were used to structure all work flow. This was radical thinking in the early part of this century. For the first time, management had a definable function in a company; to plan, organize, and direct projects in a methodical manner. Productivity could be measured and controlled.

But Taylor's methods were mechanistic. They reflected the environment of the factories in the early part of the century. Machinery and people were measured and controlled. In this early industrial environment, contemporary management techniques were conceived, developed, and implemented.

Taylor's scientific management model has been a fixture in the workplace for many years. It stresses the efficient use of manpower, breaking work down into its simplest components, and measuring output. However, this tends to dehumanize the work environment on the production line. Many of Taylor's techniques are still used by Industrial Engineers including work simplification, time/motion studies, and work measurement.

ESSENTIAL PRINCIPLES OF OP EX

There is no commonly accepted list of Op Ex principles. It seems every guru, disciple, consultant has his or her own set of beliefs. As well, there are a number of international Op Ex standards and awards. However, the following are generally accepted elements and principles of the current interpretations and uses of total Op Ex:

- **Competition is global and fierce.** This is the decade of international competitiveness. Op Ex is used as a means to position a company, its products, and services for continued profitability.

- **Competitively priced quality products and services sell.** Studies assert that operational quality products and services sell. In industrial, commercial, and consumer buying decisions, quality is either the top criterion for making the buy decision or near the top with cost, delivery, and service.
- **Op Ex becomes a strategic business issue.** Op Ex has become a part of the business landscape often included in every company's vision, mission, plans, and ethic.
- **Sales produce profits and jobs.** If quality products and services sell at sufficient profit margins, they should generate continued profits for the organization. Profits also ensure jobs.
- **Total customer satisfaction produces sales.** Total customer satisfaction means that every customer experience with an organization is positive and pleasing so the result is a repeat customer.
- **Total customer satisfaction is achieved through Op Ex.** Total quality includes all activities that involve satisfying present customer requirements but also anticipating customer expectations.
- **Total customer satisfaction is the goal of all stakeholders.** Total customer satisfaction is the goal of an organization's stakeholders including management, suppliers, employees, stockholders, community and others.
- **"Voice of the customer" is internalized.** "Voice of the customer" is internalized through quality function deployment and other techniques.
- **Continuous improvement is a basic premise of Op Ex.** Fundamental to all Op Ex is the need to continuously improve as well as to pursue "breakthrough" improvement. Basically, "what was good enough yesterday or is good enough today" is not sufficient for guaranteeing tomorrow's profitability.
- **Continuous improvement is pursued company and supplier wide.** Suppliers are assuming more importance as more business is outsourced to "world class" suppliers.
- **Auditing and other Op Ex technologies facilitate continuous improvement.** Quality auditing and other Op Ex techniques are becoming a common part of everyday business. Op Ex relies on self and group initiative. Continuous improvement and customer satisfaction requires individuals and teams to identify problems and

opportunities on their own, develop solutions, eliminate the symptom, and the root cause of the problem.

- **Benchmarks and goals are established in all activities** Op Ex objectives, baselines, and benchmarks are established for all critical operational areas.
- **Critical system, process and product parameters are measured.** To achieve benchmarks, key process and operational parameters are measured inside the organization and with key suppliers. The measurements become the metrics or milestones in the Op Ex journey.
- **Prevention is pursued company and supplier wide.** Symptomatic and root cause deficiency prevention is pursued throughout the organization. Prevention includes intervention, corrective action, and other proactive Op Ex activities.
- **Flexibility is required to cope and profit from change.** Change is a factor of life in a very competitive and changing marketplace. Customers expect more, faster, better, and cheaper. The only way to deliver total customer satisfaction is through speed, flexibility, and a sense of humor sometimes.
- **All forms of waste are eliminated.** Waste can be excess materials, inefficiencies, redundancies, poor service, duplication of efforts, or high cost.
- **All employees are empowered to improve.** Responsibility and authority for Op Ex are pushed down to the lowest organizational level. Responsibility or improving Op Ex and ensuring happy customers is now coupled with the ability and authority for ensuring the appropriate actions are taken.
- **Employees are cross-trained and compensated for learning.** Continuous and breakthrough improvement requires continuous training and development of all employees to keep up with changing customer requirements, trends, and technology.[52]

OP EX IN BUSINESS FUNCTIONS

The most outstanding business firms of the future will be those whose leadership is skilled in the interface problems - technology with economics, marketing with social change, and business with government. The time has passed when good business management can narrowly focus merely on

design, manufacture, and attempts to sell products oblivious to the broader society. Such management will satisfy neither the individuals working in their companies nor the individual buyer in the marketplace.
Simon Ramo, business person

An organization has critical functions that impact overall Op Ex. In this section, each function is capitalized, such as Engineering or Supply Management. These organizational functions are evolving into processes and have a changing interpretation of Op Ex.

The following critical organizational processes are discussed in this section:

- Sales/Marketing process
- Human resources process
- Engineering process
- Supply Management process
- Op Ex process
- Manufacturing process
- Distribution process

SALES/MARKETING PROCESS

The Sales/Marketing process starts with a customer requiring a product or service. Marketing obtains information and communicates this to Engineering. Sales/Marketing views Op Ex as identifying customer requirements and communicating these to the organization so they can be satisfied.

Marketing is the primary interface between the company and the customer. Marketing sells products to the customer, provides after-sales service, and researches the needs of different demographic groups. Marketing also has to clearly define customer needs and establish a product price the customer is willing to pay.

Marketing obtains customer information through customer surveys, customer complaints, product service, product returns, and warranty claims. This information is distilled into a customer profile.

HUMAN RESOURCES PROCESS

Human Resources views Op Ex as an organizational process involving the culture, values, principles, training, and other people related issues. Human Resources management is essential in these turbulent times. Companies, especially after the recent waves of downsizing, are realizing people are not an inventory item that can be hired and fired without consequences. The consequence in many companies has been a demoralized workforce that does what is necessary to get the job done and nothing more.

People who have survived waves of downsizings are often marking time and looking for opportunities to move. Another result of mass downsizing is that employees are reserving their best product development and innovation ideas for their next employer. These new ideas are necessary for companies to grow and prosper. Human Resources are critical to establishing, implementing and sustaining the Op Ex initiative in the following areas:

- Providing Op Ex training.
- Diagnosing organizational readiness.
- Evaluating and providing prescriptions for organizational transformation.
- Restructuring performance and compensation systems.
- Developing an Op Ex communications initiative.
- Planning and implementing a customer-oriented culture change.

ENGINEERING PROCESS

Engineering designs a product based on input from Marketing and other sources. Engineering develops realistic specifications based on understanding customer needs and existing manufacturing capabilities. Engineering sees Op Ex in terms of design, function, aesthetics, form, fit, robustness, maintainability, and reliability.

Engineering develops specifications, tolerances, and drawings for a new or modified product. Engineering looks at Op Ex in terms of appearance, serviceability, reliability, packaging, and performance characteristics.

SUPPLY MANAGEMENT PROCESS

Supply Management is responsible for acquiring Op Ex, competitively priced products to be supplied to Manufacturing just-in-time for fabrication or assembly. Supply Management obtains product requirements from Engineering, then Supply Management seeks suppliers that can supply the product. Supply Management evaluates suppliers on quality, price, availability, and service. Once a supplier has been chosen, the supplier is monitored closely and rewarded on performance. Supply Management sees Op Ex as a process of selecting, monitoring, and improving overall supplier performance which may include improving deliveries, quality, total cost, service, and other factors. Customer service sees Op Ex as answering and satisfying customer concerns.

QUALITY PROCESS

While Op Ex may have functional quality control and assurance responsibilities, quality often serves as company consultants to ensure Op Ex systems are working effectively. Quality coordinates, evaluates, and monitors the overall Op Ex system. As company consultants, the quality function is not responsible for Op Ex, rather responsibility rests with the people doing the work.

MANUFACTURING PROCESS

Manufacturing consists of production and manufacturing engineering. Manufacturing sees Op Ex in terms of monitoring, controlling, and improving production processes that are critical to customer satisfaction. Manufacturing engineering designs machinery, fixtures, jigs, and procedures to manufacture the part. Manufacturing engineering may develop these for in-house manufacturing or for a supplier to provide. Production is accountable for producing a defect-free product. Production measures and controls the process and machinery so quality products are produced.

DISTRIBUTION PROCESS

Distribution is responsible for handling, securing, storing, and shipping products to the customer. The right product has to be delivered to the right customer just-in-time for it to be used. The product cannot be damaged in shipping or handling.

CROSS FUNCTIONAL COLLABORATION

The Japanese employ open discussion with generalities that leave room for movement and compromise. They have nineteen ways of saying no - suggestive of the extreme finesse with which their language navigates the shoals of conflict, avoiding it if possible.
Richard Pascale, Professor

The functional manager or key process owner is responsible for the processes and products coming out of them. The Op Ex manager should be sensitive to these requirements. The Op Ex manager may have different objectives than the line manager or core process owner. The line manager is under daily pressure to keep customers satisfied, keep production up, improve Op Ex, meet regulatory requirements. Op Ex may sometimes fall by the way side.

Operational managers and more often self-directed teams must deal on a daily basis with the following:

- Conflicting customer requirements and messages.
- Demanding and irritable customers.
- Personnel issues.
- Regulatory constraints.
- Safety issues.
- Lack of resources.
- Process breakdowns.
- Personnel turnover.
- Grievances and other personnel challenges.

A major responsibility of the Op Ex manager is to organize and monitor company and supplier wide Op Ex projects while being sensitive to the above operational realities. Many teams and improvement project leaders probably do not have a solid line, direct reporting relationship to the Op Ex manager. However, the Op Ex manager may be responsible for organizing, facilitating, monitoring and reporting progress of these projects.

The Op Ex manager must be able to interface with functional units such as Engineering, Manufacturing, and Supply Management. The Op Ex manager or representative reports on progress, schedules activities, facilitates meetings, provides administrative support, and provides training.

The Op Ex function more often is considered a support function. The department may have a small full-time staff and a part time staff. The part time staff may be borrowed experts from Human Resources, Supply Management, Production, or Engineering. These people usually report dotted line to the Op Ex organization but are direct reports to their functional department or area. For example, Supply Management may provide a buyer to work with the Op Ex department on customer-supplier partnering, supplier auditing, and supplier training. The Human Resources function may provide training or team facilitators for special projects. Production may provide first line supervisors to assist in conducting FMEA, SPC, or capability studies. Engineering may provide engineers who conduct customer requirement planning.

NEXT CHAPTER

In the next chapter, Op Ex Human Resource Management is discussed. Companies have a distinct style of managing their employees. One management style encourages employees to be involved in the workplace and in the Op Ex system. This is called participatory management or employee involvement.

Another style is an authority-based style of management where employees are told what to do, how to do it, and when to do it. This management style relies on the manager or supervisor to know what needs to be done. This management style is top-down as contrasted to the bottom-up participatory style.

CHAPTER 10
OP EX HUMAN RESOURCE MANAGEMENT

Selecting people for employment involves finding the right person with the right skills and attitudes to perform a job. This is required of both management and hourly employees. The fit of the right person to the right job helps ensure an individual's satisfaction and subsequent error-free output. For example, a rocket scientist would probably be a poor choice for production work that requires attention to detail and exacting precision.

HUMAN RESOURCE LIFECYCLE

To me, the most important element in management is the human being. So, the first essential is to treat people with consideration.
Yoshiki Yamasaki

Error-free performance by employees cannot be guaranteed but it has a higher likelihood of being ensured if an organization is aware of the human resource (HR) lifecycle of an employee. The HR cycle of a person is usually divided into four stages:

- Selection
- Development
- Motivation
- Guidance

SELECTION

Long term Op Ex will only occur if there is a committed workforce. The selection, retention, promotion, and reward of employees has become an important improvement goal. In selecting employees, progressive companies clearly communicate job requirements in writing and orally, evaluate references carefully, evaluate the candidate's ability to solve problems, and ensure the candidate can work as part of a team.

Selecting people takes time and effort. The selection of a Chief Executive Officer requires extensive interviews and evaluations by a team of people the CEO would relate with. Equally, the selection of hourly employees involves soliciting applications, interviewing, and hiring, again by a team of employees the worker would be working with.

The selection of American employees in Japanese production facilities is notoriously rigorous. As the Japanese build and staff manufacturing plants in the United States, they want people who are committed and dedicated to Op Ex. The screening process is extensive. One applicant for an Op Ex manager position spent 25 hours proving himself by going through paper-pencil tests, workplace simulations, and probing interviews.[53]

DEVELOPMENT

Continuous employee training and development is required for continuous Op Ex. Employee development means providing knowledge and skills to people so they can achieve their potential. Development includes continuing education, on-the-job training, and personal development programs.

At various stages in their careers, senior management as well as labor personnel benefit from development programs. Senior management personnel may require several months and sometimes a year of preparation before assuming a promotion. Entry level personnel may require at least several weeks of orientation and skill building.

Many organizations encourage continuous, lifelong learning so employees do not become technologically obsolete. The rate of technological change has forced employees to learn new material. The National Research Council's Manufacturing Studies Board recently concluded that the amount of knowledge is doubling every 3-5 years in the most advanced automated factories instead of the 7-14 years that was normal several years ago.

Some organizations encourage lifelong learning. For example, IBM encourages all employees to spend 2 weeks a year upgrading skills in company sponsored classes. People are paid to learn, develop, and apply skills on the job.

MOTIVATION

Motivation refers to inspiring, coaching, and encouraging employees to participate proactively with Op Ex. Management cannot order an employee to be enthusiastic and motivated about Op Ex.

Motivation is an intangible that has to be developed and nurtured. Since motivation is largely a personal attitude, behavioral scientists believe that satisfying employee needs, wants, and expectations are keys to motivation. However, inhibitors (such as fear) often arise to dampen enthusiasm and motivation.

Motivation theories have done much to humanize the workplace. Management has applied these theories to make offices more comfortable and factories more efficient places to work. Jobs are designed to be more interesting and to fit the skill set of the worker. Also, progressive managers pay attention to the needs of the worker when assigning work. Management realizes that an organization's performance and effectiveness reflect the attitudes and motivation of the worker.

There has been much recent research of how to remove the factors that inhibit an Op Ex culture. Several years ago, an American Society for Quality survey identified the following Op Ex inhibitors: employee attitudes, training\educational level of the workforce, outdated technology, unions, and outside economic factors.[54]

Guidance

Probably the most difficult part of guiding employees is measuring performance. The purpose of performance appraisals is to ultimately encourage and guide effective behavior. Unfortunately, sometimes performance appraisals focus on individual performance instead on group Op Ex and productivity objectives.

In theory, performance appraisals should be fair and accurate so they inform and guide employees. However, performance appraisals sometimes are a tool for rewarding personal favorites. Inevitably, a loss of trust, poor attitudes, and poor Op Ex result. Properly used, appraisals can be used to redirect employee's actions if a person strays off course; acknowledge and reward special individual or group efforts; reinforce strengths; and identify and alter weaknesses.

In order to be fair and accurate, Op Ex performance appraisal systems follow a systematic process of:

- Defining task requirements and objectives.
- Defining acceptable methods to accomplish the task.
- Providing skills, tools, and knowledge to attain objectives.
- Defining expectations.
- Measuring performance.
- Providing encouragement and accurate and timely feedback.

STAFF SELECTION

One machine can do the work of fifty ordinary people. No machine can do the work of one extraordinary person.
Elbert Hubbard, Business person

Hiring people has become much more complex in the last 20 years. Employment regulations and requirements, such as affirmative action, equal opportunity, ADA, and other requirements have made hiring much more complicated.

STAFFING THE OP EX DEPARTMENT

Staffing or employee selection is one of the critical activities of an Op Ex manager. The Op Ex department is only as good as its people. While this may be true for any organizational function, it is especially true in Op Ex because it works with and through many elements of the organization. Staffing involves defining customers, identifying customer requirements, identifying human resources to meet requirements, and developing staff.

The Op Ex managers must be resourceful in leveraging the function's assets and abilities. As Op Ex responsibilities are downloaded onto operational managers, Op Ex managers must influence the Op Ex decisions. This often requires Op Ex managers to work with and through others.

The Op Ex function may be staffed with full time employees. Op Ex teams are composed of operational unit employees that address a specific project. The team reports directly to operational or functional unit managers and may or may not have an indirect reporting relationship to the Op Ex department. The result is the Op Ex organization may be at a high level but is thinly staffed.

Who should staff the Op Ex organization? The modern Op Ex department is characterized by the following:

- Is small but influential.
- Is staffed by personnel with many years of operating experience.
- Is at a high level, VP or higher with few full-time staff.
- Works through others to improve Op Ex and to satisfy customers.
- May be considered a rotating, essential position for high potential managers.
- Requires highly creative and innovative problem-solving abilities.

ROTATION PEOPLE THROUGH OP EX FUNCTION

The Op Ex function may be a line or staff function. More and more, Op Ex responsibilities are being downloaded on operational groups. The Op Ex group is often staffed by process specialists who are rotated through the Op Ex organization for exposure and promotional purposes. Since everyone is responsible for Op Ex, each operational area needs process Op Ex experts, champions, trainers, and other Op Ex professionals.

An assignment may last 6 months to two years. Usually, these rotating assignments attract the company's "best and brightest." However, this can create problems for the Op Ex manager, director or VP who also may be in a rotational mode. When people are moving in and out, the following challenges arise:

- Lack of institutional memory.
- Lack of in-depth strength.
- Little department or process allegiance.
- Continual learning and training.
- Resentment from other organizational areas over visibility, pay, or authority.
- Lack of problem-solving specialists.

On the other hand, the advantages for rotating people include:

- Getting the organization's "best and brightest".
- Spreading the Op Ex gospel.
- Developing a cadre of companywide Op Ex professionals.
- Developing contacts and relationships with managers who have rotated through department.
- Developing visibility and credibility throughout the organization.

STAFF PERFORMANCE EVALUATION

You've got to lead and not drive, inspire and not dominate, cause respect and not fear, win support and not opposition.
Anonymous

Some believe that money does not motivate people in the long term. As well, some experts argue that intrinsic motivation is more or as important as money. Regardless money is one of the critical motivators of individual and team performance and is a major inducement for organizational change. Non-money rewards, such as recognizing employee's contributions, may be equally critical for inducing people or teams.

Employee evaluations are usually written, objective, and confidential. The evaluations may be evaluated by a second level manager as well as the Human Resources department to ensure fairness and compliance to the employment regulations. Evaluations usually follow the standard management by objectives format (MBO). MBO is preferred by most Op Ex managers because it is the most objective evaluating method.

CHANGING NATURE OF HUMAN RESOURCES	
Old Approach	**New Approach**
Asian workers have Op Ex edge	American workers produce Op Ex equal or greater to the Asian
Focus is on specialized work	Focus is on flexibility
People are managed	People are empowered
Emphasis is on measuring quantity of work	Emphasis is on measuring quality and Op Ex
Authoritarian management style is adopted	Participatory styles are adopted
Punishment is accepted to modify behavior	Encouragement, open communication, and accountability guide behavior

STAFFING CHALLENGES

The freedom to make mistakes provides the best environment for creativity.
Anonymous

Every Op Ex manager or supervisor will be challenged by the following:

- Mavericks
- Prima Donnas
- Cynics

MAVERICKS

As every Op Ex manager knows, the population of individuals follows a bell curve in terms of abilities and performance. It is also a cliché that no two individuals are the same. Each person brings something to a business that could be called an individual core competency. For example, some individuals won't or can't work as part of a team.

So, what can be done with these people? These "wild ducks" may be tolerated and placed in special corporate nurturing environments. These people are sometimes not followers or team members. They flourish in entrepreneurial environments. Why? The sources of many new ideas and innovation can be found in these individuals. As well, these individuals show exemplary leadership or an uncanny ability to anticipate new markets or trends.

CRITICS AND CYNICS

The time is past when all Op Ex is considered good. Op Ex must be defined, measured, improved, and improved again. Op Ex must compete with other marketplace considerations such as cost, delivery, service, regulatory constraints, and other projects. In terms of other projects, Op Ex must return more than the purchase of a new machine or project management training.

In today's organizational atmosphere each project, head count addition, or purchase must be justified, rationalized, and measured. Op Ex for its own sake will encounter resistance. The resistance may be "why do we need this" to "this is a go no-where project." The resistance may be judgmental people, antagonists, critics, objectors, or cynics. Objectors may bring up good points. Addressing their concerns affirmatively can lend credibility and support to the project. If concerns or objections are not addressed then they may even derail the improvement project. The question is how should the Op Ex manager deal with them?

The only simple answer is with respect because:

- People may bring up legitimate objections.
- Candor and honesty are essential in an Op Ex culture.
- Critical flaws may be identified in thinking.
- Listening and hearing are critical in Op Ex.
- Respect for the individual is another element of Op Ex.
- Objectors may have critical Op Ex ownership or implementation responsibility.

PRIMA DONNAS

Op Ex function in some companies has been known to display a better or holier than thou attitude. The Op Ex group believes and vocally asserts that all Op Ex knowledge and skills resided in the group. This contradicts the conventional wisdom that everyone is responsible for the Op Ex of their operations.

Many problems have occurred when Op Ex professionals believe they have some special knowledge or skill to impart to the world and senior management does not understand the process. Op Ex professionals give talks internally, write papers, author books, and even develop commercial products outside of the organization. The Op Ex professional's employer may not understand the benefits of this public exposure, especially if it is done on company time. The employer will especially resent or resist the exposure if the person is revealing sensitive or proprietary information. In some cases, the Op Ex organization has been disbanded because the Op Ex function prided itself or took 100% ownership of some Op Ex accomplishment, such as achieving the Baldrige Award or ISO 9001:2015 registration.

The Op Ex organization should be staffed with professionals whose first responsibility is satisfying organizational stakeholders. The successful Op Ex professional realizes that Op Ex wins, stories, and effectiveness must be shared. There is also a prominent quote that states a leader is the person who can get things done while giving credit to others.

SUCCESS FACTORS

Competition, customer requirements, and other pressures can create a sense of urgency, to get things done right and on time. Management and employees realize they are all in this together. Op Ex awareness is quickly established and a sense of Op Ex ownership is developed at all organizational levels.

A recent survey identified the following as critical to the success of an Op Ex initiative:

- **Business threat.** Companies in danger of failing without dramatic changes seem to be the most successful with implementing and seeing results from an Op Ex initiative.

- **Organizational commitment.** The degree of senior management and employee commitment also determines long term Op Ex success.
- **Op Ex planning**. An Op Ex plan for how to pursue and implement Op Ex is also important. However, the plan without commitment won't guarantee long term success.
- **Progress.** If a company has been implementing Op Ex and employee involvement for years, it is less likely to be dropped
- **Op Ex strategy.** A formal Op Ex strategy integrated with the business strategy also ensures Op Ex will be pursued.

In any Op Ex initiative or project, there is some risk. The following are barriers to Op Ex success:

- Lack of senior management support.
- Lack of understanding of Op Ex purpose, goals, and objectives.
- No sense of urgency.
- Lack of employee cooperation.
- Lack of middle management support.
- No or lack of job-specific training.
- No metrics.
- No internal auditing or assessment.
- No strategic and tactical Op Ex planning.

To minimize risks, the Op Ex manager should understand:

- **Stakeholder requirements.** An Op Ex project may include a number of external or internal stakeholders. Each stakeholder may have different requirements or a different measure or understanding of success. The Op Ex manager or team leader should understand and attempt to satisfy them.
- **Competitive pressures.** Competitiveness pressures are immense. Management often wants improvement projects to be completed quickly. Time becomes a competitive weapon. Teams must attack a project quickly and effectively.

- **Organizational changes.** Organizational changes, such as downsizing, outsourcing, new management, or new initiatives, can instill confusion, despair, or cynicism. Op Ex requires total focus and commitment which may wither when the organization is going through major changes.
- **Complexity.** A project always looks easy and doable at first. Reality sets in when the team investigates the root causes and resources needed for solution. Problems may be chronic or systemic. Additional resources and management approvals may be required to root-cause solve the problem.
- **Technology changes.** Technology is the great wildcard in all business. It's clichéd to say that things change and that technology is the driver of the change. Technology can't be stopped. Its effects must be understood and applied effectively.
- **Offshore risks.** An Op Ex project may require that a team visits an offshore supplier. Language, custom, contractual, and regulatory difficulties may arise that can't be anticipated.

TERMINATION

Termination is called various names in different organizations, including reduced in force, rightsized, fired, terminated or a number of other names. Termination is probably the most difficult and necessary job for the Op Ex manager. Termination may result from a pattern of noncompliance to policies, lack of performance, theft, policy noncompliance, incompetence, involve a numerical scale, narrative by the manager, narrative by stakeholders, customer review, management by objectives, assessment center, and critical incident response.

More often, the traditional practices and assumptions of management are becoming outmoded. For example, employee selection, employee evaluation, and automatic salary increases are going by the wayside in many companies, specifically:

- **Employee selection.** Prospective employees go through grueling selection process of multiple interviews, tests, and other performance measures. In some companies, first year employees are on contract so the company can evaluate their performance.

- **Employee evaluation.** Existing employees and managers are no longer evaluated by an immediate boss. Three hundred, sixty-degree evaluations are becoming common where an employee is evaluated by bosses, peers, and subordinates.
- **Salary increases.** The guaranteed wage increase based on the consumer price index is also fading. Salary increases are based on rewarding performance, improving Op Ex, developing new products, or adding value to the organization.

OP EX LIFECYCLE COSTS

An important concept in COQ is "lifecycle cost." Lifecycle costs are incurred to maintain or improve Op Ex throughout the product lifecycle. In the middle and later stages of the product lifecycle, external failure costs such as service, repairs, warranty costs, and replacement part costs increase. The life cycle costs of Op Ex can negatively impact sales in the later stages of the product lifecycle and can also provide useful information for contingency planning. Anticipated future warranty, service, maintainability, and reliability costs can reveal information that present management can use to make better product decisions. For example, high warranty and other external failure costs can squeeze profit margins late in the product lifecycle. So, as competitors enter the market, margins are squeezed and these external failure costs cannot be passed on to the consumer.

RETURN OF OP EX

The return on Op Ex is a concept receiving more attention. Op Ex is an investment that should return a stream of income as well as lower costs over time. There is a close parallel between return on Op Ex and return on investment (ROI) which is how Op Ex initiatives and projects should be perceived. The challenge is being able to pinpoint these numbers. The common belief is that returns from reducing the cost of poor Op Ex can be substantial. The question is how substantial. Many companies don't measure the costs of Op Ex or the hard benefits of an Op Ex initiative or project because Op Ex costs are difficult to retrieve and the administrative overhead for collecting the data can be high.

Cost of Op Ex, return on Op Ex and other Op Ex related costing mechanisms are new to many organizations. Operational management may have to introduce these costing concepts as well as communicate them in understandable terms to senior management. Senior management will understand these concepts if they are communicated as a percentage of total sales or as a percentage of revenue. These costs can then be used to make Op Ex investment, project justification, capital expenditure, or cost-benefit decisions. One common method is to look at Op Ex costs through the cost of quality lens.

CONFORMANCE COSTS

Prevention costs are incurred to prevent defects or errors from occurring in the first place or before a product is produced. Prevention costs result from:

- Op Ex engineering, reliability planning, data accumulation, and quality planning.
- Design and development of measurement and control equipment.
- Op Ex planning of improvement projects.
- Op Ex training.

Appraisals ensure standards, specifications, policies, or procedures are being followed. Appraisal costs result from:

- Inspection and testing of purchased material; receiving inspection; test of materials at the supplier's facility; or at the company's receiving dock.
- Inspection and testing product conformance at set-up, first-article, in-process, and final product.
- Conducting process and product audits.

OPERATIONAL ASSURANCE

Operational assurance is responsible for monitoring decisions made by operational control or more often by some operational group. In general, operational assurance staff analyzes, plans, and coordinates improvement projects. Operational assurance engineers work with Engineering, Production, Supply Management, and suppliers to prevent design flaws early in the design cycle. Assurance staff focuses on the long-term technical areas of Op Ex. The operational assurance staff also supports operational areas to troubleshoot Op Ex problems.

At the process level, operational assurance evaluates and analyzes design, manufacturing and procurement processes to ensure Op Ex. Operational assurance analyzes blueprints, specifications, production plans, and other technical documents to ensure the product is designed properly. The design and supporting documentation must be accurate for Manufacturing to build the product.

Operational assurance also reviews contracts, drawings, plans, instructions, measuring instruments, tools, and processes to ensure product quality is maintained before, during, and after production. Operational assurance ensures a company's contractual responsibilities are fulfilled including evaluating finished product quality, availability, cost, service, safety, and maintainability. Operational assurance also reviews engineering documentation for adequacy, completeness, and currentness. Engineering documentation includes released engineering material including engineering drawings, specifications, standards, work instructions, and change orders.

Operational assurance also is directly or indirectly responsible for:

- Developing Op Ex policies, procedures, work instructions and forms.
- Controlling and updating Op Ex documentation.
- Planning Op Ex initiatives.
- Planning inspection and test.
- Controlling and conducting metrology and calibration.
- Designing and implementing process control.
- Conducting Op Ex training.
- Measuring the cost of Op Ex, efficiencies, and effectiveness.

- Acquiring systems, process, and product Op Ex data collection and reporting.
- Conducting supplier audits.

KNOWLEDGE SHALL SET YOU FREE

Data must become information to be useful for decision making. Traditionally, middle management gathered and collated data from operations. This data was distilled into information that was communicated to top management.

A major challenge is to manage the quality data and information that are being received, otherwise the data is useless unless it is used to make better decisions. A company has to have processes, and procedures for culling, collating, distilling, and transmitting the data so it is useful. Otherwise, data won't be utilized and people will be forced to rely on gut feelings where the risk of failure may be high.

Senior management and line employees may have real-time access to the same information. Computer networks have allowed people to generate and integrate information across connected and distributed computer systems. Computers have become critical by providing decision makers with real-time information that affects design, production, and service Op Ex. In the new Op Ex universe, the decision maker may not be a vice president or a top manager. A decision maker may be the person on the assembly line who needs instantaneous process or product Op Ex information. Or, a decision maker may be a customer service representative who needs a customer's order history to resolve a billing discrepancy.

CONDUCTING PERFORMANCE EVALUATIONS

Give credit where credit is due.
Proverb

Long term management is essential to a successful Op Ex initiative. One way to ensure this is to evaluate the Op Ex initiative in terms of meeting stakeholder needs and providing high returns on the Op Ex investment. An objective assessment each year of the organization's Op Ex efforts will determine if it is going in the right direction and if it is effective.

Every manager, including the Op Ex manager, must evaluate performance of different groups, employees, suppliers, Op Ex teams, day-to-day operations, and the list goes on. The challenge to the Op Ex manager is that he or she must sometimes evaluate the performance of groups and employees who don't report directly to the manager. The teams report directly to the operational manager and may not even be a dotted line reporting relationship with the Op Ex manager.

PERFORMANCE EVALUATION

Matrix organizations and loose reporting relationships can present difficulties to the Op Ex manager. The Op Ex manager may have little or no knowledge of the team's performance. The Op Ex manager may have little or no direct method by which to evaluate and reward the team but has some indirect methods, such as the following:

- **Write letter.** The Op Ex manager can write a letter of appreciation for the employee's file or attention to the unit manager.
- **Convey evaluation.** The Op Ex manager can pass the word to senior management about the performance of the team.
- **Participate directly.** The Op Ex manager can support the team through participating or championing the improvement effort.
- **Provide resources.** The Op Ex manager can provide staff resources to the effort, again signaling approval.
- **Participate directly in performance evaluation.** The Op Ex manager may become part of a team evaluating performance.

Employee evaluations are often written, objective, and confidential. The evaluations may be reviewed by second-level management as well as the Human Resources department to ensure fairness and compliance to employment regulations.

Management by Objectives (MBO) is the preferred evaluation method by most Op Ex managers. It is probably the most objective evaluating method.

A team composed of a person's stakeholders is another popular evaluation method. A person's stakeholders are those who the person works with including bosses, employees, customers, and suppliers. An evaluation by one's peers tends to present more information however it takes longer. The value of this assessment is that employees receive feedback from many sources which provide more tips for improvement.

Evaluations of professional staff may involve a numerical point scale, narrative by the manager, narrative by stakeholders, internal/external customer review, or management by objectives.

How should a supervisor evaluate negative performance? The quick answer is carefully. Too many people withhold negative information which may be important to team or individual area performance. The opposite also occurs when performance appraisals are inflated. Both are unfair to the organization, team, and employee because the individual or team is not provided accurate feedback to correct or improve performance. If this is a systemwide pattern, it can result in suboptimizing a very important organizational system - its human resources.

INDIRECT EVALUATIONS

Every manager, including the Op Ex manager must evaluate performance of different groups, employees, suppliers, Op Ex teams, day-to-day operations, and the list goes on. The Op Ex manager must evaluate the performance of groups and employees who don't report directly to him or her. This is common in matrix organizations as well as in Op Ex initiatives occurring throughout the organization. The teams report directly to the operational manager and may not report to the Op Ex manager at all.

Matrix organizations and loose reporting relationships can be difficult. Operational management sometimes has little or no knowledge of the performance of the team. The operational management has no direct method by which to reward the team but has some indirect inducements, such as writing letters of acknowledgement. The following are several ways by which the Op Ex manager can evaluate performance in a matrix or indirect reporting relationship:

- Op Ex manager can write a recommendation letter for the employee's file or attention to the unit manager.
- Op Ex manager can pass the word to senior management about the performance of the team.
- Op Ex manager can participate or champion the improvement effort. This involvement implies strong support.
- Op Ex manager can provide staff resources to the effort, again signaling approval.
- Op Ex manager may become part of a team evaluating performance.

TYPES OF RECOGNITION SYSTEMS

Recognition systems should be real and genuine to the team or individuals. People know if recognition is used to force behavior or manipulate them. Recognition may be as little as a public 'thank you' or may be as elaborate as a company and supplier wide appreciation day. Recognition is important because it is a public statement or acknowledgement of what is important. The recognition also reinforces organizational principles, values, culture, and behavior. Recognition through senior management can also be used to positively change or redirect an organization's attention to a new culture or a rededicate it to a new mission.

Recognition may be public or private. Public recognition is usually through a newsletter, meeting, or memo. Public recognition can be through the mass media if a team or a plant has accomplished something worthy of public attention. People or teams responsible for the improvement are widely quoted. Public recognition is often better than private recognition because it publicly acknowledges the improvement and the people responsible.

SHARED RISK - SHARED RETURN

Let's assume that the Op Ex initiative is succeeding. Op Ex and productivity have improved. Costs are down and profits are up. The turnaround is the result of management and labor working together. But do both share in the rewards?

Let's look at another scenario. The marketplace is forcing a company to be more competitive. To maintain profit margins, management has to lower costs. The normal method is to reduce wages by threatening plant closure. Unfortunately, threats have the opposite effect and harden already adversarial relationships. This results in lowered productivity, rising costs, and finally what nobody wanted, a plant shutdown.

Gainsharing is a method for employees to share in the profitability of the organization. Gainsharing is a broad category of programs that advocates management and labor share gains obtained through Op Ex and productivity improvements. Employees are eligible for bonuses and other perks. To illustrate how it works, when employees earning $9 an hour increase productivity by 22.2%, labor costs are reduced by $2 an hour. Sharing gains equally gives $1 to the company and $1 to the employee. The employee effectively gets $10 an hour and the labor cost to the employer is $8 an hour. The benefits of gainsharing include improved Op Ex, lower costs, increased productivity, and employee commitment.[55]

AWARD SYSTEMS

There is no standard policy or method for providing awards. One company may have an extensive award program. Awards are given for best idea, customer service beyond the call of duty, best design, and so on. Each employee may be rewarded twice or more each year. In other companies, awards and recognition are fewer and harder to achieve. Teams may have an award-off where each team presents its ideas for peer and senior management review. The best team and individual accomplishments are recognized and rewarded. Awards are given for best new design, exceptional customer service, outstanding achievement of a group or team, best suggestion, or completion of a college degree.

OP EX JOB DESCRIPTIONS

Job descriptions of the following are attached:

- Vice President - Op Ex
- Dirctor - Operational Assurance
- Manager - Supply Operations
- Operational Engineer
- Internal Operation Consultant
- Op Ex Control Technician

VICE PRESIDENT – OP EX JOB DESCRIPTION

- Directs the company-wide development of the Op Ex vision, mission, and value statements.
- Directs and coordinates the company wide Op Ex function.
- Participates in formulating and administering organizational policies and mission.
- Assists senior management in developing long-range Op Ex goals, plans, and objectives.
- Directs and coordinates Op Ex activities that support operational units.
- Reviews and analyzes Op Ex activities, costs, and operations.
- Forecasts Op Ex activities of operational departments and business units toward the attainment of company Op Ex goals and objectives.
- Confers with the Chief Executive Officer and other senior managers to review Op Ex achievements and discuss further requirements.
- Plans, directs and coordinates the Op Ex initiative and projects to ensure that Op Ex goals and objectives are accomplished within time frame and budget.

CAUSES OF POOR PERFORMANCE	
Root Cause	**Remedies**
System failure	Total Op Ex initiative
Misunderstanding of job expectations	Communication of job expec-
tations	
Lack of awareness about performance	Clear performance feedback
Lack of time, tools, resources to	Provision of appropriate time,
tools, and	
succeed	resources
Lack of necessary knowledge or skills	Implementation of an appro-
priate development	
program	
Lack of appropriate consequences for	Adjustment of consequences
performance	
Bad fit for the job	Separation of the employee
from the job[56]	

- Reviews operational project proposals and plans to determine time requirements, funding limitations, procedures for accomplishing projects, staffing requirements and authorizing resources to projects.
- Directs preparation of Op Ex policies to business unit, division, and plant administrators.
- Promotes Op Ex activities internally and throughout the supplier base.

DIRECTOR - OPERATIONAL ASSURANCE JOB DESCRIPTION

- Participates in formulating and establishing Op Ex function policies and operational procedures.
- Develops, implements, and coordinates through operational assurance staff projects to prevent or eliminate nonconformances in new and existing products.
- Develops, implements, and coordinates through operational assurance staff projects to develop controlled and capable processes.

- Analyzes, evaluates, and presents information to senior management concerning Op Ex, customer satisfaction, process capabilities, etc.
- Suggests alternative methods and procedures for resolving customer problems and meeting changing market opportunities.
- Cooperates with senior management in formulating and establishing organizational policies, operating procedures, and goals.
- Delineates areas of responsibility, personnel requirements, and operational procedures within operational assurance function consistent with organizational goals and policies.
- Evaluates Op Ex reports from operational process owners.
- Evaluates Op Ex costs from product development teams and operational department heads.
- Confers with senior management in formulating Op Ex fiscal budgets.
- Conducts management meetings to establish, delineate and review organizational policies to coordinate Op Ex functions within organization.
- Reviews technical and Op Ex problems and procedures of operating departments and recommends solutions to problems or changes in procedures.
- Establishes work plan and staffing for Op Ex projects.
- Arranges for recruitment or assignments of project personnel.
- Confers with management and supervisors on operational work plans, duties, budgets, responsibilities, and authorities.
- Coordinates Op Ex activities among operating units, functions, and other areas to increase operational efficiency and effectiveness.
- Analyzes internal Op Ex plans to identify areas of improvement.
- Reviews Op Ex status reports and modifies schedules or plans as required.
- Prepares Op Ex status reports for senior management, customers, or other stakeholders.
- Provides coaching, technical advice, and mentoring to operational personnel.
- Resolves conflicts and problems among different constituencies.

- Visits and confers with suppliers to obtain information relating to supplier Op Ex and capability to meet orders and improve product quality.
- Confers with engineers about new product designs.

MANAGER - SUPPLY OPERATIONS JOB DESCRIPTION

- Directs and coordinates supplier activities, dealing with Op Ex, delivery, compliance, service and technology.
- Assists Supply Management in selecting, monitoring, and improving suppliers.
- Directs testing of received parts, components, and materials to determine conformance to standards and specifications.
- Conducts periodic and special audits of supplier's facilities and processes to determine adequacy, control, and capability.
- Resolves operational disputes with suppliers.
- Reviews supplier operational deficiencies with Engineering, Supply Management, and Manufacturing personnel.
- Prepares periodic and special reports concerning supplier Op Ex systems, schedules, audit results, and corrective actions.
- Coordinates activities to evaluate and resolve supplier operational problems.
- Reviews Op Ex, product schedules, engineering specifications, orders, and other related information to maintain and improve Op Ex levels among suppliers.
- Confers with customers, internal engineering, supplier engineering, Sales, Supply Management and Production to provide technical and Op Ex support.
- Interprets engineering drawings and facilitates correction of errors on drawings, documents, and bills of materials during the product development cycle and throughout the product's lifecycle.
- Investigates reports of nonconforming, damaged, or malfunctioning parts, assemblies, equipment to determine nature and scope of the problem.
- Formulates corrective action plans and ensures implementation of the plan.

- Maintains records and oversees recording of Op Ex information by others to ensure drawings and other Op Ex documents are current and complete.
- Serves as a leader or member of joint Op Ex committees.
- Reviews contracts to determine contract compliance and sufficiency.
- Reviews standards, contracts, drawings, purchase orders, and other documentation to ensure customer requirements are detailed.
- Confers with suppliers to determine contract capability.

OPERATIONAL ENGINEER JOB DESCRIPTION

- Plans and directs activities concerned with the development, application, and maintenance of Op Ex standards for processes, materials, and products.
- Develops Op Ex standards and methods for product inspection, testing, and evaluation.
- Develops and initiates Op Ex standards and methods for process control and capability.
- Devises procedures, forms, and instructions for recording, evaluating, and reporting Op Ex, reliability, and maintainability data.
- Establishes Op Ex systems to evaluate calibration precision and accuracy of production and testing/inspection equipment.
- Develops and implements methods and procedures for disposition and correction of nonconforming materials.
- Directs employees and others in measuring and testing products and tabulating data concerning materials, processes, and product excellence and reliability.
- Ensures compliance with international, national, and industry standards and regulations.
- Compiles and writes Op Ex training materials.
- Conducts training in Op Ex technologies.
- Facilitates teams.
- Plans, directs, and coordinates the preparation of Op Ex documentation to ensure customer requirements are met.
- Monitors status of Op Ex documentation and Op Ex manual to ensure they are complete, current, and accurate.

- Submits Op Ex documentation to management for approval, and transmits approved documents to Op Ex stakeholders.

INTERNAL OPERATIONS CONSULTANT JOB DESCRIPTION

- Consults with customers to define Op Ex needs, requirements, and expectations.
- Conducts Op Ex studies and surveys to obtain and analyze data to advise or recommend solutions to Op Ex problems.
- Utilizes knowledge of Op Ex theory, principles, and technology to improve company and supplier wide excellence systems.
- Consults with customers to determine and define customer needs and/or to identify problem areas and to determine scope of investigation required to obtain solution.
- Conducts Op Ex customer survey.
- Works with process owners on problems to obtain data required for solution.
- Analyses data to determine solutions to problems, such as installation of alternate Op Ex methods and procedures, changes in process, new practices, modification of machines or equipment or redesign of product or services.
- Advises customers on alternate methods of solving problems and recommends specific solutions.

CALIBRATION ENGINEER OR TECHNICIAN JOB DESCRIPTION

- Develops and evaluates calibration systems that measure product characteristics, substances or phenomena, such as length, mass, time temperature, electric current, luminous intensity, chemical or other physical characteristics.
- Identifies margin of error contributing to uncertainty of results.
- Redesigns or adjusts measurement capability to minimize errors.
- Develops calibration methods and techniques based on Op Ex principles.
- Ensures calibration accuracy and precision of testing and inspection equipment.
- Ensures equipment complies with standards and procedures
- Maintains calibration records.

- Advises operating personnel on calibration equipment.
- Ensures equipment is calibrated properly and calibration is transferable to NIST.

OP EX CONTROL TECHNICIAN JOB DESCRIPTION

- Tests and inspects products at specified points of production process to determine compliance to drawings and specifications.
- Evaluates process and product statistical data to determine and maintain product quality and reliability.
- Interprets engineering drawings and formulas to determine Op Ex standards.
- Selects products for testing at specified stages of production.
- Supports line personnel in problem detection and solving.
- Assists operating personnel in controlling, monitoring, and improving operations.
- Plans, promotes, and organizes Op Ex related activities.

NEXT CHAPTER

In the next chapter, Op Ex Communications is discussed. They serve several important purposes including communicating the culture and rites of the organization. Anyone who has worked in an organization can attest that a person can be overwhelmed by meetings especially since studies indicate managers and senior executives may spend up to 70 to 80% of their time in meetings.

CHAPTER 11
OP EX COMMUNICATIONS

Conflicting or inconsistent messages result when an organization is rudderless in terms of what is important, what models will determine success, and what will be communicated to its stakeholders. For example, poor communication may be the biggest problem in developing teams. This isn't surprising. Communication problems may arise among team members, between the leader and the team, between the leader and senior management, between the leader and operational management, and the list goes. Communication problems may arise because of personal resentment, working resentments, different languages, differing priorities, resource allocation, egos, individual requirements and for a number of other reasons.

POWER OF COMMUNICATIONS

Communication problems can be positive if they are resolved quickly, effectively, and amicably. Communication problems may highlight system deficiencies. Problems may create higher levels of understanding and commitment. Early problems can provide an early glimpse into future problems. However, if communications don't improve, they will lead to long term resentment and anger which may demobilize a team.

Good communications are important for the following reasons:

- Promote understanding of the importance of Op Ex
- Communicate Op Ex benefits
- Communicate Op Ex information
- Communicate business information
- Comply with regulations

- Verify Op Ex

PROMOTE UNDERSTANDING OF THE IMPORTANCE OF OP EX

Open communication is the only way to ensure internal customers understand important concepts such as satisfying customer requirements, conforming to specifications, and adding value. For example, all employees should understand the criticality of what they do and how they affect other steps in the value-added chain. Organizationally, this means several things. Boundaries and walls between work groups and departments have to destroyed. Inter-group meetings must be held often. Problem identification and resolution becomes a joint activity.

COMMUNICATE OP EX BENEFITS

Op Ex and its benefits must be communicated to a number of stakeholders including, internal customers, suppliers, regulators, external customers, shareholders, and unions. Each stakeholder has a buy-in and some level of ownership in the Op Ex issue.

COMMUNICATE OP EX INFORMATION

One company believes in plant-wide visualization of goals, beliefs and policies. For example, capital asset utilization diagrams, Op Ex cost information, and process capability charts are posted throughout the plant identifying opportunity targets in different areas. These diagrams impart a sense of urgency. Financial and operational information is taken seriously by everyone. Line personnel are taught financial and accounting information so everyone can interpret financial goals and trends.

COMMUNICATE BUSINESS INFORMATION

Meetings are one of the most important means for communicating information. There are two basic types of meetings, one is to reflect and to think such as what occurs in staff meetings. The second type of meeting is to act such as what occurs in task groups. In these meetings, four basic processes may occur, including coming up with ideas, investing ideas with power, communicating information, and providing feedback on performance.[57]

They serve several important purposes including communicating the culture and rites of the organization. Anyone who has worked in an organization can attest that a person can be overwhelmed by meetings especially since studies indicate managers and senior executives may spend up to 70 to 80% of their time in meetings.

COMPLY WITH REGULATIONS

Op Ex documentation and records are a fundamental requirement of many Op Ex policies, standards, and specifications. For example, ISO 9001:2015 requires documentation for each of the system requirements. It seems just about everyone is becoming accustomed to the hierarchy of Op Ex documentation. The first level includes Op Ex policies which are included in an Op Ex manual. Second level documentation includes procedures while third level documentation involves work instructions. Fourth level documentation includes forms and records.

Op Ex documentation is the main evidence of Op Ex, that procedures exist and were followed consistently. If the customer wants to know that quality and value were added to a product, then documentation and records may be the only corroboration after the service has been performed or the product was produced. Documentation is a key quality system to ensure Op Ex was defined, understood, operationalized, measured, controlled, and consistently improved.

IMPORTANCE OF GOOD COMMUNICATIONS

Nothing is more central to an organization's effectiveness than its ability to transmit accurate, relevant, and understandable information among its members. All the advances of organizations - economy of scale, financial, and technical resources, diverse talents, and contacts, are of no practical value if the organization's members are unaware of what other members require of them and why.

Saul Gellerman, writer

Communication problems can be positive if they are resolved quickly, effectively, and amicably. Communication problems may highlight system deficiencies. Problems may create higher levels of understanding and commitment. Early problems can provide an early glimpse into future problems. However, if communications don't improve, they will lead to long term resentment and anger which may demobilize a team.

Conflicting or inconsistent messages result when an organization is rudderless in terms of what is important, what models will determine success, and what will be communicated to its stakeholders. For example, poor communication may be the biggest problem in developing teams. This isn't surprising. Communication problems may arise among team members, between the leader and the team, between the leader and senior management, between the leader and operational management, and the list goes. Communication problems may arise because of personal resentment, working resentments, different languages, differing priorities, resource allocation, egos, individual requirements and for a number of other reasons.

Good communications are important for the following reasons:

- Promote understanding of the importance of Op Ex
- Communicate Op Ex benefits
- Communicate Op Ex information
- Communicate business information
- Comply with regulations
- Verify Op Ex effectiveness

PROMOTE UNDERSTANDING OF THE IMPORTANCE OF OP EX

Open communication is the only way to ensure internal customers understand important concepts such as satisfying customer requirements, conforming to specifications, and adding value. For example, all employees should understand the criticality of what they do and how they affect other steps in the value-added chain. Organizationally, this means several things. Boundaries and walls between work groups and departments have to destroyed. Inter-group meetings must be held often. Problem identification and resolution becomes a joint activity.

COMMUNICATE OP EX BENEFITS

Op Ex and its benefits must be communicated to a number of stakeholders including, internal customers, suppliers, regulators, external customers, shareholders, and unions. Each stakeholder has a buy-in and some level of ownership in the Op Ex issue.

COMMUNICATE OP EX INFORMATION

One company believes in plant-wide visualization of goals, beliefs and policies. For example, capital asset utilization diagrams, Op Ex cost information, and process capability charts are posted throughout the plant identifying opportunity targets in different areas. These diagrams impart a sense of urgency. Financial and operational information is taken seriously by everyone. Line personnel are taught financial and accounting information so everyone can interpret financial goals and trends.

COMMUNICATE BUSINESS INFORMATION

Meetings are one of the most important means for communicating information. There are two basic types of meetings, one is to reflect and to think such as what occurs in staff meetings. The second type of meeting is to act such as what occurs in task groups. In these meetings, four basic processes may occur, including coming up with ideas, investing ideas with power, communicating information, and providing feedback on performance.[58]

COMPLY WITH REGULATIONS

Op Ex documentation and records are a fundamental requirement of many Op Ex policies, standards, and specifications. For example, ISO 9001:2015 requires documentation for each of the quality system requirements. It seems just about everyone is becoming accustomed to the 4-level hierarchy of Op Ex documentation. The first level includes Op Ex policies which are included in an Op Ex manual. Second level documentation includes procedures while third level documentation involves work instructions. Fourth level documentation includes forms and records.

VERIFY OP EX

Op Ex documentation is the main evidence of Op Ex, that procedures exist and were followed consistently. If the customer wants to know that quality and value were added to a product, then documentation and records may be the only corroboration after the service has been performed or the product was produced. Documentation is a key Op Ex system to ensure Op Ex was defined, understood, operationalized, measured, controlled, and consistently improved.

ADVERTISING

Give them quality. That's the best kind of advertising.
Milton Snavely Hershey

Advertising is a method to communicate tangible product and intangible service benefits to a customer. The marketplace is competitive with so many products that companies advertise to puff up product attributes, performance, or capabilities.

USES OF ADVERTISING

Advertising emphasizes such Op Ex themes as reliability, durability, and workmanship. Advertising can be used to:

- Educate people
- Promote Op Ex image
- Create brand loyalty

Educate People

Initially with any product, Marketing's challenge is to educate the consumer about a product's benefits. Advertising is used to communicate a product's novel and unique features to differentiate it from its competitors.

Promote Op Ex Image

Companies use advertising to establish or promote an Op Ex image by stressing brand preference and recognition. But, if the consumer has had a bad experience with a product, then no amount of advertising can change its image. Advertising cannot make a bad or ordinary product good. False claims or misrepresentations backfire and the effect is the opposite of what is intended. If a product is already good, then advertising can create additional market opportunities.

Create Brand Loyalty

As the marketplace becomes competitive, companies use advertising to stress dealer or consumer loyalty. Promotions may emphasize product availability, price, and service. Sometimes, a product is modified so the brand or label is still on the package but contents are different from its predecessor.

COMMUNICATION CHALLENGES

In **Follow the Yellow Brick Road,** Richard Saul Wurman identified the following causes of instruction and communication breakdown:

- Failure to translate the instruction to the perspective of the information taker
- Failure to take into account the understanding level and the needs of the information taker
- Messages phrased in abstract terms that defy mutual interpretation
- An excess of information that obscures the intent of the instruction
- Hiding the clear intent of the instruction under allusion and veiled references
- Omitting essential pieces
- Unnecessarily threatening enforcement of compliance with the instruction
- Lack of context
- Choice of an inappropriate channel to convey the content of the instruction, so the taker confuses the message
- Departure from accepted custom without adequate warning
- False claims or promises
- Lack of attention paid to human behavior
- Evoking the parent-child rebellion response
- Self-destructive instructions
- Time lapse problem
- Inadequate incentive to follow[59]

COMMUNICATING POLICY CHANGES

Op Ex documentation may change the nature of an operation or process. If it does then the organization should take steps to ensure all employees are:

- Informed of the change
- Informed for the reason
- Notified when it will take effect
- Notified who will assist in the implementation

System or process documentation or implementation changes can be announced through:

- E-mail or computerized bulletin boards
- Site bulletin boards
- Memos and newsletters
- Copies of the new procedure sent to all manual holders

WORK LIFE

Some Op Ex problems can be laid to poor communications about expectations. Lately many employees believe that organizations do not recognize, care, trust, listen or reward people appropriately. Senior management believes employees don't understand global competitive pressures or customer requirements. There are now many attempts to improve the quality of work life.

Quality-of-work-life (QWL) is a general description of a set of programs that bring management and employees together to work on common problems and to find mutually satisfactory solutions. Organizations hope if workers contribute directly to the quality of their work environment, they will be more committed to achieving product quality and delivering Op Ex service.

The quality excellence-of-work-life concept suggests that people perform their best in an environment where decisions are made jointly by management and employees. The basic idea is that Op Ex accountability is pushed to the lowest level in the organization that can handle the responsibility. Individual employees or more commonly teams control the quality of their output, request resources, develop schedules, and plan their production levels. In some cases, they evaluate the performance of individuals in the work group. Historically, management was responsible for these functions.

BREAKDOWN OF TRUST

Many U.S. organizations had a simple approach to organizational commitment - trust coming down the organization was rewarded with trust going up. The problem is this compact has recently been broken. Many employees believe trust has been broken with downsizing, reengineering and other initiatives that have resulted in many employees departing and those who remain having to work longer hours for less remuneration. Employees, including many managers, have little reason to trust senior management.

Some of the major changes occurring in the workplace include:

- Employee expectation changes
- Rise of employee participation, involvement, and empowerment
- Everyone is an Op Ex professional
- New roles for middle management and first level supervision
- Use of multiskilled teams
- Focus on quality of work life

Employee Expectation Changes

The workplace is changing. Today's young employees are more curious. They were brought up in a permissive environment where questioning was an accepted form of behavior. Authority was also questioned. These employees can be threatening to traditional managers who demand unquestionable obedience.

Both management and employees may feel threatened by changes. Management may feel threatened when they perceive a loss of authority. Employees may feel uncomfortable because of changes in work environment, emphasis on training, additional responsibilities, elimination of work rules, and new forms of supervision.

Rise of Employee Participation, Involvement, and Empowerment

Participatory management does not come easy to managers who were trained and rewarded by traditional, authority-based leadership. Today's managers are often people who paid their dues on the factory floor. These people worked hard to get into management by following accepted rules and learned to manage according to the style that got them promoted. If not flexible, these managers tend to guard their authority and resist change. But, enlightened and progressive leadership at the top can cure this problem.

Change is difficult but doable. At one company, middle managers are trained to run meetings of hourly employees, and accept their suggestions. At another, division managers reinforce the message of participatory management by promoting and rewarding managers who adopt new ways of doing things. What happens if first line managers resist change? They may have to be removed and reassigned to areas where they have no direct supervision.

Everyone Is An Op Ex Professional

In an employee involvement atmosphere, employees and teams have more responsibility and authority to control product and service quality. Organizations realize Op Ex rests with each employee. Organizations that focus on excellence attempt to create working conditions allowing employees to make decisions that enhance their work environment. Every employee becomes an Op Ex professional. In many production facilities, workers control the speed of the line and can stop the line if they believe there is a defective component. In this way, the worker has more control over his or her process and over product quality.

In a manufacturing plant, "Op Ex associates" inspect their own work and act as the quality control for the person ahead and the person behind in a process. Parts go through continuous quality inspection by each employee.

New Roles for Middle Management and First Level Supervision

In the future, management and labor will have to cooperate and learn new skills to build quality products in the "factory and office of the future." These factories will operate as integrated systems where machinery and equipment instantaneously communicate with each other to monitor and control process and product quality. The office of the future may well be at home, in the car, on the road, or at the customer's facility.

The majority of unskilled jobs and many middle-level management positions will be replaced by highly trained, technical workers. The consequences of equipment or process failure are so high that factories with advanced manufacturing technologies will require a responsible, self-motivated, and self-regulated workforce.

Since teams are self-regulating, layers of management are eliminated. If plant managers need information, they tap directly into central computers without any need of middle managers to collect, integrate, and communicate the information.

Use of Multi-Skilled Teams

To realize the potential of technology and new social systems, organizations will integrate workers and technology into sociotechnical systems. In these systems, semiautonomous teams of five to seven multiskilled members work on projects spread across functional departments. These employment systems require broad based jobs, teamwork, participative managers, and multiskilled workers. The payoff is that plants designed around worker participation and innovation teams are 30-50% more productive than conventional plants.[60]

Work in computerized environments will be arranged around processes, rather than specific tasks such as welding or machining. The work team producing the product or subassembly is responsible for its Op Ex and productivity. Responsibility is given to employees by creating positions called "owner-operator," where operators are responsible for the process and its outputs. These teams are responsible for producing defect-free products within a specific work area. Work teams tend to motivate individual members as well as complement individual team members' skills and knowledge.

Self-managed work groups accept responsibility for production schedules, quality, cost control, upgrading worker skills and assignment of work. Previously, management was responsible for these activities. Now, self-managing groups direct these activities. Many job classifications have been replaced by one work classification. The work environment has been humanized. Time clocks have been eliminated. Compensation is based on pay-for-knowledge so that workers are paid on the basis of training, experience, and knowledge.

FIRST-LEVEL SUPERVISION SUPPORT

First-level supervision is also going through the same changes as middle management. With self-managed teams, management is asking what value does first level supervision add to a work environment where teams may be responsible for hiring, promoting, and managing their work.

First level supervision must change from supervising to coaching, mentoring, and problem solving. Most importantly, the supervisor must understand and facilitate the reversal of roles between supervisor and team members. Instead of hierarchal and perhaps adversary, both groups must trust and depend on each other to get the work done. Again, this is difficult for traditional first level supervision. Some supervisors will adapt and others will fall by the way side.

In networked computer environments, what is the role of the supervising Op Ex engineer? Traditionally, this middle person evaluated designs, managed operations, and communicated results to senior management. Now, team members can evaluate designs. Teams may also self-manage design projects. And, senior management can access project files to assess progress, evaluate budgets, and check performance.

OP EX IS ONLY AS GOOD AS INFORMATION

Op Ex information should be:

- **Reliable.** Information should be from an authoritative source.
- **Valid.** Information should exist and be based on facts and preferably be written down.
- **Complete.** Decision makers should have all the critical information to support a sound and informed judgment. Reports communicate the good and the bad. Complete information frames and provides

- context to information. Complete information is also distilled and collated.
- **Verifiable.** Verifiable information can be used by two parties to arrive at the same conclusions and recommendations.
- **Relevant.** Relevant information can be used to make good decisions.
- **Usable.** Usable information results in better designs. Information is presented in a format appropriate to the customer and user. Information can be tailored to accommodate individuals with different backgrounds by being in a statistical, narrative, or graphical format.
- **Informative.** Clear and concise information provides customers with feedback for making better decisions. For example, corrective action feedback will reveal if the fix eliminated the symptom and the root cause so the problem did not recur.
- **Timely.** Timely information is available to make reliable decisions.

OP EX INFORMATION FOR DECISION MAKING

Operational management information is especially critical in the following decision-making areas:

- **Cost of quality data.** Cost of quality (COQ) data is the cost of obtaining quality and the cost of not achieving quality. Any departure from normal procedures, specifications, and standards results in additional costs to the organization. Once costs are captured, then the organization can identify areas for Op Ex.
- **Supplier history.** A large manufacturing organization may have thousands of suppliers. Suppliers are periodically evaluated for Op Ex, availability, service, price, and delivery.
- **Product failures.** Product failure information provides an organization with data on product reliability performance. Reliability problems are hazardous and costly because they can result in warranty, litigation, and call-back costs. Product failure information is used to initiate corrective action. Product failure information is supplied to Engineering to design out possible defects and to Manufacturing to

prevent defects from occurring during manufacturing. Product failure information is also collected throughout a product's life so a product can continuously be improved.

- **Status of incoming, in-process, and final material Op Ex**. Data on the number and type of defects provide information on the status of incoming, in-process, and final Op Ex. Special or assignable cause variation among products identify areas for Op Ex. Once, an Op Ex specification has been written, excessive variation especially outside the specification limits implies poor Op Ex. So, process and product uniformity is essential to maintaining customer satisfaction. Op Ex information can be reported on a daily, weekly, quarterly, and yearly basis. Information can show trends of deterioration or improvement.

INFORMATION AND DATA RELIABILITY

Management by data has become operationalized in many companies. While hunches and anecdotal information are important, the risks of a bad decision have become be too high. Managers want the right type of information and data to arrive at an optimal decision.

A major problem in the management by information process is that data may not be reliable or accurate. The reasons vary. Information may be gathered from multiple sources which may gather, collate, emphasize, and analyze information differently. This results in added variation which can cause further miscommunication.

Critical information can also be lost in background noise. Expressed in another way, the signal, the critical actionable information, has to be found amid the background noise. For example, the information coming from the field or from customers may be skewed, unimportant, or simply unknown until there is a major failure. It becomes critical to determine which data is best and which should be believed and acted upon.

Also, information does not come free. There is always a cost and a benefit to good information. The benefits, include better decisions, improved Op Ex systems, improved communications, enhanced problem solving, and more process ownership throughout the organization. Better information usually means more cost in terms of developing cost systems, buying machinery for obtaining the information, training people on how to gather and use the information, and developing systems for communicating the information so it can be used. As a rule of thumb, information is useful if the received value is higher than the cost to gather it.

TIME OUT

After an Op Ex initiative or project has been operating for a while, inertia may set in. Energy dissipates Easy pickings have been accomplished. Hard work sets in as results are harder to demonstrate. The steering committee may want to sharpen the Op Ex initiative mission. The entire organization may want to evaluate where the organization is in regards to Op Ex and where it wants to go.

QUANTUM IMPROVEMENT OBJECTIVES

- Respond to customer requests within 2 hours.
- Company and supplier wide electronic documentation.
- Six sigma Op Ex, 3.4 deficiency opportunities per million.
- Products tailored to cultural, demographic needs.
- On-line customer information.
- One-stop customer service.
- Dramatic reduction in staff, 20% or more per year.
- Reduce product development from three years to 2 years.

REASONS WHY OP EX INITIATIVES FAIL

Companies have unrealistic Op Ex vision, mission, objectives and plans:

- Companies don't link improvement to specific business result.
- Downsizing and reengineering sometimes conflict with Op Ex messages.
- Op Ex projects can result in conflicting messages.
- Companies and key personnel resist changes.
- Managers and employees are tired of new programs and become sarcastic.

- Companywide Op Ex becomes logistically difficult and removes the focus from daily operations.

- Sweeping redesign, transformation, and cultural changes can result in backlash.
- Focus is sometimes on eliminating symptoms instead of root causes.
- Op Ex tools, initiatives, ideas from other organizations are not adapted.
- Companies drift from one tool to another.
- Technical fix is applied instead of understanding the organizational process.

CHARACTERISTICS OF SUCCESSFUL OP EX INITIATIVES

If your spirits are low do something; if you have been doing something, do something different.
E. Hall

The last twenty years has seen a number of competitiveness cures being offered. When the cures don't offer instant results then faddism sets in. Faddism is the need for instant gratification when applying a new management or organizational theory. When the newest theory or cure doesn't instantly work, the organization goes on to the next.

A recent survey identified the following issues as being critical to an Op Ex initiative's success:

- **Op Ex strategy.** An Op Ex strategy integrated into the business strategy ensures Op Ex will be pursued.
- **Business threat.** Companies in danger of failing seem to be the most successful with operational management.
- **Organizational commitment.** Senior management and employee commitment also determine long term Op Ex success.

- **Op Ex planning**. An Op Ex plan for pursuing and implementing Op Ex lays out the road to success.
- **Progress.** If a company has been implementing Op Ex and employee involvement for years, it is less likely it will be dropped.

Factors that determine Op Ex success may not be under the direct control of the Op Ex manager. The Op Ex manager may have no direct influence on project objectives, budgets, approvals, authorization, direction, support, control, and implementation.

In some organizations, the Op Ex executive may be considered a technical resource, champion, facilitator, or team leader. The Op Ex manager may provide guidance, direction, and support for all projects from analysis through implementation. A major challenge for the Op Ex executive is finding creative ways for leveraging existing technologies and resources to support the organizational transformation, support the Op Ex initiative, assist suppliers, and support restructured processes.

Project success requires the efficient and effective control of four variables, people, work, resources, and time. By understanding the dynamics and interrelationships of the key variables, the Op Ex manager can better manage resources, balance time, and keep projects on course. Problems can be anticipated. New improvement projects can be launched with higher confidence of meeting schedules, budgets, and customer requirements.

OP EX PROJECTS TEAMS

The rapid rate of change in customer expectations and in competitive pressures has also created the need for new organizational structures for conducting business. Traditional hierarchical, bureaucratic structures have had to adapt to these massive changes.

The Op Ex approach to organizing, planning, implementing, and controlling work is relatively new. Op Ex is characterized by new methods of restructuring work, special management techniques, and new organizational structures. Op Ex teams thirty years ago were largely thought to work in Japanese organizations where there was a sense of community, common background, and homogeneity. Now, Op Ex teams are common in all organizations and industries including hospitals, schools, law firms, manufacturing, construction, defense, banking, food, and government. Op Ex teams are common in federal, state, and local governments.

The formation of a team involves both process and product. The process of team building includes selecting team members, building consensus, negotiating rules for the team, resolving conflicts, encouraging involvement, ensuring fairness, monitoring progress, providing direction, and reinforcing progress. The product of a team is its results. The team may have to solve an intractable problem, implement systems, or gain ISO 9001:2015 registration. The list goes on. Bottom line: the team has an objective - a measurable, deliverable which must be met.

NEXT CHAPTER

Some companies are encouraging each employee to be responsible for problem recognition, problem solving, and ultimately for improving their systems. Individuals as part of a Op Ex project team, work area, or department are responsible for the system. Teams are created as needed. For example, a team may be created for a special project or to solve a specific problem. The teams stay together as long as they are needed and then disband.

CHAPTER 12
OP EX PROJECTS

An Op Ex project can be divided into two segments, planning the project and implementing it. The project plan involves setting objectives, developing project milestones, developing a schedule, defining activities, and estimating costs. Project implementation involves directing people, communicating with stakeholders, ensuring budgets are developed, ensuring milestones are attained, and reporting progress to organizational stakeholders.

GETTING STARTED WITH A PROJECT

I am a great believer in luck. The harder I work the more of it I seem to have.
F. L. Emerson

There are many similarities between implementing an Op Ex initiative or pursuing a qualiy or lean project as indicated by the following steps:

- Select a project leader
- Understand constraints to project success
- Ensure process team or even individual is responsible for Op Ex
- Select location or site
- Select doable, important project
- Monitor project
- Measure, measure, and measure again
- Develop recognition systems

SELECT A PROJECT LEADER

As has been emphasized throughout this book, a leader has to step forward and proclaim the value of the Op Ex initiative. Sometimes, this is an act of faith. The leader bases his or her belief that Op Ex is necessary and that it works. The person puts his or her reputation on the line by steering the organization into a new direction or facilitating a transformation that is required for survival or competitiveness.

UNDERSTAND CONSTRAINTS TO PROJECT SUCCESS

"What if" scenarios look at hypothetical situations or contingencies. Scenarios outline what may occur in the near or far future. Scenarios also challenge status quo thinking and assumptions.

ENSURE PROCESS TEAM OR EVEN INDIVIDUAL IS RESPONSIBLE FOR OP EX

Team building and Op Ex require a long-term investment of commitment and resources. One approach is to focus on problems that are important to the organization or to a team. Team members are trained and are given the opportunity to work on their concerns. Teams and their members demonstrate they can change systems. Once this is accomplished, the team focuses on what concerns the organization or management. Actively engaged employees and teams developing process ownership takes time. With one success, the team focuses on a new project.

SELECT LOCATION OR SITE

The next decision is to find the best location to conduct the pilot. Candidate locations, processes, or functions are identified. Factors that often lead to success are enthusiasm and a can-do spirit. As well, site management and work teams should be totally supportive of the improvement project.

SELECT DOABLE, IMPORTANT PROJECT

While the following has been said before, it bears repeating. Select a project that is aligned, supports, and reinforces the business plans and goals of the organization. Sometimes, Op Ex tactics, objectives, and plans are isolated from the general business goals. The Op Ex project should be perceived as a critical component of and enabler of the overall business strategy.

There is no one factor that guarantees success. Success depends on a number of factors including environment, processes, culture, and a number of other factors. Usually, a successful pilot breeds further success.

MONITOR PROJECT

An Op Ex project should be continuously assessed. Continuous monitoring becomes a vehicle for sustaining long-term improvement. A project can be monitored by a project budget, schedule, plan, or other methods. The objective of a project is to meet and exceed customer requirements so internal customers may be surveyed.

MEASURE, MEASURE, AND MEASURE AGAIN

Op Ex success can be measured by a number of metrics. The basic metric is customer satisfaction. Objectives may be derived or determined by the customer, process owner or some other stakeholder. Common requirements or expectations of success include attaining process capability and control, increasing customer satisfaction, reducing time-to-market, and reducing costs. For example, process capability may be increased from 1.0 to 1.33 to 1.66 to 2.0 over several years. Or, unit product costs may be lowered 5% a year. Or, the organization may pursue stretch benchmarks involving lowering costs 20% a year, cutting product development time by 1/2 within two years, or improving customer satisfaction by 50% a year.

DEVELOP RECOGNITION SYSTEMS

Op Ex awards recognize and may award team or individual achievements. They serve similar purposes as external, customer-supplier Op Ex awards.

SUCCESSFUL PROJECTS

The orchestra as well as an athletic team are often used as a metaphor for management excellence. The orchestra is a group of individuals, each of whom has a unique talent and a distinct way of delivering it to a satisfied customer. Usually, each player is a superstar in his or her right. Each musician as an individual and an orchestra player adds value and pleasure to the theater goer.

The parallels to business excellence are strong. Each orchestra musician is chosen because of unique abilities and talents. The musician must pass an audition based on talent and ability. Once the musician is chosen, the musician must practice, rehearse, and continue to build upon his or her abilities.

The orchestra is composed of different instruments and sections. These are similar to any business or factory with its functional groups, professionals, processes, and teams. The goal of each musical section, whether it is woodwinds, strings, or brass is to be consistent but also blend with other musical sections. Each professional may also add his or her own interpretation to the music.

The orchestra conductor is more often a team leader and coach than an authoritarian manager. The conductor leads a group of professionals who are proficient with their instruments and know their capabilities. The role of the modern conductor is to interpret the musical score and to shape the orchestra's sound so it pleases the audience. The conductor leads by interpretation, example, and strength of personality rather than by edict.[61]

WHAT MAKES A SUCCESSFUL CONTINUOUS IMPROVEMENT AND OP EX PROJECT

The list of variables that make a successful improvement project would fill a book, so instead we're only going to list the most critical:

- Understand customer and other stakeholder requirements.
- Select capable team leader/facilitator.
- Recruit capable team members.
- Develop commitment, sense of mission and vision.
- Plan, plan and plan again.
- Understand team authority and responsibilities.
- Develop good relationship with line operations.

- Share information and decision making among team members.
- Secure appropriate resources for success.
- Attempt to develop consensus.
- Develop doable and realistic timelines.
- Expect the unexpected.
- Develop contingency plans.
- Train everyone in Op Ex tools and technologies.
- Establish Op Ex and performance metrics for team.
- Develop customer-friendly deliverables.
- Meet deadlines, budgets, etc.
- Provide home for team members.
- Develop plans for conflict resolution.
- Have fun.

PROJECT TEAM STAKEHOLDERS

Jeffrey Pinto and O.P. Kharbanda in **Successful Project Managers** identified the following project stakeholders:

- **Top management.** Senior management authorizes a project, provides resources, and supports it throughout its lifecycle.
- **Accountant.** The project cost accountant ensures costs and budgets are monitored and controlled.
- **Functional managers.** Op Ex projects may be staffed by people who are on temporary assignment from a line position. Operations may be disrupted. People may have to work longer hours. Or more often, team members may be doing two jobs simultaneously. So, functional managers should fully endorse the purpose and direction of the project.
- **Project team members.** Project team members want the project to achieve its objectives.
- **Clients.** Clients or customers want the project completed as quickly, effectively, and successfully as possible.

- **Competitors.** Competitors may be external or internal to the organization. A competitor's project team may be developing a similar product and first-to-market becomes a competitive battle. Or, a competitor may be a team in the organization pursuing similar objectives such as improving customer satisfaction or achieving ISO 9001:2015 registration.
- **Suppliers.** Suppliers provide resources, raw materials, or equipment to a project team. The success of the project ensures suppliers received more orders.
- **Intervenor groups.** Intervenor groups include political, regulatory, environmental, social and consumer groups that can affect a project's development and completion.

ROLE OF THE STEERING COMMITTEE

Let our advance worrying become advance thinking and planning.
Sir Winston Churchill

In a large company, each level of the organization may have different steering committees. For example there may be a corporate steering committee, as well as business unit, divisional, plant, and worksite Op Ex committees. Corporate, business unit, and division Op Ex steering committees basically focus on organizational issues including culture, ethics, policies, vision, and mission. For example, the corporate Op Ex steering committee may:

- Identify customer requirements and expectations.
- Communicate and operationalize these into the organization.
- Develop the Op Ex vision for the organization.
- Develop Op Ex policies.
- Select Op Ex function management.
- Identify Op Ex goals for the organization.
- Identify critical Op Ex objectives.
- Establish continuous improvement committees throughout organization.

- Identify organizational requirements to achieve Op Ex objectives.
- Approve and authorize resources.
- Monitor progress.
- Eliminate organizational roadblocks.
- Take actions on problems or disputes.
- Coach and counsel senior managers on Op Ex.

Plant level steering committees have similar objectives as the corporate steering committee. Often, the focus and scope of the plant level committee is tactical and specific. For example, a plant level committee may focus on targeted improvement projects. As well, the plant committee may:

- Monitor Op Ex systems and process.
- Test products.
- Monitor internal customer satisfaction.
- Identify specific process and system parameters for improvement.
- Ensure process control and capability.
- Ensure documentation is accurate, up to date, and followed.
- Establish performance improvement teams.
- Provide training.
- Plan and implement Op Ex projects.

PROJECT PLANNING

Planning is probably the most critical activity in an Op Ex, continuous improvement, Lean, or other team-oriented project. The team is working under great pressure in a tightly defined time schedule and budget constraint. The team leader or members are expected to develop a number of plans, including cost sheets, PERT charts, critical path chart, Gantt charts, and work activities chart. The methods and techniques of project planning are complex and the following is an excellent resource for further review, Harold Kerzner's **Project Management: A Systems Approach to Planning, Scheduling, and Controlling.**

Project planning consumes large amounts of time. A proper plan ensures there is a higher likelihood that the proper path will be followed, resources will be optimized, stakeholders will be satisfied, and timelines will be met. As well, proper planning minimizes the risks of going in the wrong direction, not having sufficient resources, and eliminating potential problems.

PLANNING SKILLS

An Op Ex project requires extensive planning first among the project stakeholders and then among the team members who are brought together to discuss their expectations and requirements.

In organizations with highly developed Op Ex initiatives, Op Ex planning is a high priority and is almost as critical as budgeting. Internal customer groups want to know:

- What Op Ex initiative or project is contemplated?
- How will the Op Ex initiative work?
- What resources are required?
- Will operations be disrupted?
- What are the benefits of the project?
- When will it be implemented?
- How much will it cost and who will pay for it

PROJECT TEAM STAKEHOLDERS

Jeffrey Pinto and O.P. Kharbanda in **Successful Project Managers** identified the following project stakeholders:

- **Top management.** Senior management authorizes a project, provides resources, and supports it throughout its lifecycle.
- **Accountant.** The project cost accountant ensures costs and budgets are monitored and controlled.
- **Functional managers.** Op Ex projects may be staffed by people who are on temporary assignment from a line position. Operations may be disrupted. People may have to work longer hours. Or more often, team members may be doing two jobs simultaneously. So, functional managers should fully endorse the purpose and direction of the project.
- **Project team members.** Project team members want the project to achieve its objectives.

- **Clients.** Clients or customers want the project completed as quickly, effectively, and successfully as possible.
- **Competitors.** Competitors may be external or internal to the organization. A competitor's project team may be developing a similar product and first-to-market becomes a competitive battle. Or, a competitor may be a team in the organization pursuing similar objectives such as improving customer satisfaction or achieving ISO 9001:2015 registration.
- **Suppliers.** Suppliers provide resources, raw materials, or equipment to a project team. The success of the project ensures suppliers received more orders.
- **Intervenor groups.** Intervenor groups include political, regulatory, environmental, social and consumer groups that can affect a project's development and completion.

OVER PLANNING AND POOR SCOPE DEFINITION

On the down side, an Op Ex manager can over plan. Planning may become an end unto itself. Elaborate plans are constructed but no work is accomplished. The plan is written into stone and it cannot be changed. Plans by their very nature should be elastic. They should reflect circumstances and change accordingly.

Project creep is an expression that describes the natural process of growing or changing expectations during the life of the project. Project creep results when initial customer requirements and project scope were defined poorly.

Project creep can result in budget overruns, poor direction, loss of control, and inevitably dissatisfied customers. Project scope should be well defined during upfront planning, for example before a supplier signs a customer's contract.

Project creep can be eliminated by developing a project scope document, a memo of understanding, or similar document between the customer and project team. The team can develop the memo or its leader/facilitator can.

The memo of understanding basically spells out who does what, how and when using what resources.

Self-managed or directed work teams bring their own planning challenges. Self-directed work teams are responsible for an operational area and may be responsible for a specific project. The team may be responsible for formulating the project, breaking it into manageable tasks, selecting a leader, planning its direction, requesting resources, keeping it on track, and completing it on time.

OP EX PROJECTS

Project improvement may be a one-time effort to solve a specific problem or it may become operationalized as a normal part of daily improvement efforts. Examples of Op Ex projects include:

- **Poor Customer Service.** A customer service complaint may be solved by offering counseling to a customer service representative. If there is a pattern of complaints, the solution may require extensive training of all customer service personnel.
- **Operational problem solving.** Operational problem solving is often an ongoing effort to define operational targets and to ensure consistency around the targets.
- **Improving process capability.** Capability in a machine production environment is the ability to meet product specifications. Minimizing variation at the target implies the process is improving.
- **Plant ISO 9001:2015 registration.** ISO 9001:2015 is a long-term project involving many elements of the organization. Registration may take up to two years and then require ongoing monitoring to ensure continued registration. A companywide ISO 9001:2015 effort would probably be classified as an initiative.

Permanent or Temporary Team

The process improvement team may be temporary or permanent. The permanent team is usually the process owner responsible for redesigning, stabilizing, and improving the process. In this team, membership is voluntary, open to all, and involves all members. The team may deal with supervisory

CRITICAL PROJECT SUCCESS FACTORS

Project Stage	Critical Success Factors
Formation	Personal ambition
	Senior management support
	Team motivation
	Clear objectives
	Technological advantage
Buildup	Team motivation
	Personal motivation
	Senior management support
	Technical expertise
Main phase	Team motivation
	Personal motivation
	Client/customer support
	Senior management support
Close -out	Personal motivation
	Team motivation
	Senior management support
	Financial support[62]

and managerial issues such as planning, organizing, delegating, monitoring and improving the process.

The permanent Op Ex team offers several benefits. Its members intimately know the process and its problems. The team members have a vested interest to make their work area safer and easier. Communications and coordination are enhanced. Problems get solved much quicker and more effectively than if a team were organized every time there was a problem. Everyone believes and feels there is a sense of ownership. It frees up supervisors to deal with systemic issues.

SUCCESS TIPS FOR OP EX PROJECTS

The following are tips for ensuring Op Ex project success:

- Identify customers and focus on their requirements.
- Define work as a process to be managed and improved.
- Define vision, mission, strategies, and plans.
- Develop mission statement for the project.
- Break project into subsystems and sub projects.
- Establish accountability for subsystems.
- Provide sufficient resources for success.
- Plan the project using PERT, GANTT, CPM charts.
- Monitor project and intervene when required.
- Provide technical assistance.
- Provide recognition and visibility.
- Define value added processes.
- Maintain flexibility.
- Create organizational and stakeholder consensus.
- Be inclusive, not exclusive in Op Ex initiatives.
- Measure everything of value and provide timely feedback.
- Make metrics simple, relevant, and understandable.
- Display measures.
- Redesign the organization around processes.
- Stabilize and ensure process capability.
- Maintain enthusiasm.

PROJECT BY PROJECT SUCCESS

You can't stand still.
Proverb

There is no single, perfect all-encompassing model for operational management. What should the Op Ex manager do? Op Ex managers should adopt and adapt an Op Ex model based on an approach that works well for the organization.

Op Ex projects until recently were approved based on vague promises of benefits. In these days of constrained benefits, an improvement project is evaluated as any other project that must compete for finite corporate resources.

An improvement project is characterized by:

- **Specific objective.** A specific Op Ex objective such as reducing nonconformances by 50%.
- **Specific start date.** The implementation project starts at an established time.
- **Defined or open end date.** The project may end when the goal has been achieved or when all resources have been consumed. Or, implement projects may become an ongoing process of continuous improvement.
- **Resources.** Resources, such as equipment and monies are required to complete the project.
- **Skills.** People or teams must have the skills to complete the project successfully.

USING DOCUMENTATION TO PROCEDURALIZE OPERATIONS

We think in generalities, but we live in detail.
Alfred North Whitehead

Op Ex documentation and specifically procedures should be developed to make operations more efficient and effective. Op Ex documentation can help to make operations, processes, and systems more consistent by ensuring that:

- Customer requirements are understood and defined.
- Customer requirements are internalized into the company.
- Critical product attributes are identified.
- Critical process parameters are identified.
- Processes are in control, capable, and improving.

- Operational methods are consistent and documented.
- Operators are trained in these methods.
- Operations and systems are monitored and audited.
- Deviations are symptom and root cause corrected.

The purpose of proceduralizing operations, developing consistent procedures and work instructions, is to reduce variation. Variation causes unstable operations. The secret of Op Ex is to maintain consistency and uniformity at specific targets. The basic function of a policy and procedure is to outline boundaries of acceptable and preferred behavior.

OP EX DOCUMENT ADMINISTRATION

Department and business unit heads are responsible for administering and ensuring Op Ex policies and procedures are consistently followed. The Op Ex director is responsible for coordinating with the corporate steering committee the development and deployment of Op Ex policies. The Op Ex representative will ensure the manual, procedures, and work instructions are current, complete, and accurate.

The Op Ex representative may be responsible for calling meetings, assigning drafting responsibilities, auditing Op Ex documentation, and revising documentation. Functional representatives are responsible for attending committee meetings, auditing documentation, communicating changes to respective departments, evaluating revisions, and apprising departments of changes, revisions, and additions.

Op Ex manuals are assigned to positions and may even be registered to manual holders. Manual holders are required to maintain assigned and current copies of Op Ex documentation. The holders will insert new pages when they are received and destroy superseded material. All manuals remain on company property and are not for distribution. Holders are expected to return assigned copies upon request, terminating employment, or transfer.

PROCEDURALIZATION WITHOUT INHIBITING INITIATIVE

Proceduralizing doesn't mean developing and living with stultifying work rules or procedures. Procedures should be developed to make an organization free to innovate and experiment.

Standards, procedures, and controls don't work as well in areas where creativity, innovation, and freedom are perceived as paramount such as in Sales, Engineering, and Research/Development. The issue is how to communicate that proceduralization and consistency are beneficial to them? The following are useful suggestions:

- Emphasize design Op Ex is what customers say it is.
- Discuss how their design affects safety or environmental Op Ex.
- Have customers work directly with engineers.
- Provide creative people training in operational management.[63]

However, there is a downside. The process focus may become an end in itself. Assumptions are created about what is the optimal process. Anything outside this process focus is considered heresy because it can cause unwarranted variation. A "if it ain't broke, don't fix it" mentality can set in which no one wants. Process owners won't want to analyze whether process steps are even necessary which is a fundamental question of reengineering. At the extreme, status quo thinking may discourage new ideas, testing of new assumptions, reexamining processes for value-adding opportunities, or engaging in breakthrough thinking.

OP EX PROCEDURES OBJECTIVES

- Communicate Op Ex requirements.
- Control and document key Op Ex practices.
- Train employees in Op Ex requirements.
- Indicate compliance to requirements.
- Illustrate how the company handles personnel training, engineering design changes, and other important operational information.
- Establish a reference manual of approved, standardized, and accepted procedures and practices.

- Maintain uniform and proceduralized practices.
- Indicate how to maintain capable and stabilized processes.
- Serve as a model for continuous improvement.
- Define methods and requirements for training.
- Indicate continued compliance with standards.

SOFTWARE DESIGN

To minimize software design errors, a system designer can:

- **Flowchart a program.** Flowcharts illustrate the structure of the program. Flowcharting visually shows the logic path of the program. If a program does not do what the user wants, then a programmer can follow the logic path and isolate the cause of the problem.
- **Chunk the program into manageable units.** Logic errors can be eliminated by breaking large programs into manageable chunks. Each chunk, like a link in a chain, is connected to the larger program. A software programmer tries to minimize logic errors by consistently and systematically checking and testing the program at each link.
- **Use a common language.** Commercial contractors and governmental agencies are requiring contractors to use standardized computer languages.
- **Prototype software.** Prototyping software is becoming another popular technique because it allows customers to try out and evaluate a mockup software program before a final program is written. The system considers how different users interface and respond to the system. Software design is becoming more people and user focused. By working closely with their internal customers and by quickly implementing customer feedback, software programmers can incrementally generate software that meets customer's requirements.

SOFTWARE ERRORS

Computer systems can be flawed because of poor reliability, safety, security, and privacy. These flaws can affect national security to product quality. The following are common causes of software errors:

- **Management.** Software errors may be technical problems that are caused by poor project planning. If the project scope is poorly conceived or changed in mid-stream, software may have to be totally rewritten.
- **Heightened expectations.** Specification creep is the tendency for software users to require software contractors to tighten up on specifications, forcing the programmer to rewrite the software. Software users may change their minds. As a user becomes more familiar with the problem, the user finds he or she wants something additional. The user may want information faster, presented in a special format, or sent to different locations.
- **Programming Errors.** A large program includes thousands or millions of lines of instructions or code. An error in any line of code can cause cascading errors in the rest of the program. Other errors include typing mistakes and misplaced digits.

OP EX INITIATIVE SUCCESS FACTORS

The following is a list of factors to consider when starting a company-wide Op Ex initiative:

- Understand management and stakeholder expectations.
- Identify and satisfy hot buttons.
- Develop sense of urgency.
- Select Op Ex leadership.
- Focus Op Ex initiative on improving business objectives.
- Remember organizational culture.
- Develop Op Ex infrastructure.
- Establish teams.
- Look for opportunities.
- Manage by fact.

- Adopt and adapt.
- Create synergies.
- Prioritize elements of the initiative.
- Kickstart faltering initiative.
- Fight shortsightedness.

UNDERSTAND MANAGEMENT AND STAKEHOLDER EXPECTATIONS

The first step in an Op Ex initiative should be successful. Senior management has expectations of the Op Ex initiative. These expectations should be understood, written, and preferably exceeded. It is critical the first pilots are successful and cost-effective.

IDENTIFY AND SATISFY HOT BUTTONS

If Op Ex is to be integrated in the organization, it must be meaningful to senior management, middle management, first level supervision, and work area. Operational management should recognize and deliver the wins, the hot buttons, of each stakeholder group. Each stakeholder may have a different hot button. Senior management may want to focus on customer satisfaction or profitability. Middle management may want to develop value-adding processes. First level supervision may want stable and controlled processes. Line employees may want freedom to make decisions and a safe work environment.

DEVELOP SENSE OF URGENCY

The level of urgency may determine if a company wide initiative or a localized pilot is pursued. For example, if a customer requires ISO 9001:2015 registration of all plants, then all sites of the company may have to pursue registration simultaneously.

SELECT OP EX LEADERSHIP

Op Ex leadership and support personnel may have to be recruited if an Op Ex initiative is new. The manager needs strong communication and leadership skills. As well, the manager may need operational experience, business exposure, and team building skills.

FOCUS OP EX INITIATIVE ON IMPROVING BUSINESS OBJECTIVES

The Op Ex initiative or improvement project should be integrated into the organization's strategic goals, objectives, and plans. A challenge in some companies is that Op Ex is separated from the strategic and tactical goals of the organization. At a tactical or work area level, Op Ex activities may become disconnected. Op Ex should have a synergistic effect on the organization. One success should breed other successes in the ongoing improvement journey.

REMEMBER ORGANIZATIONAL CULTURE

Culture change or transformation should unite the efforts of all employees and stakeholders in the pursuit of a common goal. It may be difficult for all employees to embrace a new philosophy unless each person realizes how he or she is affected and what's in it for him or her. Self and team empowerment are a powerful win for employees. If responsibility and authority can be shared through teamwork, then everyone's quality of work life should be enhanced.

DEVELOP OP EX INFRASTRUCTURE

Normally, when one considers infrastructure, bridges, roads, power, water, and other utilities come to mind. Without infrastructure, companies can't do business. There are no roads to distribute materials. There is no power to drive machinery. There is no water to sustain development.

In much the same way, a company needs an Op Ex infrastructure to implement an Op Ex transformation. An Op Ex infrastructure includes Op Ex standards, Op Ex policies, procedures and work instructions, favorable corporate climate, training, systems, and senior management commitment.

ESTABLISH TEAMS

The Op Ex transformation or improvement approach to organizing, planning, implementing, and controlling work is relatively new. Op Ex is characterized by new methods of restructuring work, special management techniques, and new roles. Op Ex teams, specifically Op Ex circles, twenty years ago were largely thought to work in Japanese organizations where there was a sense of community, common background, and homogeneity. Now Op Ex teams are common in all organizations and industries including hospitals, schools, law firms, manufacturing, construction, defense, banking, food, and government.

LOOK FOR OPPORTUNITIES

Operational managers and teams are only human when they focus on what is easy and positive. Looking for deficiencies or opportunities for improvement requires energy and resources. Some people take the path of least resistance and often accept chronic or systemic problems as a normal course of business. However, this is not the Op Ex way. The challenge of the Op Ex professional is to encourage operational teams and management to look for improvement opportunities and to act proactively.

MANAGE BY FACT

Sufficient and reliable information and data should be available to support intelligent decision making. Teams or operational management may make decisions based on anecdotal evidence. For example, chronic acceptance of what may seem like a minor problem may actually involve a major system deficiency. Hard data on sales, costs, capability, reliability, and customer satisfaction should be used to justify the initiative or project.

ADOPT AND ADAPT

One size Op Ex initiative does not fit all organizations. Companies adopt a particular Op Ex tool, methodology, or guru's ideas believing it can be used to make the organization more competitive or to stimulate organizational change. Management may adopt an idea based on a best-selling book or even based on a benchmarking study.

The problem is that adoption won't work unless there is adaptation. The particular technique must be tailored to the specific industry, company, plant, work area, process, and even team owners. Otherwise a new idea is adopted and is grafted onto the existing organization which may reject the imposition. The challenge, problem, deficiency, or inefficiency to the system should be understood.

CREATE SYNERGIES

A company may pursue multiple Op Ex related initiatives or projects such as ISO 9001:2015, self-management teams, reengineering, customer surveys, lean, JIT, and customer-supplier partnering. These initiatives are a little different but share the same goal, specifically to make the organization more efficient and effective. These initiatives may also be pursued as standalone projects and may not be integrated into a common purpose. Their messages are different. They also may be working at cross purposes. As much as possible, Op Ex initiatives or projects should be tied together at the top of the organization. Senior management should ensure messages, purposes, implementation, and metrics are consistent.

PRIORITIZE ELEMENTS OF THE INITIATIVE

Improvement projects should be prioritized. First, the big picture must be understood and scoped out. The big picture is the competition, customers, government regulators, risks, and business opportunities. A company also has strategic and tactical goals which may deal with cost reduction or reduced time-to-market cycle times.

The Op Ex initiative can be treated as interconnected projects and prioritized in terms of critical, major, and minor importance. They also can be categorized in terms of enhancing revenue, satisfying customers, containing risks, and complying with regulatory requirements.

KICKSTART FALTERING INITIATIVE

After starting an Op Ex initiative, the steering committee or operational management may discover that enthusiasm is beginning to flag. Energy is down. Inertia has set in. Results are harder to come by. The Op Ex initiative has to be refocused and reaffirmed. The corporate Op Ex steering committee may have to redefine Op Ex goals, reset priorities, reallocate resources, and establish overall goals again.

This may involve a minor tweaking of the system or may require major adjustments. The impact may be major but shouldn't be so severe that there is culture shock or organizational arrest. Several actions may be required, including reexamining and rewriting a company's vision, missions, and plans; new structures, such as teams, new management; new policies, procedures, and instructions; or new forms of communication.

FIGHT SHORTSIGHTEDNESS

Problems and challenges occur so frequently in business that managers and employees want instant solutions. Deming called this the "instant pudding" syndrome. Many Op Ex problems are chronic, systemic, or intractable. Quick fixes often don't work. The same problem resurfaces again or in some other form. People may believe that the problem was fixed or can be fixed. Management and employees become cynical about the entire process.

OP EX INITIATIVES

An Op Ex initiative is often company and supplier wide. Pursuing the Baldrige award or ISO 9001:2015 registration are examples of company-wide Op Ex initiatives. These require full Op Ex commitment from senior and middle management as well as the investment of substantial resources. Or, an Op Ex initiative can be based on linked Op Ex projects where each successful project paves the way and justifies the next. The first approach is often radical and transformational. The second is isolated and incremental. Both have their benefits.

What characterizes a company and supplier wide Op Ex initiative? The following are some indicators:

- Initiative involves multiple business units and plants.
- Initiative Op Ex requirements may extend into supplier base.
- Initiative may never end or large project may take a year or longer.
- Full time personnel are dedicated to the initiative or project.
- Monies, equipment, and other expensive resources are also dedicated.

- Activity may vary, from very intense to routine.
- Senior management is often the sponsor.
- Training and other full-time facilitation is required.
- Front end planning is critical.
- Communications to all stakeholders is critical.

On the other hand, a focused and successful Op Ex project will often lead to other improvement projects. One success leads to other successes. An Op Ex project is characterized by four common dimensions:

- Project is constrained by specified budget and time frame for completion.
- Project is composed of complex and interrelated activities that must be coordinated.
- Project has a clear, attainable goal.
- Each project is unique.

From the perspective of the Op Ex function, a company and supplier wide initiative is often preferred over a project by project approach because it provides:

- First step in the continuous improvement journey.
- High visibility.
- Promotional opportunities to Op Ex personnel.
- Senior management Op Ex commitment.
- Benefits of improved operations, increased customer satisfaction, etc.
- More responsibility and authority.
- Proof of the value of Op Ex.
- Enhanced teamwork.

The downside of a companywide Op Ex initiative includes:

- Failure is highly visible.
- Daily operations may be disrupted.
- Costs are high.

- Resources have to allocated or diverted.
- People work long hours.
- Frustration and tensions grow.
- Communications to all stakeholders requires more time.
- Op Ex systems and procedures have to be developed.

OP EX ATTRIBUTES

Always define your terms.
Eric Partridge

These dimensions of Op Ex can be considered product or service attributes. Sometimes, a product attribute becomes synonymous with quality initiative that evolve into operational excellence. Some of the above quality attributes are measurable and some are imprecise. For example, a quality product attribute, like aesthetics, may not be measurable. On the other hand, performance is probably measurable.

David Garvin, a professor at Harvard Business School, recognized the problem of multiple definitions and identified eight dimensions or categories of quality, which is an important element of operational excellence. The list has been revised into the following nine categories:

- Performance
- Reliability
- Conformance
- Usability
- Maintainability
- Customer service
- Aesthetics
- Environmental
- Software quality[64]

PERFORMANCE

Performance is the ability of a product to operate up to the expectations of the user. Performance is measured differently in different products. In an automobile, performance includes acceleration, braking, and handling ability and in a pair of running shoes, it includes comfort, style, durability, and weight.

Performance is a user-based definition, which means that an automobile can satisfy different expectations of different users. For example, a race car driver expects a different level of performance from an Indy Ford compared to a Ford Escort.

Suppliers also are expected to improve a product's performance, packaging, reliability, and maintainability. Improvement may vary based on the type of product, such as whether it is an industrial or consumer product. Let us look at a computer. Performance of a personal computer may be enhanced by making it operate faster and transmit more information. Packaging can be improved by making it more aesthetic, easier to operate (user friendly), lightweight, and more compact.

RELIABILITY

Reliability is long-term operational excellence and is the probability of a product failing after a specified period of time under certain operating conditions. In other words, reliability measures the likelihood that a product or assembly will work over time. Reliability is both a user-based and a conformance-based attribute of quality or operational excellence. For example, if a customer buys a lamp with an one year warranty, the customer expects it to last at least one year. Otherwise, the customer will return it for repair, refund, or replacement. The lamp manufacturer knows this and does not want to spend much money replacing defective lamps. Therefore, the lamp is designed and manufactured to last at least one year.

Reliability is measured in terms of mean-time-between-failure (MTBF) or mean-time-to-first failure (MTFF). MTBF is the average time it takes a product to fail between two successive failures. MTFF is the average time it takes a product to fail based on the first time it is put into service. For example, automobile manufacturers know what parts of an automobile will likely fail, so they suggest checking and replacing parts based on a preventive maintenance schedule.

CONFORMANCE

Conformance is the ability of a product to comply with a specification, standard, or design. There are thousands of standards that specify how a product should be designed, built, tested, installed, stored, maintained, and repaired. For example, a screw is a simple fastener that holds one part onto another. A screw specification may designate height, width, thread taper, threads per inch, material, and material strength.

Conformance is an engineering or manufacturing definition of operational excellence, because it is related to a feature of a product that can be measured. Conformance is measured in terms of defects rates or levels. For example, a specification for a screw may state that a certain type of screw should have 11 threads per inch and should be made of soft steel. If a screw randomly selected and inspected from a lot has 12 threads per inch and is made of stainless steel, then the screw has two nonconformances. These are defects, even though the screw has more threads per inch and is made of a stronger material than required by the specification.

USABILITY

Usability is a key product attribute. A product may have all the technical bells and whistles, but it should be user friendly. All of us have been frustrated in trying to use software that simply doesn't work. The reasons may be technical incompatibility, poor documentation, user inability, or a number of other reasons. One company that has tested hundreds of software products uncovered many quality blunders, including excessive technical jargon, overuse of icons, over reliance on training to overcome poor software design, cryptic error messages, and poorly conceived help systems.[65]

MAINTAINABILITY

Maintainability is the same as serviceability. It is the ability of a defective product to be repaired easily, quickly, and economically. For example, if an automotive water pump fails, it has to be replaced. But first, the automotive equipment in the way of the water pump has to be removed. Since the compact car was designed to be light, the area under the hood is tight and everything is squeezed into a small space. This decreases automobile weight and also decreases serviceability because the automobile is harder to work on.

This quality attribute is both a conformance- and user- based definition. In an engineering sense, maintainability can be measured. A common measurement is mean-time-to-repair (MTTR), which is the average time it takes to repair a defective water pump or service a customer. In a user-based sense, maintainability reflects how the customer feels about replacing the defective unit. Was it easy to replace? Did the person get bruised knuckles? Could it be done quickly? Or, if a serviceman at a repair station performed the work, was the service courteous, fast, and economical?

CUSTOMER SERVICE

Customer service is an important quality attribute used to encourage repeat sales. Therefore, companies design products that can be serviced easily and safely. And companies are providing faster turnaround service to repair defective products. For example, Caterpillar Tractor promises it will deliver repair parts anywhere in the world within 48 hours and Mercedes guarantees 24-hour service in California and Arizona.[66]

AESTHETICS

Aesthetics consist of the intangible attributes of quality and operational excellence: how a product looks, feels, sounds, tastes, or smells. Obviously, aesthetics is subjective, but they are a very important user-based attribute of operational excellence.

Many people buy a car not based on measurable, technical features of conformance or reliability, but on their perceptions of quality, fit, and finish of the vehicle. People are often more concerned about the "fit and finish" of an automobile than the technology inside, such as a new turbocharger. Or, they buy based on current and faddish styling standards. The same can be said for a number of other major consumer purchases, such as in apparel and fashion industries.

ENVIRONMENTAL

Environmental groups and regulatory authorities are important stakeholders in the Op Ex process. Many perceive that resources are being used and abused. The world's environment is changing radically as indicated through the ozone depletion, unbreathable air in American cities, toxic waste sites, and the list goes on.

Businesses are now listening as a result of the Valdez oil spill, Three Mile Island, and other environmental disasters. Environmental concerns go well beyond being better corporate citizens, companies want to improve their public-customer perceptions as well as limit their legal exposure. Compliance to regulations is becoming more proactive to prevent environmental degradation. How is this done? Companies are designing highly reliable and maintainable products. Packaging uses recycled materials. Products can be disposed cleanly and easily.

Environmental issues are also becoming more critical in determining overall project or product costs. Companies are beginning to implement Op Ex processes to improve environmental conditions. In many companies environmental issues were once the responsibility of environmental compliance specialists who were often inspection and correction oriented. Now, prevention planning, periodic auditing, and people involvement are being emphasized.

More importantly a philosophy, the quality of global life, is emerging. Articulate and fervent believers maintain the world is a finite resource which is constrained by real limits to growth. Another new philosophy is sustainable development. Assertive governments are developing mandates to improve business environmental performance. ISO is developing a series of environmental management standards, called the ISO 14000 series.

SOFTWARE QUALITY

Software specifications are an integral part of all management information systems. Software specifications are different than other specifications. But software quality, just like any tangible product, must satisfy user's requirements, comply with relevant standards, be cost-effective, and be measurable. For example, software quality must also be interoperable, intraoperable and exhibit a number of other product characteristics.

NEXT CHAPTER

In the next chapter, Op Ex Standards is discussed. Standards provide consistency. Consistency is a powerful Op Ex concept. Consistency implies that operations are running normally. Processes have been stabilized and in control. Procedures outline suggested and correct methods of operation. Employees are trained in operations. Customer requirements have been identified and are capable of being met. Equipment is properly calibrated. These concepts can be applied to almost any industry or practice. For example, hospitals can identify patient requirements and development consist patient care practices.

CHAPTER 13
OP EX STANDARDS

Organizational transformation is a daily operational challenge to companies with obsolete or obsolescent systems and structures such as vertical organizations, command and control decision making, outmoded processes, non-value adding systems, untrained personnel. dated policies, stagnant procedures, and outmoded work instructions. At a basic operational level, many end-to-end operations or processes are slow, clumsy, overly documented, redundant, and non-value adding.

ISO 9001:2015 AS A TRANSFORMATIONAL TOOL

Whoever stops creating today is dead the day before yesterday.
Nicolas Reisini

There is no one size fits all, success organizational transformation blueprint. Success can't be prescribed. As one pundit said: "If success could be cookie cutterd and if it were easy, everyone would do it." The solution is to understand the challenge and to use a menu of change methods in small areas to find the most successful one.

First, the change agent must understand the workings of the organization, its policies, culture, stakeholders, industry, and competitive environment. As well, the change agent has to see each change tool objectively. In the past, Op Ex gurus, disciples and acolytes would fight each other. Various change methods include reengineering, continuous improvement, process control, and proceduralization. For example, there is a big difference between a reengineering approach and a Deming approach, especially in terms of fear. Deming abhorred the use of fear and reengineering proponents use fear to bust the status quo. Each approach has its value, but the change agent has to tailor the approach to the needs of the organization. The appropriate change method and its implementation must be optimized for success.

ISO 9001:2015

ISO 9001:2015 proceduralization process has evolved into one of the most common and accepted transformational methods. There are several reasons for this. ISO 9001:2015 is less threatening than using the Malcolm Baldrige criteria. ISO 9001:2015 is international and promotes global Op Ex . ISO 9001:2015 is easy and doable. ISO 9001:2015 promotes Op Ex system consistency and uniformity. Finally, ISO 9001:2015 bridges the technical and the social systems in an approachable method that the biggest or smallest company can implement.

As a transformational tool, ISO 9001:2015 encourages consistency and proceduralization. ISO 9001:2015 is basically documentation intensive. As discussed, ISO 9001:2015 used to require certified companies have a quality policy manual and preferably Op Ex system procedures and work instructions. To promote consistency, the documentation details how an organization followed the precepts of "do what you say, say what you do" and "plan what you do and do what you plan."

Proceduralization is the process of ensuring critical systems are uniform and consistent. Proceduralization is much more than documentation, such as policies, procedures, and work instructions. Proceduralization encompasses the whole gamut of organizational activities. Proceduralization means processes are stabilized and are capable of meeting requirements. Proceduralizing also eliminates waiting times and waste. Proceduralization can enhance the quality of work life as well as enhance safety, the social environment, and physical environment.

Proceduralizing may involve training, documentation, or statistical controls. The most critical question in proceduralization is to ask: "Is this policy, standard, procedure, or pacification really needed and why?" The document should add value to the organization in terms of specifying quality,

AUDIT PROCEDURE
Purpose

Op Ex audits are periodically conducted to determine the efficiency and effectiveness of the organization's Op Ex activities.

Scope
This procedure applies to the all internal functions and business units.

Procedure
The quality or Op Ex is responsible for conducting the audit. Departmental managers must authorize the audit. The auditee is notified of the pending audit within two weeks. Audit supervisor or manager reviews and approves the audit plan. Op Ex audit follows three elements:

1. Planning
2. Conducting
3. Reporting

Auditor is responsible for developing audit plan. The audit plan details how the audit is conducted. The plan incorporates the following:

1. Customer/client
2. Auditor's name
3. Auditee's area and name
4. Program/project name
5. ISO 9001:2015 quality system requirement elements
6. Audit date
7. Audit plan/Course of action
8. Reporting procedure

improving efficiency, or complying with regulatory requirements. For example, a work instruction is a critical document. All organizational employees must know how their jobs affect and enhance the total satisfaction of internal customer as well as how their efforts relate to final customer satisfaction. Excess paperwork that does not relate to Op Ex or to customer satisfaction should not be developed.

The Op Ex audit seeks to determine compliance with the appropriate ISO 9001:2015 requirement. The auditor ensures Op Ex documents satisfy ISO 9001:2015 requirements. First, the Op Ex manual is reviewed for compliance. Business unit or functional area procedures and work instructions are evaluated to determine if work is performed according to documentation. The auditor may conduct the following tests:

- Compare work against work instructions.
- Test random production products to evaluate the effectiveness of test or production processes.
- Observe work methods to ensure they follow procedures.
- Analyze deviations or deficiencies to determine cause.
- Calculate stresses, reliability, or other Op Ex related problems.
- Inspect drawings, bills of material, or other technical documentation for accuracy, completeness, and understandability.

Auditor completes the operational assurance plan attached to this procedure. If deficiencies are discovered then they are reported in a corrective action request. Reports are completed within one week of conducting the audit. Quality audit reports are reviewed by the auditee and approved by audit supervision. If required, follow up audits may be conducted upon request.[67]

The quality audit seeks to determine compliance with the appropriate ISO 9001:2015 requirement. The auditor ensures Op Ex documents satisfy ISO 9001:2015 requirements. First, the Op Ex manual is reviewed for compliance. Business unit or functional area procedures and work instructions are evaluated to determine if work is performed according to documentation. The auditor may conduct the following tests:

- Compare work against work instructions.
- Test random production products to evaluate the effectiveness of test or production processes.
- Observe work methods to ensure they follow procedures.
- Analyze deviations or deficiencies to determine cause.
- Calculate stresses, reliability, or other Op Ex related problems.

ISO 9001:2015 INTERNAL AUDIT PROCEDURE
Purpose

Op Ex audits are periodically conducted to determine the efficiency and effectiveness of the organization's Op Ex activities.

Scope
This procedure applies to the all internal functions and business units.

Procedure
The Op Ex department is responsible for conducting the audit. Departmental managers must authorize the audit. The auditee is notified of the pending audit within two weeks. Audit supervisor or manager reviews and approves the audit plan. Op Ex audit follows three elements:

1. Planning
2. Conducting
3. Reporting

Auditor is responsible for developing audit plan. The audit plan details how the audit is conducted. The plan incorporates the following:

1. Customer/client
2. Auditor's name
3. Auditee's area and name
4. Program/project name
5. ISO 9001:2015 quality system requirement elements
6. Audit date
7. Audit plan/Course of action
8. Reporting procedure

- Inspect drawings, bills of material, or other technical documentation for accuracy, completeness, and understandability

Auditor completes the operational assurance plan attached to this procedure. If deficiencies are discovered then they are reported in a corrective action request. Reports are completed within one week of conducting the audit. Op Ex audit reports are reviewed by the auditee and approved by Audit supervision. If required, follow up audits may be conducted upon request.

OP EX DOCUMENTATION

Doing little things well is the way towards doing big things better.
Anonymous

Written Op Ex documentation can prevent variation, confusion, chaos, and litigation. Everyone wants to do a job right. But, the questions becomes "What is right?' Is right what the employee thinks? Is right what the supervisor believes? Is right what the customer wants or expects? A critical organizational objective is to define what is "right" through Op Ex policies and procedures.

Lack of, conflicting, or misunderstanding policies, procedures, and work instructions can result in a recall, excessive variation, contradictory practices and decisions.

NEED FOR OP EX DOCUMENTATION

Some organizations follow the credo that employees are capable of determining what is right and doing it. However, problems can arise. The person or team guided by instinct, good will, skills, and knowledge may do what it deems right or correct for the moment. But, trouble may develop if the person or team does not anticipate developments, understand upstream/downstream process requirements, or have insufficient background knowledge. Written, consensual Op Ex documentation should serve as the roadmap and milestone for Op Ex activities.

OP EX DOCUMENTATION CHALLENGES

If Op Ex policies exist, they should be used and adhered to. However, this may not be the case for several reasons:

- Policies may not have been distributed to all managers or operating groups.

- Teams may not be using them because they have not been updated.
- New employees have not been introduced to policies, procedures, or work instructions.
- In a diverse workplace, new employees may not be able to read or understand the procedures and work instructions.
- Policies have not been updated.
- Employees are not aware of the existence of work instructions.
- Op Ex policies may be contradictory.
- Departmental or workouts follow different practices than those spelled out in the Op Ex documentation.

OP EX MANUAL APPROVAL

Prior to issuing the Op Ex manual, documents should be reviewed by all affected and responsible parties to ensure clarity, accuracy, and suitability. Internal stakeholders, customers, and suppliers should have the opportunity to assess the usability of the document. Final release should be authorized by the management level responsible for its implementation. The Op Ex manual should be accessible to all internal parties. Proper distribution, control, approval, and issuance can be assured through serial copies of the documents.

Changes to the Op Ex manual are incorporated and controlled by the Op Ex department. The same review and approval process used in writing the Op Ex manual is also used when incorporating changes. In some cases, the Op Ex manual may contain sensitive information in which case it is clearly identified as a controlled copy.

The following are tips for developing an Op Ex manual:

- **Comprehensive.** The Op Ex manual addresses all the applicable Op Ex system requirements.
- **Understandable.** The Op Ex manual is written simply and directly so most employees understand and follow its policies.
- **Usable.** The manual can be used as an Op Ex guide.

- **Keep it short and simple.** As a rule, an Op Ex manual is 10 to 40 pages long and is tailored to an organization.
- **Select a template and follow it.** There are several acceptable formats for developing the Op Ex manual. There is no one best method. The important point is to follow a consistent format in terms of writing, words, Op Ex concepts, and clause numbering.
- **Make it appealing.** Op Ex manuals are sometimes used as sales documents with existing or prospective customers. If the Op Ex manual is to be used as a sales document, then it should be packaged appropriately in heavy glossary paper with perhaps 4-color pictures.
- **Make it grammatically correct.** Especially if this document is being used as a sales piece, the Op Ex manual should be grammatically correct.
- **Ensure there is a master copy.** A master copy of all Op Ex documentation should reside in the Op Ex Department. While the Op Ex manual won't change too often, Op Ex procedures, work instructions, drawings, bills of material, specifications may change often. A central clearing office ensures document changes are consistently incorporated into the document and the latest revisions are communicated to all document holders.
- **Ensure there is a one-to-one mapping between a standard and the Op Ex manual.** This is sometimes called an Op Ex manual assessment or desk audit. If the Op Ex manual is laid out like the required standard, the third party or second party auditor will have a much easier time understanding the auditee's Op Ex systems.
- **Understand external and internal stakeholder Op Ex system requirements.** An Op Ex manual should be developed that fits an organization and satisfies stakeholder requirements.
- **Tailor manual to an organization.** If an off-the-shelf manual is used, it should be tailored to the specific requirements and needs of the organization.
- **Revise and rewrite.** The Op Ex manual will require iterations until it is fully accepted and adopted. How many iterations are re

quired? It may require three or more iterations until it is fully accepted. The iterative development process is important for developing organizational buy-in.

- **Use Op Ex manual as the foundation Op Ex document.** All Op Ex documentation is tiered. At the top of the hierarchy is the Op Ex manual, then procedures, work instructions, and forms filling out the rest of the pyramid. Tie each level to the next if possible.
- **Ensure buy-in into the Op Ex manual.** The Op Ex manual is a companywide policy document.
- **Be clear, accurate, and comprehensive.** Everyone's goal is to have a clear and accurate Op Ex manual. However once the manual has been reviewed and revised, the document becomes dense reflecting everyone's requirements. Make sure there is one editor who incorporates everyone's comments. This person should maintain consistent language and style.
- **Develop an understandable and usable document.** The Op Ex manual is a companywide document. It should be understandable. Avoid fancy, awkward, complex, or unorthodox terms.
- **Use neutral language.** The language in Op Ex documentation is now gender neutral. Until a few years ago, it was common to say that "he" will do something. Now, the more common term is he/she or even better "person". Gender neutral language does not offend or discriminate.
- **Strive for a most length.** Op Ex policies should communicate the organization's position on an Op Ex topic. Op Ex procedures should communicate the proper method for implementing the policy. Op Ex work instructions should communicate how to perform a specific task. Op Ex forms should be usable by the entire organization.
- **Use the KISS principle.** KISS principle (keep it sweet and simple) applies to writing Op Ex documentation. Ideas are expressed best when they are concise, clear, and to the point. Over-precision can lead to confusion, limit creativity, or limit initiative.

OP EX MANUAL DEVELOPMENT

The Op Ex manual must fit the organization, its processes and products. It must be usable and satisfy the needs of the users. Senior management authorizes the development of the Op Ex manual. Senior management will usually assign the development and coordination to an individual or a group from one or more functional areas.

Op Ex policies should meet the needs of all departments and business units of the organization. What's the best way to develop Op Ex policies that represent the entire organization? One way is to set up a committee representing the functional areas or process owners. This ensures diverse views are heard and incorporated into the manual.

The committee should be large enough to represent all the major organizational areas. Usually, the Op Ex committee has representatives from Human Resources, Quality, Engineering, Manufacturing, Supply Management, and Sales. The development group follows a logical process in developing, preparing, and obtaining approvals of the documents. The development process consists of the following steps:

- Identify existing Op Ex system policies and procedures.
- Understand organizational requirements.
- Identify internal Op Ex systems that must comply with customer or other stakeholder requirements.
- Obtain information about the existing Op Ex systems from internal users.
- Develop and evaluate questionnaires on existing practices.
- Determine format and structure of the Op Ex manual.
- Classify existing Op Ex documents in terms of Op Ex compliance.
- Develop Op Ex policies and procedures required by statute or standard.

The actual development and writing of the Op Ex policies can be done by a coordination team, internal consultants, external consultants, or functional area employees. The coordination team ensures the manual's accuracy, completeness, and continuity.

OP EX MANUAL STRUCTURE

Situations are rarely ever black or white; they are usually varying shades of gray.
Professor Ray Brown

Op Ex documentation is often organized using several styles. The most common style is to follow a one-to-one correspondence with the numbering of an Op Ex standard, such as ISO 9001:2015/9002/9003.

LOWER LEVEL OR SITE OP EX MANUALS

The Op Ex policy manual applies to the entire organization. The manual is used by all business units, divisions, plants in a large organization. Op Ex procedural manuals can be specialized, tailored documents. They are division or plant specific because they detail procedures that may be different from business to business. Many companies are now structured along business lines. One business unit may be mining raw materials while another is processing these materials into ingots which may be machined by another business unit into finished products. Each business unit may be a separate business or plant designing or producing a separate product. Each has its own Op Ex manual.

HOW TO DEVELOP OP EX POLICIES AND PROCEDURES

ISO 9001:2015 and other customer-supplier requirements often mandate the development and implementation of documented operational systems, specifically an Op Ex manual comprised of an organization's Op Ex policies. In order to define and to develop a consistent Op Ex manual, an ISO technical committee developed a standard, ISO 10013 "Guidelines for Developing Quality Manuals." The purpose of this document is to establish a uniform structure for developing Op Ex manuals. It should be emphasized that these are general guidelines or recommendations for preparing and developing the Op Ex manual. They inevitably must be tailored to the specific needs of the user. Each major department in the organization should be included in developing Op Ex principles and policies. Whenever an operational or procedural change occurs, the committee determines if a policy revision is required. If the committee determines if a change is needed then the policy revision should go through a formal evaluation of review and approval. The committee reviews all updates and revisions to ensure there are no contradictions or inconsistencies in the documentation.

The Op Ex function or the policy committee should review the Op Ex documentation to ensure it is current. The policy manual is revised as needed. The manual should be thoroughly evaluated periodically to ensure it satisfies management intent and organizational stakeholder needs. Lower level documentation, procedures and work instructions, should be audited every six months or yearly.

THE ISO 9001:2015 REGISTRATION PROCESS

There is no one right way to pursue ISO 9001:2015 registration. Registration is a doable task for many companies if a team and project management approach is followed. Like managing any complex project, such as managing ISO 9001:2015 registration, senior management must understand and approve the project; resources must be gathered and channeled to the appropriate locations and tasks; and employees must see the benefits of the project.

The following are generalized steps for pursuing ISO 9001:2015 registration:

- **Step #1. Understand the ISO 9001:2015 registration environment.** ISO 9001:2015 registration is a global phenomenon. A company should understand what its competitors are doing, what its customers' want, and what regulatory authorities expect.
- **Step #2. Determine the benefits and challenges of ISO 9001:2015 registration.** ISO 9001:2015 registration is not easy. A company pursuing registration or implementing ISO 9001:2015 Op Ex systems should conduct a basic cost-benefit of pursuing registration.
- **Step #3. Secure management commitment.** Senior management must be fully committed to authorize resources including people, monies, and equipment. Senior management must also actively participate in the registration by establishing project teams,

maintaining organizational enthusiasm, providing direction, and reconciling differences. Middle management must be committed because they will provide the members for the project team.

- **Step #4. Plan for ISO 9001:2015 registration.** ISO 9001:2015 registration should be thoroughly planned so resources are not wasted or the team does not go down dead ends.
- **Step #5. Organize for registration.** Often, a multi-disciplinary team tackles ISO 9001:2015 registration. The team plans and develops quality system documentation. The team also verifies that systems are in place and operating properly. The team also ensures that registration is implemented on time and under budget and it satisfies stakeholder requirements.
- **Step #6. Train, Train, Train.** New Op Ex systems are implemented. Audits are conducted. Corrective actions are implemented. Procedures and work instructions are written. All of this requires training.
- **Step #7. Conduct the preassessment.** The preassessment compares the "what is" against the "what shall be" as specified by the ISO 9001:2015. This is called ISO 9001:2015 document gap analysis or simply gap analysis.
- **Step #8. Develop Op Ex documentation.** Developing Op Ex documentation is the most time consuming and expensive element of ISO 9001:2015 registration. Three levels of ISO Op Ex documentation are usually prepared, specifically Op Ex manual policies, procedures, and work instructions.
- **Step #9. Select a registrar.** Most of the effort and time is expended in planning and preparing for the registration assessment. Most registrars charge similar fees for similar services.
- **Step #10. Maintain registration.** Once a company gains registration, the company must actively maintain registration. ISO 9001:2015 registration is a long-term process of continuous auditing to ever higher revised ISO 9001:2015 Op Ex systems standards. The standards are being revised every four to five years incorporating higher Op Ex requirements. As well, the registrar conducts a surveillance audit of a company every six months or every year.[68]

BALDRIGE NATIONAL OPERATIONAL EXCELLENCE AWARD

If standards are not formulated systematically at the top, they will be formulated haphazardly and impulsively in the field.
John Biegler

The Baldrige award is the most important Op Ex and perhaps business award in the U.S. The award has helped to focus the importance of Op Ex. Pursuing and even winning the award is a great motivator for many business executives. The award is a symbol of accomplishment and may be the biggest non-monetary award business award in the U.S.

THE NATIONAL OP EX AWARD

The Baldrige award recognizes organizations that have implemented "world class" total Op Ex systems and processes. The intent of the award is to establish high standards and to harmonize total operational management criteria.

The Baldrige award is the quintessential business award. This characteristic may be its biggest benefit or may even be a liability. The award has been criticized for requiring large expenditures of resources for applying for the award and for preparing for site visits. The other major criticism is that winning the award doesn't guarantee future profits.

A major benefit of the award is that it is a living document. It incorporates the latest in business and Op Ex thinking. For example the award in recent years has shifted its emphasis from strategic Op Ex planning to strategic business planning. This change integrates and mainstreams Op Ex into a business' strategies, goals, and objectives. Op Ex goals, priorities, and targets are spelled out clearly, quantified, and substantiated.

The Baldrige changes each year to reflect the importance of Op Ex to customers and to other stakeholders. A major change in recent Baldrige criteria involves placing the criteria in the mainstream of business, specifically competitiveness. In other words, Op Ex and customer service are not important by themselves but are important in the context of business performance and of a company's competitiveness.

BALDRIGE APPLICATION PROCESS

The Baldrige award recognizes U.S. companies for business excellence based on Op Ex achievements, internal Op Ex processes, customer satisfaction, and other criteria. The award promotes awareness of Op Ex as an increasingly important element of competitiveness and for profitability. The award is granted in three areas, manufacturing companies, service companies, and small businesses.

The award application form requires applicants to describe their Op Ex systems and respond to specific categories. Each application is assigned to 3 examiners who independently evaluate and score the application. Then, senior examiners develop consensus scores and make recommendations to for site visits.

The award follows a rigorous evaluation process based on a four-stage process:

- **Stage 1** - Independent review and evaluation by at least five members of the Board of Examiners.
- **Stage 2** - Consensus review and evaluation for applications that score well in Stage 1.
- **Stage 3** - Site visits to applicants that score well in Stage 2.
- **Stage 4** - Judges review results and make recommendations.

USING EXTERNAL CONSULTANTS AS FACILITATORS

Advantages:

- Have a fresh perspective and can offer "out of box" solutions.
- Are independent and objective.
- Can offer new solutions to old problems.
- Have resources not available internally.
- Can offer tailored, cost effective services not available internally.
- Can offer small companies, big company ideas and skills.
- Can be dismissed and replaced easily.
- Can come in and offer the broad view of an issue.

Disadvantages:

- Don't understand systems, processes, and products.
- May offer universal solutions to specific problems.
- Can cause resentment for knowing everything.
- Can preempt local Op Ex efforts and take ownership of the Op Ex initiative.

OPERATIONAL MANAGEMENT OPPORTUNITIES

Marketplace changes are offering major opportunities for Op Ex managers to increase customer satisfaction and performance improvement. Op Ex managers have a solid foundation for leading and playing a key role in Op Ex, cost, technology and other related initiatives being introduced to organizations. The professional challenge for Op Ex professionals is capitalizing on opportunities instead of allowing themselves to be victimized by changes.

CAUSAL ANALYSIS AND INTERPRETATION

A process in control has all its points inside the control limits. Special causes have been eliminated from the process. Output from the machine or process cannot be improved. Any variation is due to chance causes.

A process in control has a pattern of data points that display random variation in the following manner:

- No points on the chart are above or below the control limits.

- Points are distributed randomly about the average.
- Approximately two-thirds of the values are located around the average.
- Points follow a random pattern of variation.

DIFFERENCE BETWEEN PREVENTION AND INSPECTION

SPC is one of the primary analytical tools of the prevention mode of Op Ex. The difference between the inspection mode and prevention mode of Op Ex should first be explained. While the inputs to the inspection and prevention modes are the same, the processes monitor product Op Ex differently.

Inspection catches defects only after work has been performed on a product. For example, a finished product may go through hundreds of different operations. At each step work, or in other words value, is added to the product. If inspection catches a defective product after many operations then it has to be scrapped or reworked. Both of which are expensive.

In the prevention mode, inputs are the same as the inspection mode. However, the prevention mode monitors and controls product quality during the process. If the process deviates from the center of the specification because of some identifiable reason, the operator adjusts the machine or process. Defect-free products are sent to the customer and rework is negligible.

NEXT CHAPTER

In the next chapter, Op Ex Statistical Tools is discussed. Op Ex is only as good as the information and data generated. Solving Op Ex problems requires that large amounts of data are collected, analyzed, deciphered, and acted upon. Product quality is only as good as the process information and data generated. Data and information therefore must be accessible and understandable to management, teams, and all employees. Statistics can be used to make data and information understandable for Op Ex decision making.

CHAPTER 14
OP EX STATISTICAL TOOLS

Deming introduced Walter Shewhart's ideas to the Japanese in the early 1950s. One of the more important contributions was the PDSA or sometimes called the PDCA cycle which became known as the Deming Cycle. The PDSA cycle is based on scientific management and systems theory. The cycle is a simple but powerful illustration how to approach and solve problems and then start the cycle again.

VARIABLE AND ATTRIBUTE DATA

SPC control charts are based on the type of data obtained from a process, which can be either variable data or attribute data. The diameter of a bore, thickness of this book, or today's temperature are examples of variable data. A variable is any product characteristic that can be measured over a range of values.

Variable data and information are obtained by tracking a manufacturing process over time. An operator or inspector continually samples, measures and compares dimensions of parts to ensure they comply with specification data shown on the engineering drawing.

Conforming or non-conforming, go or no/go, good or bad, and acceptable or not acceptable are examples of attribute data. An attribute is a characteristic that the product has or does not have. A surface blemish is an example of an attribute type of data. An inspector will determine whether the blemish affects the product's marketability or function and will make an accept/reject decision based on the examination.

PROBLEM SOLVING

Anticipating, controlling, and correcting problems are essential to Op Ex. Several approaches elements include:

- **Intervention.** Intervention is the process of discovering or anticipating problems then containing and eliminating them so they don't recur.
- **Proactive Op Ex auditing. Op Ex** auditing is sometimes a passive activity. Forms and procedures are checked for compliance. Products are inspected to ensure compliance with specifications. However, a more important objective of Op Ex auditing is to actively search for improvement opportunities. This is called proactive Op Ex auditing.
- **Containment.** If a critical problem occurs, such as a critical product failure that resulted in loss of life, then a team is immediately assembled to contain the damage, fix the immediate problem and ensure that it does not spread. Containment of a nonconforming shipment of products would involve segregating the shipment until permanent corrective action can be accomplished.
- **Corrective action.** Corrective action is after-the-fact actions or activities to fix a problem.
- **Preventive action.** Preventive action encompasses the set of activities to ensure that areas of risk are monitored and there are sufficient internal operational controls to prevent deficiencies from occurring.
- **Corrective action audit.** This evaluates the effectiveness of the corrective action to eliminate the symptom and root-cause of the problem.

SMALL BUSINESS OP EX

Small businesses often do not think they have the resources, including time or money, to implement a companywide Op Ex initiative unless there are immediate payoffs. A small business when implementing Op Ex usually starts small, focuses on immediate rewards, couples Op Ex with its reengineering efforts, and ensures payoffs are tangible and measurable.

A small business is often a sole proprietorship. Expensive consulting is difficult to justify to a small business owner. Often, the small business owner is focused on daily concerns such as getting products out the door and paying bills. Op Ex may be an afterthought unless the customer is requiring it as a condition of business.

The Op Ex function changes as a small business matures. A small business will transition from an entrepreneurial organization to a management run business. In the entrepreneurial mode, problems are attacked as they arrive. Long term Op Ex planning and systems development require resources that are often spent on daily concerns. As a management run business, Op Ex systems are developed and integrated into operations.

TOTAL OPERATIONAL MANAGEMENT DEFINITIONS

"Total operational management consists of continuous process improvement activities involving everyone in an organization - managers and workers - in a total integrated effort toward improving performance at every level. This improved performance is directed toward satisfying such cross functional goals as quality, cost, schedule, mission need, and suitability. Op Ex integrates fundamental management techniques, existing improvement efforts and technical tools under a disciplined approach focused on continuous process improvement. The activities are ultimately focused on increased customer/user satisfaction."[69]

OP EX STATISTIVAL TOOLS

This section discusses common Op Ex statistical tools:

BRAINSTORMING

What: An idea generation techniques for generating ideas and opinion from a small group.

Why: Brainstorming produces ideas in a short time which can be used as a starting point for identifying problems to solve. Additional advantages of brainstorming include participating, problem solving, commitment building, and structuring a plan of action.

How:

1. Outline ground rules and instructions.
2. Present the challenge or problem.
3. Generate ideas or suggestion for a specific period of time.
4. Don't judge or limit ideas.
5. Write ideas on flipchart.
6. Eliminate duplicate ideas.
7. Prioritize ideas.
8. Develop action plan.

CAUSE AND EFFECT DIAGRAMS

What: Sometimes called a Fishbone diagram because of its shape. It illustrates the relationship between an effect and possible causes. The effect is a recognized problem which may have been identified from a Pareto Diagram.

Why: Diagram is drawn to identify major and minor causes of problems and their interactions among factors affecting a process.

How:

1. Identify a critical problem.
2. Identify major categories of causes, for example methods, operator, methods, environment, machines, suppliers, tools, etc.
3. Use a group to brainstorm for additional causes.
4. Identify critical and major causes.
5. Prioritize causes.
6. Eliminate major causes.
7. Draw another cause and effect diagram using the major cause as the new problem.

TEAM BUILDING

What: Purpose of building a team is to develop, facilitate, lead, and maintain a group of people who are working towards a common goal.

Why: Empowered teams are responsible, have ownership, and have authority to manage and improve their processes.

How:

1. Identify team members through volunteers or through assignments.

2. Have team identify facilitator or leader.
3. Teach problem solving and other Op Ex techniques.
4. Identify team goals.
5. Provide support and direction.
6. Recognize team successes.
7. If required, maintain the team.

SIMULTANEOUS/CONCURRENT PRODUCT DEVELOPMENT

What: Method for integrating multi-functional disciplines and teams into developing products simultaneously instead of linearly. Concurrent product development teams may include key individuals from Engineering, Manufacturing, Supply Management, and key suppliers.

Why: Approach has been used many times to shorten development times, to reduce costs, to improve product reliability, and to increase cycle times.

How:

1. Use cross functional teams.
2. Use computers and software to communicate interactively.
3. Identify and eliminate constraints to rapid product development.

PARETO CHARTS

What: A bar chart that identifies and displays the major causes of a problem starting from the largest cause to the left bar on the chart to the least on the right.

Why: Pareto principles, sometimes called the 80-20 rule, states that a few of the causes, 20%, account for most of the effects. These "vital" few are addressed and eliminated first.

How:

1. Identify a problem.
2. Measure all the causes of the problem.
3. List the causes according to their magnitude, starting from the left.
4. Create a cumulative distribution for the number of causes measures.
5. Construct a bar graph.
6. Focus and eliminate the most significant cause first.

QUALITY FUNCTION DEPLOYMENT (SHORT EXPLANTION)

What: QFD is a conceptual map (house of quality) that outlines the linkages among a number of key variables including customer requirements and product characteristics. The objective is to transform customer wants and needs into quantitative design characteristics.

Why: Products should be designed to satisfy customer requirements. QFD is a structured methodology for ensuring that customer requirements are translated directly into engineering drawings. Marketing, design engineering, production and Supply Management work closely together to develop a QFD chart.

How:

1. Identify customer requirements.
2. Prioritize requirements.
3. Translate requirements into product characteristics.
4. Understand the relationships among product characteristics.

COST OF QUALITY

What: Method for acquiring and analyzing cost data usually not available in the chart of accounts. Cost of Quality consists of conformance and nonconformance costs. Conformance costs deal with the nonconformance of prevention and appraisal. Nonconformances costs consist of internal and external failure costs.

Why: These costs are often hidden and a high percentage of overall sales.

How:

1. Identify operational excellence costs.
2. Use multidisciplinary team to analyze COQ and implement solution.
3. Priority the most significant costs.
4. Identify the causes or sources of these significant costs.
5. Identify solutions for reducing these causes.
6. Implement solution.
7. Analyze cost savings.
8. Start again with another significant cost.

STATISTICAL PROCESS CONTROL

What: Method for determining the cause of process variation based on statistical analysis. Operators use SPC to stabilize and improve processes. SPC allows identification of common and special causes of variation. Common causes are random. Special causes are identified and can be eliminated.

Why: SPC can be used to control and improve almost any process. SPC allows operators to identify special cause variation and to eliminate it quickly and accurately. SPC also provides data for operational decision making, provides a baseline for improvement, and encourages workplace participation.

How:

1. Identify process.
2. Identify special and common causes of variation.
3. Construct a cause and effect diagram.
4. Collect data.
5. Analyze variations.
6. Take corrective action.

DESIGN OF EXPERIMENTS

What: Statistical approach used to understand and improve a process by identifying major causes of operational variation.

Why: Design of experiments is used to eliminate unwanted causes of variation. DOE optimizes product design and production processes by understanding the major causes. DOE reduces costs, stabilizes production, and ensures robust design.

How:

1. Identify products functional characteristics and key process parameters relating to these characteristics.
2. Identify controllable and uncontrollable factors of a process.
3. Develop experiments to discover interaction among controllable and uncontrollable factors.
4. Optimize factors relating to a product's functional characteristics and minimize the influence of uncontrollable factors.

STATISTICAL PROCESS CONTROL

Statistician: A person who can go directly from an unwarranted assumption to a preconceived conclusion.

Anonymous

Statistics consists of powerful decision-making tools. However as the above quote illustrates, they should be used carefully. Statistical Process Control (SPC) involves the collection, analysis, and interpretation of data from a machine or process being monitored. SPC illustrates many of the lessons of this chapter, including process control, capability, stability, prevention, and improvement. SPC is an objective system for evaluating machine or process performance. It eliminates subjective evaluations and lets the team or operator monitor and control a machine or process.

Traditionally, operational control personnel performed SPC studies to evaluate whether a machine or process was capable of making products within the specification limits. Now, production teams or operators use process charts to maintain and improve Op Ex.

STATISTICS AND VARIATION

Statistics involves collecting, processing, and then presenting data in an understandable form. Statistical analysis provides techniques and tools for studying variation and patterns by examining data samples to estimate characteristics of the larger population.

Statistics by themselves should be used and interpreted carefully. For example, some data even though it is reported to six significant decimal places, may be suspect. Data may be generated by a measurement instrument to 0.00001 in. but if the instrument has not been calibrated properly or recently, measurements may be inaccurate. Or, a worker or team may not have been instructed in its use. Also, data may not represent typical conditions or circumstances.

SPC IMPLEMENTATION

Common sense in an uncommon degree is what the world calls wisdom.
Samuel Taylor Coleridge

The following are the steps for implementing SPC:

- Flowchart operation.
- Identify equipment and specifications.
- Identify critical product characteristics.
- Identify locations that can cause variation in product characteristics.
- Monitor accuracy of measuring equipment.
- Obtain data.
- Construct charts.

FLOWCHART OPERATION

An operation to produce a product or deliver a service can be 1 or 100 steps. If 100 steps, an operation can be understood by flowcharting the steps. The flowchart is a road map of what occurs in the process.

IDENTIFY EQUIPMENT AND SPECIFICATIONS

A complex product can go through successive steps, such as assembly, fabrication, test, painting, and inspection. Each discrete operation can include machines and test equipment of a different vintage, manufacturer, and amount of usage. Each has a different capability to meet specifications.

IDENTIFY CRITICAL PRODUCT CHARACTERISTICS

Engineering may design a product to satisfy an identified market need. Engineering will specify product characteristics on a drawing. Or, Engineering, Manufacturing, and Op Ex departments may jointly identify characteristics and plans for controlling Op Ex. Or the customer may specify the Op Ex characteristics, specifications, and tolerances if the customer uses the supplied part or component in another product.

IDENTIFY LOCATIONS WHERE PRODUCT CHARACTERISTICS ARE MADE

Once product characteristics are identified, machines are identified to produce these characteristics. The operator or process engineer will identify the capability of the machine or set of machines to meet specifications. If a customer or final inspector finds flaws, discrepancies, or defects, they must be traceable to the machine so the causes of errors can be eliminated.

MONITOR ACCURACY OF MEASURING EQUIPMENT

Measurement equipment can err through use, misuse, or abuse. Inaccurate measuring equipment can bias measurements and make all operational control efforts questionable. Depending on criticality, test and measuring equipment must be calibrated periodically and properly stored and secured.

OBTAIN DATA

Finally, data are obtained from pulling and measuring samples during production. The inspector or operator can manually measure one or more characteristics during production. In flexible machining centers or computer-controlled machinery, many product characteristics can be checked through automatic measurement techniques. Automatic SPC measuring equipment samples and measures product characteristics. SPC charts are then constructed and the operator simply monitors out-of-control points or suspicious trends.

THE SEVEN DEADLY SINS OF PROCESS IMPROVEMENT

Process is the hot buzz-word of the 2000's. Process defines how organizations are structured, how work gets done, and how products are developed. Every Op Ex person should be aware of these 7 sins of process improvement:

1. Process improvement is not tied to the strategic issues the business face.
2. The process improvement initiative does not involve the right people.
3. Process improvement teams are not provided with clear directions and are not held accountable for their objectives.

4. Senior managers think if they are not carving away at the existing organization, they are not making significant improvements.
5. Process designers do not consider how the changes will affect people.
6. The organization focuses more on process redesign than on improvement implementation.
7. Teams fail to develop a measurement system and other elements of a continuous improvement infrastructure.[70]

VOICE OF THE PROCESS

The voice of the process is an expression referring to measuring process output. Process data is statistically collected to determine process stability and process control. If process output is outlined, the upper and lower control limits, then the operator, team or process engineer stop the process and determine the cause of the assignable variation. The goal of any process is to be on target and to have its assignable variation controlled and minimized around the target. A company should follow the 5 basic Op Ex principles when attempting to hear the voice of the process:

- Know why something is being measuring.
- Ask customers what end results should be measured.
- Continuously monitor how competitors and one's company are doing.
- Develop and track internal procedures and systems that satisfy customer requirements.
- Share with employees why processes are being measured.

The target of the specification should relate to some attribute that is critical to the customer. These characteristics may be physical, chemical, or dimensional. The critical point is to understand customer's requirements so they are identified on an engineering print and this information is communicated to a process where it can be statistically monitored and controlled.

ALIGNMENT OF TEAM OBJECTIVES WITH THE ORGANIZATION'S

There has to be a strong supporting link between the team's objectives and the organization's strategic goals. A team can sometimes develop a life of its own and its reason for existence may not support the thrust of the organization. For example, a long-standing team, such as a process team or maintenance team, may become stalled over time when mission, objectives, and initiative drivers are misunderstood or diffused. The best team talent, collaboration or leadership may not be able to recognize the root cause of the problem which may be lack of senior management support. Senior management doesn't understand why the team is still there.

STATISTICAL DECISION MAKING

Statistics are no substitute for judgment.
Henry Clay

The concepts of statistics and variation were not on management's radar screen until recently and only until Walter Shewhart and W. Edwards Deming introduced their business benefits. In particular, W. Edwards Deming popularized the concept that variation is an indispensable part of all business decisions.

The study of Op Ex often becomes the study of variation, how to detect, measure, and control it. For example, quality, specified in terms of a dimensional tolerance or a surface finish, is a variable that can be controlled and ensured. If a target product dimension can be kept in the middle of the specification spread and the variation of measurements are distributed inside the specification limits and process control limits, then dimensional quality can be controlled.

So, quality as a variable, measurable characteristic can be understood if variation and its causes are understood. Variation can be controlled by monitoring it using statistical techniques including Statistical Process Control (SPC). Variation can be caused by any of the factors identified in the cause and effect diagram, such as factors as materials, machines/process, methods, operator, and environment. In this way, a team or process operator can work on ensuring the system or machine is stable. If the machine or process shows unexpected variation, then the operator examines the cause, eliminates the symptom and root cause, and stabilizes the process again. This becomes a form of management by exception where the supervisor, team or operator focus on the unexpected process variation.

PRINCIPLES OF SPC

Statistical Process Control is based on the following fundamental Op Ex principles:

- Products and processes vary.
- Variation in products and processes can be measured.
- Variation in measurements follows identifiable frequency distribution patterns - specifically the bell-shaped curve.
- Variations due to assignable causes distort a bell-shaped distribution.
- Causes of variation can be isolated and identified.

Products and Processes Vary

Products and processes vary. No two products or processes are exactly alike. Even if two parts are interchangeable, the parts will be different, maybe at a very minute level.

Variation in Products and Processes can be Measured

Variation, however minute, in products is detectable and can be measured. Precision measurement instruments may be required to notice the differences, such as electronic instruments that measure to millionths of an inch.

Variation Follows Identifiable Patterns

Variation shows up as recognizable patterns or shapes, including bell shaped curves and histograms. If measurements are taken of a particular product characteristic from the same process and operator, the distribution generally looks like a bell curve. While the curve may be distorted, the shape still looks like a bell.

Variation Due to Special Causes Distorts Curve Shapes

Variations distort the shape of the bell curve. If measurements tend to form a bell shape and if the shape is distorted, then the variation is caused by special factors. SPC is used to detect, isolate, and eliminate special causes.

Causes of Variation can be Isolated and Identified

Causes of variation can be identified by constructing a Cause-Effect diagram. Special variation is used to pinpoint and predict the behavior of a process. Once special or assignable root causes are identified and eliminated, the process can be improved.

MEASUREMENT OF OP EX INDICATORS

Management usually establishes measurable Op Ex standards and specifications for an organization. Op Ex objectives should be tied to financial measures which are the common language of business. Common measures of Op Ex include:

- Customer satisfaction
- Project savings
- Defect levels
- Cost of quality (COQ)

CUSTOMER SATISFACTION

Customer satisfac-tion is measured by surveys, customer complaints, and warranty claims. Manufacturers and service organizations can directly or indirectly solicit customer feedback.

PROJECT SAVINGS

Cost savings are the most common and effective yardstick for measuring quality. Once costs are identified, areas with the highest costs are singled out for analysis and for improvement projects. Any Op Ex initiative or improvement project has to be cost-effective. Op Ex for its own sake cannot be justified and should not be pursued.

DEFECT LEVELS

Defect or nonconformance levels are a direct measure of Op Ex. A product can have a critical, major, or minor defect depending on the criticality of the deficiency. Defect levels are measured on a production line or in the field. Defect rates on the production line are determined through visual examination or measurement of a product. Defect rates from the field are indicated by product returns, field failure rates, reliability rates, and warranty claims.

COST OF QUALITY

Quality costs are important because the value of any Op Ex effort is based on its contribution to company profits, whether through reduced costs or increased sales. The cost of quality (COQ) is a system that measures the costs of various components of Op Ex.

The cost of quality (COQ) are costs associated with obtaining acceptable Op Ex and as a result of not achieving this Op Ex. Operational excellence or quality costs include scrap, rework, dissatisfied customers, loss of sales, etc. Costs can be incurred by any cost center or work unit and these costs can be high.

Philip Crosby in his book **Quality is Free** maintained that Op Ex achievement pays for itself. This is counter intuitive, because most people think that Op Ex costs more than it recovers. Philip Crosby believed the cost of poor quality can amount to 25% of sales in manufac-turing companies and up to 40% of operating costs in service companies. Other experts as well provide similar numbers. If these numbers are accurate, then the COQ is larger than pretax earnings of many companies.

COQ is such an important Op Ex indicator that it is often integrated into the strategic and tactical Op Ex planning process. Many Op Ex costs can be identified by examining the chart of accounts in cost accounting systems. Other Op Ex costs are derived by examining cost centers, allocating costs, and estimating them.

MEASUREMENT

Following World War II, American industry operated in an environment where raw material costs were low, shortages of resources were unknown; American Op Ex was unquestioned; and market demand for American made goods was high. Poor product Op Ex did not deter American products from being sold. So, reasonable costs were directly passed on to the customer.

This is now history. Raw materials are expensive. American quality is not always well perceived. The ability of emerging nations and the industrial nations to produce goods far exceeds demand. To contain costs and maintain a competitive edge, companies measure all costs that lead to product or service improvement.

IMPORTANCE OF MEASUREMENT

An Op Ex initiative is initially expensive. People are hired and trained. Policies, standards, and procedures are developed and written. Measuring and test equipment are purchased. Facilities are built.

Until recently, management believed that maintaining and achieving high levels of Op Ex cost more than cost savings or revenue generated. This was largely because the relationship between Op Ex and cost was not available in conventional cost accounting systems. Managers thought that Op Ex could not be measured and therefore was not important.

Op Ex measurement is now as essential as productivity measurement and product costing. Op Ex measurement can:

- Focus management's attention on areas of im-provement
- Prioritize improvement projects
- Verify effects of corrective action
- Measure progress

TYPICAL OP EX MEASURES

The following are typical Op Ex measures:

- Reliability
- Maintainability
- Product Op Ex characteristics
- Process capability
- Cost of Op Ex
- Return on Op Ex
- First pass yields
- Time to market
- Manufacturing costs
- Design costs
- Customer defined Op Ex
- Fit and function

OP EX GOALS AND OBJECTIVES

Doing little things well is the way towards doing big things better.
Anonymous

Op Ex objectives are statements of how an organization intends to meet its Op Ex goals, including customer satisfaction. An objective can be thought of as a doable, tactical goal to be achieved in the near future. Objectives usually include intended results, units of measurement, plans for action, and timetable.

Goals may be realistic or even outrageous. The pursuit of outrageous goals is a concept that is gaining much credence as companies are not satisfied with incremental improvement. Incremental improvements of 10 or 20% a year are no longer acceptable in many companies where 100% quantum improvement is common.

Regardless, Op Ex goals focus on delivering value and satisfaction to an organization's stakeholders. Op Ex goals serve several important purposes:

- **Can provide a sense of urgency.** Realistic and attainable goals can create a sense of urgency for the entire organization.

- **Provide organizational focus.** Many Op Ex and continuous improvement initiatives emphasize process over results or deliverables. Op Ex initiatives were kicked off with lots of training with a mandate to improve systems and make customers happy. There was little or no focus on how these would benefit the corporation. Now, Op Ex goals are tied to the organization's mission and overall strategy.
- **Provide the basis for measurement.** Continuous improvement can only be achieved through establishing baselines and benchmarks and through measuring improvement.[71]

OP EX CONTROL AND ASSURANCE FUNCTIONS

Authority and responsibility are rarely balanced.
Joe Kelly

The terms operational control and operational assurance have sometimes been used interchangeably. As the Op Ex function evolved, the difference between the two terms became significant. As responsibility for Op Ex was transferred to those responsible for the tasks, operational control's main functions became measurement, problem solving, and inspection. These include the inspection and measurement of product and processes throughout the product lifecycle to determine that specifications are being met and standards are being followed.

In the inspection mode, operational control staff was sometimes perceived as the "policeman." This has bred resentment and sometimes resulted in inferior products. As a problem solver, Op Ex staff is more often perceived as facilitators in the process to produce defect-free products.

Operational control responsibilities are often being transferred to the functions responsible for conducting the activity. The supplier is responsible for providing defect-free products, thereby eliminating the need for incoming material inspection. An outgoing product is no longer inspected unless regulations or special applications require it. Manufacturing is responsible for measuring, controlling, and ensuring the consistency of measurements of the key quality characteristics.

DESIGN ASSURANCE TECHNIQUES

Several common design assurance and control methods are:

- Manufacturability evaluation
- Test plan evaluation
- Engineering change control
- Product testing
- Design review

Manufacturability Evaluation

Manufacturability assesses whether a product can be produced in a cost-effective manner. Before finalizing a design, the development team evaluates manufacturing capabilities, costs, and limitations.

The development team needs feedback from Manufacturing on design elements that will help eliminate defects during production. If new or non-standard components are used, then Manufacturing may have to design new tooling and fixtures.

Test Plan Evaluation

As mechanical and electronic products become more complex, products are automatically inspected and tested as they move down a production line. Test plans are prepared before production to ensure a product is testable before, during, and following production. A complete test plan evaluates equipment, personnel, calibration accuracy, and diagnostic instructions.

Engineering Change Control

Engineering change control is a process that checks, monitors, and ensures design integrity if a product is modified. The engineering change control board investigates and then approves/disapproves requests for design changes. The board consists of representatives from the development team including Marketing, Engineering, Supply Management, and Distribution.

Product Testing

Even though a product meets all customer requirements and product specifications at one point in time, subtle changes in a production process may force a drift in dimensions that initial product testing would not catch, but can lead to premature failure once in the hands of the customer.

So, the purpose of reliability testing is to ensure that long term customer needs are satisfied as well as limit a company's exposure to warranty and product liability claims. Testing can take place in the laboratory under controlled conditions or in the field. Testing under field conditions subjects a product to real-world conditions. The types of product testing are numerous including physical, chemical, and mechanical measurements. The tests can be destructive or nondestructive.

Testing can be performed at the supplier's facility, customer's warehouse, or independent testing laboratory. Op Ex staff usually performs test and measurement and supplies the results to Supply Management. Also, independent contractors can perform plant or site inspection.

Design Review

Up to 80% of production decisions and costs are determined by a product's design. This is why it is critical that Manufacturing staff provides input during the product development process. Time-to-market requirements are accelerating the product development decision making process. Design iterations are minimized.

Design reviews are systematic and planned activities at critical points throughout the product development process which analyze design objectives, process inputs, process capability, process outputs, documentation, suppliers, and a multitude of other critical design criteria. Design review is being used as a continuous empowerment, improvement, and corrective tool. Design review is conducted throughout the product development process to evaluate customer requirements, designs, calculations, bills of material, and other documents that may affect Op Ex, warranties, and production costs.

DESIGN CONTROL AND ASSURANCE

Keep in mind the fact that Ralph Nader could be the first customer for your new product.
Anonymous

Product changes are inevitable throughout the development lifecycle. However, product change requests, waivers on specifications, or product deviations can adversely affect product quality unless they are approved, monitored, and documented. Otherwise, exceptions and deviations become the accepted mode of operation.

The reason for any change must be studied in order to decide whether the change is warranted. If a change is warranted, then it should be implemented so product integrity is not sacrificed. Any changes have to be approved by knowledgeable personnel, properly documented, and monitored throughout the development lifecycle.

Specifically, design control, assurance and review are the application of practices, procedures, and specifications for preventing defects from occurring in the development cycle. Specifically, design control, assurance, and review ensure:

- Drawings, calculations, bills of material, and specifications are checked.
- Drawings, specifications, engineering changes, procedures, and manufacturing instructions are consistently followed.
- Standard methods for data sheets, drawings, and work packages are developed.

- Design changes or modifications are properly reflected in drawings, bills of material, parts lists, and instructions.
- Engineering design is pursued in a logical fashion.
- Drawings, procedures and ancillary materials are reviewed and signed by designated parties at appropriate point of the design cycle.
- Deviations are properly documented.
- Deviations are properly authorized.
- Engineering documentation is systematically numbered, identified, filed, updated, and secured.

DESIGN FOR MANUFACTURE AND ASSEMBLY

Design for manufacture and assembly (DFMA) is a structured analysis to simplify and to accelerate the design and product development processes while decreasing overall costs, improving product quality, developing quality systems, and decreasing time-to-market. DFMA is also a multidisciplinary effort because time-to-market can't be enhanced without considering all the factors in the design and production cycle.

In DFMA, the following are addressed before a product goes to prototyping:

- What is the function of the product?
- What does the product look like?
- What parts and materials are going into a product?
- How many parts are requiring for each product?
- How will the product be produced?
- How much will the product sell for and cost to product?
- What are the sources of materials and services?
- What systems and processes are required to build and test the product?

SPECIFICATIONS AND MEASUREMENT

Measure a thousand times and cut once.

Proverb

The product development team takes often poorly articulated customer requirements and designs a product that customers will buy. Before a product is developed, the team agrees that product requirements will satisfy the customer, including attributes such as performance, manufacturability, features, maintainability, reliability, and appearance. At first these requirements are broad, then are refined as customer needs and wants are better understood.

SPECIFICATION DEVELOPMENT

Product requirements lead to product specifications which are spelled out in a product brief. The brief is an initial attempt to distill the customer's wants, needs, and expectations into a preliminary set of requirements. These requirements are then translated into technical specifications that detail how the product is dimensioned, manufactured, assembled, and tested for the whole product, assembly, subassembly, and even component.

A complex product may consist of levels of parts. Performance and reliability specifications are first developed at the product level and then for each sublevel, from assembly to subassembly to component. Because, each level has to interact and act dynamically with other system components, dimensional tolerances for mating pieces are carefully specified so mating parts and assemblies fit and function reliably.

SPECIFICATION AND CONTROL LIMITS

If measurement points are within the upper and lower control limits of the chart, then the process is in statistical control and capable of meeting specifications. If a process is capable of meeting specifications, we simply say that the process is capable. Statistical control means that only random variation exists in the process. Random variation is caused by chance factors and not by any special cause variation.

Specification limits and control limits are independent of each other on the control chart. Product designers establish specifications and tolerances. Control limits are based and calculated on the variation found in

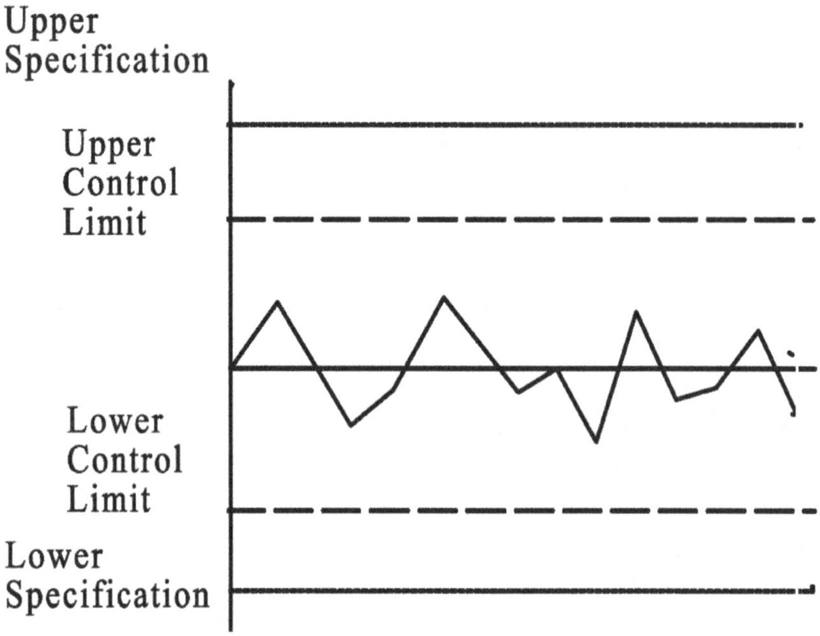

the process. Once control limits are determined, they are compared against the specification spread to determine how many parts are inside the tolerance band. The figure shows two lines of dashes which are the upper and lower control limits.

Control limits are used to evaluate the status of the process. If a point is outside the control limits, it is assumed that a special cause is present. This cause will be identified and eliminated by the operator or process engineer. If a point is inside the control limits, it is assumed that a random cause is present and the process is stable. The process will then be left alone and not adjusted.

Control limits are established at plus or minus three standard deviations from the mean or central line. This means that if all the plotted data points are between the upper control limit (at plus three standard deviations) and the lower control limit (at minus three standard deviations), then only three measurements in one thousand are out of control. When a measured point is outside the control limits, the process is out of control and an assignable cause is present and should be eliminated.

CHALLENGES OF SPECIFICATION DEVELOPMENT

Product quality can deteriorate if the team develops specifications that are:

- **Tight or loose specifications.** If specifications are too tight, Manufacturing may be forced to build special tooling or purchase new equipment in order to produce products that conform to specifications. If specifications are too loose, Manufacturing may build a product that will not fit or function properly when parts are assembled.

- **Not applied uniformly.** Product specifications are useful only if they are applied uniformly. Too often, tight specifications are loosely enforced. If Op Ex gets the word not to enforce tight specifications, nonconforming products may slip through the door. On the other hand, loose specifications tightly enforced also result in poor Op Ex. Parts that should mate smoothly do not, either interfering with each other or operating with so much slop that the product fails prematurely.

Result of Poor Specifications

Design errors, miscalculations, tight specifications, and loose specifications early in the design lifecycle can result in reliability problems later in the product lifecycle. Early design errors introduced into the product are thus replicated in each manufactured product.

Also, specifications must be balanced between detailed precision and practical application. Unrealistic specifications can result in silly consequences. For example, military suppliers maintain that the reason for $400 hammers and $3,000 toilet seats is that military specifications are unrealistic, inflexible, and rigid.

LATHAM AND LOCKE GOAL SETTING

Gary Latham and Ed Locke have recently developed a new theory of motivation based on goal setting. They believe that individuals are motivated to satisfy various needs on the job. A major need of people is to strive for and achieve goals. The goal motivates an employee to develop marketable skills that are used to fulfill job requirements and to improve work performance. If employees believe they have the abilities and resources to meet a job requirement, they will be motivated to attain higher goals.

A work-related goal must have three characteristics. The goal should be specific, meaningful, and attainable. A specific goal is well defined. Improving product reliability is a general goal. Increasing the mean time between failures (MTBF) 20% in a year is a specific, well defined goal. If the goal is too general, it is also meaningless.

If increasing product reliability 20% lowers repair costs by 50% then the goal is meaningful if the reliability engineer considers it important for his or her job security. The engineer must consider it personally important so it becomes a personal challenge.

Finally, the reliability goal must be attainable. A difficult and stretch goal is acceptable. However, if the goal is beyond the grasp and abilities of an individual then he or she will only pay lip service to achieve it.

STANDARD DEVIATION

Standard deviation (SD) is a measure of variation, the spreading tendency of data. A large standard deviation shows greater variation in data than a small standard deviation. The symbol for standard deviation is a sigma.

Standard deviation affects the shape of a normal curve. A large standard deviation results in a flat and broad normal curve. A smaller standard deviation results in a peaked and narrower normal curve. However, the relative shapes of the two normal curves are the same, both bell-shaped, symmetrical around the measurements, and diminishing toward the tails of the curves.

The figure on the next page illustrates the shape, symmetry, average, and standard deviations of a generalized normal curve. As seen in the figure, the laws of probability state that a specific percentage of the measurable population will fit within certain standard deviation (S.D.) limits:

- Plus or minus 1 standard deviation has 68.27% of the data

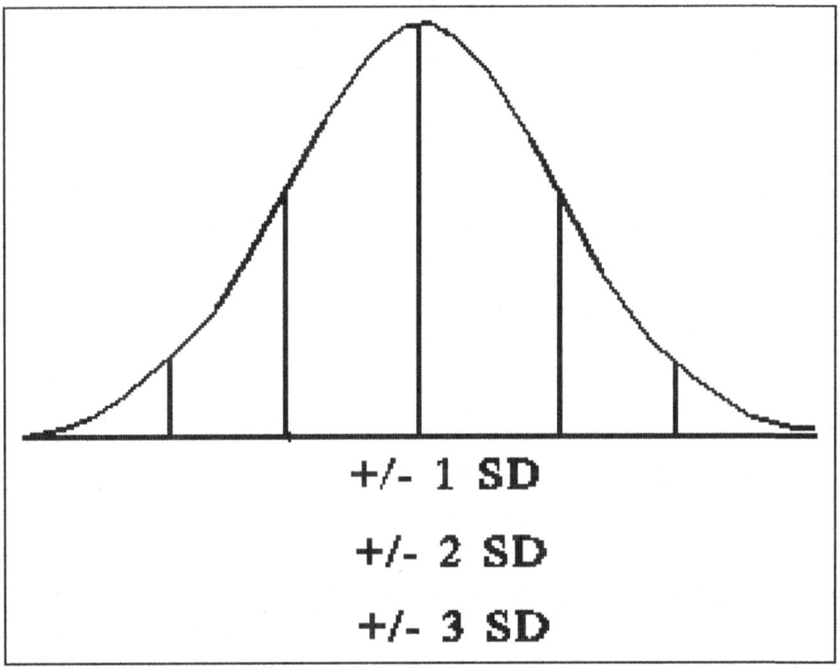

- Plus or minus 2 standard deviations have 95.45% of the data
- Plus or minus 3 standard deviations have 99.73% of the data

TYPES OF INSPECTION

Statistical inspection involves pulling a sample of incoming products from a shipment, batch, or lot and comparing critical product characteristics, features, and properties against specifications. If a product dimension falls within an acceptable tolerance spread or range, the product is accepted.

If the sample consists of sufficient acceptable products, then the whole shipment is accepted and products are sent directly to manufacturing or placed in inventory. If enough defective products are found, then the whole shipment is rejected, segregated, and shipped back to the supplier.

Statistical sampling inspection is more reliable and effective than 100% inspection in finding defective products but statistical sampling still assumes that some defective parts will slip through the inspection net. Inspection can be either:

- 100% inspection
- Statistical inspection

100% Inspection

In 100% sampling, an inspector checks, inspects, or tests all products in a shipment, lot, or batch. One hundred percent sampling is performed to comply with government regulations, special customer requirements, one of a kind products, or very expensive products.

The problems with 100% sampling are:

- It is expensive.
- It is inaccurate; inspectors become hypnotized by repetitive procedures and accept nonconforming parts.
- It is sometimes impractical; some sampling involves destructive testing.
- It becomes a sorting or screening procedure.

Statistical Sampling

Statistical sampling is preferred if inspection is required to conform to contractual commitments or government regulations. Statistical sampling involves pulling a sample of items from a homogeneous lot, batch, or shipment. The sample is assumed to be representative of the entire shipment. The inspector rejects or accepts the batch based on looking at or measuring critical features in a statistically derived number of products.

SAMPLING PLANS AND INSPECTION

A pinch of probability is worth a pound of perhaps.
James Thurber

Sampling is used to estimate the behavior of a population of data by studying measurements taken from samples. For example, the natural tendency of a population of measurements is to cluster around a central point and to spread. If the sample size is sufficiently large and representative of the population, the same clustering and spreading tendencies will be revealed in the sample. This tendency is important in Op Ex, decision making, prevention, and Statistical Process Control.

As we've stressed, prevention is preferred over inspection. Inspection takes the responsibility for operational excellence off the person, provider, department or supplier that is ultimately responsible for Op Ex. The burden for Op Ex should remain on the person or firm performing work or supplying this service.

Inspection even 100% inspection does not catch all defective products. The customer ends up with a defective product which inevitably leads to customer dissatisfaction and loss of repeat sales.

Inspection should be performed only as long as it accomplishes its intended purpose. Inspection may be necessary and justifiable if the product is life-enhancing, one-of-a-kind, costly, or required by Federal regulations to be tested.

If inspection is required, then the choice between 100% inspection and no inspection may be statistical sampling. Statistical sampling is between the two extremes and is a way to establish an Op Ex history of a new product, process or supplier. Statistical sampling also is a move towards defect prevention by using Statistical Process Control (SPC).

DISVANTAGES AND DISADVANTAGES OF SAMPLING

Statistical sampling is preferred over 100% sampling because:

- It is less expensive than 100% sampling.
- It is more efficient because item-by-item inspection is monotonous and results in errors.
- There is less handling damage.
- It requires less inspectors, time, space and equipment.
- It is a strong signal and strong motivator for the supplier to improve quality if lots are rejected.

However, statistical sampling is still inspection not prevention and has the following problems:

- Risk of accepting bad lots and rejecting good lots.
- Statistical sampling requires more planning, educating, and documentation than 100% inspection.
- It communicates to the supplier that the customer company will accept defective products.

Sampling Assumptions

Sampling plans assume inspectors follow procedures exactly and that lots are homogeneous. These assumptions are not always correct. In the name of expediency, inspectors may perform cursory inspection or testing because the "product has to be out the door." This compromises accuracy and signals to inspectors that errors and defects are tolerated. Also, sampling plans assume incoming lots consist of uniform homogeneous material. This may be false. Products can originate from different sources, processes, shifts, and suppliers.

Process Control

Statistical Process Control is required if higher levels of Op Ex are necessary. Many manufacturers want to achieve zero defects or parts-per-million (PPM) defect rates. Product inspection and sampling cannot achieve this level of operational excellence. Sampling plans are predicated upon accepting a certain level of defects through inspection. This level of defects is unacceptable in industries requiring zero defects or parts-per-million defect rates.

CAUSES OF INSPECTION ERRORS

Any inspection, whether 100% or statistical sampling, can result in errors where nonconforming items are accepted or conforming items are rejected. Common causes of inspection error are:

- Inspection, especially visual inspection in poorly lit areas, is fatiguing.
- Continuous, visual inspection of similar products is hypnotizing.

- Inspectors rely upon memory for instructions or procedures.
- Inspectors receive poor instruction on measurement and inspection
- Gages are worn, damaged, or not calibrated.
- Inspectors are not trained with new measurement equipment.
- Inspectors are not familiar with new products or parts being inspected.
- Inspectors may not fully inspect routine or normally acceptable products.

TREND ANALYSIS

A hunch is creativity trying to tell you something.
Frank Capra

If deficiencies or problems continue, this indicates that the symptom was fixed but the root cause of the problem was not discovered and eliminated. When a deficiency or nonconformance is discovered, the problem and data should be entered into a data base for future examination and trend analysis. Was this a recurrence? How often and in what area did it recur? Could the recurrence be due to multiple factors?

These and a number of other questions arise when a problem occurs:

- **Type and number of deficiencies.** Deficiencies can be a customer complaint, cost overrun, ISO 9001:2015 noncompliance, or product field failure. This data may indicate if the problem is isolated or if it is an early warning of a widespread problem.
- **Location of deficiency.** The location of the deficiency also reveals if the problem is isolated to a specific physical location, instrument, or use. This data when collated or analyzed can provide more clues for isolating the problem and finding the root-cause.
- **Corrective action analysis.** Corrective action analysis focuses on investigating the deficiency and determining actions to eliminate the cause of the deficiency.
- **Preventive action analysis.** Preventive analysis is a proactive analysis of data and information such as of Op Ex records, quality

results, service reports and customer complaints to detect, analyze, and eliminate potential causes of deficiencies. Once these are identified, then steps are identified to implement internal controls to prevent their occurrence or recurrence.

- **Cost analysis.** Op Ex, process, product, customer, and operational cost analysis indicates where there are existing and/or potential problems waiting to occur.
- **Risk analysis.** Areas of high risk are identified and internal controls are developed to minimize or eliminate the risk.
- **Trend analysis.** Trend analysis indicates if the deficiency or problem recurred. If it did then it may indicate the problem was not totally understood and there were multiple causes that were not eliminated. Trend analysis is important because it can be used to establish Op Ex baselines, indicate Op Ex, make comparisons, use for tactical Op Ex planning, and indicate historical patterns.
- **Management review.** Management review is the periodic review of the suitability and effectiveness of a company's Op Ex systems, including ISO 9001:2015 compliance and Op Ex.

COMMON OR SPECIAL CAUSES OF VARIATION

Facts speak louder than statistics.
Justice Streatfield

There are basically two types of variation:

- **Common causes.** Common cause variation, also called chance cause variation, is due to the natural and random changes in a process. There can be a number of sources of this type of variation.
- **Special causes.** Special cause variation, also called assignable cause variation, is due to unusual or identifiable causes in a system. These causes of variation can be detected and usually can be identified as an outlying point or as an abnormal trend in a process.

Variation can be caused by common (chance) or special (assignable) causes. Chance causes occur at random. While, assignable causes occur because of some identifiable reason. Assignable causes can be detected, reduced, eliminated, and thus controlled.

COMMON OR CHANCE CAUSES

Chance causes are an inherent part of the process and usually cannot be identified or eliminated by an operator simply adjusting a machine. Fluctuations of material composition within a piece of raw material, changes in tool deflection, or variations in weld penetration are examples of chance causes.

Deming and Juran maintained that 85% of the chance or system causes are the responsibility of management. These problems can only be reduced by management action. For example, an operator cannot consistently machine products so they conform to specifications if the machine is old and shows inherent vibration. The solution is to buy a new machine or widen the specification spread. Both actions require management attention and action.

ASSIGNABLE OR SPECIAL CAUSES

Assignable causes of variation are introduced from outside a process. These causes either increase or shift variation in unpredictable ways. Assignable causes result from untrained operators, poor instructions, or poor equipment.

INTERPRETING VARIABLE CHARTS

The trouble with facts is that there are so many of them.
Samuel Crothers, author

The development team establishes specifications independently of machine process limits. When the variable charts are drawn, three situations may result between process and specification spreads:

- Process spread is the equal to the specification spread.
- Process spread is less than the specification spread.

- Process spread is greater than the specification spread.

The process spread is the upper control limit minus the lower control limit and for the purposes of this example are the limits of the bell curves in the example to the right. Similarly, the specification spread is the upper specification limit (USL) minus the lower specification limit (LSL).

PROCESS SPREAD IS EQUAL TO SPECIFICATION SPREAD
If the process spread is equal to the specification spread and both are centered at the same point, then the process is capable. This means that 99.7% of the manufactured products conform to specifications. Approximately, three out of every thousand products are outside the specification band of the specification and this is indicated as a) in the above figure.

PROCESS SPREAD IS LESS THAN SPECIFICATION SPREAD
The ideal situation is to have the process spread less than the specification spread and to have it centered in the middle of the specification spread. Then, the process is capable. The curve is centered in the middle of the specification and is well inside the specification spread.

PROCESS SPREAD IS GREATER THAN SPECIFICATION SPREAD
If the process spread is greater than the specification spread or if the process spread is centered sufficiently above or below the specification center line, then an unacceptable number of defective products are produced. The process is out of control and not capable of meeting specifications.

Sometimes, the operator cannot find any special causes to eliminate, so the process spread cannot be narrowed. The specifications are so narrow that the process or machine is not capable of making products that conform to specifications. This occurs if a development team or engineer developed specifications without consulting Manufacturing about the capability of the machine or process to make a product to certain dimensions. New machines have to be purchased or the engineer increases the specification spread to accommodate the inherent capability of the machine.

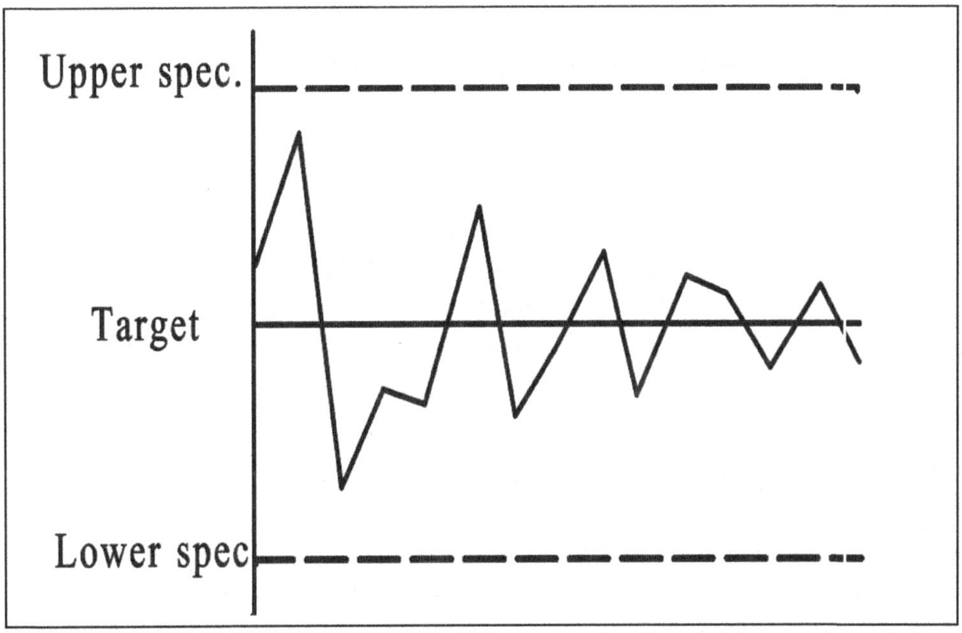

PRODUCTION PROCESS CONTROL

operational control is sometimes called the study of variation. Once a specification is written, process variation can be monitored and controlled around the specification target. The following are the steps for specifying, measuring, monitoring, and improving manufacturing process Op Ex so variation is minimized:

- Product and process specifications are developed.
- Classification of characteristics is defined.
- Inspection and test instructions are developed.
- Measuring and test equipment are available.
- Sampling system is established.
- Work instructions are written.
- People are trained.
- Documentation is developed.
- Progress is monitored and verified.
- Continuous Op Ex is pursued.

Product and Process Specifications are Developed

Procedures and work instructions are developed for all activities, including product, process, and service activities. Specifications define the optimum target and accepted limits of performance. As well, procedures are developed for test, inspection, material movement, material handling, storage, packaging, and costing.

The development team may write specifications or specifications can be derived from engineering, a customer, government requirements, or industry standards. Product specifications have to be realistic, measurable, and attainable. Product specifications specify product dimensions, reliability, workmanship, appearance, maintainability, and performance.

Process specifications detail how product specifications are met. Specifications also include physical dimensions, tolerances, surface finish, mechanical, chemical, and physical properties. Each of these can be ranked in terms of product nonconformance levels. Service specifications detail acceptable objectives for performing or delivering a service, including such operational excellence or quality attributes as courtesy, effectiveness, and reliability.

Classification of Characteristics is Defined

Manufacturing, Operational Excellence, and Engineering may jointly establish operational excellence levels for each significant product operational excellence characteristic. For example, important characteristics for a threaded fastener may be pitch depth, number of threads per inch, major pitch diameter, and minor pitch diameter.

Deficiencies or nonconformances can be classified in terms of their relative importance. The following three categories are often used, critical, major, and minor. Critical nonconformances can adversely affect product function and can result in a loss of life. A material crack that compromises structural integrity would be a critical defect. Major nonconformances can cause a product to malfunction without a loss of life. A major nonconformance lowers performance or decreases product marketability. A minor nonconformance does not meet a specification but does not affect performance, "fitness for use" or customer acceptance. A surface blemish on the inside of a product is an example of a minor defect.

A product may have different types of defects. A product with 100 quality characteristics may have 10 critical, 10 major, and 80 minor nonconforming classifications. One nonconformance in a critical product characteristic always rejects the product. One major or critical defect is usually sufficient for a product to be rejected.

Inspection and Test Instructions are Developed

As more organizations adopt an operational excellence system, mass inspection is being dropped in favor of third-party registration, operational excellence auditing, process control, or selective testing. Inspection and test instructions specify how to inspect and test parts, subassemblies, assemblies, and finished products. Instructions may be generated for incoming, in process, and final inspection.

The following must be known for developing inspection and test instructions:

- Sampling criteria to be used.
- Product, service, or process characteristics to be checked.
- Inspection or test equipment used.
- Inspection identification method used.
- Specification documents used.
- Accept and reject numbers.
- Name of the fixture, gage, or equipment needed for inspection.

Detailed instructions may also include drawings, specifications, and test procedures. Test and inspection equipment is specified for each test or inspection point in a production line.

Measuring and Test Equipment are Available

Measuring and test equipment are used to measure, gage, test, inspect, compare, and examine components to determine compliance to specifications. Operational excellence is only as good as the measuring and test equipment used to measure a key process characteristic. If measuring instruments are inaccurate, there is little confidence in decisions based on measurement data. So, gages, instruments, and test equipment must be calibrated and software diagnosed. Calibration is the process of comparing and measuring test equipment against measurement standards of known accuracy to detect and adjust deviations from known standards.

Sampling System is Established

Operational control sampling is a statistical process of determining how many products should be drawn and inspected from a batch or shipment. The number of products is mainly determined by the producer's risk of making nonconforming products, the consumer's risk of receiving defective products, cost of sampling, and sampling effectiveness.

Work Instructions are Written

A product, an assembly, or subassembly can be composed of many components. Detailed instructions for assembly and fabrication are prepared for fabricating and assembling component parts. The work instruction package for a machine operation may include drawings, work orders, standards, specifications, and sequence of operations.

People are Trained

People are trained in machine operations, measurement, product handling, and problem solving. While the mechanics of production is fairly routine and easy to comprehend, developing, and instilling a conscientious attitude and care about product quality and process consistency is more difficult.

First-line supervision must communicate that operational excellence is everyone's responsibility and that it rests with the team or person performing the work. Senior management also reinforces this attitude with consistent messages, coaching, and rewards.

Documentation is Developed

All manufacturing operational excellence decisions have to be planned, specified, and documented. Documentation includes equipment, specifications, workmanship standards, and other information critical to controlling and ensuring operational excellence.

Progress is Monitored and Verified

Process, product, or material status is verified at critical points in the production process. Verification can be accomplished through process controls, automatic inspection, tollgate inspection, or random auditing. By checking operational excellence status charts or graphs, operators and process engineers monitor a machine or process. If there are any abnormal deviations or trends, these can be root-cause solved.

Continuous Operational Excellence is Pursued

The goal of any operational excellence process is continuous improvement. Manufacturing operational excellence control and assurance can become a static program. Specified defect-levels or process capability can become instituted in an organization when it becomes satisfied with status-quo operational excellence and does not want to change. Pushing products out the door becomes more important than improving process or product operational excellence.

NEXT CHAPTER

In the next chapter, Op Ex Time Tools is discussed. Time is an essential element of all areas of lean, six sigma, supply management, quality, and for Op Ex managers. For example, effective and efficient time management for an Op Ex manager includes delivering projects on time, setting an example for the organization, being seen talking about and doing Op Ex, cheerleading, planning Op Ex, resolving conflicts and differences, and attending meetings.

CHAPTER 15
OP EX TIME TOOLS

Time is a resource, just like a machine, people, equipment, and monies. Time is finite. Time has value. Time must be managed in the face of constraints. Time management is probably one of the more persistent challenges facing the Op Ex manager. Time is involved in all operational management activities from planning, staffing, and getting projects done on time and within budget. The following discussion deals with time issues.

TIME MANAGEMENT

Hindsight is good, foresight is better; but second sight is best of all.
Evan Esar

Sixty hours or more work weeks gets old. Pressures build up at work. The tension may be taken home. Tension is a real killer of Op Ex managers. The level of authority and responsibility has risen as the Op Ex function expanded from inspection, control, assurance to companywide operational management. Working smart these days means managing one's time smartly. The Op Ex manager can't over promise and under deliver without losing credibility and authority.

TIME MANAGEMENT TIPS

What's the solution? Time management. Time management is the ability to manage work, responsibilities, and people to get work done. Technology is also coming to the rescue. Assistance is available through palm computers, time planners, wrist watch beepers, cellular phones, and beepers. Often, effective time management involves some simple steps as:

- Saying no to new projects.

- Delegating as much as possible.
- Training personnel to do multiple tasks.
- Prioritizing work.
- Following schedules and plans.
- Making meetings short and sweet.
- Planning work.
- Inspiring confidence in others to get the job done.
- Not over promising and under delivering.
- Evaluating mental and physical status periodically.

IMPORTANCE OF JUST-IN-TIME

FISH: First in. Still Here.
Anonymous

Just-in-time, lean, Supply Management, distribution and logistics are important systems of the total Op Ex process. The broad goal of JIT and lean is to eliminate waste, add value, and optimize the entire chain of value added activities from understanding customer requirements to quickly delivering a product. Cycle reduction and just-in-time systems are complementary processes to offer companies the advances of increased production flexibility, faster customer response, and lower costs.

Just-in-time (JIT) is a broad philosophy covering many operational areas. Just-in-time broadly is the design and management of a customer-supplier value-added system to minimize cycle and lead times. The precise arrival of parts to the specific location is the conventional interpretation and understanding of just-in-time. However, it is but one example of the very broad impact and involvement of JIT and lean. JIT and lean are often illustrated as rocks in a stream or a large boulder. As water is lowered, more chronic problems are discovered which must be corrected.

JIT AND LEAN PROCESS ELEMENTS

JIT and lean broadly involve:

- **Just-in-time deliveries.** Products are delivered just-in-time to be used on the manufacturing floor. Deliveries are in small quantities, supplied more frequently, and have an exact count.
- **Suppliers located close to the plant.** In order that shipments are delivered reliably, suppliers of perishable, critical, or heavy products are located near the customer. Light-weight products may be flown on overnight delivery.
- **High quality goods.** As well, JIT delivery requires products are defect free. If defective products end up on the line then the customer's production line will stop.
- **Reengineered internal operations.** Internal operations are examined and if necessary reengineered to improve them. Smoothing and streamlining operations add value and eliminate waste which are core values of all just-in-time processes.
- **Total Op Ex.** Total Op Ex in its broadest sense is the goal and objective of every element of the value-adding process stream.
- **Controlled and capable processes.** Critical processes are stable and capable. Stable processes are in control. Capable processes are able to meet customer requirements and specifications. The goal of all controlled and capable processes is to improve consistency over time.
- **Customer-supplier partnering.** An important element in JIT and lean is the need for fewer suppliers. Multiple product suppliers can result in increased product, delivery, cost, and quality variation. These may be caused by lack of understanding, poor communication, or differences in capabilities. Whatever the cause, the results are the same - poor quality products and service result in dissatisfied customers. This is the reason for reducing the supplier base to a prime supplier or one supplier and an approved alternate.
- **Worker and management commitment to work together.** The entire process from order taking to product/service delivery is streamlined in process JIT and lean. Many disparate parts of the organization must work together as smoothly as an expensive Swiss watch. If there are problems, they are root cause solved and eliminated. For this to work, management and employee teams must be empowered, trained, and committed.

- **Dock to production delivery.** Dock-to-stock was the prevailing wisdom for many years. Now, companies want to eliminate all inventory and move incoming parts directly onto the production line.
- **Sequenced delivery.** The right parts have to arrive at the right location in the proper amount, at the right time, and in the right order. Even the packing of the parts in a truck or railcar is critical. For example, parts are packed in the truck in the reverse order in which they will be used. To minimize handling and storage, parts are pulled from the truck in the sequence they will be used on the assembly line. Trucks can be unloaded quickly; parts go directly onto the production line; trucks don't have to wait to unload; costs are reduced; queues are eliminated; space is not required to repalettize or shift parts; and loading dock efficiency is increased.
- **Proper packaging.** If parts are packaged loosely then products can be damaged. If parts are packaged too robustly then additional personnel, equipment and time may be required to break down the packaging.

TIME AS A COMPETITIVE WEAPON

The first person gets the oyster; the second person gets the shell.
Andrew Carnegie, business person

The first company often has a dramatic market advantage. The list of firsts are extensive - the first to market, the first to become ISO 9001:2015 registered, the first to win the Malcolm Baldrige, the first to implement just-in-time systems, and the first to deliver a product to market. Markets are fragmented with customers with diverse needs who want them fulfilled instantly with products or processes that not only exceed their expectations but please them in every way.

A company that can satisfy customers with lower cost, high quality products and services delivered just-in-time and in the right manner has a higher probability of beating its competition. Delivering products and services faster requires a company does the right things right the first time and every time. Op Ex must be ingrained in the organization. Operations are proceduralized, in control, and capable. Everyone is trained to do their jobs right. All non-value added processes and systems are eliminated.

HIGH OP EX IS NO LONGER SUFFICIENT

Conventional business wisdom now says quality by itself is not enough to please customers. Now, it must be the right bundle of price-competitive, products and services delivered just-in-time and in the right manner to the customer. Time is as or more important than Op Ex. For example, software developers are offering buggy software for their first product release that is debugged in subsequent revisions.

Business hurdles and barriers are higher than five years ago. In only several years, low price, high quality products and services don't guarantee success. Products must be developed and delivered quickly to satisfy fickle customer tastes. As well, the risks are higher. Customers want cost-competitive, tailored products quickly. Companies must invest more resources in products and service development.

Often a benchmarking study is the impetus for a company to discover that something is wrong. The competition is doing something critical in half the time and are reaping tremendous profits from this strategy. Evaluating and if necessary redesigning internal processes is the first step to increasing time-to-market. First a company eliminates nonproductive internal tasks and redesigns processes. Once this is done, they are monitored, stabilized and improved over time.

CRITICAL CYCLE TIME REDUCTION AREAS

One consequence of postwar technology has been the acceleration of change in our society, so that we seem to produce a new generation of products about every five years.
Ross Macdonald

Cycle time reduction is critical to resolving chronic problems; improving customer deliveries; supplier deliveries; responding to fashions, trends, tastes; eliminating waste; responding to product recalls; implementing ISO 9001:2015 quality systems; and introducing products to market.

Time as a competitive advantage can be illustrated in the following examples:

- Product development partnerships
- Just-in-time production
- Just-in-time delivery

PRODUCT DEVELOPMENT PARTNERSHIPS

World class product and services sell. Few companies have the resources to be the best in all areas and activities. Also, few companies have the abilities to create by themselves the products they need to be a globally competitive and to satisfy all its customers. Large companies are now scanning the horizon for small companies with new ideas, lots of energy, and special skills they want but don't have. Sometimes, large companies will buy smaller, entrepreneurial companies. Sometimes, large companies will license technology and sometimes the bigger companies will partner with smaller companies. These partnerships are called strategic alliances, strategic partnerships, or even virtual corporations. They exist as long as value is being added by each partner and as long as revenues are being produced. Partnering is becoming the favorite option because entrepreneurs choke in the larger organizations where initiatives and invention are often stymied.

JUST-IN-TIME PRODUCTION

Just-in-time (JIT) production or manufacturing is the systematic elimination of waste throughout the product or service delivery stream. Just-in-time often starts with suppliers and is driven throughout the value added delivery stream. The goal of JIT and lean is to eliminate waste in all resources including people, equipment, technology, and systems. Superfluous raw material, extra material handling, inventory, extra labor, inadequate supervision, all add unnecessary costs to the process.

JUST-IN-TIME DELIVERY

The marketplace changes quickly. New competitors arise. Customers are fickle. Customers want products delivered over night. In general, everything in business seems to be accelerating at electronic speed.

The windows of opportunity are shrinking as stakeholders are linked electronically. Parts must be delivered just-in-time for assembly or test. Inventories are held down to close to zero. The time between a customer order and product delivery is reduced to a minimum. Products across the world are delivered within 24 hours of being ordered.

JUST-IN-TIME METRICS

Nothing is more satisfying when timing and delivery occur in perfect sequence.
Anonymous

Lean and Just in time are used synomously. Just-in-time can be defined and measured in terms of Op Ex attributes or lean dimensions, such as:

- Timeliness
- Reliability
- Product integrity
- Customer service
- Accurate and complete information
- Flexibility

TIMELINESS

Timeliness is the ability to deliver a product when and where the customer wants it. Speed is the key to delivery. Especially in JIT and lean distribution, the internal customer wants products delivered onto the production line at precise schedules.

RELIABILITY

Reliability is the ability to deliver products at regular time intervals. Delivery reliability is measured in terms of transit time which is compared to promised delivery. Supply Management can contract for supplies to be drop shipped on a monthly basis at a specific location. The manufacturer relies on the supplier to meet delivery obligations every month, otherwise a missed shipment shuts the production line. If missed shipments become a habit, then the customer is required to carry additional inventory to meet unexpected demands. This is expensive because of high inventory, storage, and handling costs.

PRODUCT INTEGRITY

Product integrity means that a defect-free product is delivered intact to the customer. There is no storage, shipping, or handling damage. Once delivered, the product functions as the customer expects.

CUSTOMER SERVICE

Customer service keeps the customer advised of delivery problems, providing notice of product changes and price changes, providing accurate invoicing, satisfying warranty claims, reconciling billing differences, and supplying technical assistance.

The sales engineer provides current and accurate information of a product's special features, maintenance, and performance. An order desk clerk provides prompt and efficient order taking. If product integrity has been compromised, then problems need to be resolved courteously, quickly, and satisfactorily.

ACCURATE AND COMPLETE INFORMATION

Product delivery is not complete if support documentation is not current, accurate, and complete. This is especially important for a complex industrial product. Support documentation includes product certifications, parts lists, engineering prints, spares list, operating instructions, maintenance instructions, inspection reports, and other product information.

FLEXIBILITY

Flexibility is the ability to respond to sudden customer needs. For example, a customer requires a rush delivery to satisfy unexpected demands. Sudden needs may require substituting material, rescheduling shipments, or changing carriers.

JIT AND LEAN ADVANTAGES

JIT and lean are different than traditional distribution management. In JIT and lean, material distribution, transportation, storage, and handling become more critical as requirements for reliable and consistent delivery of product increase. Customer inventory is reduced drastically and it is hoped eliminated. Product warehousing requirements are also reduced.

Specifically, JIT Supply Management and distribution result in:

- Fewer suppliers
- Improved product quality
- Reduced inventory
- Fewer nonproductive personnel

Fewer Suppliers

JIT and lean require fewer suppliers. JIT and lean have little room for error. Products have to be supplied on time and be defect-free. Otherwise, a late shipment or one with defective products shuts down a customer's production line.

The trend is to reduce the supplier list to those that can comply with contractual commitments. Compliant suppliers are offered inducements, such as predictable orders for their products.

Suppliers of critical products are often the most compliant, willing to learn, and try new techniques. These suppliers have major accounts and have the largest incentive to change.

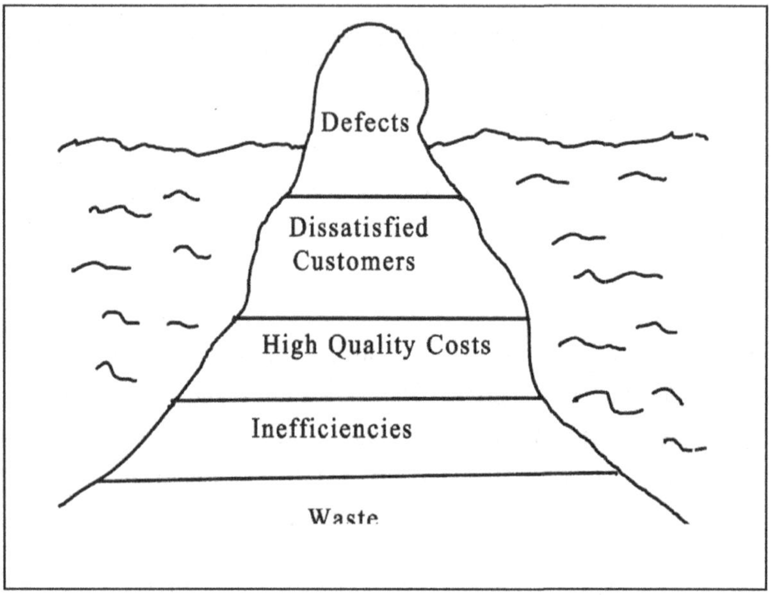

Improved Product Quality

Quality, as 100% conforming material shipments, is required for the proper functioning of JIT. The customer does not inspect any incoming material. If a supplier delivers a shipment with defective products, then the customer's production line stops. This is expensive. Once suppliers understand the consequences of failure, they must be able to deliver on-time, defect-free material.

Reduced Inventory

The goal of JIT and lean is to progressively reduce all types of inventory. Traditionally, by maintaining high inventory levels, a supplier could provide a high level of customer service by supplying products on demand. Inventory was a buffer to balance unpredictable levels of supply and demand.

Fewer Nonproductive Personnel

As inventories are reduced, the number of material handlers, parts inspectors, supervisors, and other employees, who do not produce anything, is reduced.

ROCKS IN THE LAKE

As inventory is reduced, problems are exposed. The analogy is often made of rocks in a lake. The water in the lake represents inventory and rocks in the lake represent various types of Op Ex and productivity problems. A lake with deep water (high inventory) hides rocks (problems) that remain below the surface, hidden from view.

Eliminating inventory forces an organization to acknowledge and solve problems. Inventory hides operational problems including machine downtime, scrap, work in process buffer inventories, engineering design redundancies, change orders, inspection backlog, paper backlog, poor material Op Ex, high scrap rates, late supplier deliveries, transaction errors, double orders, safety stock, and rejected materials.

NEXT CHAPTER

In the next chapter, Op Ex Process Tools is discussed. Proces tools focus on process management, defect prevention, and problem solving. For example, defect prevention is a major Op Ex objective. As a product is made or a service is delivered, value is added. Value is the labor, machinery, material, or facilities required to do work. For example, it is expensive to scrap a porous casting after it has gone through 10 or more manufacturing steps. Or, it is counterproductive to manufacture a highly reliable product if the delivery system is inefficient.

CHAPTER 16

OP EX PROCESS TOOLS

Process tools are the basis for Op Ex, lean, six sigma, and quality problem solving and decision making. It all starts with understanding the PDSA cycle.

PDSA CYCLE

How do I work? I grope.
Albert Einstein
The four stages of the cycle are:

- **Plan.** Study the current situation to determine what should be improved including safety, quality, delivery, cost, or productivity.
- **Do.** Implement a small improvement project, design a prototype, or do something similarly in a small scale.
- **Study.** Determine or examine the results of the implementation.
- **Act.** Adopt the change, modify it, or abandon it depending on the observed results. Start the process again, if there is insufficient information or data. Or, start the process again to improve the system.

The PDSA cycle conveys the powerful message that there is a continuous search for improvement. The Japanese called this kaizen and became a critical element of all of their Op Ex initiatives and projects. The status-quo was never good enough. Things could always be done better.

Coupled with the above message is that the cycle never stops. Once a team has studied and implemented changes, the team or another one improves the existing problem or pursues another project.

QUALITY FUNCTION DEPLOYMENT

Quality Function Deployment is a technique developed by the Japanese to translate the "voice of the customer" into the organization. The voice of the customer has become the most important mission and goal for almost any company. Many companies have gone beyond simply satisfying customers to pleasing and even delighting them at every turn.

QFD is a structured process to understand customer requirements in terms of specific product and service characteristics, features, and performance and then translating these into measurable engineering and production specifications. The customer may want a bundle of quality features, performance, and characteristics such as visual aesthetics, safety, performance, ease of use, and after sales support. The purpose of this process is to ensure that all internal groups can understand and identify critical customer requirements and then deliver them.

The QFD process consists of four main steps:

- **Capturing the voice of the customer.** The steps for capturing the voice of the customer were discussed in the previous section. Usually market research or some other proactive method is used to obtain the information.
- **Transferring customer requirements and expectations into an Op Ex matrix.** This step looks at the "hows", the specific steps of how these customer Op Ex requirements can be met. The product development team may brainstorm, analyze, and develop a consensus decision of the "hows" which are sometimes called QFD measures. QFD incorporates a series of matrices that resemble a number of houses, hence the "house of quality" description of QFD.
- **Cascade the first matrix results into subsequent matrices.** This step defines how a customer's requirements will be satisfied and will cascade through the organization. The product development team will analyze the relationships between customer wants and hows and prioritize them into strong, moderate or weak relationships. Strong relationships are critical for ensuring customer satisfaction. The QFD process focuses on the customer at each step.

The measures or "hows" of each process step or matrix becomes the wants of the next step of the cascading matrices. For example, the customer requirements in the first house of quality become product characteristics. In the design matrix, technical requirements are converted to assembly or part characteristics. In the process matrix, these technical requirements are converted to process characteristics which evolve to actual production control requirements.

- **Act on the results.** The QFD process becomes thoroughly integrated into the product planning and development process so a cost-competitive, high-quality product or service that the customer wants can be developed.

BREAKTHROUGH PROBLEM SOLVING

Give a man a fish and you feed him for one day. Teach a man to fish and you feed him for a lifetime.
Chinese proverb

Many organizations solve problems using a fire fighting approach. The fire-fighting approach means reacting to emergencies by doing what needs to be done to solve a problem. The fire-fighting approach is exciting because everyone stops what they are doing to work on the problem. This approach solves isolated problems but usually does not solve recurring minor or major problems.

Continuous operational excellence requires what Joseph Juran called "breakthrough management." Organizations and management must "breakthrough" the accepted level of chronic problems and focus their efforts to improve the foundation of the operational excellence system. For example, if a development team discovered a process only had a 90% yield, this would be clearly unacceptable. As a result, the development team may have to redesign the product in order to eliminate the defect

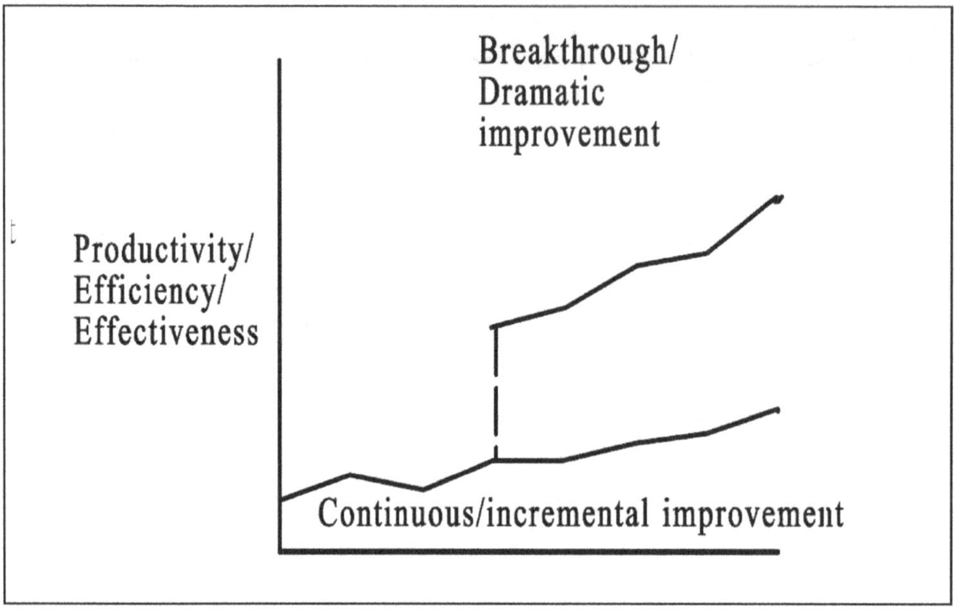

which could not be achieved by simply adjusting or designing the production process.

TYPES OF PROBLEMS

Major recurring or isolated problems require immediate attention and resolution. These problems compromise operational or product integrity. A major problem involves product safety or reliability such as automobile brake reliability. Otherwise, an accident due to faulty brakes can result in costly litigation.

Less critical, minor recurring or isolated material problems also require immediate attention. These problems do not affect operating integrity. More often, they are nuisances that lower operational efficiency or effectiveness. Minor recurring or isolated problems are usually fixed as they occur. However, they can lower operational efficiency and become a part of the system.

PREVENTION AND PROCESS IMPROVEMENT

Problem solving and constructive innovation are what business is all about.
Randall Meyer

However, Op Ex as "conformance to specifications" cannot be assured or controlled by inspecting Op Ex into the product. Inspectors inspect, sort, rework, rehandle, and reinspect defective products. This is wasteful, because it consumes time, effort, expense, material, personnel, and facilities.

Customer satisfaction cannot be guaranteed by instructing a salesperson in courtesy after the sale. The salesperson or receptionist should have been instructed in policies and procedures before the assignment.

The long-term goal is to improve the process. A process consists of a series to steps, each of which has an input, process, and output. An internal supplier provides input to an internal customer who processes it to another internal customer. Each process step adds value in the process chain. Each process step is responsible for the Op Ex of effort as well as ensuring that downstream customers are satisfied.

The following are the assumptions of a process:

- Every work activity is a process.
- Each process has inputs and outputs.
- Each process has a supplier(s) and customer(s).
- Each process can be controlled, made consistent, and improved.
- Each process adds value.
- Op Ex, service, delivery, service, performance, efficiency and economics are measured.
- Each process can be documented and measured.
- If process works as intended, the outputs should conform to customer requirements.
- Process thinking and doing are essential to all process Op Ex.

Process redesign requires management commitment, external or internal urgency, process understanding, employee motivation, and problem-solving abilities. Business process improvement involves understanding the process, eliminating nonvalue-added steps, stabilizing the process, determining process capability, and finally improving the process over time.

THE AUDIT PROCESS

The big things you can see with one eye closed. But keep both eyes wide open for the little things. Little things mark the great dividing line between success and failure.
Jacob Braude

Op Ex auditing and corrective/preventive actions are probably the two most important ISO 9001:2015 Op Ex system requirements. They form the basis of monitoring, correcting, and improving Op Ex systems.

INTERNAL AUDIT PROCESS STEPS

Auditors must know the basic Op Ex tools, speak the language of Op Ex, and know operations. As well, auditors must be sensitive to the culture of the organization. Auditors assume different roles including inspectors, independent reviewers, and even internal consultants. Auditors in some total Op Ex environments are seen as business partners who can serve as internal consultants to improve operations.

An audit, particularly a process audit, is a snapshot of an operation at a given point in time. An operation is really a moving picture. The auditee may present an over optimistic image that does not reflect the realities of the operation. On the other hand, a minor problem can be blown out of proportion and not reflect the general conditions of the operation.

To avoid these extreme reactions, an audit team follows a systematic process of:

- Preparation
- Preliminary conference
- Data acquisition
- Data interpretation
- Closing conference

- Feedback and action

Preparation
The auditee is first notified of the impending audit. The auditee is advised when it will be performed, who and how many people will be performing it, and why it is being performed.

The team obtains background information on the auditee. Background information is obtained from financial statements, industry descriptions, and trade journal articles. For specific information, the team evaluates the Op Ex manual, specifications, drawings, layouts, flowcharts, reliability test reports, and customer service history.

Preliminary Conference
The preliminary conference at the auditee's facility establishes audit ground rules. Any auditee fears are dispelled in this conference.

Data Acquisition
The team collects program, process, people, and product information. The team interviews management and employees. The team reviews Op Ex policies, procedures, plans, procedures, standards, and specifications.

Data Interpretation
The team interprets and tries to understand the data collected during the audit. This is time consuming and labor intensive. The team should understand the client's industry, internal processes, and product. With this knowledge, the team attempts to identify unusual variations or unusual conditions in the organization and may recommend corrective actions.

Closing Conference
The closing conference reviews preliminary impressions, compliance problems, preliminary conclusions, and preliminary recommendations. If there are substantive areas of disagreement, these may be appealed to the customer's corporate management.

Feedback and Action

Finally, the auditee is formally notified of audit results in writing. If deficiencies are found, the auditee is asked to correct them prior to approval. If the auditee does not agree with the recommendations and conclusions, then customer and auditee management may resolve the difference.

If the auditee is a supplier and is being evaluated for the first time, the audit team may approve the supplier, reject the supplier, or recommend further evaluation. If the supplier has been supplying products for some time, the audit is used as a monitoring tool to encourage continuous improvement.

Eliminate Root Cause

Root cause analysis investigates the cause and the chain of events that resulted in the problem. Each process step is investigated, possible causes are identified and examined until a root cause is determined. Once this process becomes institutionalized, system problem solving becomes a normal course of business. The challenge is that a problem may have multiple causes and it becomes difficult to determine the prime cause.

FEEDBACK LOOPS

No progress is going back.
Proverb

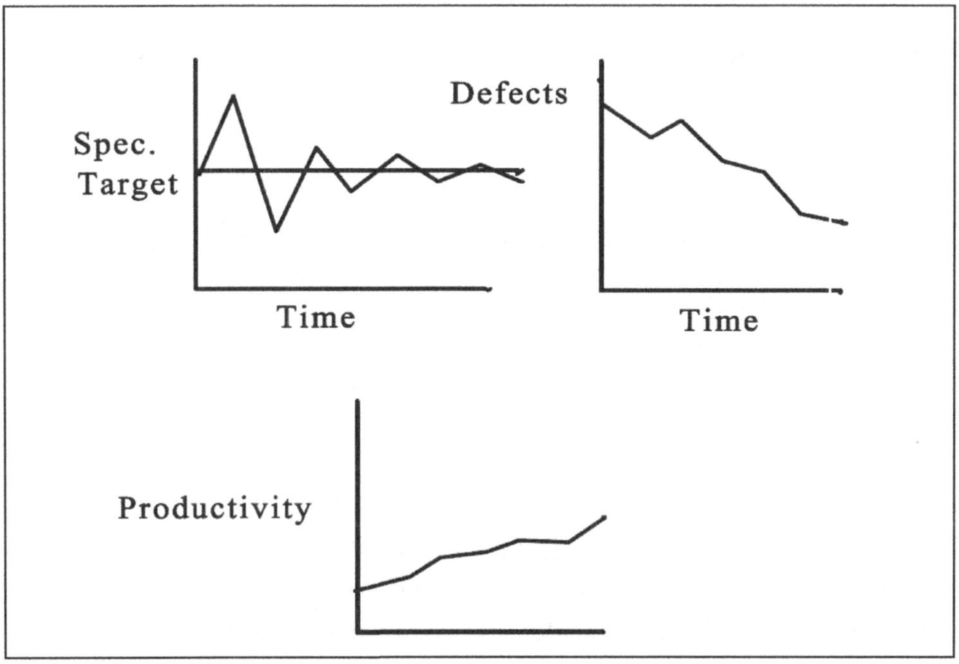

The goal of continuous improvement is to evolve from an ad hoc process to formal, controlled, operational systems that are capable of meeting internal and external customer requirements. Operational control is a fundamental element of Op Ex. Teams and process personnel attempt to proceduralize and stabilize operations that are also capable of satisfying requirements and customers. If there is an unusual occurrence then the process is stopped and the source of the problem is discovered and eliminated. Control depends on people using their best judgment to make the right decisions to solve the problem.

Process improvement can include a number of things, process variation is being minimized at the specification target. Defects are decreasing over time and the bottom figure shows productivity improving over time.

PROCESS IMPROVEMENT

Jack Welch, the CEO of General Electric, popularized the concept of the boundaryless organization where artificial boundaries to resources, communication and cooperation are removed in order to improve business processes. Technology and instant communication facilitate the redesign of organizations through the removal of horizontal barriers within the organization, the vertical barriers in the organizational hierarchy, and the external barriers outside a department or business unit.

CONTINUOUS IMPROVEMENT METHODOLOGY

Businesses aren't run by geniuses. It is a matter of putting one foot after another in a logical fashion. The trick is in knowing what direction you want to go.
James R. Barker

There is no one officially sanctioned or approved continuous improvement methodology. It seems that every consultant to differentiate himself or herself recommends something a little different. The following methodology is a plain vanilla model that incorporate many common and useful steps suggested by many.

A typical continuous improvement model is similar to the following eight steps:

- **Step 1.** Understand competitive and business environment.
- **Step 2.** Establish operational management and cultural environment.
- **Step 3.** Define the business and Op Ex mission of each component of the organization.
- **Step 4.** Set performance improvement goals and priorities.
- **Step 5.** Develop project improvement action plans.
- **Step 6.** Implement project using improvement methodologies.
- **Step 7.** Evaluate results and improvement.
- **Step 8.** Review and Recycle (Go back to Step 1).[72]

STEP 1: UNDERSTAND COMPETITIVE AND BUSINESS ENVIRONMENT

The purpose of the competitive analysis is to identify competitors and to gather information about the environment in which an organization competes. The competitive analysis guides the development of strategies and plans.

Competitive analysis is an ongoing process. As a company develops and implements strategies, the results can be monitored on an ongoing basis to ensure the right things are being done at the right time. Continuous feedback monitoring allows for nonconformances to be corrected, establishes Op Ex systems so nonconformances can be prevented, and promotes searching for opportunities to improve the system.

Questions and factors to consider in a competitive analysis include:

- What are the major and macro-economic, social, cultural, and political trends impacting a business over ten, five, three, and one year?
- Who are today's competitors?
- What are their relative strengths and weaknesses?
- Who may be tomorrow's competitors?
- In terms of today's competitor's which point of weakness can provide the greatest competitive leverage?

STEP 2: ESTABLISH OPERATIONAL MANAGEMENT AND CULTURAL ENVIRONMENT

Continuous process improvement (CPI) is a total business, organizational, and technical approach towards developing systems, processes, and products that please customers. Senior management commitment and involvement is essential to establish the organizational conditions for CPI to flourish. Senior management takes the lead for creating a flexible work environment, defining the culture, and encouraging change.

Senior management is responsible for:

- Vision
- Long term commitment
- Active and visible support
- People involvement and empowerment
- Goals and objectives definition
- Methodologies
- Support systems
- Training
- Organizational roadblock elimination

Vision

Senior management and critical stakeholders assist in establishing an organizational vision of where it wants the organization to go and what it thinks the organization should be. The visioning process attempts to link external market requirements, opportunities, and challenges to internal core capabilities. If internal capabilities don't exist, then they are developed or acquired.

Long Term Commitment

Op Ex and customer satisfaction require long term commitment. Customer requirements change over time and Op Ex must also change to accommodate today's customers as well as tomorrow's. For example, a few years ago Op Ex was largely defined in terms of conformance to requirements. Now, niche customers must be pleased with cost competitive, aesthetically pleasing products and services that are delivered courteously and quickly.

Senior management commitment involves a number of visible activities and products including providing:

- Long term perspective and drive.
- Focus on innovation, reengineering, and continuously improving results.
- Policies defining the direction of the organization.
- Procedures specifying what is expected and accepted.

- Talks, speeches, and rewards.
- Monies, facilities, people, equipment and other resources.
- Value added training.
- Reward and recognition for approved and expected accomplishments.

People Involvement and Empowerment

People are the means of implementing any continuous improvement project. People must feel sufficiently comfortable and responsible to own their processes. Senior management establishes, supports, and reinforces the systems for encouraging and empowering employees to initiate ideas and to implement them within their areas of expertise without fear of reprisal.

Individual and team self-direction and self-management sometimes require a change if not an organizational and cultural transformation. It takes time and patience. The process may start with low-level participation and move towards involvement, empowerment and finally ownership of systems and processes.

The critical elements of success are faith, trust, and results. Faith is required to start the process. Trust between management and employees and among team members is required to ensure the process will proceed satisfactorily. Finally, demonstrable results ensure the next Op Ex project will be funded.

Goals and Objectives

The goals and objectives of the continuous improvement initiative and the individual improvement projects must link, support, and reinforce the organizational and business vision, mission, plans, and objectives. This linkage must be demonstrable, timely, definable, and measurable.

Until recently, many Op Ex initiatives were basically approved because they were viewed as good for the customer, organization, or work area. Monies were allocated and spent with few results. Now, senior manage ment and other stakeholders are smarter and regard Op Ex as an investment that must demonstrate sufficient financial return. Most importantly, these returns must support the organizational business imperatives.

Methodologies

Continuous process improvement must follow a disciplined and integrated approach using the proper tools, methodologies, principles, and techniques. The right approach and tool must be used for the right challenge and consider the culture of the organization. CPI professionals must be able to recognize the problem, intervene appropriately with the right approach, tools and techniques to solve the problem or remove the deficiency.

A typical systems approach to technical problem solving involves:

- Analyzing organizational, management, team, and individual issues.
- Analyzing systems, processes and products.
- Solving the problem.
- Stabilizing and documenting the system.
- Ensuring the system is capable.
- Improving the system and process.
- Auditing the system for improvement.

Problem solving is difficult because it requires discipline, time, resources, and energy. The status quo must often be challenged. Change is also difficult. Process owners must control and improve their systems.

Support Systems

Support systems are the organizational links for transferring Op Ex throughout the organization and into the supplier base. The improvement process starts with senior management which assists in cascading goals, objectives, values, and training down the organization.

An Op Ex steering committee or a similar group may start the process. The corporate steering committee is composed of senior management. The committee may develop the organizational vision and the goals for the Op Ex initiative. Similar steering committees may be established in divisions, business units, and plants to cascade the Op Ex messages and improvement activities throughout the organization and into the supplier base.

Training

Changing customer requirements and new product development require continuous employee training in Op Ex, processes, procedures, and techniques. New employees at a minimum are trained in the importance of Op Ex for ensuring customer satisfaction. Employees are then trained in Op Ex tools and techniques. The level and expense of the training is determined by the type of organization, its culture, customer requirements, processes, systems, and products.

STEP 3: DEFINE THE BUSINESS AND OP EX MISSION OF EACH COMPONENT OF THE ORGANIZATION

Vision and mission are sometimes confused or used interchangeably. The vision is the end goal of where the organization is headed. The mission defines how it is going to get there. The mission of a business defines how it meets its objectives of satisfying stakeholders which may include shareholders, bondholders, management, employees, community, and suppliers.

The organizational mission is usually distilled in a simple statement. This mission statement then cascades down the organization. Each business unit, plant, function, work area, and team may develop a mission which is consistent and supportive of the organizational mission.

STEP 4: IDENTIFY PERFORMANCE IMPROVEMENT GOALS AND OBJECTIVES

More often, continuous Op Ex initiatives or projects are performance driven in terms of showing demonstrable results that are tied to strategic business objectives. A hierarchy links improvement efforts down into the organization and across functional boundaries. The entire organization is interlinked with reinforcing Op Ex projects that support the strategic goals of the organization. Overall goals are set by senior management which support the mission of the organization. Then middle and line operational managers develop business unit, division, and plant business and Op Ex goals which are translated to team and individual performance objectives.

Typical performance improvement projects or opportunities may involve:

- Improving process capability
- Improving product maintainability or reliability
- Reengineering processes
- Establishing ISO 9001:2015 systems
- Pursuing ISO 9001:2015 registration
- Lowering costs
- Improving delivery and service
- Improving customer satisfaction

STEP 5: DEVELOP PROJECT IMPROVEMENT ACTION PLANS

The company wide Op Ex initiative should spawn interlinked and coordinated improvement projects throughout the organization. As discussed in step 3, there may be two or more coordinating groups which may include:

- Corporate steering group
- Business unit steering group
- Process improvement teams

Corporate Steering Group

This senior level business management group focuses on the strategic direction of the CPI initiative. As well, this group:

- Establishes the operational excellence vision.
- Develops guiding principles.
- Provides resources.
- Establishes rewards and recognition.
- Establishes metrics.
- Identifies operational excellence owners in business units.

Business Unit Steering Group

This operational management group focuses on the tactical direction of the CPI teams at the business unit or at the plant level. As well, this group:

- Analyzes systems and processes.
- Identifies specific improvement opportunities.
- Establishes plans for achieving objectives and capitalizing on opportunities.
- Provides resources.
- Develops improvement plans.
- Measures and reports on progress.
- Provides operational coaching and mentoring.
- Develops team leaders and facilitators.
- Monitors system and process control and capability.
- Intervenes when required.

Process Improvement Teams

These teams implement the improvement project using established operational excellence methodologies and techniques at the plant or work area level. The teams often focus on process or workplace issues.

STEP 6: IMPLEMENT PROJECT USING IMPROVEMENT METHODOLOGIES

The basic steps in an operational excellence projects are:

- **Identify and prioritize improvement opportunities.** Opportunities can be identified and prioritized through Pareto analysis, cost of operational excellence, return on investment, risk analysis, and force field analysis. Projects with the highest return, quickest return, or the highest risk are chosen and pursued first.
- **Understand process culture.** Each process has stakeholders, process owners, and a culture. The culture at the process, function, or team level says how things are done. This culture has to be understood before improvement initiatives can be implemented. Process owners may form the bulk of the CPI team because they will be responsible for ensuring long term process improvement.

- **Flow chart process.** A process flowchart shows the process as a series of steps. Each step has a customer and supplier. The flowchart can then be used to understand the process and to identify redundancies, waste, or other non-value added activities. Specific techniques to use include: block diagrams, input/output analysis, benchmarking, and reengineering.
- **Assess fulfillment of customer needs.** Each process step has a customer whose needs must be satisfied. Process customer satisfaction determines if the process is doing what it is supposed to be doing. Customer satisfaction may be determined by satisfying a number of process requirements such as speed, operational excellence, cost, efficiency, or effectiveness. Processes can be controlled and proceduralized. Specific process parameters can be controlled, capability can be ensured, and the process should be improved. Specific techniques to use include statistical methods, inspection, sampling, and capability analysis.
- **Identify process steps.** A process may consist of one or a hundred steps in a series or series-parallel configuration.
- **Identify inputs and outputs of each process step.** Each process step has inputs from a supplier and each step has outputs sent to a customer.
- **Develop and establish process measures.** The inputs, process, and outputs of the process can be measured. Measures may be process or product specific. Process measures include capability indices, costs, or time related measures. Product measures include critical dimensions, physical characteristics, or chemical characteristics.
- **Understand variation.** The measurement and control of variation is fundamental to all continuous operational excellence. Once data is collected and reviewed, then special causes of variation can be eliminated. Once the process is in control, then common causes of variation can be identified and eliminated.
- **Implement improvement.** Process improvement involves several objectives. One major objective of improvement is to establish con

trolled and capable processes. The process should also be improved over time through minimizing variation or pursuing breakthrough improvement.

STEP 7: EVALUATE RESULTS AND IMPROVEMENT

Measurement, monitoring, and evaluation of results are essential to the continuous improvement process. Measurement identifies the effectiveness, efficiency, and economy of the operational excellence. From a business decision, it determines if the investment was worth it. Results may involve lower costs, elimination of a deficiency, cycle reduction, improved productivity, improved customer satisfaction, or other specific factors. All measurements should be meaningful to the process team, plant/business unit steering team stakeholders, and corporate steering committee stakeholders.

Measurement may include:

- **Process measurements.** Process measures include internal customer and supplier satisfaction, process control, and process capability.
- **Product measurements.** Product measurements include complying with dimensional, physical, or chemical specifications.
- **Project measurements.** Project measurements involve meeting budgets, completing the project on time, and complying with contractual requirements.
- **Product development measurements.** Product development measurements involve external customer satisfaction, cycle time reduction, and safety.
- **Behavioral/organizational measurements.** Behavioral measurements include increased customer satisfaction, improved quality of work life, and increased safety.

STEP 8: REVIEW AND RECYCLE (GO BACK TO STEP 1)

One of Deming's 14 points is constancy of purpose which meant that quality was not instant pudding or a silver bullet but required continuous attention and application. Op Ex requires long term commitment and effort from senior management and day-to-day commitment from each organizational employee.

Continuous improvement implies the process starts again when an improvement project has been completed. The process may start with another company wide initiative or a targeted Op Ex project. Companywide initiatives may include cost reduction, improving customer service, or decreasing cycle times.

PROCESS OUT OF CONTROL

Process charts indicate when a process is out of control and provide clues as to the cause. When a measurement point is outside the control limits, the process is out of control. A special cause of variation is present. The cause is not random and unnatural to the process. Special causes are then identified and eliminated.

Out of control conditions can be identified by recognizing certain patterns on SPC charts, such as:

- Sudden changes
- Runs
- Cycles
- Multiple populations
- Errors

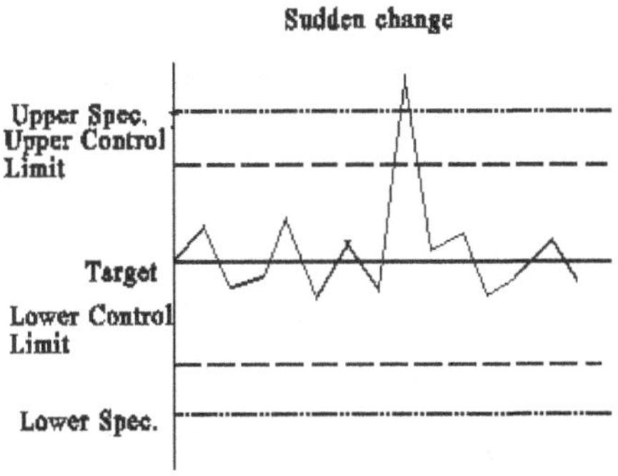

Sudden Changes

A sudden change or jump in the level of points in the SPC chart may indicate a change in the setting of the process or machine as seen in the above figure. Possible causes of this condition may be:

- **Operator.** An inexperienced operator may have changed the process.
- **Machine.** Machine, tool, die or fixture may have been bumped.
- **Method.** Method for making the product may have been changed.
- **Material.** Raw material may be varied.
- **Environment.** Environmental changes in the plant may cause sudden jumps.

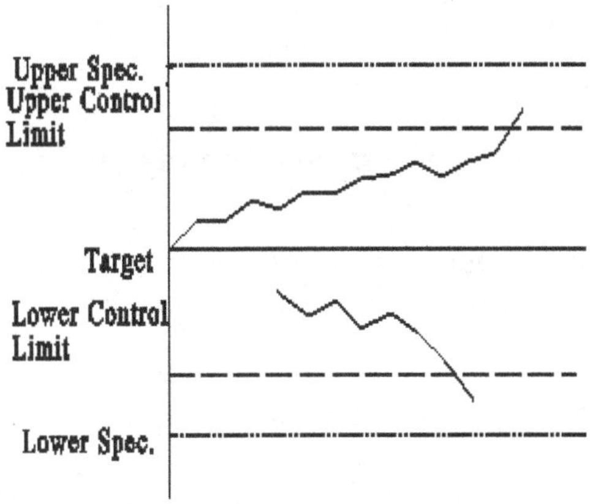

Runs

Trend or steady changes in the level of the points on the chart indicate problematic conditions. The trend may be in an upward or downward direction. Possible causes are:

- **Operator.** Inexperienced operator may allow the process to drift up.
- **Machine.** Tools and dies may wear out.
- **Method.** Methods and procedures are improved and understood. The points trend toward the average line.
- **Material.** Quality of raw material may improve and be less varied.
- **Environment.** Changes in temperature or humidity may cause a deterioration in quality.

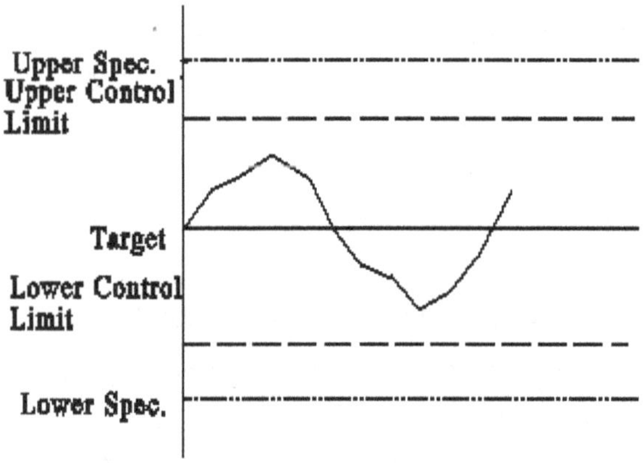

Recurring Cycles

Recurring cycles show patterns of low or high points. This is shown in the above figure. Possible causes are:

- **Operator.** Different operators, skills and shifts show different patterns.
- **Machine.** Changes in machinery occur at regular intervals.
- **Method.** Different operators may use different methods and procedures to perform a task.
- **Material.** Lots or batches of raw material may have different properties.
- **Environment.** Environment, such as temperature and humidity may change the quality of the material.

Multiple Populations

Two populations of data points have similar patterns on the chart shown below. The patterns may be regular or irregular and either near the center line or near the control limits.

- **Operator.** Different workers with different abilities display different patterns of data points.
- **Machine.** Different machines may be on the same chart.
- **Method.** Different methods may be used by different workers.
- **Material.** Raw material may be significantly different.
- **Environment.** Night and day environmental variations may cause changes in the process.

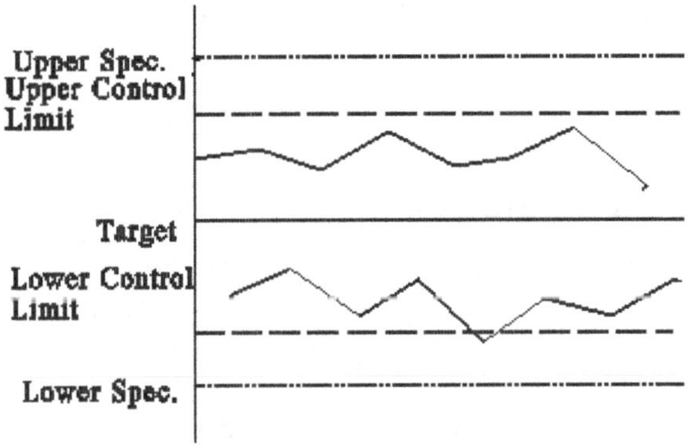

Mistakes

Mistakes can cause dramatic changes in a chart. The mistakes may be intentional or unintentional.

- **Operator.** Operators may make mistakes because of poor instructions or supervision. Operators may edit the charts because of poor attitudes. In the examples shown in the above figure, the operator over-adjusted the process in the first example. In the right example, the operator over adjusts the process again resulting in a saw-tooth pattern.
- **Machine.** Measuring equipment may not be calibrated.
- **Method.** Methods used by the operators to run, measure, or calibrate equipment may be wrong.

- **Material.** Material used in the process may not have uniform characteristics.
- **Environment.** Environment, such as high humidity or temperature, can change the characteristics of the raw material or affect measuring equipment.

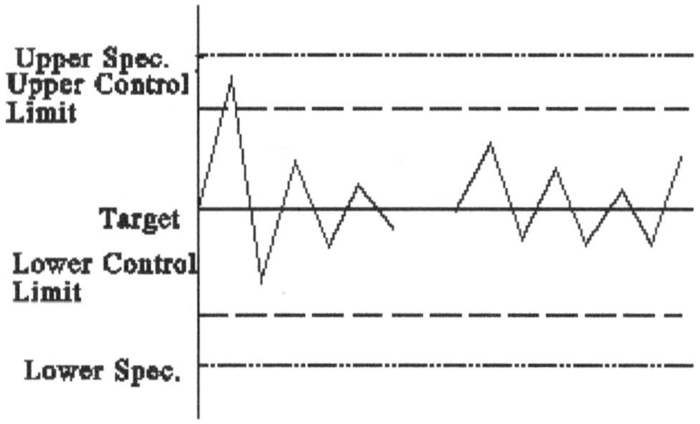

PROBLEMS AND CHALLENGES

A small leak will sink a great ship.
Thomas Fuller

Problems and challenges occur so frequently that managers and employees want instant solutions. Deming called this the "instant pudding" syndrome. Many Op Ex problems are chronic, systemic, or intractable. Quick fixes often don't work. The problem resurfaces again exactly or in some other form. People may believe the problem was fixed or can't be fixed. Management and employees become cynical about the entire process.

Feedback loops ensure that the responsible parties were notified of the problem and that if a correction was implemented, the problem did not recur. Feedback loops may involve reporting the status of:

- Product development.
- Nonconforming material disposition.
- Effective corrective action.

- Occurrence or recurrence of deficiencies.
- Resource utilization, including people, budgets, and progress.
- Project progress.

In any of the above instances, a decision must be made. For example if there are nonconforming products or a design mistake, products or designs must be rerouted to an earlier process step for corrective action, disposition, or some other decision. This backward looping is costly and wasteful. The further a product or design moves from the source of the mistake, the more value has been added to the product and the more it costs to rectify the problem.

If a problem occurs frequently, this chronic problem becomes an opportunity for improvement. When even a problem, error, or other deficiency is detected, the root cause should be detected and root-cause corrected. There should be closed-action feedback loops where the deficiency is discovered and eliminated so the deficiency does not recur.

CORRECTIVE AND PREVENTIVE ACTION

Continuous Op Ex auditing is critical in all organizational activities to ensure a project is progressing smoothly, processes are controlled and capable, product development considers all critical and major customer requirements, and customers are satisfied. For example in improvement projects, monitoring may involve weekly progress meetings with the team leader or team members; periodic review of project controls, such as budgets, project management charts; and periodic auditing of the Op Ex team.

Corrective and preventive actions are essential elements of all Op Ex systems. Corrective and preventive actions ensure symptoms as well as their root causes are eliminated so the problems do not recur. ISO 9001:2015 and other Op Ex standards state the goal is to eliminate the causes of actual and potential nonconformances depending on the magnitude of the problem as well as potential risks.

In general, corrective action is doing what needs to be done to resolve differences or disputes between two or more parties, such as between a supplier and a customer. Once the cause of the difference or discrepancy is discovered, corrective action is undertaken to eliminate the recurrence of the detect, flaw, problem, or discrepancy.

Corrective action may involve:

- Redesigning or modifying the product.
- Redesigning or modifying fixtures and dies.
- Training suppliers.
- Updating specifications or changing tolerances.
- Increasing incoming material inspection.

Preventive Action
On the other hand, preventive action is anticipating a potential problem and identifying steps to eliminate its possible occurrence. How can potential problems be anticipated is the key question? One method is to identify the areas of highest risk and to ensure there are compensating controls to minimize or eliminate the risk. Another method is to use internal resources to see if there are any trends which may indicate a potential problem. Typical examples of trends that may indicate potential problems include high rework, customer service reports, high product waivers, inspection problems, and high waste.

Corrective and preventive action are sometimes confused. Corrective action is the process of eliminating a nonconformance and ensuring that it doesn't recur. To do so, Op Ex or process personnel must understand the nature of the problem and be able to suggest a solution such as Supply Management a new fixture, developing a new procedure, or training employees. Corrective action is indicated by recurring customer complaints, nonconformances, unstable processes, or product rework.

COST-BENEFIT ANALYSIS

Profits are part of the mechanism by which society decides what it wants to see produced

Henry Wallich

Not too many years, every Op Ex project was unconditionally accepted. Management authorized it and resources were allocated. The project was assumed to be critical to the organization.

Times have changed. Senior management now wants, or more accurately demands, to know the value of Op Ex and especially how Op Ex is correlated with revenues, customer satisfaction, market share or other important strategic metrics. Resources are harder to obtain and authorization is harder to justify. Top management requires that project benefits and costs are evaluated. The purpose of the cost-benefit analysis is to maximize returns and to limit risks, costs, and exposures. In other words, Op Ex projects are seen as investments where benefits must exceed costs at a higher return than comparable projects.

Cost benefit analysis attempts to evaluate the benefits and costs associated with a project or initiative. Two type of costs can be evaluated, direct and indirect costs. Direct costs include equipment, labor, training, machinery, and salaries. Indirect costs include downtime, opportunity costs, pollution, and displaced workers.

As well, two types of benefits can be evaluated, direct and indirect benefits. Direct benefits include increased production, higher quality, reduced delivery costs, higher reliability, lower deficiencies, and lower warrantee costs. Indirect benefits include improved sales, improved quality of work life, increased internal customer satisfaction, and better trained employees.

Cost benefit analysis justifies Op Ex decisions and the allocation of scarce corporate resources. However, many indirect benefits and costs can't be quantified.

ADVANTAGES OF COST-BENEFIT ANALYSIS

As companies have increased their Op Ex levels, it has become more difficult to differentiate and position themselves by using their Op Ex. Many companies already are providing this value to the customer, specifically in

terms of providing cost-competitive, high quality products and services that are delivered courteously and just-in-time.

Cost reduction has now become as important as Op Ex for many companies as they try to find ways to do things right the first time at the lowest possible cost. Aggressive cost reduction as well as Op Ex are now in many strategic plans.

Cost benefit analysis is conducted to do "what if" analysis:

- Compare the benefits, costs, and risks of competing projects.
- Allocate resources among projects.
- Justify expenditures for equipment, products, or people.

Cost-benefit decision making can be used to purchase a new machine, add a new process line, justify outsourcing parts instead of making them in-house, or determine the best Op Ex projects. The essence of all cost-benefit is determining whether and how much accrued benefits surpass costs.

The major problem with cost-benefit analysis is that the benefits and costs of many Op Ex projects can't be determined. There are many indirect, inaccessible, and unknowable costs and benefits that can't be anticipated.

The variety of Op Ex initiatives are astounding. If left unchecked, Op Ex initiatives can divert resources from critical organizational activities. The Op Ex manager should ensure economic benefits and communicate these to senior management.

COST OF OP EX

If you are possessed by an idea, you find it expressed everywhere, you even smell it.

Thomas Mann, writer

The cost of quality or Op Ex is high. Studies indicate that the cost of poor Op Ex can be as high as 25% of sales. Lack of Op Ex results in wasted resources throughout the organization.

Op Ex costs are an important element of understanding operational performance. Product or service Op Ex is basically measured in terms of how well something satisfies requirements. Op Ex costs are incurred as a result of an organization trying to meet customer expectations and requirements.

The cost of Op Ex concept is important to the Op Ex system because it:

- Assesses and measures effectiveness of Op Ex projects and processes.
- Identifies and prioritizes projects for action.
- Identifies appropriate balance between prevention/appraisal and failure costs.
- Analyzes benefits of effective corrective action efforts.

Op Ex or quality costs are divided into 2 broad quality related categories: conformance and nonconformance costs. Conformance costs are further broken down into prevention and appraisal costs. Nonconformance costs are broken down into external and internal failure costs.

NONCONFORMANCE COSTS

Internal failure costs are associated with rework, repair, scrap, reinspection, retesting, failure analysis, and material review. Internal failure costs are incurred when products, parts and raw material fail to meet Op Ex requirements just before a product is shipped to the customer. These costs would disappear if there were no product nonconformance's or system deficiencies.

External failure costs are associated with processing complaints, warranty claims, repair of returned material, replacement of returned material, handling, liability, storage, and shipping. External failure costs are incurred when the product does not perform satisfactorily after the customer has bought the product.

BALANCING APPRAISAL, PREVENTION, INTERNAL, AND EXTERNAL COSTS

The cost of quality or Op Ex will never be zero. Companies try to balance appraisal/prevention costs with internal/external failure costs by emphasizing appraisal and prevention to reduce internal and external nonconformance costs. At a certain point, reduction of internal and external nonconformance costs will reach an optimum level which will depend on a company's systems, processes, and products.

The Op Ex professional has to be careful in obtaining data. Op Ex costing may be perceived as a threat to operating managers because a person may use the numbers to discredit others. Op Ex costs should be used like cost accounting to monitor and check operational progress, to identify areas for improvement, and to make better management decisions.

CONTINUOUS REVIEW

Less is more. God is in the details.
Mies van der Rohe

ISO 9001:2015 and other customer-supplier standards require that a company takes direct responsibility for the Op Ex of its processes and products. What does this mean? The company must designate a manager with executive responsibility to be responsible for defining and documenting an Op Ex plan including Op Ex objectives and Op Ex commitment.

ISO 9001:2015 say that internal personnel must have the organizational freedom and responsibility to:

- Initiate corrective actions to prevent process or product nonconformances.
- Identify and record Op Ex system, process, and product deficiencies.

- Initiate and recommend solutions to problems through approved channels.
- Verify implementation of the solution so the deficiency doesn't recur.
- Control processing and delivery to ensure deficiency is root-cause corrected.

Op Ex audits are one of the most effective and extensive monitoring and improvement techniques used by organizations. Op Ex audits are an official examination of the Op Ex initiative, processes, product, or people to verify effectiveness and compliance to policies, procedures, work instructions, specifications, and so on. Audits can be performed on a periodic or random basis and can be performed unannounced or upon request.

Once the audit is conducted, audit findings are documented in a report that is circulated to authorized clients. The audit report may recommend corrective action or no action. Usually, if corrective action is indicated, a corrective action request (CAR) is written to initiate further action.

The following are advantages of auditing:

- Supply independent and objective advice to management.
- Monitor corporate, plant, supplier operations, and products.
- Provide follow up on corrective action.
- Identify areas of Op Ex.
- Measure effectiveness of people, processes, product, and program.

PROCESS IMPROVEMENT

It is a capital mistake to theorize before one has data. Insensibly one begins to twist facts to suit theories, instead of theories to suit facts.
Sir Arthur Conan Doyle, writer

The improvement process model can be illustrated by a production process. The production process incorporates many previously discussed elements of the process model as well as illustrates important ideas associated with variation. In much the same way, policies, procedures, and work instructions are developed to specify approved, preferred, and reinforced behaviors in a service environment.

In the prevention mode, a manufacturing process or machinery is monitored continuously to keep a process in control so defect-free parts conform to specifications and internal customers are satisfied. Statistical Process Control (SPC) maintains process stability, so when changes are noticed, the operator adjusts the process to bring it under control.

Statistical Process Control is a statistical technique that allows a team or machine operator to monitor and control process variation. Variation caused by differences in material, operators, or methods is common to any industrial, service, or administrative process. The operator or automatic machinery plot test measurements over time. The operator can look at the charts to determine whether variations are a normal part of the system or are abnormal and require correction.

SIX SIGMA OP EX

Companies in competitive environments expect parts per million (PPM) Op Ex levels from suppliers. Historically, firms purchased parts according to acceptable quality level (AQL) criteria. Using AQLs firms usually accepted defective products with defect levels of parts per 100 or parts per 1000.

In electronics such defect rates cannot be tolerated. For example, many electronic components are wired in series. If one series component fails then the whole component can fail. In a hypothetical computer that had 10 printed circuits boards each containing 10 components, if the parts were 1% defective, then as many as 97% of the computers would end up with at least one defective part. Depending on the configuration of the wiring, one defective component could create a malfunction making the whole computer inoperable. Electronic buyers are thus requiring suppliers to ship parts with no more than 10 parts per million defect rates.

FROM INSPECTION TO TOTAL OP EX

The graveyard of business is littered with companies that failed to recognize the inevitable changes.
Anonymous

Op Ex has evolved from a product inspection task to a companywide management system. The following discuss the transition from inspection to companywide and supplier wide management:

- Inspection
- Quality control
- Operational assurance
- Operational management

INSPECTION

The first quality function was an inspection organization whose main responsibility was to direct the work of factory inspectors. Factory inspectors policed the quality of incoming, in-process, and outgoing products. The department had no independence because it reported to the head of Manufacturing.

QUALITY CONTROL

The Inspection Department was replaced by a department called operational control. As the name suggests, prevention through control was emphasized. Operational control, now independent of Manufacturing, monitored manufacturing performance. Quality control could no longer be overruled or second guessed by the department it was supposed to monitor. However, operational control still focused on manufacturing control and had no independence to monitor engineering design.

QUALITY ASSURANCE

As the issue of quality became more important, management realized it needed an independent and objective group to monitor quality in other functions, such as Engineering, Supply Management, and Distribution. So, a separate but equal department was created called operational assurance.

The department responsible for quality activities has many titles these days. The department is called operational excellence, operational assurance, operational control, engineering, reliability engineering, or product

assurance. In the service sector, it is called customer service and customer operational excellence. Regardless of the name, the departments have the same responsibilities which are to coordinate, maintain, and monitor Op Ex activities throughout the organization and into the supplier base.

OPERATIONAL MANAGEMENT

As Op Ex becomes a strategic business issue, it is evolving into an officer level position reporting to the Chief Executive Officer or Chief Operations Officer. The Op Ex function coordinates the efforts of people, information, and processes so Op Ex is maintained, pursued, and improved throughout the organization and the supplier base.

Op Ex is still prevention oriented, but its scope has increased to integrate Op Ex into the whole company instead of focusing on manufacturing excellence. Op Ex has the corporate mandate to develop and implement the organization's Op Ex mission in staff and operational areas. A major change has been less reliance on technical skills and more emphasis on management skills. Traditionally, the Op Ex function stressed technical analysis, including laboratory analysis, product testing, process inspection, and incoming material inspection. Now, emphasis is more organizational and managerial, focusing on solving systemwide Op Ex problems and coordinating the Op Ex system while meeting the needs of the customer.

ESSENCE OF TODAY'S OP EX PHILOSOPHY

Op Ex performance is everyone's responsibility. The responsibility for Op Ex rests with the person or work unit performing the work. This may be a person on the line or a person who delivers product to the customer. Only this person is able to add or degrade the value or Op Ex of the product or service.

Op Ex function consults with elements inside the company to provide Op Ex guidance and direction. If problems arise, Op Ex assists people to solve their own problems. Op Ex intervenes at the proper time; aids in the solution; trains people to solve recurring, systemic problems; and then leaves knowing the people responsible for Op Ex have the tools to solve future operational excellence problems. Since Op Ex is everyone's responsibility,

all employees are responsible for verifying and correcting the Op Ex of their work through a self-evaluation program.

OP EX FUNCTION'S RESPONSIBILITIES THROUGH PRODUCT LIFE CYCLE

Throughout the product lifecycle (PLC) and design lifecycle (DLC), the operational excellence function now owns the internal "voice of the customer", always reminding the organization to satisfy customer needs. Operational ly, the operational control group establishes acceptable limits of variation in product quality characteristics and monitors and reports on the compliance to those limits. Variation can be caused by people, material, methods, machinery, and environment.

Early in the design lifecycle, operational control evaluates product safety, maintainability, performance, safety, and other important factors. Once these are known, requirements are quantified into specifications. Operational control works with the development team to create precise, accurate, and complete specifications that can be translated into manufacturable products. Once specifications are developed operational control prepares general procedures and specific inspection instructions.

Early in the product lifecycle, operational control analyzes the manufacturing process to evaluate whether a product can be manufactured to design specifications, cost limitations, and delivery dates. As so often happens, unforeseen difficulties arise and operational control engineers develop new specifications, new processes or machine tolerances, estimate new costs, or change delivery dates.

In the growth stage, operational control evaluates field failures. Operational control identifies root cause solutions of the field failures and then initiates corrective action to eliminate the deficiency. Operational control tries to eliminate any recurrence of the problem in any products being manufactured as well as minimize field problems. If a deficiency is discovered, operational control will warn buyers of the defect and if it sufficiently severe, even recommend a recall.

In the mature stage, products are continuously modified by enhancing performance or by adding value to the products. Op Ex and engineering groups evaluate each improvement and enhancement to determine if the

desired Op Ex is being maintained. Product improvement and Op Ex are emphasized so products can be differentiated from the competition. Product reliability is high as standardized products dominate the market. Employees develop specialized skills.

In the decline stage, sales and production decline steadily. Products are standardized and eventually become commodities. Product lines with low profit margins are eliminated. Manufacturing is highly efficient, costs are reduced. Processes are controlled. Operational assurance reviews field failure reports, customer complaints, and warranty claims to ensure that products are not failing catastrophically.

FROM INSPECTION TO TOTAL OP EX

The graveyard of business is littered with companies that failed to recognize the inevitable changes.
Anonymous

Op Ex has evolved from a product inspection task to a companywide management system. The following discuss the transition from inspection to companywide and supplier wide management:

- Inspection
- Quality control
- Operational assurance
- Operational management

INSPECTION

The first quality function was an inspection organization whose main responsibility was to direct the work of factory inspectors. Factory inspectors policed the quality of incoming, in-process, and outgoing products. The department had no independence because it reported to the head of Manufacturing.

QUALITY CONTROL

The Inspection Department was replaced by a department called operational control. As the name suggests, prevention through control was em phasized. Operational control, now independent of Manufacturing, monitored manufacturing performance. Quality control could no longer be overruled or second guessed by the department it was supposed to monitor. However, operational control still focused on manufacturing control and had no independence to monitor engineering design.

QUALITY ASSURANCE

As the issue of quality became more important, management realized it needed an independent and objective group to monitor quality in other functions, such as Engineering, Supply Management, and Distribution. So, a separate but equal department was created called operational assurance.

The department responsible for quality activities has many titles these days. The department is called operational excellence, operational assurance, operational control, engineering, reliability engineering, or product assurance. In the service sector, it is called customer service and customer operational excellence. Regardless of the name, the departments have the same responsibilities which are to coordinate, maintain, and monitor Op Ex activities throughout the organization and into the supplier base.

OPERATIONAL MANAGEMENT

As Op Ex becomes a strategic business issue, it is evolving into an officer level position reporting to the Chief Executive Officer or Chief Operations Officer. The Op Ex function coordinates the efforts of people, information, and processes so Op Ex is maintained, pursued, and improved throughout the organization and the supplier base.

Op Ex is still prevention oriented, but its scope has increased to integrate Op Ex into the whole company instead of focusing on manufacturing excellence. Op Ex has the corporate mandate to develop and implement the organization's Op Ex mission in staff and operational areas. A major change has been less reliance on technical skills and more emphasis on management skills. Traditionally, the Op Ex function stressed technical analysis, including laboratory analysis, product testing, process inspection, and incoming material inspection. Now, emphasis is more organizational

and managerial, focusing on solving systemwide Op Ex problems and coordinating the Op Ex system while meeting the needs of the customer.

ESSENCE OF TODAY'S OP EX PHILOSOPHY

Op Ex performance is everyone's responsibility. The responsibility for Op Ex rests with the person or work unit performing the work. This may be a person on the line or a person who delivers product to the customer. Only this person is able to add or degrade the value or Op Ex of the product or service.

Op Ex function consults with elements inside the company to provide Op Ex guidance and direction. If problems arise, Op Ex assists people to solve their own problems. Op Ex intervenes at the proper time; aids in the solution; trains people to solve recurring, systemic problems; and then leaves knowing the people responsible for Op Ex have the tools to solve future operational excellence problems. Since Op Ex is everyone's responsibility, all employees are responsible for verifying and correcting the Op Ex of their work through a self-evaluation program.

OP EX FUNCTION'S RESPONSIBILITIES THROUGH PRODUCT LIFE CYCLE

Throughout the product lifecycle (PLC) and design lifecycle (DLC), the operational excellence function now owns the internal "voice of the customer", always reminding the organization to satisfy customer needs. Operational ly, the operational control group establishes acceptable limits of variation in product quality characteristics and monitors and reports on the compliance to those limits. Variation can be caused by people, material, methods, machinery, and environment.

Early in the design lifecycle, operational control evaluates product safety, maintainability, performance, safety, and other important factors. Once these are known, requirements are quantified into specifications. Operational control works with the development team to create precise, accurate, and complete specifications that can be translated into manufacturable products. Once specifications are developed operational control prepares general procedures and specific inspection instructions.

Early in the product lifecycle, operational control analyzes the manufacturing process to evaluate whether a product can be manufactured to design specifications, cost limitations, and delivery dates. As so often happens, unforeseen difficulties arise and operational control engineers develop new specifications, new processes or machine tolerances, estimate new costs, or change delivery dates.

In the growth stage, operational control evaluates field failures. Operational control identifies root cause solutions of the field failures and then initiates corrective action to eliminate the deficiency. Operational control tries to eliminate any recurrence of the problem in any products being manufactured as well as minimize field problems. If a deficiency is discovered, operational control will warn buyers of the defect and if it sufficiently severe, even recommend a recall.

In the mature stage, products are continuously modified by enhancing performance or by adding value to the products. Op Ex and engineering groups evaluate each improvement and enhancement to determine if the desired Op Ex is being maintained. Product improvement and Op Ex are emphasized so products can be differentiated from the competition. Product reliability is high as standardized products dominate the market. Employees develop specialized skills.

In the decline stage, sales and production decline steadily. Products are standardized and eventually become commodities. Product lines with low profit margins are eliminated. Manufacturing is highly efficient, costs are reduced. Processes are controlled. Operational assurance reviews field failure reports, customer complaints, and warranty claims to ensure that products are not failing catastrophically.

BENCHMARKING

Knowledge is power.
Proverb

Benchmarking is a critical method for justifying change and for establishing a direction for the change. Benchmarking is the continuous process of

comparing and measuring processes, systems, services, practices, and products against leading companies inside or outside one's industry sector. The benchmarking process forces an organization to look outside the box or outside the organization for best practices. This process results in breakthrough thinking and doing.

Companies can benchmark just about any activity. In Supply Management, the following can be benchmarked: electronic data interchange (EDI), supplier certification, manufacturing resource planning (MRP), JIT delivery, lean, and customer-supplier partnering.

There are 4 basic types of benchmarking, internal, competitive benchmarking, industry, and competitive benchmarking. Often, benchmarking companies look for tips outside an industry sector because it is easier to gather this information. These companies aren't paranoid about a competitor stealing a secret and are more willing to share information.

Benchmarking may be a one-time effort or it may be a continuous process of comparing a company against its competitors. Companies that continuously benchmark learn to adapt and to adopt new principles to make operations more efficient. It's critical that benchmarking companies look for companies that have "world class" processes. A benchmarking project as any operational excellence related project should reinforce the organization's strategic direction and be consistent with the operational excellence plans, policies and procedures, and be doable.

Unfortunately, the above requirements are not always followed. The benchmarking study is very broad and not easily achievable. For example, a study to benchmark the best practices of a wafer fab production operation is difficult if not impossible. These plants may cost a billion dollars. They have state-of-the-art technologies that companies don't want to share with competitors.

HOW TO BENCHMARK

The telephone book is full of facts, but it doesn't contain a single idea.
Mortimer Adler

Robert C. Camp, the author of the best-selling **Benchmarking,** outlined the following steps of a successful benchmarking project:

- **Identify what is to be benchmarked.** Define the mission, deliverables, and performance measurements of the benchmarking project. Articulate the objective and plan for benchmarking project. Understand the process, product, or procedure to be benchmarked.
- **Identify comparative companies.** Identify the best competitors or industry leaders from whom lessons can be learned. As well, determine appropriate form of benchmarking, i.e. competitive, internal, functional, or generic benchmarking. Approach selected companies to be benchmarked and have backup companies. Identify constraints to benchmarking within or outside one's industry.
- **Determine data collection method and collect data.** Determine how information is to be gathered. Information can be collected from internal sources such as internal experts or through public domain information such as external experts and consultants.
- **Determine current performance "gap".** Gap analysis investigates differences in practices, performance, cost, operational excellence, or efficiency.

- **Project future performance levels.** Is the gap widening or closing and at what rate? This analysis allows understanding of the gap and what can be done to close it in terms of developing new practices or procedures.
- **Communicate benchmark findings and gain acceptance.** The results of the benchmarking study have to be communicated to the appropriate stakeholders in terms of specific recommended actions.
- **Establish functional goals.** Benchmarking results are then operationalized, translated into functional, attainable goals.
- **Develop action plans.** The actions to achieve functional plans and goals may involve implementing process controls, establishing process capability, developing new training methods, or pursuing other system/process improvements.
- **Implement specific actions and monitor progress.** Specific actions are implemented to achieve goals. Implementation can be through line management, project management, or performance teams. Progress is also monitored and reported periodically.
- **Recalibrate benchmarks.** Progress reports determine if the benchmarking practices are being implemented according to plan. If not, the system is corrected or recalibrated.[73]

TEN BENCHMARKING WARNING SIGNS

Benchmarking is widely accepted as a competitive tool. The concept is easy to comprehend. Basically, a company looks at best practices and finds ways to internalize these. However, the following common mistakes should be avoided:

- Lack of senior management sponsorship.
- Wrong people on the benchmarking team.
- Lack of true understanding of how target companies implemented practices.
- Unmanageable benchmarking team.
- Underestimation of time, resources, and efforts required to complete and implement benchmarking results.

- Over emphasis on reaching performance targets instead of focusing on improvement processes.
- Use of benchmarking as a tool, instead of a positioning strategy.
- Use of benchmarking for minor challenges instead of furthering strategic objectives.
- Too many site visits especially when information can be researched or is a phone call away.
- Failure to follow up on benchmarking implementation.[74]

ESSENTIAL FOUNDATION OP EX ELEMENTS

The Conference Board years ago analyzed a number of qualities initiatives and asked what determines success in an initiative. The responses follow:

1. A clear, compelling vision of what quality means to the organization.
2. Quality planning process.
3. Company-wide customer focus.
4. Companywide process-improvement focus.
5. Innovation in all aspects of the business.
6. Employee participation in management and change.
7. Healthy competition to improve performance.
8. Strong participative leadership from the top of the organization and throughout it.
9. Dedication to training and learning, for both employees and managers.
10. Use of teams for many improvement projects.
11. Benchmarking against superior role models.
12. Measurement of the costs of bad quality and the results of quality.
13. Extensive use of process management methods and tools.[75]

NEXT CHAPTER

In the next chapter, Op Ex Outsourcing Strategy is discussed. Fewer and better suppliers are becoming the norm for many companies. This is sometimes called single-source partnering. This trend is evidenced by a number of factors. Customer-supplier certifications are very common. ISO

9001:2015 registration is becoming a requirement to be on the customer's approved bidder's list.

CHAPTER 17
OP EX OUTSOURCING STRATEGY

The supply chain has become a popular concept to describe how employees, suppliers, and others provide a chain of value-added activities at each step of the process. The objective is to ensure the right value is being added at each process step.

Many companies are partnering with suppliers. Some are single-sourcing, Supply Management products and services from one "world class" supplier. With fewer suppliers, both parties have much to gain and to lose.

OUTSOURCING STRATEGY

Most of the companies that rated among the top 100 today were not there 20 or even 10 years ago and some had not even started.
Anonymous

These days Supply Management focuses on:

- Selecting, monitoring and improving suppliers.
- Using multidisciplinary customer-supplier teams to improve processes and develop products.
- Using ISO 9001:2015 registration as a supplier requirement to be on the approved bidder's list.
- Reducing the supplier base, sometimes to single-source partners.

SELECTING SUPPLIERS

There's no such thing as "zero risk."
William Driver

Procurement follows a cycle that starts with selecting a supplier and ends with encouraging supplier improvement. The procurement lifecycle starts in the development stage of the product development cycle (see Chapter 6). In this stage, the development team, which includes representatives from Op Ex and Supply Management, looks for possible product or service providers. As a product changes through the product lifecycle, changes in design or specifications are communicated to suppliers.

The procurement cycle is discussed in the following sections:

- Select supplier
- Monitor supplier
- Maintain supplier
- Correct supplier

SUPPLIER SELECTION

The process of selecting a supplier can be compared to a series of hurdles that a supplier must jump over. At each hurdle, the supplier satisfies a customer procurement requirement. A prospective or candidate supplier has to deliver a quality product at a competitive price that represents the state of the art as well as service it on demand.

The following are steps in selecting a new supplier:

- Identify candidate suppliers
- Narrow the supplier list
- Narrow the supplier list further
- Select suppliers

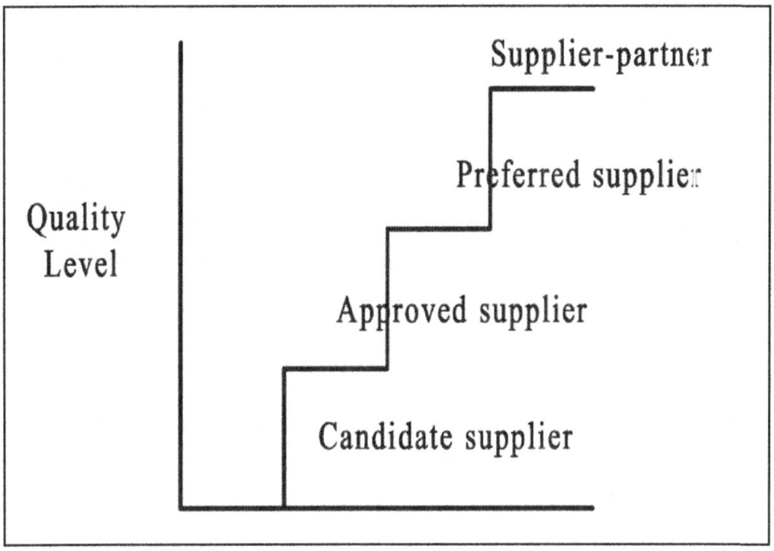

Identify Candidate Suppliers

The first step is to identify prospective suppliers who can manufacture the required products. Suppliers can either be domestic or foreign. A domestic-supplier list can be generated from personal knowledge, industry contacts, catalogs, phone books, trade publications, advertisements, or directories. The foreign supplier list can be generated from chambers of commerce, departments of economic development, U.S. State Department, U.S. Commerce Department, trade representatives, foreign consulates, and trade publications.

Data from these sources is then collected to develop a master list of candidate suppliers. While many U.S. companies prefer to buy American products, a global economy and the need for competitiveness has forced companies to go overseas to obtain the best products at the most competitive price.

NARROW SUPPLIER LIST

The second step is to evaluate candidate suppliers and to narrow the list to those acceptable to the customer. This is the first cut. Approval depends on factors, such as:

1. **Location.** Location is important because logistical, plant location, just-in-time delivery, or technical assistance requirements mandate

the supplier is located near the customer, not half way around the world. If problems arise and they always do, then it is easier to resolve them if the supplier is located down the street.

2. **Supplier performance.** Supplier performance history reveals if the supplier has been responsive in complying with contractual commitments. If a supplier has a history of satisfactory performance, this provides a degree of assurance that material will be supplied just-in-time and at the specified Op Ex levels. If the supplier is new, then a reference check of previous customers is essential.
3. **Financial stability.** Financial stability indicates the supplier has been a going concern for several years. This implies continuity and stability. A customer does not want a supplier of critical components to go bankrupt. A wayward second-tier supplier providing a critical component can disrupt contractual commitments of the prime contractor.
4. **Supplier motivation.** Supplier motivation is the supplier's attitude to work with the customer to resolve disputes in a timely and mutually beneficial manner. Disputes in supplier-customer relations always arise. If the supplier is motivated, these differences can be resolved quickly and amicably.

NARROW SUPPLIER LIST FURTHER

The third step is to narrow the supplier list to those capable of manufacturing a product that conforms to specifications. One measure often used in manufacturing is process capability which refers to the supplier's ability to control a process and consistently meet specifications. Capability implies the supplier has the technical and manufacturing competence to satisfy requirements. Capability is verified through interviews, inspection of product characteristics, review of past manufacturing performance, visit to the plant to audit the manufacturing process, or exchange of product samples.

To evaluate capability, the supplier must have drawings, specifications, standards, and all relevant information to make a conforming product. Otherwise, the supplier can manufacture a product but not to the quality, performance, or reliability levels required by the customer.

SELECT PRIME SUPPLIER

The last step is to select the prime supplier and maybe another acceptable alternate. As opposed to single sourcing, two sources are sometimes preferred to reduce the risk of receiving unacceptable products and to help ensure future price competition. Supply Management coordinates this effort with Op Ex and Engineering. The final decision of selecting the prime supplier rests with the Supply Management function, because they are responsible if quality products are not delivered on time and at the specified quality level.

Formal evaluation plans are useful for making the supplier aware of quality requirements and Op Ex levels that the customer expects the supplier to maintain. Details for the evaluation are outlined and attached to the purchase order.

WHAT TO LOOK FOR IN A STRATEGIC SUPPLIER-PARTNER

A company can't be all things to all people or to all customers. The only way to penetrate a number of markets with high quality products and services may be through collaborative relationships. These relationships are also called strategic alliances. This type of partnering has successfully been used to penetrate new markets, offer a local presence, enhance quality, lower exposure, create a market for new products, establish a local distribution network, resell products, integrate suppliers, and share process innovations.

In exploring these partnering relationships, it is critical to:

- Understand partnering requirements and expectations.
- Ensure both parties can deliver.
- Understand how fulfilling requirements assists the other party in measurable ways.
- Develop performance, quality, or other metrics for each party.
- Understand today's partners may be tomorrow's competitors.
- Evaluate past performance of the partners.
- Evaluate partner's state-of-the-art capabilities.

MAINTAINING SUPPLIERS

The difficult we do immediately. The impossible takes a little longer.
Anonymous

The following are goals for maintaining a long-term customer-supplier relationship:

- Open and honest communication
- Mutually beneficial relationship
- Continuous improvement

OPEN AND HONEST COMMUNICATION

The key to maintaining a good customer-supplier relationship is open and honest communication that anticipates difficulties and establishes trust. The customer keeps the supplier informed of order changes and design modifications. The supplier keeps the customer informed of changes in delivery dates and production problems. Clear communication settles issues before they become problems or disputes.

Trust is the hopeful outcome of clear communication. If the customer and supplier trust each other to maintain a positive working relationship, each party knows it will be mutually beneficial. The customer consistently receives a defect-free product and knows the supplier will work toward improving product reliability and cost. And the supplier obtains a long-term contract.

MUTUALLY BENEFICIAL RELATIONSHIP

The customer tries to establish a mutually beneficial long-term relationship. It is easier to maintain a relationship than to start one from scratch. If a supplier has been providing a unique product at a reasonable price with good service, then it is just good business to keep a supplier.

CHANGING NATURE OF SUPPLY MANAGEMENT	
Old Approach	**New Approach**
Price is major factor in buy decision	Op Ex is equal to price in buy decision
Multiple suppliers provide products	Single or acceptable alternate supplier provides products
Product is simply accepted from supplier	Processes are extensively and intensively audited
Supply Management department is tactical	Supply Management is strategic
Products are purchased from local suppliers	Products are purchased from all over the world
Suppliers are adversaries	Suppliers are partners in procurement process

CONTINUOUS IMPROVEMENT

Suppliers are asked to continuously improve product quality, delivery, and service through prevention. Prevention hopes to eliminate routine incoming material inspection. If a supplier can demonstrate a history of defect-free shipments for a period of time, the supplier is audited periodically to ensure internal operational controls are followed and documented.

At this point, shipments go directly into production or inventory. Supplied product samples may be periodically evaluated or certificates of compliance reviewed. If a number of successive shipments have been accepted and the supplier can prove internal controls are in place to ensure product Op Ex, then a supplier becomes certified and all shipments are sent directly to production. If a shipment is rejected, then shipments are immediately canceled. The supplier is reinstated when delivery or Op Ex issues are resolved.

CUSTOMER-SUPPLIER PARTNERSHIPS

Everything is connected to everything else.
Barry Commoner

In terms of total dollar amount, external suppliers provide a significant portion of a manufacturer's product. For U.S. firms, 50% or more of the final price of a product can be the cost of purchased goods. In Japan, it can be even higher. For these reasons, supplier management is critical to a company's competitiveness.

As products require specialized components, companies ask: "Should we make or buy the component?" The "make or buy" decision becomes a financial one where companies ask: "Do we have the expertise to manufacture a quality product at a competitive price?" Since some industrial tasks cannot be effectively accomplished in-house because of lack of equipment, trained personnel, or material, the answer to the question is often "no." So, many products and services are contracted to outside suppliers.

CUSTOMER-SUPPLIER PARTNERING

Large companies are outsourcing products to world-class suppliers. The auto companies are sourcing up to 70% of their manufacturing dollar. What does "world-class" mean? Customers now want these suppliers to tell them how to improve parts, assemblies or systems instead of vice versa. These suppliers have Op Ex systems and processes in place and fully documented to provide world-class products on time, at the right location. Partnering allows a customer to bring key suppliers into the product development process to take advantage of the supplier's skills, knowledge, tooling and service.

Many North American companies have established partnering arrangements with their suppliers to improve product and service Op Ex. Traditional customer and suppler relations were based on survey data or anecdotal evidence to draw conclusions about supplier Op Ex, cost, delivery, and technology. The trend now is to rely on more objective information, such as ISO 9001:2015 registration upon which to base purchase decisions.

The following are the requirements for a true customer-supplier partnership:

- Mutual benefits should be real, tangible, and quantifiable.
- Partnership should be based on a formal and binding contract.
- Each party should meet its obligations.
- Continuous improvement of cost, Op Ex, deliver and service are critical elements of the partnership.

The benefits of being a supplier to a large organization are enormous. Aside from the prestige of being a supplier to a major company, large contracts, manufacturing and technical assistance, and even financing for special capital equipment are awarded to supplier-partners.

For the supplier, there are partnership risks. A large company may structure its supplier relationships in such a way that suppliers become captive, in other words the supplier only has one customer. A customer may require high-volume suppliers modify management and operational methods to comply with its requirements. A large company may require suppliers to invest in additional property, plant, and equipment to increase or to improve production capacity. A company may monitor its supplier's performance and tie future order levels to Op Ex and delivery targets.

To limit the exposure to risk of a single supplier not being able to deliver, some companies (customers) are working with a prime and an acceptable alternate supplier. One supplier gets the lion's share of the business. These two suppliers at the end of the year are objectively evaluated and business is allocated to each depending on the year's performance. These arrangements are often called single-source, customer-supplier partnerships.

PRODUCT IS ONLY AS RELIABLE AS ITS COMPONENTS

Supply Management's role is changing from a function whose mission was mainly to procure products and material at the lowest price to an important operating function. Its new mission is to procure products that optimize Op Ex, service, availability, and price.

In this sourcing environment, the buyer or user is considered the customer. All purchased material, parts, and assemblies must conform to specifications, blueprints, and/or industry standards. In addition, Supply Management expects products to be competitively priced, delivered on time, available as needed, and innovative. These factors are usually spelled out in a contract or purchase order.

Reliable and defect-free goods from suppliers are important because a finished product is only as reliable as its smallest component. Since a finished product is the sum of many small parts which form a subassembly, assembly, and finally, a finished product, the smallest component can cause the whole unit to fail. For example, if a tiny rivet on an aircraft bulkhead fails, there can be a cascading effect where the pressurized bulkhead fails and causes the pilot to lose control of the aircraft. If a manufacturer obtains many small components from suppliers, each component has to be as reliable as the finished product.

CUSTOMER AND SUPPLIER PARTNERSHIPS

Supply Management, in partnership with Op Ex, has evolved to become the prime assurance of purchased products. This is important to an organization that spends a large part of its manufacturing dollar buying products from suppliers.

Suppliers are often considered partners in the product development process. Suppliers are expected to continuously improve their manufacturing capabilities so the customer can maintain an Op Ex edge in the competitive marketplace.

Companies look to suppliers to control the Op Ex of their incoming goods, implement just-in-time delivery, and eliminate incoming material inspection. Companies increasingly audit suppliers, certify them, and expect zero-defect levels. If suppliers comply, rewards are shared. Suppliers get larger and longer-term contracts, technical assistance, and special equipment.

As the primary interface with suppliers, Supply Management and Op Ex departments review specifications with suppliers to ensure requirements are properly spelled out and understood. Questions about the appropriateness, tightness, and looseness of the specifications are discussed with the supplier's and customer's engineering representatives. This is important because specifications of complex equipment can be many pages and can include Op Ex requirements that second, third, and even fourth-tier suppliers must conform to.

In the supplier selection process, Supply Management plans, coordinates, and consults with Engineering, Op Ex, and Manufacturing functions. Engineering supplies material specifications. Op Ex audits supplier's Op Ex systems to ensure the selected supplier can manufacture products that meet specifications. And Manufacturing provides feedback on any changes that may be required of the supplier.

Supply Management and Op Ex functions are more visible and are attracting highly trained and educated personnel. Companies require Op Ex personnel to have engineering degrees, professional certifications, and be cross trained. Experience in development/design engineering allows Op Ex professionals to challenge supplier's specifications, which may be restrictive from a sourcing point of view. Operations and design experience allow Op Ex professionals to obtain the respect of engineers and manufacturing personnel while providing input to design and Op Ex decisions.

CUSTOMERS AND OTHER INTERESTED PARTIES

Public sector Op Ex managers have different customers than those in the private sector. For example a public Op Ex manager has 1) consumers, those who use its services, 2) clients, those who are funding sources and 3) constituents, those with an interest in an agency's work.

Public sector Op Ex managers have a more difficult time determining who the customer is and determining actual needs and requirements. Public administrators often provide a number of services to many public customers, some are known while others are unknown. The other major challenge is determining whose requirements are the most important? This is critical because if a need remains unfulfilled the public administrator may hear of it the next day in the local newspaper or on the five o'clock news.

LINKING CUSTOMERS AND SUPPLIERS

Partner-supplier alliances will become more common as more companies understand the benefits of partnering especially to bring products to market quickly. More often, a design-development team works with key suppliers to develop a product through a concurrent or simultaneous design process.

Companies are now linking and partnering with their stakeholders, including suppliers, customers, distributors, transporters, designers, and other strategic partners. Good telecommunications and exchange of information have allowed these networks to share information, designs, procedures, and other critical information almost seamlessly. An engineer, for example, can use these transparent information systems to acquire SPC information, check bills of material, and provide input into a new product development. Or a Supply Management agent can check a supplier's order, delivery dates, invoices, payments, and receipts.

Networked computers are critical in this process. Engineering, Supply Management, Op Ex, Manufacturing, Customer Service, Sales, and suppliers can evaluate and review design information. These groups and others can view the product on the computer, check calculations, evaluate critical characteristics, conduct tests, evaluate the bills of material, and evaluate the product. Once a design is developed, special instructions can be downloaded from the computer to production machinery as well as to automatic inspection and testing machinery. What-if and how questions can be answered though the computer often without having to build multiple prototypes.

SUPPLIER INVOLVEMENT IN DESIGN

As more products are being outsourced, early involvement of suppliers is required to develop a quality product quickly. Supplier involvement is especially critical as up to 80% of the manufacturing dollar is outsourced to "world-class" suppliers. Key suppliers are brought in as integral partners of the concurrent development product team. Suppliers have specialized knowledge or testing facilities. Suppliers can suggest alternatives so a better product is designed. Suppliers can provide information on design modifications, design reviews, component testing, tooling modifications, process modifications, and simplified design configurations.

For example, a design engineer may want a special seal for a complicated, new product. The seal must fit into the complicated part. A knowledgeable supplier may suggest a moldable component instead of a more expensive machined component. The moldable part allows for more stringent dimensions, eliminates nicks, and permits a more controlled manufacturing process.

SUPPLIER PROBLEMS

Successful collaborative negotiation lies in finding out what the other side really wants and showing them a way to get it, while you get what you want.
Herb Cohen

Even in the best of customer-supplier relationships, problems arise. Either the customer or supplier can be the source of problems. The customer can modify a drawing so the supplier can no longer make the part. The customer may want a sudden increase of products shipped to the plant, but the supplier is already running three shifts at capacity. The customer may tighten up specifications and tolerances so the supplier simply cannot make the product. This occurs when the customer wants improved Op Ex and reliability too quickly and the supplier does not have the equipment or internal discipline to make products to specification.

The supplier can also have problems. A supplier can have a strike, a fire, capacity problems, financial problems, or even supplier problems of its own. Any of these can disrupt or stop operations.

SOLVING SUPPLIER PROBLEMS

A problem supplier is one who is unresponsive about solving quality problems. A problem supplier is monitored more closely than other suppliers. Close monitoring may involve more frequent plant visits to intensified process monitoring. Close monitoring usually ends when the supplier has shipped acceptable products over a period of time. If nonconforming products continue to be shipped, the supplier is removed from the approved supplier's list.

So what can be done with recalcitrant suppliers? Systems and procedures have to be established so disputes can be settled with suppliers. The following are options that companies can pursue:

- Work with existing suppliers
- Manufacture component in house
- Find new suppliers

Work with Existing Suppliers

If more products, tighter tolerances, lower prices, and faster delivery are needed, the preferred option is to work with existing suppliers. Existing suppliers already know customer needs and wants. If the customer anticipates the need for more products and the supplier is running at capacity or the supplier cannot manufacture products to specifications then the customer may provide the supplier with financial and technical incentives.

Manufacture Component In-House

A less preferred option is to manufacture components in-house. This is done if the supplier cannot consistently make conforming products because of material, technology, or personnel problems. Critical or state-of-the-art products may require additional investment in property, plant, equipment, and extensive personnel training.

Find a New Supplier

The third option is to find a new supplier. The process of evaluating and selecting a new supplier was covered earlier. The process is long and tedious, so it is less preferred than negotiating with existing suppliers.

WORLD CLASS SUPPLIERS

Companies want to partner with "world class" suppliers." What does "world class" mean to a buyer? The following are criteria a buyer or customer may look for in a "world class" supplier:

- ISO 9001:2015 registration

- Improving processes
- Extensive use of Op Ex metrics
- Desire to do business on a long-term basis
- Long term financial stability
- Advanced material requirement practices
- Computerized Supply Management
- Facilities
- Extensive use of cost controls
- Advanced techniques employed in QC
- Research and development
- Recent investments
- Management progressiveness
- Willingness to share costs

MONITORING SUPPLIERS

Trust, but verify.
President Ronald Reagan

During the selection process and during the life of a contract, a supplier is monitored to assure on-going quality, delivery, and contractual compliance.

The following are commonly used techniques to monitor a supplier:

- Audits
- Product samples
- Process capability analysis
- Incoming material inspection
- First-article inspection
- Certification

AUDITS

Audits check and verify that suppliers are producing and supplying what is called for in the contract. Audits review suppliers' performance based on objective criteria such as delivery, defect levels, and reliability.

Audits are conducted by the Op Ex function for minor suppliers. Major supplier audits may be conducted by a team representing Op Ex, Manufacturing, Engineering, and Supply Management function. Major suppliers are those that provide a large dollar volume of products or supply key components. A major reason for the recent adoption of ISO 9001:2015 standards and requirement of being registered is the ability to check a register of certified suppliers and to avoid duplicative audits.

Audits are usually formal and highly structured. They begin with an initial discussion about the purpose, scope, and intent of the audit. Depending on the intent and scope of the audit, the following areas can be investigated:

- Op Ex manual, procedures, and work instructions
- Op Ex organization
- Training and certifications
- Op Ex planning
- Op Ex documentation
- In-coming material control
- In-process product control
- Final product test and evaluation
- Corrective action
- Measuring equipment and calibration
- Storage and delivery

PRODUCT SAMPLES

Customers may send a sample product to suppliers when specifications are difficult to develop, such as for products with intricate shapes. Samples are also sent to suppliers to determine if they can be manufactured to specifications and tolerances.

Sometimes, parts cannot be specified in writing or depicted in drawings because of intricate geometric shapes. Instead, it is easier to produce a sample product and give this to suppliers to duplicate. Suppliers then make a similar product and submit this to the customer with critical dimensions clearly marked. Then duplicate measurements using similar instruments are made by both supplier and customer. Appearance, critical measurements, and product performance are verified and any differences are checked. The problem with samples is that product reliability can't be tested. So, a product may conform to all specified measurements but not survive prolonged use.

PROCESS CAPABILITY ANALYSIS

Process capability analysis is a statistical study of dimensional variation in a product characteristic. The customer provides the supplier with a small number of parts. Dimensions on parts are measured and compared against the specification. Deviations between the actual measurements and the specifications are analyzed. If measurements are inside and centered in the middle of the specification spread, products are accepted for use. If measurements are outside the specification, products are returned to the supplier.

INCOMING MATERIAL INSPECTION

Incoming material inspection measures, tests, or checks material from suppliers. Incoming material inspection is time consuming and costly. By checking for nonconformances, the customer is ensuring the Op Ex of the supplier's work. Material is accepted, rejected, or corrected. If accepted, material goes into inventory or directly into production. If rejected, material is used as is, reworked, or returned to the supplier.

FIRST ARTICLE INSPECTION

First article inspection is used for inspecting, testing, and measuring the first of a series of products or a significantly modified product manufactured by a new or existing supplier. First-article inspection can be a cursory check of critical product dimensions or a comprehensive investigation of all physical, functional, and dimensional characteristics of the part or assembly. The degree of the investigation depends on the complexity of the product, the familiarity of the supplier, and time constraints.

First article inspection can:

- Detect early discrepancies, defects, or flaws in the prototype product.

- Serve as proof that specifications can be met.
- Serve as proof that manufacturing set-up is correct.
- Confirm that corrective action modifications have been made.

However, first article inspection can provide misleading results because it:
- Is a snapshot of one item and does not indicate the conformance of following products?
- Does not indicate the reliability of a product?
- Does not allow for any process variation that may move dimensions out of the acceptable specification spread?

CERTIFICATION

Once selected, suppliers are expected to improve product quality, service, delivery, and price. Companies establish formal supplier certification programs to induce suppliers to improve. Suppliers are classified into categories based on history of operational performance. Categories include candidate, approved, and preferred suppliers.

Supplier-partners, the highest certification category, usually have in-house Op Ex initiatives that are equal or more stringent than the customers. Preferred suppliers are audited periodically to ensure a supplied product is defect-free. Preferred supplier parts are also sent directly into production. ISO 9001:2015 registration is becoming a condition of business for candidate as well as approved suppliers.

MEASURING SUPPLIER PERFORMANCE

Measurement is essential in evaluating on-going supplier performance. Without complete and accurate data, decisions cannot be made of a supplier's performance. Common Op Ex measures used to track and monitor suppliers include:

- Process improvement
- Parts per million Op Ex levels
- Rejects of incoming material
- Rework in dollars or hours
- Production stoppages
- End customer complaints

- Amount of material accepted on-waivers
- Scrap generated in use
- Warranty costs due to product failure
- Number of late shipments

PARTNERING BENEFITS AND CHALLENGES

Partnering is a dream come true for many suppliers. But, partnering comes with some costs as the following illustrates:

Upside:

- High volumes.
- High recognition.
- Preferred access to future projects.
- Improved manufacturing processes.
- Op Ex gains and lower costs.
- Access to specialized designs.
- Access to production expertise.
- Lower costs.
- Ability to synchronize just-in-time operations.
- Quicker cards.
- Order levels turnaround time.
- Quick change over.
- Fewer problems in design and product change-overs.

Down side:

- Minute scrutinization and operational pressures.
- Customer presence.
- ISO 9001:2015 or other certifications.
- Customer required controls.
- Annual "report tied to performance.
- Ever tighter requirements.
- Vulnerability to sharp demand swings.
- Possible loss of other customers.

- Evaluation of past history.
- Assessing security of information.
- Loss of sensitive or proprietary information.
- Loss of customer confidence if failure occurs.
- High opportunity costs.
- Loss of market share.
- Loss of credibility among stakeholders and competitors.
- High entry costs.

TYPES OF CONFLICTS

Conflicts can range from a major disagreement to a minor difference of opinion. Examples of conflicts include:

- Differences in interpreting documents.
- Differences in implementing corrective action.
- Differences in prioritizing Op Ex projects.
- Policies about offering waivers.
- Politics among internal and/or external stakeholders.
- Likes/dislikes.
- Conflicting messages/signals.
- Lack of resources.
- Conflicting upper management directives.
- Conflicting orders.
- Lack of or poor documentation and policies.
- Time conflicts.
- Customer demands.
- Regulatory mandates.
- People conflicts.
- Team member selection.
- Vague objectives.
- Competition for the use of resources.
- Multiple goals.
- Lack of senior management support.
- Lack of middle management support.
- Lack of first level supervision support.

- Lack of team member commitment.
- Communication problems.

NEGOTIATE, LITIGATE, OR ACCEPT

Conflicts, with suppliers always arise and can be resolved in three ways:

- Litigate
- Accept
- Negotiate

Litigate

The least-preferred option is to rely on lawyers and the courts to settle differences. Litigation is expensive and requires time to adjudicate and, unfortunately, the outcome is usually ill-will between parties.

Accept

Another option is to accept the problem. Not resolving disputes or problems in the short-term results in larger, long term problems. A TV commercial sums up the situation by warning "pay me now or pay me later." When problems have an opportunity to fester for years, the only way to resolve a dispute is through litigation and the cost of litigation can threaten a firm's survival.

Negotiate

The preferred option is to negotiate or arbitrate differences through negotiation. Differences can be resolved quickly and inexpensively. A win-win partnership can slowly evolve where the customer gets quality products delivered just-in-time and the supplier gets a long-term contract.[76]

DISPUTE RESOLUTION

Disputes and disagreements should be resolved quickly, fairly, and amicably. Disputes are sometimes seen as a personal battle, where the outcome is binary, one party wins and the other party loses. A better approach is to use the disagreement to establish trust and rapport with the other party, to understand each other's requirements.

All too often, people resolve disputes by litigation. Alternate dispute resolution is gaining more favor as a means to resolve differences. Alternate dispute resolution including negotiation, arbitration and mediation is usually less expensive, fairer, and quicker than litigation. Litigation results in many counterproductive problems. Litigation drains the finances of all parties. It is adversarial and minimizes the win-win potentials of an agreement. Litigation is disruptive to operations because it can keep management from focusing on customers and on operations.

The goal of dispute resolution is to find a method that maintains the relationship among the disputing parties and fosters reconciliation and further understanding. Disputes can then be resolved quickly, cheaply, and fairly. People problems are often intractable and are not conducive to easy solution. Op Ex professionals are taught to find the root source and use whatever methods to eliminate the root cause of the problem. Human issues and challenges are often much more complex. Finding a win-win solution may require deemphasizing the win-lose attitude, creating a positive atmosphere, attempting to simplify the conflict, and doing whatever possible to resolve the conflict.[77]

CONFLICT RESOLUTION

Always do right. This will surprise some people and astonish the rest.
Mark Twain

Misunderstandings, waivers, miscommunication, deficiencies, and nonconformances are a part of the Op Ex manager's life. They are unavoidable and must be resolved quickly and effectively. It seems the life of an Op Ex manager is to fight fires (eliminate symptoms) and get right to the problem (eliminate root causes).

Problems don't come to the operational manager. The operational manager's job is largely to ferret and attack systemic and chronic problems. Some would say the better the Op Ex manager attacks problems, the better he or she is doing the job. The Op Ex manager must have a plan to find, intervene, and attack the root-cause of problems and if necessary have a plan to deal with the fallout. The fallout are the conflicts that may arise because others may see operational personnel intruding on their turf, disrupting operations, or hurting people's feelings.

Conflicts can be dealt with in the following ways:

- **Fight.** A fight doesn't have to be physical. A fight can be an irreconcilable confrontation.
- **Finesse.** Finessing means the participants find areas of agreement and focus on them. In other words, they agree to disagree.
- **Compromise.** Compromising is the process of finding common ground.
- **Mandate.** Mandating has one party imposing his or her will on the other party. This person often is in a position of authority or power.
- **Ultimatum.** The ultimatum is the "my way or the roadway" approach.
- **Mediation/arbitration.** There are a number of alternate dispute resolution techniques where a third party facilitates resolution.

COMPETITION AND TRAINING

Too often the American dream is interrupted by the Japanese alarm clock.
Anonymous

There is mounting recognition that training and adaptation are required to remain competitive in a constantly changing environment. Training is one of the critical means by which a company ensures there is a skills match for present and future business. It would be catastrophic if a company is developing a new product or is planning a new process and doesn't have the human resource capabilities to implement its plan.

The marketplace is changing the method by which organizations are preparing their human resources for the future. Learning and training is following two routes, preemptive and maintenance learning. Preemptive learning emphasizes training that supports the strategic direction of the company. People and suppliers are sufficiently trained to support new products and services as they are developed. Preemptive training becomes a competitive tool to assist a company to position itself in the marketplace. Maintenance learning is also critical since it ensures that employees of existing projects, systems, or processes are capable of problem solving and continuous improvement.

HAVING FUN

One ingredient of successful, long term Op Ex projects seems to be enthusiasm. When the going gets tough, enthusiasm and long-term commitment keeps the process moving. There are always stumbling blocks in the Op Ex journey. Enthusiasm and can-do attitude are the engine for success.

The following is a list of things that can be done for defusing tension, ensuring fun, and focusing on end-results:

- Address concerns at each meeting.
- Resolve conflicts and disagreements quickly.
- Reinforce and encourage constantly.
- Have Friday casual dress days.
- Have weekly pizza and Coke get-togethers.
- Provide comp time.
- Use a flex schedule.
- Be affirmative and enthusiastic.
- Reward and recognize team and individual accomplishments.
- Develop a fun, informal and serious work culture.
- Celebrate the weekend.

CONTINUOUS IMPROVEMENT REQUIRES CONTINUOUS LEARNING

Continuous learning doesn't come easy to organizations. Companies often don't learn from experiences, whether positive or negative. It is critical for their survival and prosperity that organizations learn how the marketplace works, how competitors compete, and how regulators regulate. Internally, all employees need to learn how the organizational systems work as well as how work processes add value in an unbroken chain of product and service delivery. The ability to learn is also a litmus test to how likely a company is to develop new products, lower costs, improve safety and lower time to market.

Employee training is expensive. Some industries have a high turnover, such as hospitality, fast food, healthcare, manufacturing. There are a number of reasons for the high turnover. Wages are low and hours are long. Educational levels are also low reflecting the nature of the work. This is now changing as customer requirements become higher and the skill level of prospective employees is lower.

Training is a value adding investment because it allows a company to maintain its competitiveness. Employees need to learn new techniques, Op Ex tools, team management skills, and new machinery. Employees need the new skills and knowledge, and attitudes to successfully master the changing competitive and workplace environment.

Training also serves other important competitive purposes, including:

- Allows employees to understand a company's culture and requirements.
- Allows people to control and manage change.
- Allows employees to be competitive.
- Provides a sense of worth and workplace partnership.
- Communicates company protocols for conducting business.
- Enhances the quality of work life.
- Provides a person with the required skills and confidence to get the job done.
- Instructs employees how to work as teams.

NEW CONTRACT BETWEEN EMPLOYER AND EMPLOYEE

We are entering a very radical world of discontinuities.
Eugene Cafiero

The essence of employee empowerment is to have employees think and act like company owners and more specifically like process owners. This is often difficult because companies are rightsizing. Why should a person feel a sense of ownership when his or her job may be in jeopardy?

EMPLOYEE EMPOWERMENT

Most employee training deals with problem solving, team building, and preventing nonconformances. This is tactical learning, highly focused on searching for better ways of doing daily jobs. But strategic learning, the big picture, is not usually provided to employees. The big picture is how the business runs, its financial status, and competitive posture. Employees have the chance to learn their jobs but also to understand the company's goals, customer requirements, and overall costs. It's believed the more understanding employees have, the more they should be committed to improving their jobs as well as the performance of the company.

One method for ensuring there is a sense of ownership is to share financial information with employees including product cost, cost of quality, profits, and risk information. Even though the information may leak to competitors, companies believe there is value in employees knowing the current state of the company because there may be more operational buy in and ownership.

This view is not universally shared among companies. Some companies don't want employees to upgrade their skills. These companies, often small businesses insist that training is an employee's responsibility. It sometimes is difficult to convince a small business owner that an educated employee should be a valuable resource to improve Op Ex, productivity and organizational performance.

EMPLOYEE SELF DEVELOPMENT

Traditionally companies told employees what is necessary to perform a task or job satisfactorily. As well, the company provided resources and training to ensure the task was performed according to company policies, procedures, and expectations. This has now changed as more companies are moving towards a system of developing employee potential through a process of self-development.

Self-development means that employees are encouraged to enhance their skills, knowledge and capabilities. A company can tell the employee what needs to be done but the employee is ultimately responsible for ensuring he or she has the skills to get the job done. The employee also has the information, resources, broad direction, networks, and even mentors to pursue self-development.

There are several major assumptions in self-development. First, the companies are relying on the individual to determine what is the best method to do a job and to find the right career path to get there. The company is relying on the individual's skills, resources, and abilities to ensure that he or she will get the job done. As well, the company is saying that accountability for success is now shared between the company and the individual. The employee assumes more responsibility as the contract between employee and company changes. The employee must show initiative, be resourceful, and get the job done. In other words, value must be added. If not, the employee may be downsized. Tough talk for tough times.

Another message being sent to all employees is that everyone is responsible for his or her own career. The employee is offered options and it is up to the employee to avail himself or herself of the opportunities for educational advancement. Additional education and training have become the carrots or inducements for promotion or lateral transfer within the organization. As more companies are rightsizing, employers are also recognizing and communicating to workers that life time employment may not be an option so employees must avail themselves of the training if not for self-development but also for self-survival.

As more job postings detail specific requirements. Employees can look at the requirements and understand what needs to be done to get the next promotion or job transfer. This empowers the employee to be responsible for his or her own career. The problem is that these tend to be lateral moves as many companies flatten their hierarchies.

TECHNICAL SKILLS AND TRAINING

Management authority today is derived more from personal qualities - possession of knowledge, skills, and values - than on ownership of capital or property.
John Mee

Sometimes, the best and brightest engineers are promoted to Op Ex manager. While this person may have technical skills, business and organizational skills may be lacking. Sometimes, Op Ex professionals with technical skills fail as managers or leaders. They were excellent engineers or first level supervisors who were not exposed to business dynamics, customer service requirements, or the human side of Op Ex. These technically oriented managers may fail because they became too enamored with the technical problem and solution to the detriment of the organizational or customer requirements.

GENERAL TECHNICAL SKILLS

Some Op Ex managerial positions require a technical background. For example, Op Ex engineering and metrology require technical skills and experience. Op Ex auditing and customer-supplier relations require technical, managerial, and other multi-disciplinary skills.

The Op Ex manager needs general technical skills and knowledge. The Op Ex manager will be working intimately with different functional areas such as Supply Management, Engineering, Production, Planning, Accounting, Customer Service, Marketing, and Sales. The Op Ex manager should be familiar with the people, processes, systems, technologies, and products of these areas. This is especially critical as work is organized around processes instead of functional departments.

The Op Ex manager should be familiar with:

- Functional customer departments.
- Key supplier-partners.
- Engineering and information technology tools and techniques.
- Regulatory requirements.
- Product applications.
- Processes and products.
- Technological trends and applications.

How does a person acquire these technical skills and knowledge? Several methods include classes and on the job training as part of a special project team or through a lateral assignment. A manager can be assigned as a technical expert, process expert, or team leader to different organizational areas. Not only does the manager get exposed to other department's problems but is also sensitive to key player's needs and requirements. Another way to get exposure to different functional areas is through lateral transfers.

OPERATIONAL MANAGEMENT DEVELOPMENT

Keep an ear to the ground and watch the handwriting on the wall.
Herbert Prochnow

Total operational management and other principles offer insights and ideas to better management and higher profitability. However, these new ideas seem to fail for a number of reasons. Often, they fail because the ideas are new, change is resisted, and the new ideas aren't integrated into the daily workings of the organization.

As well, new ideas are threatening to the status quo of almost every element of the organization. Middle managers are afraid of losing responsibility or authority. Line workers don't have the time or the inclination to take on new responsibilities. Senior management tends to bow to the newest management fads.

LEARNING ORGANIZATION

Innovation thrives on encouragement and dies with routine.
Anonymous

Many organizational structures are in a transition from a hierarchical to more of a horizontal one where responsibility is pushed to the lowest organizational levels. In this structure, employees are challenged to expand and to take on more authority and responsibility. A critical assumption is the individual must add value to the organization.

Information and knowledge are where real value is being added. Knowledge allows for a smarter organization that can deliver products and services faster and better than competitors. Arie de Geus, a management strategist, once said that "the ability to learn faster than your competitors may be the only sustainable competitive advantage."

OP EX AND THE LEARNING ORGANIZATION

It has been said that people, their ideas, and motivation are an organization's greatest asset. People develop ideas which are turned into products or service that generate profits. The challenge is most people don't work at even close to their potential. Employees can add much more value and performance to their work. The question for senior management is how would this be done? A preferred method is now the learning organization.

Learning organization is characterized by the following:

- Risk based problem solving.
- Risk based decision making.
- Systematic problem solving.
- Experimentation with new approaches.
- Learning from past experience.
- Learning form the best practices.
- Transferring knowledge quickly and efficiently throughout the organization.

Operational management and the learning organization link nicely and create synergies. As a company implements and finishes an Op Ex initiative or project, lessons are learned and can be shared throughout the organization. Each new lesson allows the organization to develop products faster, involve employees in decisions, and become more competitive.

The learning organization is flexible, using its human resources, systems, and processes to deliver new, pleasing products quickly. The learning organization encourages employees to be innovative and improving. The learning organization is adaptable and strives to constantly satisfy existing and new customers.

Learning is simply not cosmetic or abstract. A learning organization is excellent in creating, acquiring, transferring and implementing knowledge and skills. These new skills are used to improve operations as well as modify systems, processes, products, and documentation to make the organization more competitive. Benefits of the learning organization include:

- Integrating information, knowledge, and skills to the organization.
- Avoiding repeating old mistakes.
- Benchmarking and learning from "best" practices.

IMPORTANCE OF TRAINING

Knowledge is a treasure, but practice is the key to it.
Thomas Fuller

According to the Fortune Magazine, the technician is becoming the core employee of the digital information age. Production workers will disappear and knowledge workers will rise. Two forces are converging to increase the importance of technicians. Versatile, and user-friendly technologies are eliminating routine, time consuming tasks. Second, front-line workers are more conscious of eliminating Op Ex nonconformances, producing Op Ex service, answering customer questions courteously, and delivering products quickly and efficiently. The line employee must now use technology to work smarter, not particularly faster. These forces require that workers are more actively engaged in their work which requires a high level of judgment and skills. To harness employee commitment, the work environment must be conducive to identifying, harnessing, acknowledging and rewarding talents.

MANAGER AND LEADERSHIP DEVELOPMENT

Despite all of the educational and analytical infrastructure that has been built up around the alleged science of management, it still reduced itself to homework, common sense, and good communication.
Donn Tatum

Old management rules no longer seem to apply. Management pundits call this the management paradigm shift. New roles and rules are replacing new ones. The question is which ones are critical. And, that's the crux of the issue for management and leadership training. New rules and roles have to be learned and accepted. For example, middle managers are cheerleaders, facilitators, coaches, and hand holders.

Motorola, Coca Cola, Ford Motor Co. and others have built universities to train company's suppliers, employees and other important organizational stakeholders. Motorola, for example, offers Op Ex, technical, Supply Management, customer service, marketing and a full range of courses. At Motorola, the average employee receives about 50 hours of training per year which can range up to 80 or more hours in some companies.

EXECUTIVE EDUCATION

In this changing competitive environment, leadership training is ever more critical. The business environment is global and more competitive. Even small companies are competing directly or indirectly with foreign suppliers. The requirements for success for management and employees are even different from five years ago. Leaders share common attributes, specifically they are technically proficient, opportunistic, globally aware, culturally sensitive, multilingual, and team builders. The global perspective is especially critical to those moving up large global organizations with plants, divisions, and business units throughout the world.

Leadership training is not just for managers but for line employees. Line employees may become project leaders, team facilitators, or assume other leadership roles. Op Ex leadership training includes team and people empowerment, team facilitation, and coaching techniques.

SENIOR MANAGEMENT SURVEY BUY-IN

Senior management should have a vested interest in planning, conducting, reporting, and acting upon a customer satisfaction survey. Senior management will ensure the survey is successful, focuses on business needs, and provides value to the organization.

Many companies use customer satisfaction to evaluate and compensate employees, especially senior managers. Management interest and involvement in customer satisfaction surveys is guaranteed because customer satisfaction affects their incentives, bonus, or even base salary.

Enhancing customer satisfaction can also be used to increase sales and revenues. There is often a positive correlation between customer satisfaction and revenues. As well, customer service metric is an excellent way to align tactical Op Ex interests with a company's strategic goals and plans. Some companies measure customer satisfaction performance, customer retention, customer loyalty, and business results. Business managers are also expected to develop objectives and a plan on how he or she will meet specific objectives such as increasing external or internal service quality.

WHAT NEW EMPLOYEES NEED TO LEARN

New employees need basic Op Ex and customer information that can be divided into three basic areas:

Knowledge:

- Information about the internal and external customer requirements.
- Standards of performance, product Op Ex, service quality, lean, process Op Ex.
- Professionalism, information of company expectations protocols, accepted practices, dress codes, values, and principles.
- Job information, specific information of what is expected on-the-job, resources provided, and assistance.
- Company information on values, principles, and financial status.

Skills:

- Step-by-step instructions on how to get the job done.
- Models that illustrate the best way to get the job done.
- Criteria or standards of performance.
- Tools or equipment to get the job done.
- Safe work environment.

- Current, accurate, and relevant job expectations and requirements.

Attitudes:

- Fairness, basically the golden rule.
- Openness, sharing information to get the job done.
- Respect, for individual and team differences.
- Compassion, identifying and helping others inside and outside the organization.
- Staff support, providing support for new activities and processes.
- Management support, walking and talking the part.
- Leadership, providing active and financial support.
- Responsiveness, meeting internal and external customer requirements.[78]

BUSINESS SKILLS AND KNOWLEDGE

Business expertise is sometimes under rated in the Op Ex function. On the other hand, operational, technical, and organizational skills and expertise are highly recognized and rated. With the rapid development of products and service in the global organization and the critical role of Op Ex to satisfy customers, the manager has to understand fundamental business principles and practices.

For example, the Op Ex manager as part of the total customer satisfaction team may be involved in:

- Setting Op Ex directions for the department, business unit or even the entire organization.
- Searching for new marketing opportunities.
- Conducting cost-benefit analyses of proposed Op Ex projects.
- Analyzing customer needs and expectations.
- Benchmarking new products or processes.
- Analyzing competitors.
- Selecting, monitoring and evaluating suppliers.
- Working with and satisfying regulators.

HOW TO TRAIN, EDUCATE AND DEVELOP OPERATIONAL EXCELLENCE MANAGERS

The following are common methods for training, educating, and developing Op Ex managers:

On the job

- Job rotation.
- Special assignments.
- Mentoring, guidance from experienced managers.
- Op Ex team facilitation or leadership.
- Customer contact and problem solving.
- Supplier contact and problem solving.
- Working with experienced managers.
- Participating in multidisciplinary teams.

Education/schooling

- Accredited university operational management programs
- Professional certification
- Certification
- Seminars

Professional activities

- Technical societies
- Professional societies
- Courses, seminars, or workshops
- Hands on training
- Books, workshops, etc.

OP EX FUNCTION AS LINE OR STAFF

The Op Ex organization may have both staff and line responsibilities. Line responsibilities for the Op Ex function include Op Ex auditing; incoming, in process, and final inspection; and metrology. As well, the Op Ex function may have staff responsibilities including training and Op Ex auditing.

Responsibility for process control and product Op Ex often rests with the people doing the work. The responsibility of the staff Op Ex group then is to objectively and independently monitor the Op Ex work performance. Monitoring responsibility for the Op Ex system is thus separated from responsibility of the implementing the system and process.

In many organizations, the best Op Ex organizations are populated by self-managed, self-motivated problem-solving teams. The Op Ex function representative is an advisor, coach, or facilitator of team. Op Ex professionals must be versatile, must be broadly trained, have more operational knowledge, have internal consultant skills, and be empowered to improve processes. How do Op Ex professionals acquire this knowledge and understanding of the organization's systems? One method is to loan existing employees to operating departments to ensure that Op Ex function employees are exposed and understand internal customer requirements.

IMPORTANCE OF CONTINUOUS TRAINING

A global marketplace and discerning custom-ers require an organization to be flexible in order to satisfy changing customer needs. Flexibility involves designing, producing, and delivering innovative products and requires a workforce educated in Op Ex techniques.

Training can create an awareness of the importance of Op Ex, help people identify Op Ex problems, provide tools to solve problems, and develop systems to measure improvements. Bottom line: training is now seen as an investment to make an organization more competitive.

To stay current, everyone from the CEO to the person on the line requires extensive training. For example:

- **Marketing and customer service personnel.** Learn how to listen to the customer as well as provide courte-ous service.

- **Engineering personnel.** Learn about Op Ex engineer-ing, reliability, design of experiments, project management, maintainability engineering, reliability engineering, statistics, product testing, and design.
- **Human resource personnel.** Learn how to develop and nurture a cooperative corporate climate, facilitate empowerment groups, and assess the corporate climate for change.
- **Supply Management personnel.** Learn just-in-time, supplier evaluation, supplier auditing, contract management, and material requirement planning.
- **Manufacturing personnel.** Learn statistics, process control, robotics, just-in-time manufacturing, updated manufacturing techniques, and automation.
- **Op Ex personnel.** Learn statistics, process control, project management, Op Ex systems, Op Ex engineering, reliability, and maintainability.
- **Distribution personnel.** Learn just-in-time, handling, shipping, and storage techniques.

EMPLOYER OF CHOICE

Companies in competitive marketplace value their employees. These "world class" companies compete aggressively to attract the best and brightest employees. These companies are aware that employees have a choice of companies for which to work. Employees will gravitate to companies whose workplace is safe, challenging, rewarding, and more importantly fun.

A common way to become the "employer of choice" is to establish a culture and quality of work life that is conducive to the talents and direction of the high-potential employees. In terms of quality of work life, the company embraces and nurtures a culture that allows an employee to develop new skills and knowledge.

HOW TO LEARN MANAGEMENT

How do managers or supervisors learn who to manage and lead? One method to learning and building skills is through executive development, education and training. A formal degree, like an MBA is also helpful. More often, a manager or supervisor learns the organizational culture by observing how managers handle problems successfully. Newly minted mangers handle their own situations by trial and error, finally adopting a successful style that is congruent with the needs of the workplace, the individual, and teams.

Executive education is becoming an important perquisite of high potential managers. Executive education is sometimes conducted on site or at prestigious universities. These programs offer tips and ideas on competitive strategies, productivity, remuneration, cycle time reduction, Op Ex, reengineering, and culture management. The common feature of these programs is that they are highly tailored to the needs of the client organization. These programs emphasize global perspective, integrated on-the-job and classroom learning, are team based and participatory, and offer holistic solutions to problems.

Most major universities have executive education programs. Often universities and companies partner to deliver tailored or customized programs to a business. These customer courses address the company's concerns and problems.

CHANGING NATURE OF DISTRIBUTION	
Old Approach	**New Approach**
Inventories are acceptable	Inventories are not acceptable
Warehouses store people's mistakes	Warehouses are minimized
Supplied material is nonconforming	Supplied material is defect free
Inspection is performed in warehouses	No incoming material inspection is performed
Buffer inventory maintains continuous production	All inventory is costly

OP EX FUNCTION AS LINE OR STAFF

The Op Ex organization may have both staff and line responsibilities. Line responsibilities for the Op Ex function include operational auditing; incoming, in process, and final inspection; and metrology. As well, the Op Ex function may have staff responsibilities including training and Op Ex auditing.

Responsibility for process control and product quality often rests with the people doing the work. The responsibility of the staff Op Ex group then is to objectively and independently monitor the Op Ex work performance. Monitoring responsibility for the Op Ex system is thus separated from responsibility of the implementing the system and process.

In many organizations, the best Op Ex organizations are populated by self-managed, self-motivated problem-solving teams. The Op Ex function representative is an advisor, coach, or facilitator of team. Op Ex professionals must be versatile, must be broadly trained, have more operational knowledge, have internal consultant skills, and be empowered to improve processes. How do Op Ex professionals acquire this knowledge and understanding of the organization's systems? One method is to loan existing employees to operating departments to ensure that Op Ex function employees are exposed and understand internal customer requirements.

QUALTY OF WORK LIFE

The perspective of Op Ex as being a good physical place to work has a powerful appeal. If people are happy or content with their physical surroundings and respect their management, then this should translate into concern for product and service quality. Then Op Ex can rest with the people and management doing the work instead of any department or any inspector. The spirit of cooperation facilitates the goal of continuous Op Ex.

Technology, specifically automation, provides workers with a greater span of control and authority in their work area. However, does the worker want the additional responsibility? Many workers resist change. Sociologists believe that by creating a quality work environment that takes into account worker's needs, resistance and fear may be reduced.

Quality of work life is being enhanced by:

- Improving internal communications and through active listening.
- Reinforcing the positive and confronting the negative.
- Developing employee friendly procedures.
- Offering liberal family benefits including child care.
- Providing extensive training and career counseling.
- Offering support.
- Making the work environment a pleasant place to work.

Quality of work life is intangible. Its definition relies on the perceptions of people. How does a company solicit information on these perceptions? One method is to perform a climate assessment of the organization. A climate assessment surveys employee Op Ex attitudes, Op Ex expectations, customer service, and product quality.

NEXT CHAPTER

In the next chapter, Op Ex Leaders is discussed. The chapter focuses on 3 leaders that defined quality, Lean, and Six Sigma over the last 50 years: Phil Crosby, W. Edwards Deming, and Joseph Juran.

CHAPTER 18

OP EX LEADERS

In this chapter, the following are discussed in detail:

- Joseph Juran
- W. Edwards Deming
- Phil Crosby

JOSEPH M. JURAN

The task of management is not to apply a formula but to decide issues on a case-by-case basis. No fixed, inflexible rule can ever be substituted for the exercise of sound business judgment in the decision-making process.
Alfred P. Sloan, Executive

Joseph M. Juran went to Japan in 1954 to lecture on how to manage quality. Previously, he was chief of the electrical division of Western Electric and a professor at New York University. Eventually, the Japanese incorporated many of his ideas into their companywide Op Ex initiatives.

While Op Ex technology had evolved, operational management and quality had stood still. Juran believed that operational excellence should be managed. Juran's operational management ideas focused on organization, communication, and coordination of internal functions. Communication and coordination across functional departments could solve Op Ex problems that technical approaches cannot.

FITNESS FOR USE

According to Juran, there are two definitions of quality. The first is "conformance to specifications". The second definition is "fitness for use." Problems arise when a product conforms to engineering specifications but may not be "fit for use." For example, Manufacturing builds a product that conforms to engineering specifications, but the product is not what the customer wants. Marketing did not properly communicate customer needs and wants to engineering. However, a customer does not care about specifications. The customer wants a particular need fulfilled, such as clear TV reception, dependable telephone service, or a reliable toaster.

JURAN'S TRILOGY

Juran believed there was a quality and Op Ex crisis which won't go away in the foreseeable future. The quality of Japanese goods had been increasing at a faster rate than the West. While both Japanese and western quality levels had approved appreciably in the last decade, the difference between the two has remained constant. This difference in Op Ex levels had resulted in the loss of market share for many products in the U.S. and throughout the world.

Juran developed a methodology, the Trilogy, to explain his approach to solving broad management problems. Juran's Trilogy consisted of three basic quality and Op Ex elements:

- Operational (quality) planning
- Operational (quality) control
- Operational (quality) improvement

Operational Planning

Op Ex planning is the process to develop quality plans to meet organizational goals. This is done by identifying the customer, determining needs, and delivering a product that satisfies these needs.

Operational Control

Operational control is the process to maintain organizational processes at optimal levels. Because systemic deficiencies, company processes may run at high levels of waste. Waste becomes planned into the system. Operational control consists of identifying the variables to control, finding an unit of measurement, and controlling the process to limit any unnatural variation that leads to waste.

Operational improvement

Op Ex occurs when waste, losses, or deficiencies are reduced through improvement projects. Management or teams first identify areas for improvement, organize to implement the project, and then implement solutions. Juran believed that Op Ex improves through a sequence of breakthroughs from one project to another. Improvements were measured. If improvements returned more than the cost of a project, then this served to justify the next project. After a series of successful projects, a company developed a habit or culture of quality and Op Ex. Chronic problems became correctable and manageable.

However, Op Ex and quality could be pursued only if the corporate climate is conducive to change and implementation. Management must be aware of the need and benefits of an Op Ex program. Management must lead and support the initiative, otherwise it will fail. Like Deming, Juran believed that 15% of the quality problems were caused by hourly employees and 85% by management.

Op Ex projects must have attainable goals. Once these are established, progress is monitored. Op Ex required investment in time and money. Successful projects reduce costs or generate revenue.

MAJOR ELEMENTS OF JURAN'S IMPROVEMENT PHILOSOPHY

Major elements of Juran's improvement philosophy included:

- Project structure to pursue projects
- Big picture orientation
- Doable and measurable projects
- Group focus
- Measure improvements

Project Structure to Pursue Projects

A corporate steering committee or council monitored and facilitated progress of the Op Ex and quality teams. Management organized a project structure, such as a corporate council, as well as teams to achieve Op Ex goals. The corporate council identified problems, selected projects, appointed teams, and designated facilitators. Once teams were formed, people were trained in communications, statistical operational control, customer-supplier relations, and engineering principles.

Big-Picture Orientation

Juran focused on the big picture, emphasizing the role of senior management and integrating Op Ex throughout the organization. For example, he believed that training in operational management for everyone benefits the organization.

Doable and Measurable Projects

Juran believed that doable and measurable projects contrasted to large initiatives are the way to achieve Op Ex. General and broad programs resulted in objectives that are difficult to measure. A project-by-project, problem solving approach to Op Ex was measurable and easier to implement.

Group Focus

Improvement should be rewarded and recognized through highlighting group accomplishments. Genuine recognition fostered trust and respect within the organization. Progress reports gave project management visibility and ease implementation.

Measure Improvements

Finally, it wasimportant to keep score. Measurement and benchmarks indicated improvements, provided goals to teams, and justified the next improvement project. When sufficient successful projects had been implemented, a momentum was achieved. Then an Op Ex culture could be integrated into the organization.

Juran Approach to Quality and Op Ex

Joseph M. Juran had been espousing that Op Ex should be based on integrated and reinforcing Op Ex projects. The advantages of this approach included:

- One project lead onto another, until the entire organization was focusing on continuous improvement and innovation.
- Approach involved top-down and bottom-up commitment.
- It was self-reinforcing.
- Approach required multi-disciplinary teams.
- Project management tools could be used in Op Ex projects.

JURAN'S TRILOGY

Operational excellence and quality planning could:

- Identify the customers, both external and internal.
- Determine customer needs.
- Develop product features that respond to customer needs.
- Establish Op Ex and quality goals that could meet the needs of customers and suppliers alike, and do so at a minimum combined cost.
- Develop a process that can produce the needed product features.
- Improve process capability prove that the process could meet the Op Ex goals under operating conditions.

Control:

- Choose subjects what to control.
- Choose units of measurement.
- Establish measurement.
- Establish standards of performance.
- Measure actual performance.
- Interpret the difference (actual versus standard).
- Take action on the difference.

Improvement:

- Prove the need for improvement.
- Identify specific projects for improvement.
- Organize to guide the projects.
- Organize for diagnosis for discovery of causes.
- Diagnose to find the causes.

- Provide remedies.
- Prove that the remedies are effective under operating conditions.
- Provide for control to hold the gains.

PHILIP B. CROSBY

In the days ahead, the management of any consumer goods company is going to have only two options: build a trouble free product or be ready to fix the product fast.
S. E. Knudsen, business person

Philip Crosby was the founder of Quality College, a school on operational management for executives. Quality College graduates had a successful track record of implementing Op Ex in many Fortune 500 companies. Crosby believed that management did not put quality and Op Ex on an equal footing with other corporate objectives. Controlling costs and keeping production on schedule were more important than Op Ex.

Crosby's philosophy centered around "doing it right the first time" (DIRFT). He believeed DIRFT can be achieved at any level of an organization. His converts credited his methods for saving their company's millions of dollars.

MANAGEMENT PRINCIPLES

The four major principles of Crosby's philosophy were:

- Definition of quality is "conformance to requirements".
- Management system is prevention.
- Performance standard is zero defects.
- Measurement system is the cost of Op Ex.

Conformance to Requirements

Quality is defined as "conformance to requirements and to specifications." It is measured in terms of the cost of not conforming to specifications, procedures, and policy. The cost on nonconformance could be very high, anywhere from 10% to 30% of a company's gross sales. Crosby believed if a company adopted an Op Ex program, the program could pay for itself through savings in Op Ex. As a result, Crosby believed that "quality is free."

Prevention
Prevention is the preferred method for managing quality and Op Ex. By the time a product is manufactured, time, labor, and material have been invested in the product. If product deficiencies are found during inspection, then the investment has to be scrapped and that may be expensive.

Zero Defects
The performance standard is Zero Defects (ZD). The ZD philosophy says that management and all employees should strive for nothing less than zero defects in everything they do. Zero defects are the cornerstone of Crosby's philosophy. Zero defects are encouraged internally as well with external suppliers. A zero defects program requires self-discipline to change old habits, to completely eliminate defects. If a company accepts a certain level of defects, then everyone's expectations are conditioned to operate at that level of nonconformances. This makes it difficult to establish zero defects as the expected level of performance.

The second element is to communicate the importance of quality and Op Ex to suppliers. The ZD program requires vendors to supply acceptable, defect-free parts. If a large portion of the manufacturing dollar goes to outside suppliers, then supplied products must be defect free. Suppliers have to be educated to share the responsibility of ensuring defect-free parts.

Cost of Op Ex
The measurement system is the cost of Quality (COQ). Money is the yardstick that every company uses to justify projects and programs. And Op Ex programs are no different. The cost of Quality is the cost of not doing things right. The Cost of Quality is important, because it gets management's attention and it serves as a guide to prioritize projects.

CROSBY'S 14 STEPS TO QUALITY

1. Obtain management commitment for quality.
2. Form quality teams with representatives from each department.
3. Find where current and potential quality problems are.
4. Evaluate the cost of quality and explain its use as a management tool.
5. Raise the awareness of quality among all employees.
6. Act to correct problems identified through previous steps.
7. Establish a committee for the Zero Defects program.
8. Train supervisors to carry out their part of the quality program.
9. Hold a "Zero Defects day" to communicate to all employees that there has been a change.
10. Encourage individuals to establish measurable and attainable improvement goals for themselves and their groups.
11. Encourage employees to communicate to management the obstacles in the way of achieving their improvement goals.
12. Recognize, appreciate, and reward those who meet goals.
13. Establish quality councils to communicate quality on a regular basis.
14. Do it all over again to emphasize that the quality program is continue.

W. EDWARDS DEMING

Skilled leaders share traits that elevate them above the majority of managers. While most managers concern themselves with doing things right, leaders focus on doing the right thing.
Warren Bennis, educator

W. Edwards Deming is considered the dean of quality and Op Ex gurus in the west. In 1950, Deming conducted a population census in Japan. While there, Deming spoke to Japanese leaders on statistical operational control. They listened, learned, and implemented his ideas. Part of the myth surrounding Deming is that by doing this, quality and Op Ex evolved into a national ethic in Japan. In recognition of his contributions to the economy of Japan, the Union of Japanese Science and Engineering (JUSE) instituted the annual Deming Prize awarded for advances in the Op Ex and reliability of products.

MANAGEMENT IS THE CAUSE OF MOST OPERATIONAL PROBLEMS

Deming distilled his philosophy into 14 points of management. The major principle behind Deming's 14 points is that management is the cause of 85% of a company's problems and only management has the resources, such as time, material, and money to remedy the systemic problems that they created.

Deming believed institutional, systemwide problems can only be solved through long-range planning and improvement programs that attack fundamental causes. Therefore, top management must be responsible for actively steering and reinforcing the Op Ex process.
According to Deming, the major problems with American management are:

- Inspection mode of management.
- Short term business goals.
- Fixation on the quick fix.

Inspection Mode of Management

Management depends on mass inspection instead of prevention to find nonconforming products. But mass inspection communicates that a company tolerates mistakes and nonconforming products by assuming that mistakes will be made.

Even then, inspection only catches a small representative sample of the mistakes. Deming argued that top management should communicate to all company employees and stakeholders that deficiencies and mistakes can no longer tolerated.

Short Term Business Goals

In regards to business goals, American management focuses on improving quarterly earnings reports. Management can manipulate statistics to make financial statements look healthy in the short-term but this does nothing for the long-term strength of the company. Focus on short term paper profits does not improve a company's infrastructure, which is its economic foundation. If management wants to improve Op Ex and productivity, they must focus on the factors that lead to long-term Op Ex, such as investing in new property, plant, and equipment; designing more reliable products; or requiring suppliers to supply defect-free products.

Fixation on the Quick Fix

Op Ex is not just a one-time fix, but is a continuous improvement process. Hourly employees can achieve a small portion of the required improvement, management achieves the rest.

Only management can communicate a sense of urgency on Op Ex. With proper encouragement and incentives, management can create a company structure and culture that encourages continuing improvement in Marketing, Engineering, Supply Management, Manufacturing, Op Ex, and Distribution functions.

STATISTICS AS A PROBLEM SOLVING AND MANAGEMENT TOOL

According to Deming, quality as part of Op Ex is the sum of those characteristics in a product or service that a customer recognizes as important. With a product, characteristics are identified, written into a specification and then measured. If measurements are within the tolerance spread of a specification, then the product is accepted. If not, it is deficient. With a service, characteristics are compared to a policy or procedure. If a service conforms to the procedure, then that service behavior is reinforced. If the service does not conform to the procedure, then the employee is guided on how to deliver the expected level of service.

CONTROL VARIATION

An important theme that weaved throughout Deming's writing is that statistics can be used to monitor and control product variation. Product variation is controlled by reducing measurement variation and by having measurements at the target which is in the middle of the specification spread. If this is achieved, there is less chance for the product to be outside the specification limits. This is called Statistical Process Control (SPC).

CAUSES OF VARIATION

There are two causes of variation, chance and assignable causes. Chance and assignable causes are also called respectively common and special causes. Chance causes exist in the system and are usually so minute they cannot readily be identified or controlled.

On the other hand, assignable causes are caused by known factors, such as a worn cutting tool, poorly trained operator, or faulty jig. Statistics can be used to measure and control assignable variation in manufacturing and administrative services.

FEAR

Another theme in Deming's philosophy was the need for management to eliminate the prevailing emotion inside their organizations, which is fear. He stated that fear would disappear if mutual trust were developed between management and employees.

Deming argued that employees are an underutilized resource and that employees are not allowed to achieve their full potential. Fear of retaliation, retribution, and punishment promote only limited solutions to recurring problems alone. Safe solutions attack isolated problems while leaving alone recurring problems. Most employees become risk averse and lose any natural interest in improving the system.

If management broke down barriers among departments, including Engineering, Manufacturing, Op Ex, Quality, and Supply Management, then a team spirit could prevail. Instead, company departments are fiefdoms that do not communicate with each other. Managers fear loss of authority or power and the result is bureaucratic infighting. The loser is the company and inevitably, the customer.

BARRIERS TO OP EX

Since senior management is removed by layers of supervision from what happens on the production floor, they do not understand the causes of poor Op Ex. Deming maintained that bureaucracy and entrenched interests create barriers for employees to achieve their potential. These barriers are the most significant obstacle to improving Op Ex and reducing manufacturing and service costs in the United States.

Deming believed that management can eliminate barriers hindering hourly employees from achieving pride of workmanship and the knowledge that a job is done well. These barriers stifle employee initiative and innovation and result in an "I don't care" attitude. These barriers include:

- Fear of reprisal
- Production standards
- Exhortations

Fear of Reprisal

Supervisors and employees can be encouraged to inform senior management of conditions that require correction without fear of reprisal. Supervisors and employees would initiate change if they believed management is serious about listening and implementing new ideas. Unfortunately, the opposite is often the case. Employees are disciplined for taking initiative.

Production Standards

Industrial engineers develop standards and quotas to measure productivity. Unfortunately, emphasis on productivity often depreciates Op Ex. A work standard may state that "there will be no more than 10% nonconforming products." A numerical quota may state that "30 units will be produced every hour." These messages reinforce productivity at the expense of Op Ex, in other words, working harder instead of working smarter.

Work standards send the message that a level of nonconforming products is tolerated and even expected. If an employee knows that, then only this level is achieved and no room exists for improvement. Also, work standards and production quotas rob the employee of pride of workmanship. The result is resentment and poor product quality.

Exhortations

Op Ex is also improved if management eliminates production slogans. Deming wanted management to eliminate Op Ex posters, pictures, and anything else that encourages employees to be aware of Op Ex. He believed that exhortations, such as "Do it right the first time" and "Quality is Job #1," sound good but do not tell someone in practical terms how to improve Op

Ex. Slogans insult the employee's intelligence. Management is abdicating its responsibility for product quality by not demonstrating how to accomplish it.

EVALUATION OF OP EX GURUS

The best prophet is common sense.
Euripedes

The quality and Op Ex gurus share the following common beliefs:

- Management should be involved in Op Ex if permanent and continuous improvement is expected.
- Defect prevention is preferred over inspection.

DEMING'S 14 POINTS OF OPERATIONAL MANAGEMENT

1. Create constancy of purpose towards improvement of product and services.
2. Adopt the new philosophy. We can no longer live with commonly accepted levels of delays, mistakes, defective materials, and defective workmanship.
3. Cease dependence on mass inspection. Require, instead, statistical evidence that quality is built in.
4. End the practice of awarding business on the basis of price tag.
5. Find problems. It is management's job to work continually on the system.
6. Institute modern methods of training on the job.
7. Institute modern methods of supervision of production workers. The responsibility of foremen must be changed from numbers to quality.
8. Drive out fear, so that everyone may work effectively for the company.
9. Break down barriers between departments.
10. Eliminate numerical goals, posters, and slogans for the work force, asking for new levels of productivity without providing methods.
11. Eliminate work standards that prescribe numerical quotas.
12. Remove barriers that stand between the hourly worker and his or her right to pride of workmanship.
13. Institute a vigorous program of education and retraining.
14. Create a structure in top management that will push every day on the above 13 points.

- Continuously setting and achieving higher Op Ex goals results in higher productivity and lower costs.
- Achieving higher Op Ex levels requires commitment and takes time.
- Higher Op Ex requires a structured improvement process that is a never-ending cycle.

Some companies exclusively have used a particular guru's philosophy. A more common practice is to integrate the best and the most applicable approach to a specific operation. For example, a corporate culture, systems, people, and customer may require a tailored approach.

Deming was probably the most sought-after consultant in the 1980s because of his remarkable success in Japan. Early in his consulting career, Deming focused on statistical operational control exclusively. In his later years, he focused on a broader management philosophy based on his 14 points.

Crosby's well-accepted program for quality had been used successfully by IBM, Tennant Co., and others. He provides an easily applied, participative approach to problem solving and a clear, step-by-step approach for Op Ex awareness and top-management commitment. The program initially starts at the top, but the concept of "zero defects" can be understood by everyone. Senior management is involved from the first day to promote and implement the program. Crosby precisely defines objectives, responsibilities, and performance standards. Progress is then directly measured.

Juran is more sympathetic toward management. He favors continuous Op Ex projects. The first step is picking specific annual goals and then setting up teams to work on them. As a company attacks one project after another, the culture and habit of Op Ex are integrated into the organization. Juran's approach is attractive to management because it is simple and easily taught. He also believes that moderate "fear can bring out the best in people."

VALUE OF OP EX AWARDS

There has been an amazing proliferation of Op Ex awards in the last ten years. The notable American Op Ex award is the Baldrige Award.

Various states have designed Op Ex awards. New York state had the Excelsior Award which recognized Op Ex in the private, public, and education sectors. The award process was similar to the Baldrige. Guidelines and applications were distributed and applications were reviewed first by individual examiners and then by a team of examiners until winners were chosen.

What do these awards do? In general, Op Ex awards provide the following benefits:

- Promote a company's Op Ex initiatives and excellence.
- Motivate continuous Op Ex and customer satisfaction.
- Benchmark the best in the nation, state, or industry segment.
- Recognize the safety, health, environmental consciousness, consumer satisfaction for the company.
- Promote recognition of a job well done.

A criticism of awards is that once a company pursues and wins an award, what is left to do? A company may rest on its laurels. The goal of any business is to pursue continuous improvement and profitability. Any award should serve as an important benchmark or milepost in the improvement journey not the journey's end. This has occurred in some companies that have won prestigious awards. Goals have been met and the Op Ex initiative flounders.

NEXT CHAPTER

In the next chapter, Op Ex Truths is covered. Op Ex challenges and the future of Op Ex are discussed.

CHAPTER 19
OP EX TRUTHS

Large and small organization are implementing Op Ex initiatives. In some ways, they are fundamentally different.

- Large companies normally have Op Ex staff. Small companies may have one person assuming multiple responsibilities. For example, the Op Ex manager may also be the engineering director.
- In the large organization, Op Ex systems and processes are further developed than in a small organization.
- Large companies have more resources to attack an Op Ex problem than a small company.
- Larger organizations make communications, consensus building, decision making, and action more difficult.
- Large companies usually have better documentation, paper trails, auditing system, and corrective action systems than small companies.
- A small company may not have a full-time person in the Op Ex function. This can result in reactive Op Ex.
- In a small company, inspection may still be extensively used and operational controls are basic.

Op Ex has acquired some associated truths, specifically:

- Op Ex is increasingly important.
- Op Ex is objective and precise.
- Op Ex is an investment.
- Op Ex enhances productivity.
- Worldwide Op Ex is steadily improving.

OP EX IS INCREASINGLY IMPORTANT

Because it has become a necessary condition of business. Op Ex will not disappear. Customers want cost-competitive, aesthetically pleasing, quality products and services. If a firm does not make a good product, customers will buy another firm's products or services. They will not come back and may even tell their friends to avoid the poor-quality products.

OP EX IS OBJECTIVE AND PRECISE

Many people think that Op Ex is subjective and that it is a concept that relies "on the eyes of the beholder" or "on the hands of the user." While the subjective component of Op Ex is an important consideration, Op Ex can be defined objectively, so it is precise and measurable. If a product conforms to customer specifications or requirements, we say a product is Op Ex-made.

OP EX IS AN INVESTMENT

Many people think it costs more to make a quality product than a defective one. This is false. A company saves money by doing the job right the first time, which saves money by eliminating rework, scrap, or defects. And instead of adding cost, Op Ex pays for itself by the savings it generates.

OP EX ENHANCES PRODUCTIVITY

Senior managers sometimes think that stressing product qualitylowers factory productivity. In an industrial engineering sense, productivity is the difference between the output and input of an operation or process. Productivity was thought to decrease because it took more input to increase product excellence, while output remained constant. The opposite is actually true. When Op Ex increases, output of defect-free products increases. Rework, rejects, defects, and scrap decrease.

Also, the impacts of a company-wide operational ethic are long-term, because Op Ex develops into a "state of mind." People become involved, "doing the right thing right, the first time and every time" is encouraged. Op Ex becomes everyone's personal responsibility, not the responsibility of someone else.

WORLDWIDE OP EX IS STEADILY IMPROVING

Some American products that had been considered superior are considered of lower Op Ex. Why? The challenge is from offshore manufacturers who have increased their Op Ex at a faster rate than U.S. manufacturers. Examples include the manufacturers of textiles, electronic consumer equipment, and steel.

FUTURE OF OP EX

If I were a manager of a store today and one of my clerks told a lie to sell merchandise, I would fire him - or her - on the spot. Not only would it be wrong. It would be poor business.
J. C. Penney

Operational management implies doing the right things right all the time. This is the ideal, the ethical benchmark. However, this is becoming more difficult as stakeholder requirements differ. More companies are providing ethics training and are making ethics a condition of employment. Ethics training emphasizes doing what's right - right for the organization, the individual, the customer, the community, the environment, the supplier, and to all stakeholders.

MANAGEMENT PRESCRIPTIONS

Is Op Ex a fad? A number of well publicized Op Ex initiatives have been disappointing. Instant gratification, or what Deming called instant pudding syndrome, is common to American management. Nostrums and prescriptions are always being tried and applied with varying degrees of success. The list in the last decade is long, including the pursuit of excellence, empowerment, self-management, reengineering and even total operational management.

Prescriptions from gurus have been common. An Op Ex guru prescribes a formula or path to follow. The guru collects disciples and acolytes who preach the virtues of one method while criticizing a competitor's approach. This has created disharmony and confusion in the marketplace.

Another method has been the prescriptive or descriptive standards approach. When Op Ex standards have been applied to a specific situation, a company has failed to tailor them to the existing organizational environment. This usually leads to failure. Often, it has been more practical and effective to focus on broad Op Ex principles, such as pleasing customers and rely on organizational stakeholders to determine the most appropriate approach.

The overall goal of an Op Ex initiative or project is securing customer satisfaction which is achieved through implementing and pursuing continuous improvement plans and objectives throughout the organization and the supplier base.

REDESIGNING THE WORKPLACE

Redesigning the workplace means much more than eliminating process steps and people. In some circles, reengineering implies eliminating non-value adding process steps. But, what happens to the reengineered workers. Often, they are fired. To these workers, reengineering may imply being fired.

Redesigning the workplace in progressive organizations is a conscious and humanistic effort to make processes more effective, efficient, and economic. The challenge is to rethink the purpose of the work area and to ask how things can be done better. Workplace redesign may mean examining the managerial, social, and technical aspects of the Op Ex system. The goal is to optimize and improve the systems so they work more efficiently. Redesigning the workplace may emphasize and involve self-managed teams, total employee involvement, high-performance teams, extensive training, new procedural systems, and multi-skilled employees.

NO QUICK OP EX FIX

Both Deming and Juran believed slogans such as "do it right the first time" can backfire. Exhortations without senior level commitment and resources are just words that result in cynicism. Sometimes, companies will use the Op Ex theme as skillful propaganda to arouse awareness among subordinates that Op Ex is important. But the implied goal of Op Ex is vague, not specific. Crosby counters that anything else other than a commitment to zero defects sets up an environment where close enough is good enough.

When management hears about the success of a competitor's Op Ex initiative, they want to replicate the success instantly. However, commitment to the new program is required for it to work. A common scenario follows. A corporate officer hears about Op Ex, reads a book about it, or hears of tremendous achievement of other companies and then says he wanted it yesterday. The quick-fix mentality prevails. Or, a larger company may give an ultimatum to a supplier to achieve ISO 9001:2015 registration by tomorrow.

There is little motivation to implement the Op Ex initiative slowly in order to build trust in the process. All too often, programs get imposed from top-down, and the result is failure. There is no long-standing commitment to transform the organizational culture.

REDESIGNING THE WORKPLACE

Redesigning the workplace means much more than eliminating process steps and people. In some circles, reengineering implies eliminating non-value adding process steps. But, what happens to the reengineered workers. Often, they are fired. To these workers, reengineering may imply being fired.

Redesigning the workplace in progressive organizations is a conscious and humanistic effort to make processes more effective, efficient, and economic. The challenge is to rethink the purpose of the work area and to ask how things can be done better. Workplace redesign may mean examining the managerial, social, and technical aspects of the Op Ex system. The goal is to optimize and improve the systems so they work more efficiently. Redesigning the workplace may emphasize and involve self-managed teams, total employee involvement, high-performance teams, extensive training, new procedural systems, and multi-skilled employees.

TEN REASONS WHY OP EX DOESN'T WORK

Op ex managers must know the good and bad. Oren harari, a management consultant, has identified ten reasons why total operational management doesn't work, specifically:

1. Op Ex focuses people's attention on internal processes rather than on external results.
2. Op Ex focuses on minimum standards.
3. Op Ex develops its own cumbersome bureaucracy.
4. Op Ex delegates Op Ex to consultants rather than to real people.
5. Op Ex[79] does not demand radical organizational change.
6. Op Ex does not demand changes in management compensation.
7. Op Ex does not demand entirely new relationships with outside partners.
8. Op Ex appeals to faddism, egotism, and quick fixism.
9. Op Ex drains entrepreneurship and innovation from corporate culture.
10. Op Ex has no place for love.[80]

INDEX

M

Q

R

ENDNOTES

1. Global Competition: The New Reality, The Report of the President's Commission on Industrial Competitiveness, Washington, DC: Superintendent of Documents, 1985.

2. Ibid., Vol. 2, p. 28.

3. The four attributes are derived from the definition in B. Enis, Marketing Principles, Glenview, IL: Scott, Foresman, 1980, p. 5.

4. Pearson, Andrall E., "Corporate Redemption and the Seven Deadly Sins," Harvard Business Review, May/Jun, 1992, p: 65-75.

5. "Behind the Eight Ball," American Society for operational excellence Control," 1987, p. 10.

6. Lear, Robert W, "The Obsolescent CEO," Chief Executive, September, 1993 p:?.

7. Pennington, Randy G., "The Personal Commitment to operational excellence," HR Magazine, March, 1993, p: 100-101.

8. Hersey, Paul, The Situational Leader, NY: Warner Books, 1984.

9. Block, Peter, Stewardship, San Francisco: Berrett-Koehler, 1993.

10. Crutchley, Peter, "Management by Objectives," Credit Management, May, 1994, p. 36-38.

11. "Brown, Tom, "Re-inventing Yourself, Industry Week, November 21, 1994, pp. 20-24.

[12] Osterman, Paul, "How Common is Workplace Source Transformation and Who Adopts it?" Industrial & Labor Relations Review, January, 1994, p: 173 188.

13. Osterman, Paul, "How Common is Workplace Transformation and Who Adopts it?" Industrial & Labor Relations Review, January, 1994, p: 173-188.

14. Blackman, Ted, "Team Concept' Involves Crews in All Aspects of Mills," Journal: Forest Industries, November, 1991, p. 14-15.

15. Russell, Grant, "Prerequisites for Accountability," CMA Magazine, February, 1993, p. 7.

16. LaBar, Gregg, "Safety at Saturn: A team Effort," Occupational Hazards, March. 1994 p: 41-44.

17. Lenckus, Dave, "Safety Awareness Alone Not Enough to Sow the Seeds for Fewer Injuries," October 17, 1994, p. 15.

18. Krause, Thomas R., "Safety and operational excellence: Two Sides of the Same Coin," Quality Progress, October, 1994, pp. 51-55.
19. Bresler, Samuel J; Thacker, Rebecca, "Four-Point Plan Helps Solve Harassment Problems," HRMagazine, May, 1993, p. 117-124.
20. D Quinn Mills, The Rebirth f the Corporation, John Wiley & Sons, New York, 1991.
[21] Source: Dessler, Gary, "Value-Based Hiring Builds Commitment," Personnel Journal, November, 1993,
22. Meyers, Ken and Killeen, Bob, "Building Union-Management Partnerships," Quality Progress, April, 1994, pp. 95-97.
23. Milas, Gene, "How to Develop a Meaningful Employee Recognition Program," Quality Progress, May 1995, p. 139-142.
24. Sadler, Philip, "Designing an Organizational Structure," Management International Review, Vol. 11. No6, 1971, pp.19-33.
25. F. Herzberg, B. Mausner, and D. B. Snyderman, The Motivation to Work, NY: John Wiley and Sons, 1959.
26. J. Sears, "Changing role of the operational excellence Inspection Function," Quality Progress, July 1983, p. 14.
27. Lancaster, Hal, "Managers Beware: You're Not Ready for Tomorrow's Jobs," Wall Street Journal, January 24, 1995, p. B1.
[28] H. J. Harrington, The Improvement Process: How America's Leading Companies Improve Quality, Milwaukee, NY: McGraw-Hill, Inc. 1987, p. 11.
29. Harari, Oren, "The Lab Test: A Tale of operational excellence," Management Review, February, 1993 p: 55-58.
[30] Rosander, A. C., Applications of Quality Control in the Service Industries, NY: Marcel Dekker, 1985, p.6
31. H. Takeuchi and J. Quelch, "operational excellence is More Than Making a Good Product," Harvard Business Review, July-August, 1983, pp. 139-143.
32. Mukund, Mike, "Fitness for Use in Theory and in Practice," Quality Progress, June, 1989.
33. Kirker, Tracy "The Voice of the Customer," Industry Week, January 17, 1994, p. 11.
34. Goodman, John, Bargatze, Gary, and Grimm, Cynthia, "The Key Problem with OPERATONAL EXCELLENCE," Quality Progress, January, 1994, pp. 45-48.
35. Reid, Robert, "The Five Voices of operational excellence," Journal for operational excellence & Participation, June, 1993, p: 76-81.

36. See E. J. McCarthy and W. Perreault, Basic Marketing, Homewood, IL: Richard D.
Irwin, 1984, pp. 224-225.
37. N. Karabatsos, "World-Class operational excellence," operational excellence, January, 1986, p. 14.
[38] Desatnick, Robert, "Inside the Baldrige Award Guidelines," Quality Progress, December, 1992, pp. 69-74
[39] Furlong, Carla B. "12 Rules for Customer Retention," Bank Marketing, January, 1993, pp. 14 18.
40. Maher, Dan, "Service Guarantees," Training, June, 1991, pp. 27-30.
41. F. Scanlon and J. Hagan, "operational management for the Service Industries, Part 1," Quality Progress, May 1983, p. 18.
42. Yoshida, Kosaku, "The Joy of Work: Optimizing Service operational excellence Through Education and Training," Quality Progress, November, 1993, pp. 29-33.
[43] Albrecht, K.; Zemke, R., Service America, NY: Dow Jones Irwin, 1985, p. 27.
44. B. White, "Marketing operational excellence," operational excellence, June, 1984, p. 84.
45. Griffin, Abbie; Hauser, John R. "The Voice of the Customer," Marketing Science, Winter, 1993, pp. 1-27.
46. H. Takeuchi and J. Quelch, "operational excellence is More Than Making a Good Product," Harvard Business Review, July-August, 1983, p. 141-142.
47. "operational management and operational excellence System Elements - Guidelines," ANSI\ASQC Q94-1987, p.7.
[48] Source: B. Cochran and G. Thompson, "Why ProductsFail," The National Conference Board of Record 1, October 1964, p. 14.
[49] Source: Cooper, Robert, "New products: The factors that drive success," International Marketing Review, 1994, pp: 60-76
50. Marketing Definitions: A Glossary of Marketing Terms, Chicago: American Marketing Association, 1960.
[51] Desatnick, Robert, "Inside the Baldrige Award Guidelines," Quality Progress, December, 1992, pp. 69-74
52. Hutchins, Greg, Standard Manual of operational excellence Auditing, Englewood Cliffs, NJ: Prentice Hall, 1993.
53. R. Koenig, "Exacting Employer: Toyota Takes Pains and Time Filling Jobs at Its Kentucky Plant", Wall Street Journal, December 1, 1987, p. 1.

54. "ASQC-Gallup Attitude Survey," Milwaukee, WI: ASQC, 1987.
55. Industrial Engineering, October, 1983, p. 50-63.
[56] Source: Barone, Orlando R, "Curing the Seven Causes of Poor Staff Performance," Corporate Controller," Jan/Feb, 1993, p: 54 57.
57. Johann, Bernard, "The Meeting as a Lever for Organizational Improvement," National Productivity Review, Summer, 1994, p. 369-377.
58. Johann, Bernard, "The Meeting as a Lever for Organizational Improvement," National Productivity Review, Summer, 1994, p. 369-377.
[59] Wurman, Richard, Follow the Yellow Brick Road, Bantam Books, 1992, pp.217.
60. "Management Discovers the Human Side of Automation," Business Week, September 29, 1986, p. 71.
61. Hammons, Charles and Maddux, Gary, "The FineTuned Organization," Quality Progress, February, 1992, pp. 47-48.
[62] Morris, P. W. G., "Managing Project Interfaces - Key Point for Project Success," in D.I. Cleland, W. R. King Project Management Handbook, 2nd ed. NY: Van Nostrand Reinhold, pp. 16-18.
63. Whiting, Rick, "Engineers Say 'Prove It!'" Electronic Business, October 7, 1991, p: 89-92.
64. D. Garvin, Managing operational excellence, NY: Free Press, 1988, pp. 49-69.
65. Johnson, Sharon, "Tour the Software Chamber of Horrors," Technology Review, June, 1994, p. 6.
66. D. Garvin, "What Does Product operational excellence Really Mean?", Sloan Management Review, Fall, 1984, p.32.
[67] Hutchins, Greg, ISO 9001:2015 Toolkit, VT. OMNEO, 1994.
68. Hutchins, Greg, ISO 9001:2015, Vermont: Essex Junction, OMNEO, 1993, pp. 145-177.
[69] "Total operational management - A Guide for Implementation," Superintendent of Documents, DOD 5000.51G, 1989, p. 1.
[70] Popoff, Frank; Brache, Alan P., "The Seven Deadly Sins of Process Improvement," Chief Executive, June, 1994, p: 22-26.
71. Bohan, George, "Focus the Strategy to Achieve Results," Quality Progress, July, 1995, pp. 89-92.
72. Adapted from "Total operational management - A Guide for Implementation," Superintendent of Documents, DOD 5000.51G, 1989, p. 15.
[73] Ibid. Camp.

---

[74] De Toro, Irving, "The Ten Pitfalls of Benchmarking," Quality Progress, January, 1995, pp. 61-63.
[75] Hiam, Alexander, Closing the quality Gap: Lessons from America's Leading Companies, 1992, p. viii.
76. This chapter was excepted from Hutchins, Greg, Supply Management Strategies for Total operational excellence, NY: Dow Jones Irwin, 1992.
77. Denton, D. Keith, "Four Steps to Resolving Conflicts," Quality Progress, April, 1989, pp. 29-34.
[78] Nilson, Carolyn, Training for Non-Trainers, New York: AMACOM, 1990, pp. 11-14.

[80]Harari, Oren, "Ten Reasons Why OPERATONAL EXCELLENCE Doesn't Work," Management Review, January, 1993, p: 33 38.

Made in the USA
Monee, IL
01 May 2026

49295370R00280